Springer Series in Fashion Business

Series Editor

Jason Tsan-Ming Choi, Institute of Textiles and Clothing, The Hong Kong Polytechnic University, Hung Hom, Kowloon, Hong Kong

This book series publishes monographs and edited volumes from leading scholars and established practitioners in the fashion business. Specific focus areas such as luxury fashion branding, fashion operations management, and fashion finance and economics, are covered in volumes published in the series. These perspectives of the fashion industry, one of the world's most important businesses, offer unique research contributions among business and economics researchers and practitioners. Given that the fashion industry has become global, highly dynamic, and green, the book series responds to calls for more in-depth research about it from commercial points of views, such as sourcing, manufacturing, and retailing. In addition, volumes published in Springer Series in Fashion Business explore deeply each part of the fashion industry's supply chain associated with the many other critical issues.

Rajkishore Nayak · Huy Truong · Rudrajeet Pal
Editors

Use of Digital and Advanced Technologies in the Fashion Supply Chain

Springer

Editors
Rajkishore Nayak
School of Communication and Design
RMIT University
Ho Chi Minh City, Vietnam

Huy Truong
The Business School
RMIT University
Ho Chi Minh City, Vietnam

Rudrajeet Pal
The Swedish School of Textiles
University of Borås
Borås, Sweden

ISSN 2366-8776 ISSN 2366-8784 (electronic)
Springer Series in Fashion Business
ISBN 978-981-97-7527-9 ISBN 978-981-97-7528-6 (eBook)
https://doi.org/10.1007/978-981-97-7528-6

This Springer imprint is published by the registered company Springer Nature Singapore Pte Ltd.
The registered company address is: 152 Beach Road, #21-01/04 Gateway East, Singapore 189721, Singapore

Contents

Chapter 1
Recent Trends in the Role of Digital Technologies in Fashion and Textile Manufacturing

Rajkishore Nayak, Huy Truong Quang, and Rudrajeet Pal

Abstract The manufacturing of fashion and textiles is still labour intensive in many countries despite the advancements in technology. Unlike other sectors such as automotive and pharmaceutical, several operations in manufacturing of fashion and textiles follow manual methods of production. Availability of cheap labour, high investment cost for new technologies and low cost of the garments are some of the factors that hinder the use of technology in the manufacturing of fashion and textiles. There is a potential for various technologies to revolutionise the fashion and textile sector. This chapter has focused on various digital technologies and their potential applications/impacts in the fashion and textile manufacturing. A brief history of industrial revolution has been given in the beginning of the chapter. Subsequently, the use of various technologies is illustrated with major application areas. The benefits of using technologies are also highlighted. Further, the sustainable benefits of using the technologies are discussed in brief. The chapter has been prepared mainly from the secondary data and some primary data from the projects the authors have completed. This chapter will provide concise knowledge on the use of advanced technologies in the manufacturing of fashion and textiles.

Keywords Advanced technology · Sustainability · Artificial intelligence · Industrial revolution · Transparency and traceability

---

R. Nayak (✉)
School of Communication & Design, RMIT University, Ho Chi Minh City, Vietnam
e-mail: rajkishore.nayak@rmit.edu.vn

H. T. Quang
The Business School, RMIT University, Ho Chi Minh City, Vietnam
e-mail: huytruong.quang@rmit.edu.vn

R. Pal
Swedish School of Textiles, University of Borås, Borås, Sweden

Department of Industrial Engineering and Management, University of Gävle, Gävle, Sweden

R. Pal
e-mail: rudrajeet.pal@hb.se

R. Nayak et al. (eds.), *Use of Digital and Advanced Technologies in the Fashion Supply Chain*, Springer Series in Fashion Business,
https://doi.org/10.1007/978-981-97-7528-6_1

1.1 Introduction

Fashion manufacturing sector is considered to be the third largest sector in the world following the electronic and automotive sectors. Starting from providing the second necessity for human lives after food (which is clothing), this sector brings new innovative lifesaving products such as scaffolds and tissue-like structures for medical applications. This sector, comprising textile, clothing and fashion (TCF), provides employment to approximately 430 million people, which is 12.6% of the global working population (Center 2019). Further, this sector provides a range of job opportunities in the production (e.g., sewing, spinning and weaving), logistics, communication, advertising and retailing (Nayak and Padhye 2015). The TCF sector is one of the most important sectors in the economic development of several countries contributing 2% of the global gross domestic product (GDP). Due to significant economic contribution, this sector should be updated with the latest technologies (such as automation and artificial intelligence) to improve the productivity and efficiency.

Automation is playing a pivotal role to improve the productivity and efficiency of several manufacturing sectors (Stylios 2013). When developed countries are considered, it is a requirement to implement automation to save the rising labour costs. However, several manufacturing industries for fashion and textiles are located in the developing countries such as Vietnam, Bangladesh, India, Laos and Cambodia (Nayak and Padhye 2017). These countries lack automation, the use of artificial intelligence and robotics in the manufacturing of fashion and textiles. The major reason can be attributed to the availability of cheap labour in these countries. Other reasons can be huge financial investment to implement newer technologies, high skill level for running and maintenance of these systems, frequent style changes in garment manufacturing and low cost of garments (Salahuddin and Lee 2022; Nayak and Padhye 2018; Nayak et al. 2019). There have been several research publications on the application of Industry 4.0 in fashion and textiles. However, there is a dearth of literature explaining the recent trends in Industry 4.0.

This chapter highlights the recent trends in the use of digital technologies in fashion and textile sectors under Industry 4.0. The first section of the chapter discusses a brief history of the digital technologies and industrial revolutions. Some of the important innovations that transformed the fashion and textiles have been discussed. In the next section, various digital technologies that are being applied in fashion manufacturing and transportation are highlighted. The sustainable benefits of using various advanced technologies are also a main focus of this chapter. The chapter has been prepared with secondary data and the experience of the authors in some of the advanced technologies.

1.2 Traditional Technologies and Challenges

The use of textiles and clothing dates back to the pre-historic era when the humans were using natural materials, bark and animal hides to cover their body. Later, in the ancient civilisation people used products from hemp, silk and wool fibres in addition to the use of cotton fibres (Schwarz and Kovačević 2017). Industrial revolution brought the inventions in textiles such as spinning jenny, mechanised shuttle looms and sewing machines, which changed the way clothing was produced (Styles 2020; Hahn 2020). In the twentieth century, there were several new inventions such as the synthetic fibres, the use of open-end spinning, integration of computerised production techniques and the use of synthetic dyeing, which were some of the prominent ones (Shaw and Simpson 2002).

The twenty-first century is the age of technologies, which focus on Industry 4.0, nanotechnology, smart and intelligent textiles (Kaounides et al. 2007; Duarte et al. 2018). The chronological development of textile sector (Fig. 1.1) shows how the human creativity has been integrated with the progression of technology to alter the aesthetics and functionality of clothing and textiles. Significant growth of sustainability has also necessitated to use technology for saving energy and resources, and to improve the efficiency of processes.

Until now several garment manufacturing industries still use traditional technologies due to cost constraints, lack of awareness of the benefits or resistance to adapt

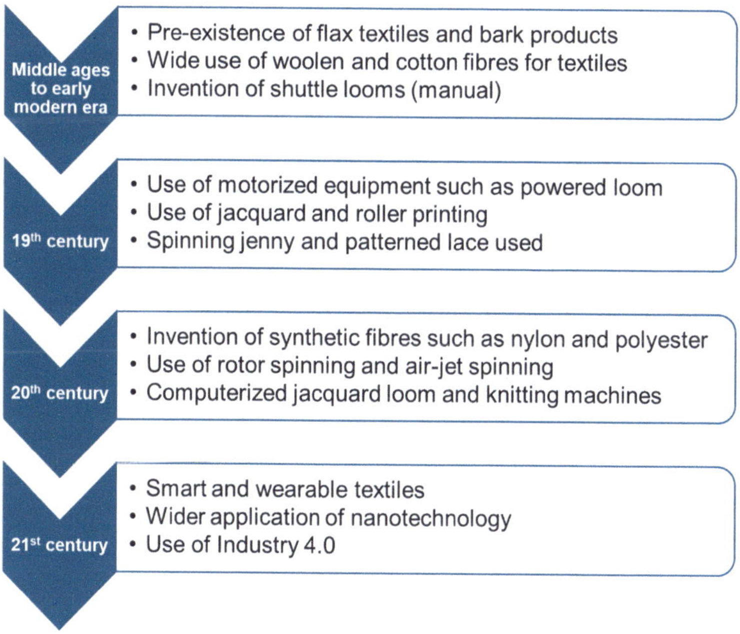

Fig. 1.1 Chronological developments of textile sector

new technologies (Nayak and Padhye 2017). In several instances, cost is a major factor for the industries that are operating with a low margin or are struggling to survive due to financial issues. These types of industries don't have enough budget to implement the latest technologies. The lack of awareness on the benefits of using new technologies can be ascribed for using traditional technologies (Nayak et al. 2020). Further, the resistance to adapting new technologies is also another reason that contributes towards the use of traditional technologies.

The traditional technologies used for manufacturing fashion and textiles have several drawbacks. Some of the major drawbacks include excessive use of resources, large amount of waste creation, slower production (low productivity and efficiency), energy and labour intensive, negative environmental impacts, ethical issues and lack of sustainable practices. Textile and clothing manufacturing is associated with excessive resource consumption in addition to creating large amounts of solid waste and wastewater. Spinning and weaving industries produce significant amount of yarn and fabric wastes, respectively. Similarly, chemical processing units produce large amounts of wastewater or effluent that is directly discharged to the water courses.

Excessive reliance on the traditional technologies affects the productivity, efficiency and quality of garment manufacturing industries. The traditional machineries are rather slow and often produce products that can't meet the quality produced by the newer technologies. Further, these machineries consume higher energy due to the use of older driving systems and mechanisms. These machineries rely on use of labour rather than using the technology. They also pose safety risks for the workers working in the machineries. Fashion and textile manufacturing has been reported for not following corporate social responsibility (CSR) practices in the manufacturing and supply chain process. Some of the common ethical issues include child labour, forced labour and discrimination. It has been reported that the use of various technologies can help to achieve benefits relating to the TBL of sustainability (Nayak et al. 2022).

Traditional technologies have higher environmental impacts due to excessive waste creation (solid waste and effluent), chemical and energy consumption. The solid wastes from many textile manufacturing industries are directly dumped into the landfill leading to greenhouse gas emission (GHG). Further, the effluent from chemical processing units is also directly discharged without any purification, which leads to massive water pollution. The use of excessive chemical and energy (derived from coal) is also a major source of environmental pollution in many countries. Further, incidents of ethical practices not being followed in some fashion and textile manufacturing industries have been reported in the past. Notable among these are forced labour, child labour, low wages, and health and safety issues. Although some brands are trying to address these issues, the complexity of the supply chain, traceability issues and other challenges do not make this sector completely sustainable (Nayak 2020).

These obstacles mentioned above demonstrate the need for a more innovative and ecological approach to textile manufacturing, usage and disposal. By embracing technological advancements, implementing sustainable practices and promoting awareness, the textile industry can lessen these problems and create a new opportunity for more responsible and forward-thinking textiles.

1.3 Digital Technologies

Starting from the later part of the eighteenth century till today, we have witnessed four industrial revolutions. These industrial revolutions transformed the way the goods were manufactured and transported from one to the other place. One of the significant achievements during the first industrial revolution is the discovery of coal and its extraction (Evans and Rydén 2017). Further, the invention of steam engine in addition to metal forging transformed the manufacturing sector. These inventions helped the integration of machines for manufacturing products, which was running through manual operations.

The first mechanised operation that was invented was the spinning jenny, which changed the way to produce yarns (Styles 2020). Later, weaving looms were invented to produce fabrics which was done by flying shuttle handlooms (Rai 2015). The second industrial revolution features invention of electricity, gas and oil, which revolutionised the transportation sector. With the assembly line production, mechanised production grew to mass production to meet the growing demand. The third industrial revolution is well-known for the integration of computers, electronics and automation. The fourth industrial revolution is notably known for the application of advanced technologies, artificial intelligence, cloud computing and robotics (Groumpos 2021).

Like the other sectors, the fashion and textile sector has evolved to its current stage through the four industrial revolutions. Majority of the technological developments in spinning and weaving happened during the first and second industrial revolutions. The first invention, spinning jenny, helped to produce yarns from cotton, flax and wool with much higher speed, which reduced the cost of production (Humphries and Schneider 2019). The demand for clothes from these fibres was significantly increased, which necessitated the creation of spinning and weaving industries.

The other notable inventions during this period (first industrial revolution) were cotton gin, spinning frame or water frame and the spinning mule (Maw et al. 2022). With these inventions, the yarn production was significantly improved in relation to productivity and quality. The notable invention during the second industrial revolution was the developments in power looms to produce fabrics with better quality and higher efficiency (Hahn 2020). Increase in the speed and automatic weft-replenishment were notable advancements in the looms for producing fabrics. The third industrial revolution is known for the integration of electronics for automation with the help of computers. The use of computers replaced manual operations and further improved speed and efficiency. Various important inventions during the four industrial revolutions are summarised in Fig. 1.2.

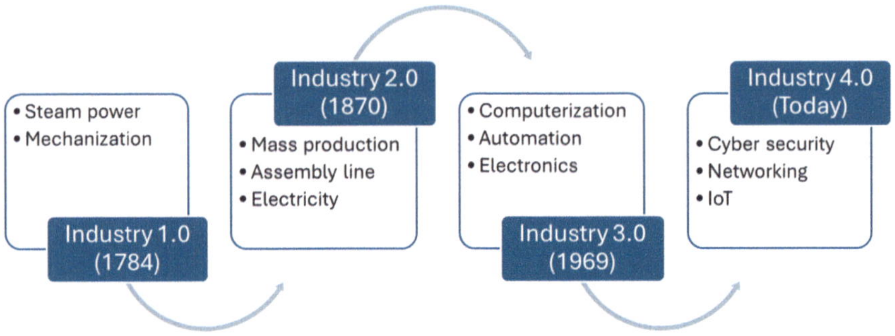

Fig. 1.2 The four industrial revolutions and important inventions

In the recent era of manufacturing fashion and textiles, automation is gaining increasing attention from researchers and fashion brands. Industrial automation involves replacing the manual and labour-intensive operations with the automatic machines. One such example from garment manufacturing industries is automatic spreading and cutting of fabrics. In the traditional process, the fabric spreading is done by several workers layer by layer, which is time-consuming and tiring for the workers (Nayak and Padhye 2017; Salahuddin and Lee 2022). The introduction of automation can help to complete the work more accurately and with increased efficiency.

In the twenty-first century, there have been rapid developments in digital technologies that have revolutionised the fashion and textile manufacturing sector. Commonly known as industrial revolution 4.0, it has influenced many of the industries including fashion and textiles (Bertola and Teunissen 2018). The features of Industry 4.0 include data storage, improved communication, transparency and automation of processes using various technologies. Industry 4.0 is the integration of automation with computer-based systems, which is a result of the developments in science, technology and robotics. Some of the promising technologies that are mainly implemented in Industry 4.0 are block chain technology (BCT), Internet of Things (IoT); radio frequency identification (RFID); big data, cloud computing; augmented reality and virtual reality (AR/VR); and artificial intelligence (AI) (Jin and Shin 2021). This chapter discusses briefly about these technologies, whereas the corresponding chapters, following chapter 1, discuss the technologies more in detail (Fig. 1.3).

In a fashion enterprise, BCT is used as an advanced database system that can share transparent information with the stakeholders (Tripathi et al. 2021). In BCT, continuously growing list of ordered records is maintained by a distributed database, which is also known as blocks and these blocks are linked using cryptography. In fashion and textile sector, BCT is becoming popular due to its capacity to function in large networks and robustness to prevent data manipulations. The recent applications of BCT in fashion involve product traceability (from fibre to final garment stage), prevent counterfeit products, customer relationship management (CRM) and meeting the sustainability commitments (Caldarelli et al. 2021). The major challenges of

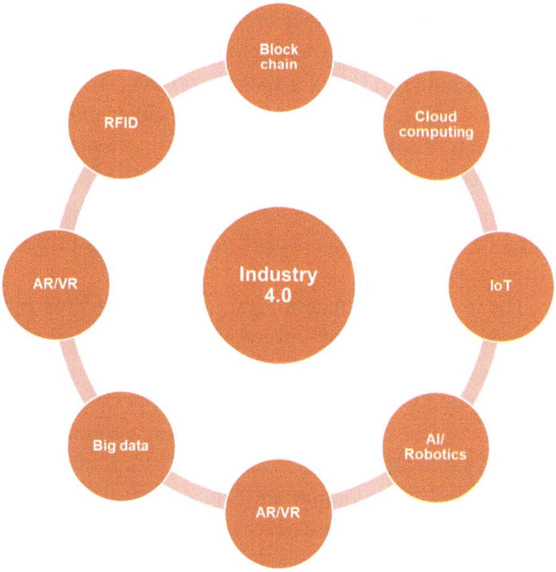

Fig. 1.3 Application of Industry 4.0 in fashion and textiles

traceability in complex supply chain can be addressed by BCT, as it can provide required information to the consumers when necessary.

The global counterfeit market segment is leading to the loss of millions of dollars by fashion brands. It is much easier to produce counterfeit products in fashion compared to other products as fashion products are easy to duplicate. The use of BCT can prevent counterfeit products and defend the authenticity of the products (Lee and Yeon 2021). The product movement can be monitored by using BCT in the supply chain that can help to achieve accurate information. The use of BCT can facilitate data storage and sharing with the business stakeholders. Further, in the sustainability marketplace, BCT can be used to source fashion products made ethically and sustainably (Chen 2023).

Internet of Things (IoT) indicates a network of systems connected to appliances, accessories, products and machines that are embedded with sensors to facilitate sharing of information (Akram et al. 2022). While designing IoT for industrial applications, machines and sensors can be connected wirelessly to create a system that can monitor the entire production process, which can facilitate quick decision-making. There are several applications of IoT in fashion, and wearable electronics is one of the applications gaining increased importance from consumers (Fernández-Caramés and Fraga-Lamas 2018; Sucharitha et al. 2022). Devices such as smartwatches (to monitor heart rate) or sneakers with sensors (to count the steps) can be included in this category, which can monitor the health and daily activity levels, respectively. Global brands such as Levi's and Yves Saint Laurent, in collaboration with Google's Project Jacquard, are working on smart accessories to improve consumer experience in wearable electronics.

Smart mirror is another area under IoT applications, which can help customers to find the best product with virtual try-on (Maizi and Bendavid 2021). Rather than spending hours to select a specific product, the customers can get the right product without wasting significant time. The other major areas of IoT application involve prevention of fake products and inventory management in retail operations. Integration of RFID technology with IoT can help to store the accurate information about a product (Nayak 2019a). When the customers buy any product, the information stored in the RFID tag can be checked with the brand information to check the authenticity of the products.

The use of RFID technology is helping fashion businesses in many aspects such as providing real-time information, stock reconciliation, inventory management, reducing counterfeit products and reducing shrinkage (Nayak et al. 2015; Garrido Azevedo and Carvalho 2012). In retail operations, RFID tags can store the information on the fast selling and slow-moving products. This can help to facilitate better inventory management to avoid out-of-stock situations or excessive stock. The accuracy in stock information and stock control can improve the return on investment (ROI) and profit. The use of RFID technology also makes the process of stock reconciliation much faster and accurate (Nayak et al. 2007). When the products enter or leave the retail store, RFID system automatically updates the stock level, which can facilitate the process of vendor managed inventory (VMI).

Big data consists of a large amount of data, which can support business activities in fashion. There are three components of big data, which are volume, variety and velocity (Jain et al. 2017). Big data analysis can help to identify the causes of various problems relating to fashion forecasting, and decision-making, which can improve the efficiency of these processes. The collection of a wide range of data on the colour, design and style can help to accurately forecast the fashion trend. Further, big data can identify abnormality in the supply chain that will help to reduce cost and save time. Big data can act as a product passport for customers providing the detailed information to them, which can improve transparency in supply chain (Silva et al. 2020). Big data can also be used to gather information on consumer choices from the history and customised styling suggestions can be created for individual customers.

Cloud computing is the use of remotely connected servers, and databases, which are hosted over the internet for data storage and sharing. Rather than designing their own network, the fashion businesses can use cloud computing for designing, manufacturing and retailing operations. Cloud computing can improve the collaboration between various supply chain stakeholders and improve efficiency of supply chains in addition to cost saving (Ma et al. 2017). The three major flows of supply chain process, such as material flow, information flow and financial flow can be better managed using cloud computing. Cloud computing can be used for inventory and warehouse management by using enterprise resource planning (ERP) software. The integration of cloud computing in creating bill of materials (BOMs) and Tech packs can improve the sourcing and designing process much faster. Operations such as production planning, operations management and order fulfilment can be managed more efficiently with the use of cloud computing (Majeed and Rupasinghe 2017).

Augmented reality and virtual reality (AR/VR) have the potential to transform fashion industry (Goel et al. 2023). These technologies are not only supporting the apparel designing process, but also redefining the retail experience (Akram et al. 2022). For example, AR technology can be used by global fashion retailers to improve the shopping experience of customers. Customers can use the AR technology to try various garments and accessories virtually even sitting at their homes. Similarly, the use of VR technology can generate virtual fashion shows, where global fashion brands can witness the latest trends using digital platforms, removing the barrier of physical locations. 3D garments can be designed using a range of software in the digital realm much faster than the traditional process of fabric manufacturing and garment designing using real physical samples, which can save both time and cost.

Artificial intelligence, or commonly known as AI, is a new trend in many manufacturing sectors. Artificial intelligence can simulate human intelligence and problem-solving capabilities in computers or machines. Artificial intelligence can be applied in product development, supply chain optimisation, retailing and many other fashion business processes (Ren et al. 2018). Trend forecasting can be more accurate through the integration of AI, which harness the power of data and predictive analytics. Data analytics and machine learning techniques can be efficiently integrated for accurate demand forecasting that can reduce the wastage at the end of a product season. Generative designs can be used to explore numerous design possibilities by leveraging computational power and algorithms. AI can play a crucial role in sustainability by right material selection, accurate sales forecasting, process optimisation and reducing waste (Ramos et al. 2023).

AI can be used for logistics optimisation in the supply chain process (Boute and Udenio 2022). The tracking and tracing of information by AI can ensure delivery of the product in the most efficient manner. Furthermore, AI can be used to reduce the instances of stockouts, eliminate excessive sock and facilitate markdown to maximise profit (Oosthuizen et al. 2021; Luce 2018). AI can also be used for customised shopping experience, which was not possible earlier. Based on the history of purchasing behaviour of each customer, AI can provide personal recommendations to improving the customer relationship management. Integration of AI can also facilitate in the quality control of garments. The AI integrated manufacturing can facilitate streamlining various operation during garment manufacturing. AI-based machine vision can be used in inspecting the quality of fabrics and garments, which is more efficient and accurate than manual operations (Abd Jelil 2018). Further, AI can be used in virtual sample designing of apparels, which can eliminate the lengthy process of physical sample development. A summary of AI applications in fashion and textile sector is given in Fig. 1.4.

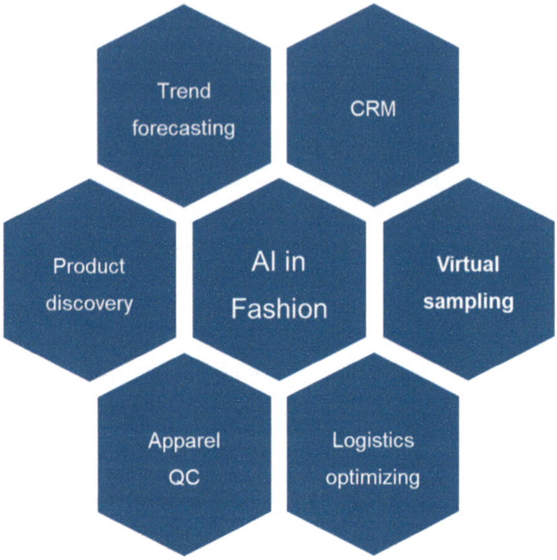

Fig. 1.4 Application of AI in fashion

1.4 Benefits of Digital Technologies

1.4.1 Benefits-Productivity, Efficiency, Quality and Cost Aspects

A revolution is now taking place in the constantly evolving fashion sector. The integration of digital technologies into the supply chain has evolved from a minor enhancement to a major driver of change (Büyüközkan and Göçer 2018). This integration represents a significant transformation in the operational and competitive strategies of fashion enterprises in the contemporary, increasingly linked world rather than just a mere recognition of innovation. Fashion companies have effectively reassessed conventional procedures and recognised new opportunities for expansion and distinction via the use of digital technology, such as enhanced analytics and automated production techniques (Li et al. 2020).

In this ever-changing environment, the primary emphasis is on maximising production, optimising efficiency, ensuring high quality and minimising costs. These pillars serve as the basis for digital technology to provide concrete value for fashion firms, allowing them to simplify processes, improve product offers and optimise resource allocation (Hora et al. 2023). Digital tools and platforms enable smooth collaboration and communication throughout all stages of the business process, from design and manufacturing to distribution and retail. This helps to eliminate barriers and promote a culture of innovation and adaptability (Zutshi and Grilo 2019). This change in paradigm is not just a reaction to the requirements of a swiftly changing industry but also a proactive approach to stimulate sustainable expansion and competitiveness (Agarwal et al. 2023).

1.4.1.1 Enhancing Productivity and Competitiveness

The incorporation of digital technology in the fashion industry has led to a significant boost in productivity, radically transforming the implementation of tasks and the allocation of resources throughout the whole value chain (Casciani et al. 2022). By using artificial intelligence and machine learning, fashion companies can automate repetitive operations and improve workflows with exceptional precision and effectiveness. This enables the allocation of valuable time and resources to more significant pursuits (Ng et al. 2021).

Moreover, digital design software has wholly transformed the prototype stage, enabling designers to investigate a multitude of imaginative possibilities (Schäper et al. 2024). By digitising the design process, fashion firms may quickly and continuously improve concepts and get creative ideas to the market faster (Marion and Fixson 2021). Moreover, cutting-edge supply chain management solutions use up-to-the-minute data to enhance logistics, hence reducing delays and inefficiencies (Lehmacher 2021). Furthermore, these digital solutions facilitate smooth communication and cooperation, eliminating the barriers that previously impeded the effective transmission of information (Shojaei and Burgess 2022). As a result, the fashion ecosystem undergoes a multiplier impact on production, which is characterised by shorter cycle times, less waste and improved ability to meet market needs. In the end, digital transformation enables the industry to attain enhanced agility, flexibility and competitiveness in a constantly changing environment (Huynh 2021).

1.4.1.2 Operational Optimisation

The fashion industry, once known for its scattered information and isolated processes, is now being digitally integrated with a focus on efficiency (Shah et al. 2022). Companies may proactively anticipate market trends, recognise evolving customer preferences and coordinate their product offers by using advanced technologies like digital design platforms and predictive analytics (Gupta et al. 2020). This proactive strategy not only reduces the likelihood of inventory becoming obsolete but also allows firms to take advantage of new prospects for development and expansion by ensuring that designs are appealing to customers from the beginning (Rahman 2021).

Furthermore, the utilisation of real-time data analysis and insights empowers fashion firms to make educated selections swiftly and decisively. Using advanced data analysis tools, organisations may optimise inventory management, pricing strategies and promotional campaigns, maximising their financial benefits and overall profitability (Song and Lim 2021). Furthermore, the digital transformation process facilitates seamless communication and collaboration across many teams and departments, therefore removing historical obstacles that hinder the efficient interchange of information within the supply chain (Butt 2020). By coordinating several departments, not only does the decision-making process speed up, but it also promotes a culture of innovation and ongoing improvement. Through the application of digital technology, fashion firms may optimise their operational efficiency, foster cooperation and swiftly respond to dynamic market circumstances, thus establishing themselves for enduring success in the ever-churning fashion industry (Huynh 2021).

The story is brought to life by means of perceptive case studies and examples, which demonstrate the pragmatic use of digital technology in the fashion business. Every instance of achievement acts as a guiding light of motivation, showcasing how various enterprises use digital resources to conquer obstacles and accomplish extraordinary outcomes. For instance, using 3D modelling to iterate on designs online might decrease physical sample manufacturing by 50% and get an impeccable fit prior to commencing production (Prashar et al. 2023). These real-world instances underscore the immense transformative power of embracing digital technologies, offering tangible proof of their ability to optimise processes, enhance quality and unlock new creative possibilities (Allioui and Mourdi 2023).

1.4.1.3 Elevating Fashion Excellence: The Fusion of Creativity and Digital Technology

The emergence of digital technology has introduced a new element to the fabric of fashion excellence, distinguished by rigorous attention to detail and exceptional artistry. The combination of 3D modelling and virtual prototyping is a significant advancement that allows designers to see and improve their concepts with exceptional accuracy (Real et al. 2021). This technical breakthrough surpasses conventional constraints by providing designers with a thorough comprehension of the garment's structure, fit and functioning before actual manufacturing, thereby reducing the likelihood of expensive mistakes and inefficiencies (Liu et al. 2022a).

Furthermore, the use of digital quality control systems signifies a noteworthy achievement in the pursuit of unwavering perfection. These innovative systems use complex algorithms and sensor technologies to carefully examine every part of the garment's production, guaranteeing compliance with strict quality and consistency criteria (Hossain et al. 2024). Digital quality control systems routinely detect and correct flaws at each step of manufacturing, reducing the chances of faults and inconsistencies. This helps protect the brand's reputation and build customer confidence (Javaid et al. 2021).

As a result, the combination of creativity and technology brings forth a new way of thinking where the total excellence of fashion items is raised to levels previously unattainable. By effectively using digital tools and processes, fashion enterprises can maintain high standards of quality while also exploring new frontiers of innovation and creativity (Hongyun et al. 2023).

1.4.1.4 Revolutionising Inventory Management

Digital solutions are crucial in transforming inventory management procedures, equipping fashion firms with the means to maintain ideal stock levels, lower excess inventory and predict prospective stock deficiencies (Ahmad et al. 2020). By combining real-time data analytics and predictive modelling, organisations get important insights into the intricacies of consumer demand patterns, enabling more accurate demand forecasting and inventory management techniques (Pal 2023). Implementing proactive methodologies not only decreases expenses associated with storing inventory and disposing of outdated products but also improves the ability to adjust to changes in market demand quickly, thus fostering a supply chain characterised by increased adaptability and resilience (Mohsen 2023).

For example, a fashion business that utilises AI-driven demand forecasting may decrease surplus inventory by 20%, reducing waste and releasing resources for creative innovation (Balasubramanian et al. 2023). This exceeds the constraints of conventional forecasting techniques, which often depend on subjective assessments and historical data (Banerjee et al. 2021). The data unequivocally demonstrates that digital technologies in the fashion industry are not only about adjusting to change; rather, they signify a groundbreaking advancement that introduces unparalleled levels of creativity, efficiency and sustainability (Balasubramanian et al. 2023).

1.4.2 Benefits from Sustainability Standpoint

In the contemporary milieu of the fashion industry, the imperative of cost efficiency underscores the critical convergence of sustainability and profitability within a highly competitive market environment (Sharma and Singh 2023). The implementation of digital technologies in the fashion industry is viewed as a crucial approach to meet the urgent need for change. This signifies a period of transformation characterised by efficient operational structures, effective resource management and strategic decision-making models (Ghobakhloo and Iranmanesh 2021). The core of this transformation is optimising industrial processes and integrating digital technology to minimise waste, improve productivity and decrease operating costs. By using cutting-edge technologies like artificial intelligence and machine learning, fashion companies can optimise production schedules, streamline procedural processes and pinpoint opportunities for process improvement with exceptional accuracy and efficiency (Perifanis and Kitsios 2023).

Moreover, the integration of sustainable practices represents an indispensable determinant in realising cost-effectiveness throughout the digital revolution of the fashion sector (Alkaraan et al. 2023). Fashion establishments can attenuate their ecological footprint and economise costs by harnessing digital technologies to optimise resource allocation, curtail waste generation and advocate for ethically sourced and sustainable production methodologies (Javaid et al. 2022). The sector's concerted emphasis on both sustainability and cost-efficiency positions it favourably to attain enduring growth and profitability trajectories. This framework harmonises economic imperatives with environmental stewardship and societal responsibility. In essence, the utilisation of digital technology not only augments the cost-efficiency quotient of fashion enterprises but also engenders a sustainable and resilient trajectory for the industry at large (Allioui and Mourdi 2023).

1.4.2.1 Environmental Benefits

At the forefront of sustainable practices facilitated by advanced technologies is the reduction of environmental impact. Digital technologies provide avenues to streamline production processes, minimise waste and optimise resource utilisation (Scaturro 2008). Through the implementation of sophisticated algorithms and machine learning, fashion businesses can precisely forecast demand, thereby curtailing overproduction and diminishing the carbon footprint associated with excess inventory. Additionally, digital tools enable the efficient management of textile waste, promoting circularity and sustainability in the fashion ecosystem (Nayak 2019b).

New technologies offer a variety of tools for optimising resource utilisation throughout the fashion value chain, going beyond demand forecasting. In the field of materials science, artificial intelligence (AI) has the remarkable ability to predict the characteristics of innovative fibres (Guo et al. 2021b). This breakthrough has enabled the creation of fabrics that are not only lighter and stronger but also more durable, all while minimising resource consumption during the manufacturing process. Designers can effectively develop and enhance their conceptual ideas using digital design tools such as 3D modelling and simulation. This eliminates the need for physical prototypes and the wasteful use of materials associated with them (Sikka et al. 2024). Furthermore, robotic automation could reduce waste and energy consumption while streamlining production processes in comparison to manual methods (Adrita et al. 2021).

1.4.2.2 Material Innovation for Sustainability

The realm of materials and fabric innovation is undergoing a metamorphosis, with digital technologies acting as the catalyst for a shift towards greener pastures. The days of large-scale prototypes and redundant use of fabric are obsolete (Coombs et al. 2018). Modern technologies such as digital weaving and 3D printing enable designers to create complex structures and patterns with extreme accuracy, reducing material waste and maximising the consumption of resources (Ngo et al. 2018). Also, digital platforms function as vibrant marketplaces, connecting designers with a plethora of sustainable fibres and eco-friendly materials, namely, instantly accessing information on organic cotton grown with rainwater harvesting techniques or mycelium leather cultivated from recycled waste streams (Ian Gibson 2015). This transparency and ease of sourcing encourage a shift towards corporate ethical and environmentally responsible practices, empowering designers to make satisfactory choices throughout the material selection process (Hossain et al. 2024).

In addition, machine learning algorithms are of the utmost importance in harnessing the full potential of recycled materials (Guo et al. 2021a). Through the analysis of extensive datasets, these algorithms have the ability to discover the most efficient methods for processing and reusing recycled fibres. This process revitalises old materials and reduces the need for new resources (Rejeb et al. 2022). For instance, the remarkable garments made from recycled plastic bottles not only excel in performance and aesthetics but also serve as a testament to the immense possibilities of circularity within the fashion industry. The impact extends beyond aesthetics and functionality. Bio-based materials like algae-derived fibres and spider silk alternatives are being explored, offering sustainable and potentially high-performance options. Imagine garments grown from renewable resources or woven with ethically sourced biomaterials, pushing the boundaries of what's possible in a sustainable fashion (Aakko and Koskennurmi-Sivonen 2013).

1.4.2.3 Smart Textiles

The concept of 'smart textiles' emerges as a prominent sustainable benefit catalysed by digital technologies (Schwarz et al. 2010). The prospect of smart textiles, imbued with sensors and responsive capabilities, transcends the boundaries of mere user experience and energy efficiency, weaving a tapestry of sustainability benefits that impact individuals and the environment alike (Ruckdashel et al. 2021). Such futuristic materials embrace the potential to revolutionise healthcare, resource management and even self-sufficiency, offering a glimpse into a more sustainable future for the fashion industry (Ramlow et al. 2021).

The potential of bio-integrated textiles, which seamlessly combine technology and biology, is to obtain a vast amount of health data, including heart rate, respiration and blood sugar levels (Liu et al. 2022b). This personalised information empowers individuals to take control of their well-being, facilitating proactive disease management and preventive measures. It is expected to enable athletes to fine-tune their performance using instant feedback from their attire or people with chronic illnesses receiving customised notifications about their well-being. The implications have far-reaching effects, extending beyond individual health and making significant contributions to resource management on a larger scale (Ray et al. 2019).

Meanwhile, self-cleaning textiles that are infused with nano-coatings have the ability to repel dirt and bacteria, which in turn reduces the frequency of laundering required (Busi et al. 2016). This results in a significant decrease in water usage, estimated to be approximately 80% for a single washing cycle, that fabrics remain clean and odour-free for extended periods, significantly reducing the environmental impact of conventional laundry practices (Toprak and Anis 2017). This not only conserves valuable water resources but also decreases the energy usage linked to operating and heating washing machines (Roy et al. 2020).

Self-healing textiles push the boundaries of resource conservation (Khan et al. 2020). This fabric possesses the remarkable ability to repair itself when subjected to small tears or abrasions, thanks to the presence of tiny capsules filled with healing agents and prolonging their durability. This helps reduce the environmental impact linked to the production, disposal and rapid turnover of garments. In addition, the potential of self-healing textiles to transform industries such as sports apparel and outdoor gear, where garments are susceptible to damage, is remarkable (Ramesh et al. 2022).

More importantly, the field of solar-powered textiles has seen remarkable advancements, with the integration of miniature photovoltaic cells that efficiently capture energy from sunlight (Arbaud et al. 2024). Picture clothing that can energise built-in electronics or even recharge your portable devices, eliminating the necessity for external power supplies. This paves the way for the advancement of self-sustaining clothing, especially in remote regions or areas affected by disasters where the availability of conventional energy sources might be restricted. This even enables self-sufficiency of energy for work and life in unfavourable situations such as adventures, long-haul travels or backpacking (Sharma et al. 2023).

1.4.2.4 Transparency and Traceability

The fashion industry, which was once known for its concealment, is currently experiencing a shift towards transparency thanks to the breakthroughs in digital technologies (Garcia-Torres et al. 2022). Consumers now have an exclusive chance to delve into the production journey of their garments as they become more cognizant of the environmental and social consequences of what they choose to wear (Ospital et al. 2023). This emerging visibility is not only enabling but also leading to a substantial shift towards sustainable practices. As an illustration, blockchain technology serves as an emblem of transparency, functioning as an unchangeable record that documents each stage a garment goes through, from its raw materials to the final item of clothing. This distributed ledger system safeguards the credibility of sustainable claims, thwarting deceptive practices and cultivating a sense of confidence between brands and consumers (Guo et al. 2020). Thus, thanks to advanced technology integration, the customer is now able to scan a clothing tag and uncover a detailed account of its origins, the labour conditions involved in its production and the environmental impact of its journey to its destination. Consumers are now able to make informed decisions and support brands that align with their principles under the high level of transparency in the fashion industry that has led to a growing demand for ethically and sustainably manufactured fashion (Ospital et al. 2023).

However, acquiring a comprehensive understanding of production involves more than simply being aware of the ‘who’ and ‘where’. Utilising digital tools such as satellite imagery and sensor technology, valuable insights can be gained regarding the environmental impact of various stages in the supply chain (McGrath et al. 2021). This consists of understanding the water usage involved in the cultivation of cotton and the carbon emissions produced during fabric dyeing (Karunathilake et al. 2023).

This detailed information enables individuals to grasp the actual expenses associated with their clothing decisions and encourages business enterprises to embrace more eco-friendly methods in order to minimise their ecological footprint (Garcia-Torres et al. 2022). Notwithstanding, transparency is a two-way avenue. Through the utilisation of social media platforms and online communities, individuals have the chance to participate in active interaction with brands and advocate for change (Jestratijevic et al. 2022). This can be seen in the participation of online forums where consumers discuss the sustainability practices of various brands, exchange personal experiences and hold brands responsible for their commitments. This interactive exchange promotes teamwork and expedites the industry's advancement towards sustainability (Rinaldi et al. 2022).

1.4.2.5 Consumer Engagement and Connectivity for Amplifying Impact

The incorporation of digital technologies into sustainable fashion practices extends to the domain of consumer engagement and education. Augmented Reality (AR) and Virtual Reality (VR) applications provide users with immersive experiences with features that assist them gain insight into the environmental impact of their personal fashion choices (Wu and Kim 2022). This heightened consciousness, combined with the advocacy for sustainable fashion on digital platforms, is driving a shift in culture towards more conscious consumption. In addition to demand forecasting, modern technologies offer a variety of tools to enhance the efficiency of resource utilisation in the middle of the fashion value chain. This process minimises the requirement for physical prototypes and the associated wastage of materials (Chen et al. 2015). Furthermore, in comparison with conventional methods, the implementation of automated procedures has the potential to enhance manufacturing operations while minimising waste and energy consumption (Mawson and Hughes 2019).

Collaboration and connectivity, enabled by digital technologies, are essential for improving the efficacy of sustainable practices (Omrany et al. 2023). The platforms that facilitate the relationship between designers, manufacturers and consumers enhance a culture of collaboration, where ideas, innovations and best practices are exchanged without restriction. This complicated framework promotes the dissemination of sustainable knowledge and accelerates the implementation of environmentally conscious practices within the fashion industry (Rizos et al. 2016). Similarly, online platforms have the potential to not only enable the exchange of information but also foster collaborative innovation (Esposito De Falco et al. 2017). Open-source platforms provide a valuable opportunity for designers as well as producers to collaborate and exchange ideas on environmentally conscious design principles. By sharing best practices, these platforms can help accelerate the development and adoption of eco-friendly alternatives (Bonvoisin 2016). In addition, crowdfunding platforms have the ability to connect environmentally friendly apparel projects with investors and consumers, offering crucial financial support and cultivating a community centred around sustainable fashion (Yáñez-Valdés and Guerrero 2023).

1.5 Conclusions

Fashion and textile manufacturing is still labour-based process in many countries. The use of various digital technologies has the potential to revolutionise fashion and textile manufacturing. The objective of this chapter is to discuss the use of various digital technologies in fashion and textiles. By researching various secondary resources and primary data collection, this chapter has highlighted various new technologies covered under Industry 4.0. A brief of the industrial revolutions focusing on some of the innovations in each industrial revolution is illustrated. There have been brief discussions on RFID, IoT, blockchain and how they can improve the manufacturing processes. Sustainable benefits achieved by the manufacturing industries are also discussed in this chapter.

The recent trend is moving towards integration of digital technologies in various manufacturing sectors. Some of the global brands have already been in the forefront of technology drive by implementing the latest technologies in manufacturing, sourcing, warehousing and retailing operations. However, several large fashion enterprises, manufacturing industries and small and medium sized enterprises (SMEs) are still in the infancy to implement the latest technologies. Several factors create hindrance to the implementation of digital technologies. The major factor is the high cost of implementing these technologies. The SMEs face challenges in terms of availability of sufficient funding for installing the software. There are several other challenges such as low cost of garments, availability of cheap labour, shortage of skilled labour, several variations in styles of fashion and textiles. Investment by famous fashion brands, financial support from government and financial institutions, training of labour force and changing the strategies towards new technologies can help to improve the adaption of new technologies in fashion and textile sector.

References

Aakko M, Koskennurmi-Sivonen R (2013) Designing sustainable fashion: possibilities and challenges. Res J Textile Apparel 17:13–22

Abd Jelil R (2018) Review of artificial intelligence applications in garment manufacturing. In: Artificial Intelligence for fashion industry in the big data era, pp 97–123

Adrita MM, Brem A, O'Sullivan D, Allen E, Bruton K (2021) Methodology for data-informed process improvement to enable automated manufacturing in current manual processes. Appl Sci 11:3889

Agarwal V, Hameed AZ, Malhotra S, Mathiyazhagan K, Alathur S, Appolloni A (2023) Role of Industry 4.0 in agile manufacturing to achieve sustainable development. Bus Strategy Environ 32:3671–3688

Akram SV, Malik PK, Singh R, Gehlot A, Juyal A, Ghafoor KZ, Shrestha S (2022) Implementation of digitalized technologies for fashion industry 4.0: opportunities and challenges. Sci Program

Alkaraan F, Elmarzouky M, Hussainey K, Venkatesh V (2023) Sustainable strategic investment decision-making practices in UK companies: the influence of governance mechanisms on synergy between industry 4.0 and circular economy. Technol Forecast Soc Change 187:122187

Allioui H, Mourdi Y (2023) Exploring the full potentials of IoT for better financial growth and stability: a comprehensive survey. Sensors 23:8015
Arbaud R, Najafi M, Gandarias JM, Lorenzini M, Paul UC, Zych A, Athanassiou A, Cataldi P, Ajoudani A (2024) Toward sustainable haptics: a wearable vibrotactile solar-powered system with biodegradable components. Adv Mater Technol 2301265
Balasubramanian S, Shukla V, Kavanancheeri L (2023) Improving supply chain sustainability using artificial intelligence: evidence from the manufacturing sector. In: Industry 4.0 technologies: sustainable manufacturing supply chains. Methods for transition and trends, vol II. Springer, Belrin
Banerjee SS, Mohapatra S, Saha G (2021) Developing a framework of artificial intelligence for fashion forecasting and validating with a case study. Int J Enterp Network Manag 12:165–180
Bertola P, Teunissen J (2018) Fashion 4.0. Innovating fashion industry through digital transformation. Res J Text Apparel 22:352–369
Bonvoisin J (2016) Implications of open source design for sustainability. In: Sustainable design and manufacturing. Springer, Berlin, pp 49–59
Boute RN, Udenio M (2022) AI in logistics and supply chain management. In: Global logistics and supply chain strategies for the 2020s: vital skills for the next generation. Springer, Berlin
Busi E, Maranghi S, Corsi L, Basosi R (2016) Environmental sustainability evaluation of innovative self-cleaning textiles. J Cleaner Prod 133:439–450
Butt J (2020) A conceptual framework to support digital transformation in manufacturing using an integrated business process management approach. Designs 4:17
Büyüközkan G, Göçer F (2018) Digital supply chain: literature review and a proposed framework for future research. Comput Ind 97:157–177
Caldarelli G, Zardini A, Rossignoli C (2021) Blockchain adoption in the fashion sustainable supply chain: pragmatically addressing barriers. J Organ Change Manag 34:507–524
Casciani D, Chkanikova O, Pal R (2022) Exploring the nature of digital transformation in the fashion industry: opportunities for supply chains, business models, and sustainability-oriented innovations. Sustain Sci Pract Policy 18:773–795
Center S (2019) Global garment and textile industries. Workers, rights and working conditions
Chen Y (2023) How blockchain adoption affects supply chain sustainability in the fashion industry: a systematic review and case studies. Int Trans Oper Res
Chen DQ, Preston DS, Swink M (2015) How the use of big data analytics affects value creation in supply chain management. J Manag Inf Syst 32:4–39
Coombs G, McNamara A, Sade G (2018) Undesign: critical practices at the intersection of art and design. Routledge
Duarte AYS, Sanches RA, Dedini FG (2018) Assessment and technological forecasting in the textile industry: From first industrial revolution to the Industry 4.0. Strateg Design Res J 11:193
Esposito De Falco S, Renzi A, Orlando B, Cucari N (2017) Open collaborative innovation and digital platforms. Prod Plann Control 28:1344–1353
Evans C, Rydén G (2017) The industrial revolution in iron: the impact of British coal technology in nineteenth-century Europe. Taylor & Francis
Fernández-Caramés TM, Fraga-Lamas P (2018) Towards the Internet of smart clothing: a review on IoT wearables and garments for creating intelligent connected e-textiles. Electronics 7:405
Garcia-Torres S, Rey-Garcia M, Sáenz J, Seuring S (2022) Traceability and transparency for sustainable fashion-apparel supply chains. J Fashion Mark Manag Int J 26:344–364
Garrido Azevedo S, Carvalho H (2012) Contribution of RFID technology to better management of fashion supply chains. Int J Retail Distrib Manag 40:128–156
Ghobakhloo M, Iranmanesh M (2021) Digital transformation success under Industry 4.0: a strategic guideline for manufacturing SMEs. J Manuf Technol Manag 32:1533–1556
Goel P, Mahadevan K, Punjani KK (2023) Augmented and virtual reality in apparel industry: a bibliometric review and future research agenda. foresight 25:167–184
Groumpos PP (2021) A critical historical and scientific overview of all industrial revolutions. IFAC-PapersOnLine 54:464–471

Guo S, Sun X, Lam HK (2020) Applications of blockchain technology in sustainable fashion supply chains: operational transparency and environmental efforts. IEEE Trans Eng Manag
Guo H-N, Wu S-B, Tian Y-J, Zhang J, Liu H-T (2021a) Application of machine learning methods for the prediction of organic solid waste treatment and recycling processes: a review. Bioresour Technol 319:124114
Guo K, Yang Z, Yu C-H, Buehler MJ (2021b) Artificial intelligence and machine learning in design of mechanical materials. Mater Horiz 8:1153–1172
Gupta S, Leszkiewicz A, Kumar V, Bijmolt T, Potapov D (2020) Digital analytics: modeling for insights and new methods. J Interact Mark 51:26–43
Hahn B (2020) Technology in the industrial revolution. Cambridge University Press
Hongyun T, Sohu JM, Khan AU, Junejo I, Shaikh SN, Akhtar S, Bilal M (2023) Navigating the digital landscape: examining the interdependencies of digital transformation and big data in driving SMEs' innovation performance. Kybernetes
Hora ST, Bungau C, Negru PA, Radu A-F (2023) Implementing circular economy elements in the textile industry: a bibliometric analysis. Sustainability 15:15130
Hossain MT, Shahid MA, Limon MGM, Hossain I, Mahmud N (2024) Techniques, applications, and challenges in textiles for sustainable future. J Open Innov Technol Market Complexity 100230
Humphries J, Schneider B (2019) Spinning the industrial revolution. Econ History Rev 72:126–155
Huynh PH (2021) Enabling circular business models in the fashion industry: the role of digital innovation. Int J Prod Performance Manag 71:870–895
Ian Gibson IG (2015) Additive manufacturing technologies 3D printing, rapid prototyping, and direct digital manufacturing. Springer, Berlin
Jain S, Bruniaux J, Zeng X, Bruniaux P (2017) Big data in fashion industry. IOP Conf Ser Mater Sci Eng 152005
Javaid M, Haleem A, Singh RP, Suman R (2021) Significance of quality 4.0 towards comprehensive enhancement in manufacturing sector. Sens Int 2:100109
Javaid M, Haleem A, Singh RP, Khan S, Suman R (2022) Sustainability 4.0 and its applications in the field of manufacturing. Internet Things Cyber Phys Syst 2:82–90
Jestratijevic I, Uanhoro JO, Creighton R (2022) To disclose or not to disclose? Fashion brands' strategies for transparency in sustainability reporting. J Fashion Mark Manag Int J 26:36–50
Jin BE, Shin DC (2021) The power of 4th industrial revolution in the fashion industry: what, why, and how has the industry changed? Fashion Text 8:31
Kaounides L, Yu H, Harper T (2007) Nanotechnology innovation and applications in textiles industry: current markets and future growth trends. Mater Technol 22:209–237
Karunathilake E, Le AT, Heo S, Chung YS, Mansoor S (2023) The path to smart farming: innovations and opportunities in precision agriculture. Agriculture 13:1593
Khan A, Ahmed N, Rabnawaz M (2020) Covalent adaptable network and self-healing materials: current trends and future prospects in sustainability. Polymers 12:2027
Lee H, Yeon C (2021) Blockchain-based traceability for anti-counterfeit in cross-border e-commerce transactions. Sustainability 13:11057
Lehmacher W (2021) Digitizing and automating processes in logistics. In: Disrupting logistics: startups, technologies, and investors building future supply chains, pp 9–27
Li K, Kim DJ, Lang KR, Kauffman RJ, Naldi M (2020) How should we understand the digital economy in Asia? Critical assessment and research agenda. Electron Commer Res Appl 44:101004
Liu K, Wu H, Zhu C, Wang J, Zeng X, Tao X, Bruniaux P (2022a) An evaluation of garment fit to improve customer body fit of fashion design clothing. Int J Adv Manuf Technol 120:2685–2699
Liu M, Zhang Y, Tao TH (2022b) Recent progress in bio-integrated intelligent sensing system. Adv Intell Syst 4:2100280
Luce L (2018) Artificial intelligence for fashion: how AI is revolutionizing the fashion industry. Apress

Ma K, Wang L, Chen Y (2017) A collaborative cloud service platform for realizing sustainable make-to-order apparel supply chain. Sustainability 10:11
Maizi Y, Bendavid Y (2021) Building a digital twin for IoT smart stores: a case in retail and apparel industry. Int J Simul Process Model 16:147–160
Majeed AA, Rupasinghe TD (2017) Internet of things (IoT) embedded future supply chains for industry 4.0: an assessment from an ERP-based fashion apparel and footwear industry. Int J Supply Chain Manag 6:25–40
Marion TJ, Fixson SK (2021) The transformation of the innovation process: how digital tools are changing work, collaboration, and organizations in new product development. J Prod Innov Manag 38:192–215
Maw P, Solar P, Kane A, Lyons JS (2022) After the great inventions: technological change in UK cotton spinning, 1780–1835. Econ Hist Rev 75:22–55
Mawson VJ, Hughes BR (2019) The development of modelling tools to improve energy efficiency in manufacturing processes and systems. J Manuf Syst 51:95–105
McGrath P, McCarthy L, Marshall D, Rehme J (2021) Tools and technologies of transparency in sustainable global supply chains. Calif Manag Rev 64:67–89
Mohsen BM (2023) Impact of artificial intelligence on supply chain management performance. J Ser Sci Manag 16(1):44–58
Nayak R (2019a) Radio frequency identification (RFID) technology and application in fashion and textile supply chain. CRC Press, Boca Raton
Nayak R (2019b) Sustainable technologies for fashion and textiles. Woodhead Publishing
Nayak R (2020) Supply chain management and logistics in the global fashion sector: the sustainability challenge. Routledge, London
Nayak R, Padhye R (2015) Garment manufacturing technology. Elsevier, Amsterdam
Nayak R, Padhye R (2017) Automation in garment manufacturing. Elsevier, Amsterdam
Nayak R, Padhye R (2018) Introduction to automation in garment manufacturing. In: Automation in garment manufacturing. Elsevier, Amsterdam
Nayak R, Chatterjee K, Khurana G, Khandual A (2007) RFID: tagging the new ERA. Man-Made Text India 50
Nayak R, Singh A, Padhye R, Wang L (2015) RFID in textile and clothing manufacturing: technology and challenges. Fashion Text 2:9
Nayak R, Akbari M, Far SM (2019) Recent sustainable trends in Vietnam's fashion supply chain. J Cleaner Prod 225:291–303
Nayak R, Panwar T, Nguyen LVT (2020) Sustainability in fashion and textiles: a survey from developing country. In: Sustainable technologies for fashion and textiles. Elsevier, Amsterdam
Nayak R, George M, Haq IU, Pham HC (2022) Sustainability benefits of RFID technology in Vietnamese fashion supply chain. Cleaner Logistics Supply Chain 5:1–12
Ng KK, Chen C-H, Lee CK, Jiao JR, Yang Z-X (2021) A systematic literature review on intelligent automation: aligning concepts from theory, practice, and future perspectives. Adv Eng Inform 47:101246
Ngo TD, Kashani A, Imbalzano G, Nguyen KT, Hui D (2018) Additive manufacturing (3D printing): a review of materials, methods, applications and challenges. Compos Part B: Eng 143:172–196
Omrany H, Al-Obaidi KM, Husain A, Ghaffarianhoseini A (2023) Digital twins in the construction industry: a comprehensive review of current implementations, enabling technologies, and future directions. Sustainability 15:10908
Oosthuizen K, Botha E, Robertson J, Montecchi M (2021) Artificial intelligence in retail: the AI-enabled value chain. Australas Mark J 29:264–273
Ospital P, Masson D, Beler C, Legardeur J (2023) Toward product transparency: communicating traceability information to consumers. Int J Fashion Des Technol Educ 16:186–197
Pal S (2023) Advancements in AI-Enhanced just-In-time inventory: Elevating demand forecasting accuracy. Int J Res Appl Sci Eng Technol 11:282–289
Perifanis N-A, Kitsios F (2023) Investigating the influence of artificial intelligence on business value in the digital era of strategy: a literature review. Information 14:85

Prashar G, Vasudev H, Bhuddhi D (2023) Additive manufacturing: expanding 3D printing horizon in industry 4.0. Int J Interact Des Manuf (IJIDeM) 17:2221–2235
Rahman MM (2021) Applications of the digital technologies in textile and fashion manufacturing industry. Technium Rom J Appl Sci Technol 3:114–127
Rai SK (2015) Ways to modernisation and adaptation: the state, weaving training schools and handloom weavers in early twentieth century united provinces, India. Indian Hist Rev 42:261–287
Ramesh S, Khan S, Park Y, Ford E, Menegatti S, Genzer J (2022) Self-healing and repair of fabrics: a comprehensive review of the application toolkit. Mater Today 54:90–109
Ramlow H, Andrade KL, Immich APS (2021) Smart textiles: an overview of recent progress on chromic textiles. J Text Inst 112:152–171
Ramos L, Rivas-Echeverría F, Pérez AG, Casas E (2023) Artificial intelligence and sustainability in the fashion industry: a review from 2010 to 2022. SN Appl Sci 5:387
Ray TR, Choi J, Bandodkar AJ, Krishnan S, Gutruf P, Tian L, Ghaffari R, Rogers JA (2019) Bio-integrated wearable systems: a comprehensive review. Chem Rev 119:5461–5533
Real R, Snider C, Goudswaard M, Hicks B (2021) Dimensions of knowledge in prototyping: a review and characterisation of prototyping methods and their contributions to design knowledge. Proc Des Soc 1:1303–1312
Rejeb A, Rejeb K, Zailani S, Keogh JG, Appolloni A (2022) Examining the interplay between artificial intelligence and the agri-food industry. Artif Intell Agric
Ren S, Patrick Hui, C-L, Jason Choi T-M (2018) AI-based fashion sales forecasting methods in big data era. In: Artificial intelligence for fashion industry in the big data era, pp 9–26
Rinaldi FR, di Bernardino C, Cram-Martos V, Pisani MT (2022) Traceability and transparency: enhancing sustainability and circularity in garment and footwear. Sustain Sci Pract Policy 18:132–141
Rizos V, Behrens A, van der Gaast W, Hofman E, Ioannou A, Kafyeke T, Flamos A, Rinaldi R, Papadelis S, Hirschnitz-Garbers M (2016) Implementation of circular economy business models by small and medium-sized enterprises (SMEs): barriers and enablers. Sustainability 8:1212
Roy S, Zhai L, Kim JW, Kim HC, Kim J (2020) A novel approach of developing sustainable cellulose coating for self-cleaning-healing fabric. Prog Org Coat 140:105500
Ruckdashel RR, Venkataraman D, Park JH (2021) Smart textiles: a toolkit to fashion the future. J Appl Phys 129
Salahuddin M, Lee Y-A (2022) Automation with robotics in garment manufacturing. In: Leading edge technologies in fashion innovation: product design and development process from materials to the end products to consumers. Springer, Berlin
Scaturro S (2008) Eco-tech fashion: rationalizing technology in sustainable fashion. Fashion Theory 12:469–488
Schäper T, Foege JN, Nüesch S (2024) Toolkits for innovation: how digital technologies empower users in new product development. Res Dev Manag 54:95–117
Schwarz I, Kovačević S (2017) Textile application: from need to imagination. In: Textiles for advanced applications. IntechOpen
Schwarz A, van Langenhove L, Guermonprez P, Deguillemont D (2010) A roadmap on smart textiles. Text Prog 42:99–180
Shah MA, Pirzada BM, Price G, Shibiru AL, Qurashi A (2022) Applications of nanotechnology in smart textile industry: a critical review. J Adv Res 38:55–75
Sharma A, Singh BJ (2023) Evolution of modified LSS 4.0 model for sustainable Indian textile industry: a narrative review. Inter J Interact Des Manuf (IJIDeM) 1–20
Sharma M, Tyagi V, Chopra K, Kothari R, Singh HM, Pandey A (2023) Advancement in solar energy-based technologies for sustainable treatment of textile wastewater: reuse, recovery and current perspectives. J Water Process Eng 56:104241
Shaw R, Simpson P (2002) Synthetic fibres. In: The structure of British industry. Routledge
Shojaei RS, Burgess G (2022) Non-technical inhibitors: exploring the adoption of digital innovation in the UK construction industry. Technol Forecast Soc Chang 185:122036

Sikka MP, Sarkar A, Garg S (2024) Artificial intelligence (AI) in textile industry operational modernization. Res J Text Apparel 28:67–83

Silva ES, Hassani H, Madsen DØ (2020) Big data in fashion: transforming the retail sector. J Bus Strategy 41:21–27

Song E-Y, Lim H-S (2021) Perceptions and trends of digital fashion technology—a big data analysis. Fashion Text Res J 23:380–389

Styles J (2020) The rise and fall of the Spinning Jenny: domestic mechanisation in eighteenth-century cotton spinning. Text Hist 51:195–236

Stylios GK (2013) Intelligent sewing systems for garment automation and robotics. In: Joining textiles. Elsevier, Amsterdam

Sucharitha G, Tannmayee B, Dwarakamai K (2022) Revolution in IoT: smart wearable technology. In: Internet of things and its applications, pp 407–425

Toprak T, Anis P (2017) Textile industry's environmental effects and approaching cleaner production and sustainability, an overview. J Text Eng Fashion Technol 2:429–442

Tripathi G, Tripathi Nautiyal V, Ahad MA, Feroz N (2021) Blockchain technology and fashion industry-opportunities and challenges. In: Blockchain technology: applications and challenges, pp 201–220

Wu YF, Kim EY (2022) Users' perceptions of technological features in augmented reality (AR) and virtual reality (VR) in fashion retailing: a qualitative content analysis. Mob Inf Syst

Yáñez-Valdés C, Guerrero M (2023) Equity crowdfunding platforms and sustainable impacts: encountering investors and technological initiatives for tackling social and environmental challenges. Eur J Innov Manag

Zutshi A, Grilo A (2019) The emergence of digital platforms: a conceptual platform architecture and impact on industrial engineering. Elsevier, Amsterdam

Chapter 2
VR/AR and Metaverse in Fashion Industry

Md. Mahbubor Rahman, Ghada Soliman, Faisal Ahmed, Md. Mazedul Islam, and Abu Sadat Muhammad Sayem

Abstract Metaverse is no more a science fiction today. Rapid advancements of the digital technologies like digital twins, internet of things (IoT), artificial intelligence (AI) and machine learning (ML); edge and cloud computing; digital networks (5G/6G); blockchain; virtual reality (VR) and augmented reality (AR) are making the parallel existence of human civilization in a virtual platform in addition its existence on the real world. Instead of connecting with the social media on internet with the help of mouse and keyboard as it is done at present by the netizens, Metaverse will take them within the internet as avatars roaming virtually, socialising and living in a parallel world. This creates a new avenue for digital fashion and establishes a new industry and market for fashion professionals. This chapter digs into the development of VR/AR and Metaverse technologies and explores the opportunities for fashion industry in Metaverse. While reading this chapter, the readers will travel from the historical background of VR/AR and Metaverse technologies through their present state of the art to their foreseeable outlook.

Keywords Extended reality (XR) · Virtual reality · 3D CAD · Digital fashion · Digital twin · Block chain · Virtual runway

---

Md. Mahbubor Rahman · F. Ahmed
Bangladesh University of Textiles, Dhaka, Bangladesh
e-mail: mahbub@tfd.butex.edu.bd

G. Soliman · Md. Mazedul Islam
University of Manchester, Manchester, UK
e-mail: ghada.soliman@manchester.ac.uk

Md. Mazedul Islam
e-mail: m.m.islam@soton.ac.uk

A. S. M. Sayem (✉)
Manchester Metropolitan University, Manchester, UK
e-mail: asm.sayem@mmu.ac.uk

R. Nayak et al. (eds.), *Use of Digital and Advanced Technologies in the Fashion Supply Chain*, Springer Series in Fashion Business,
https://doi.org/10.1007/978-981-97-7528-6_2

2.1 Introduction

The key technologies that are enabling the industrial and consumer metaverse to flourish are digital twins, internet of things (IoT), artificial intelligence (AI) and machine learning (ML); edge and cloud computing; digital networks (5G/6G); blockchain; virtual reality (VR) and augmented reality (AR) (MIT Technology Review Insights 2023). VR technology provides the gateway for the users to dive into the metaverse by setting up an immersive simulated 3D environment for them to interact with. AR tools further enhance the user experience taking it as close to reality as possible. VR/AR gadgets that facilitate this immersive journey for the users are headsets, controllers, remote controls, etc. VR/AR phenomena are commonly discussed under the umbrella term of extended reality (XR), which is explored in the next section before moving on to the metaverse. This chapter also examines the applications of VR/AR technologies in the fashion industry while section five presents the fashion business opportunities in the metaverse.

2.2 Extended Reality (XR)

Extended Reality (XR), also referred to as cross reality, comprises a diverse array of immersive technologies along with their associated human–machine interactions and environments, such as the metaverse, which relies on these technologies. XR utilises spatial computing to facilitate and enhance operations within these systems. XR technology merges the physical and digital worlds incorporating various aspects of VR, AR and mixed reality (MR) as shown in Fig. 2.1. It can connect the users with the metaverse (Chuah 2018; Lee et al. 2021). XR devices are portable computers that might be worn and have processors, storage media and the ability to send and receive data with other entities (Ko and Rogers 2021).

In the 1960s, a scientist named "Ivan Sutherland" created the initial headset, which initiated the advancement of immersive technology XR (Marr 2021b). In 1975, Myron Krueger developed Videoplace, a virtual reality system enabled by the use of projectors and video cameras. Following that, there were rapid advancements, resulting in the launch of multiple XR applications for iOS, Android, Windows and Mac operating systems (Reiners et al. 2021). Following 2010, several industries began introducing their XR product lines on a global scale, coinciding with the increasing popularity of the term "XR" (Intelligence 2021). In 2014, prominent companies such as Facebook, Sony, Samsung and Google introduced their virtual reality head-mounted displays or headsets, resulting in a substantial advancement for the sector. In 2016, Microsoft unveiled the HoloLens headset, which is based on mixed reality technology. This groundbreaking device allowed for the integration of real and virtual objects, creating unprecedented experiences.

Currently, XR systems that are accessible include transparent screens capable of displaying controls and images in the space between the user and the real world. These

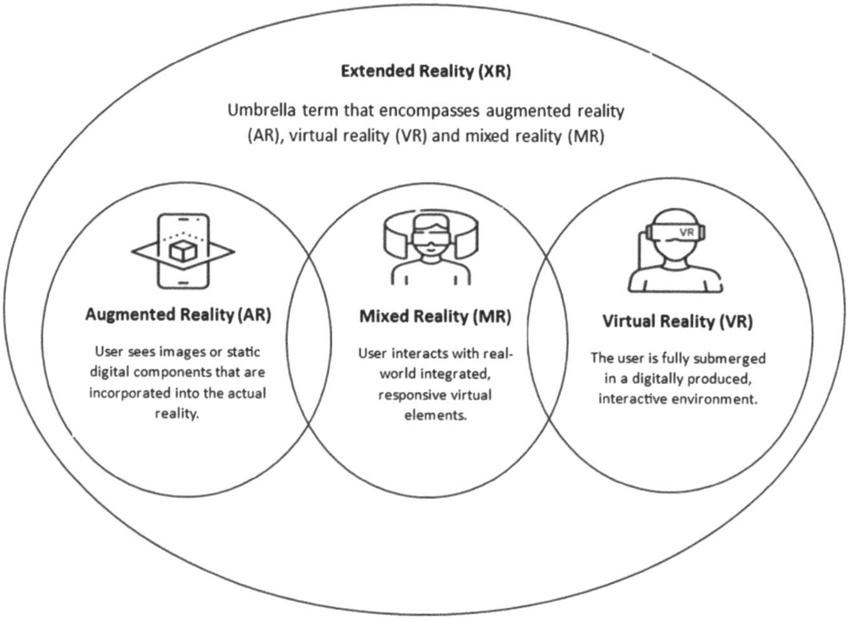

Fig. 2.1 Extended reality (XR) concept (Helmold 2023)

displays can also provide feedback cues and menu icons (Becker et al. 2020). XR devices utilise several sensors and displays, allowing them to analyse data from the sensors and generate appropriate visual outputs to provide an immersive experience. XR technologies aim to elicit specific feelings and emotions in the user, which are then captured by sensory devices embedded in the body. This creates the illusion that the user is fully engaged in a virtual environment.

The XR devices utilise thermo-haptic and vibro-haptic sensors to generate temperature and vibrational stimuli in the virtual environment, imitating the tactile sensations experienced on human skin (Ko and Rogers 2021). The advanced computer graphics (CG) and expanding bandwidth of XR technology are crucial for users to effortlessly interact with digital entities in the digital world, thanks to their ability to render realistic objects. The usability, performance, efficiency and productivity of XR products are undergoing rapid advancements (Muñoz-Saavedra et al. 2020).

Over the last twenty years, there has been an increasing emphasis on XR systems in both academic and industrial settings. Recent technology breakthroughs have enhanced the sophistication of XR. The term "reality-virtuality continuum" refers to a wide range of technologies that span from completely real to entirely virtual experiences (Gong et al. 2021).

Multiple studies have shown how XR technologies can be used to improve many manufacturing activities, including design, operation and maintenance, as documented by Phoon et al. (2017). The realisation of Industry 4.0 hinges on the seamless incorporation of XR systems, which is vital for the digitisation of the industrial sector. Engineers use a limited number of XR equipment in their everyday work routines, even though published research has demonstrated significant potential for XR applications in manufacturing (Kim and Dey 2010).

The integration of XR systems in the manufacturing sector is a complex and demanding task. With multiple existing systems, various stakeholders, and stringent quality, safety, and reliability requirements, XR systems not only provide expected benefits but also introduce novel methods of human–computer interaction for system developers and end users. The COVID-19 pandemic in 2020 has resulted in a rise in the practice of social distancing and remote meetings. This trend is likely to increase the utilisation of XR across several sectors, such as education, tourism and healthcare. Additionally, it could accelerate technological progress in the manufacturing industry (Gong et al. 2021).

Nowadays, wearables and computer technology have created habitats in both the real and virtual worlds. XR technologies have been applied in a variety of businesses and fields, including the military, psychology, marketing, retail, education, manufacturing, medicine and entertainment (Paris et al. 2022). They can also be used for specific medical applications, such as spinal medicine (Morimoto et al. 2022).

Businesses are increasingly introducing their products through virtual means and promoting client engagment from distant regions (Marr 2021a). The proliferation of cellular infrastructure to accommodate 5G and 6G will enhance the development and availability of XR applications. According to PwC (2024), worldwide XR market had a valuation of $46.4 billion in 2019, with an anticipated increase to $476.4 billion by 2025, representing a compound annual growth rate (CAGR) of 62% from 2020 to 2025 (PwC 2019). It has been predicted that XR technology would contribute $1.5 trillion to the global economy by 2030 (PwC 2019).

Emerging XR applications have become ubiquitous in real life, providing functionality in a wide range of disciplines. For these applications to function properly, they need to have access to large volumes of streaming data. The sensitive data that XR applications gather includes personal information about a person's appearance, biometrics and facts about their assets, lifestyle, occupation and social activities. Due to the sensitive nature of the data collected and the quick spread of XR applications by many tech companies, there is an increased danger of cyber-attacks, privacy violations, account theft, data exfiltration and other ethical dilemmas. In addition, raises concerns regarding physical security, motion sickness, digital sovereignty, invasions of individuals' virtual identities and the potential exploitation of connected technology and personal data (Ko and Rogers 2021; Qamar et al. 2023).

2.3 Metaverse

The concept of the metaverse was first brought into the literary realm by Neal Stephenson in his groundbreaking science fiction novel "Snow Crash," released in 1992 (Stephenson 1994; Chapman et al. 2022; Peukert et al. 2022). It represented a unique virtual reality formed using computer-generated imagery, enabling users worldwide to interact and connect utilising head-mounted displays and auditory devices. The 1984 science fiction novel Neuromancer by William Gibson introduces Matrix, a virtual reality cyberspace that acts as a literary forerunner to the Metaverse (Dionisio et al. 2013; Mystakidis 2022).

Lee et al. (2021) explained that since its initial emergence, the metaverse has been defined by a diverse range of concepts, including life logging, collective virtual space, embodied internet/spatial internet, a mirror world and an omniverse, establishing it as a space for simulation and collaboration within computer-generated universes. According to Weinberger (2022), the metaverse constitutes a network of interconnected virtual realms that, in part, intersect with and augment the real world. Within these virtual domains, users, represented by avatars, can engage in connections, interactions, and immersive consumption of user-generated content in a scalable, synchronous, and enduring environment. Additionally, there exists an economic structure incentivizing contribution to the metaverse.

Several technology companies have ventured into the Metaverse arena, with Meta, previously known as Facebook, emerging as a prominent player (Cheng et al. 2022). In September 2019, Meta introduced Facebook Horizon, a social virtual reality platform. By July 2021, the company revealed an ambitious strategy to transition into a Metaverse-centric entity within the next five years, leading to the official rebranding to Meta in October 2021. Meta considers VR as a crucial foundational element for the Metaverse, and its Oculus Quest 2 VR headset has achieved notable success, surpassing 10 million units in sales. Moreover, other major entities like Nvidia, Epic Games, Apple and Microsoft are actively participating in the advancement of the Metaverse industry.

The Metaverse, while offering societal opportunities, also confronts significant challenges (Wang et al. 2023). Current technology limitations might hinder its global functionality, posing issues of compatibility and scalability. Economically, its impact extends into the real world, intertwining virtual and actual economies. Ethical concerns arise, given its role as an expanded human habitat, introducing new moral dilemmas. Individuals face heightened privacy risks due to vast data presence, and the immersive nature of the Metaverse could exacerbate cyber-related health issues, impacting both physical and mental well-being and blurring the lines between virtual and real life.

2.4 VR/AR Applications in Fashion and Metaverse

The fashion sector has gone through significant changes over the last decade in design and manufacturing processes through a number of innovative 3D CAD software applications like Lectra, Optitex, CLO3D, Browzwear, etc. and in marketing segments with different XR tools like AR, VR and so on (Sarakatsanos et al. 2021). The leading technological innovations like AR and VR are being used extensively in fashion branding and retailing, along with other prime sectors including entertainment, education, tourism, transportation, real estate and beauty products (Boardman et al. 2020).

Fashion brands are adopting AR and VR technology on a greater scale to improve consumer shopping experience and to ensure that their products meet the desire features of their customers. Companies like Nike, ASOS, IKEA and Amazon implement AR and VR service technology to enhance the way customers interact with their products and assist them in making purchasing decisions (Heller et al. 2019; Hilken et al. 2020). When making decisions about purchasing new items, customers often rely on digitally produced product visualisation (McLean et al. 2018; Pizzi et al. 2019).

Shopping has become one of the increasingly popular online activities in the past couple of years, owing to the influence of these technological advances in the retail sector as a whole. Prominent fashion brands notably H&M, ZARA, Gucci, Myer Department Store and Nike, as well as cosmatic brands such as L'Oreal, Sephora, Oliveyoung and Estee Lauder are proactively establishing AR and VR marketplaces to maximise the buying experience (Makarov 2022) and increase consumption since evaluating clothing and fashion accessories involves various sensory inputs (Blázquez 2014).

Customers can readily explore the stores in the VR environment, and increasingly realistic and enjoyable buying experiences can satisfy their emotional requirements as well (Chittaro and Ranon 2000). A significant amount of the effort has been focused on showcasing the newest fashion trends through VR runways and presentations. For instance, the VR runway exhibition "*The Fabric of Reality*" attempts to guide spectators on an exploration to uncover the backstory as well as the context underlying the designs presented (Fashion Innovation Agency 2024).

VR has also embraced fashion in the classroom. Students studying creative arts and fashion design use simulated brushes and palettes for designing their party gowns, and instantly develop their creations employing Google Tilt Brush (Heckel 2020). VR marketing tools have been employed in recent years by different fashion brands to promote themselves (Boyd and Koles 2019; Caboni and Hagberg 2019; Rauschnabel et al. 2019). Improving customer experiences with VR campaigns is a smart approach as well as an excellent promotional channel (Alcañiz et al. 2019; Loureiro et al. 2019; Dwivedi et al. 2021).

Fashion stores can upgrade their services with VR to generate new revenue streams and boost the economy. A few fashion brands are now making efforts to employ VR tools in their promotions. In a collaborative effort, The retail brand Myer and American online shopping brand eBay launched the first VR departmental store in the world in May 2016. Their VR headgear "*Shoptical*" allows their customers to browse and purchase approximately 125,000 items at their VR retail shop (Ebay Press Release 2016). VR marketplaces for smartphones, PCs and head-mounted devices have also been introduced by Oliveyoung, a Korean top beauty products collection retailer (Wu and Kim 2022).

Alternatively, it becomes more important for customers to comprehend how well a fashionable item fits them. Through the use of AR try-on technology, customers

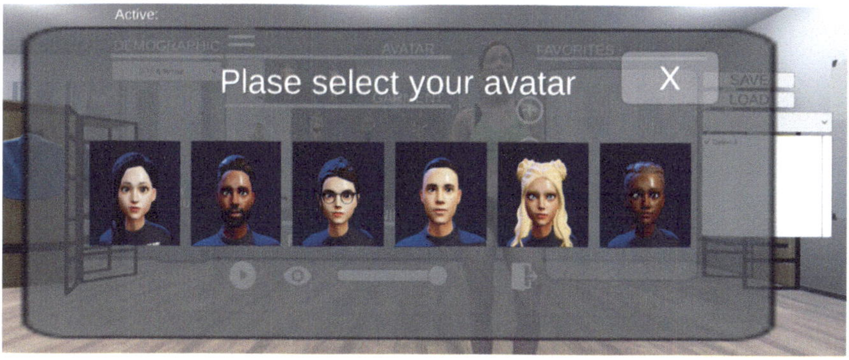

Fig. 2.2 VR Designer—multiuser avatar selection. *Source* https://link.springer.com/article/10.1007/s10055-024-00945-w#Fig5

might virtually experience things in a real-world setting that resembles the sensation of being able to try them on (Kim and Forsythe 2008). Its ability to require a significant amount of physical engagement such as clothing and cosmetic products makes AR an excellent instrument for product promotion (Baker et al. 2018). In order to improve consumer experiences in real-time (Rauschnabel et al. 2018; Dwivedi et al. 2022), AR offers a user-friendly interface and improves contextual details regarding design, satisfaction and functionality (Cummings and Bailenson 2016; Nanda and Banerjee 2020).

The inclusion of multiuser functionality can improve the experience of customers (Sarakatsanos et al. 2024). Multiple users can join the same VR session in the same virtual room and can actively interact with each other in the virtual space. Further, the use of VR empowers designers to host comprehensive design collection presentations to a group of users. Through the application of "VR Designer" multiuser mode, consumers can personalise their avatars and select products from a range of choices. The VR Designer—Multiuser avatar selection functionality has been shown in Fig. 2.2.

Integrating AR technology into different industrial settings is made more accessible to entrepreneurs through the development of cutting-edge technologies like Apple AR and 5G glasses (Javornik 2016; Pantano et al. 2020; Roggeveen et al. 2020). From the late 2000s forward, augmented reality has been utilised to investigate marketing strategies (Javornik 2016), especially the fashion retail sector reaping the positive effects of this research. Customers who shop online may acquire information about items in a manner comparable to physically handling them by utilising try-on sensory responses (Kim and Forsythe 2008). VR designer can be used to create garment props, mannequins and ceiling lights, which is quite similar to the realistic physical retail store as shown in Fig. 2.3 (Sarakatsanos et al. 2024).

AR promotional tools have evolved into fresh types of digital marketing techniques as more and more companies include AR in their advertising campaigns (Scholz and Duffy 2018; Heller et al. 2019; Rauschnabel et al. 2019). By merging

Fig. 2.3 VR Designer—retail space designed by VR. *Source* https://link.springer.com/article/10.1007/s10055-024-00945-w#Fig1

electronically stored information with the real world, AR in promotional applications offers customer experiences and illustrates customer advantages (Rauschnabel 2018). Gucci, a high-end Italian fashion brand, introduced AR-based retailing in 2019 using its customised mobile app. Customers have the option of selecting their preferred clothing and other fashion items, and attempting to virtually wear them by utilising their smartphone camera.

Through the integration of the AR marketing assistant app, ZARA realistically shows off model-wearing clothing as the camera is positioned at the retail location. Nike, the global sportswear leader, recently introduced an assistance program that uses AR to detect the consumers' feet measurements and recommend appropriate shoe sizes. Employing face scanning technology, the "*Make-up Genius*" app was released by L'Oreal, the leading beauty products brand in the world, enabling women to virtually use L'Oreal cosmetics.

VR/AR technologies have the potential for shaping the future of digital fashion within Metaverse. While purchasing digital garments in a virtual store in Metaverse, consumers may virtually try-on them with the help of AR solutions using their smartphones or AR-enabled devices in real time. On the other hand, VR may help the Metaverse residents to take part in virtual fashion shows, exhibitions and social gatherings in Metaverse.

2.5 Fashion Business Opportunities in Metaverse

Tipped to be the next generation of the current internet, Metaverse is envisioned to be an immersive alternative reality where fashion businesses and stakeholders can enter (Chrimes and Boardman 2023; Yoo et al. 2023). The fashion business in the Metaverse is a burgeoning and exciting frontier, offering unique opportunities for innovation, creativity and entrepreneurship. The innovative virtual platform allows fashion stakeholders to connect, communicate and interact through digital twins of the physical world of the fashion business (Giraldi 2023).

Research indicates ample opportunities for fashion business in the Metaverse including, better design and creativity, new ways to reach target customers and greater engagement, lowering cost, more revenue stream, and contributions to sustainable practices with less environmental and social impact (Joy et al. 2022; Chrimes and Boardman 2023). The following section provides a brief outline of the fashion business in the Metaverse.

Firstly, the Metaverse gives clothes designers more creative and innovative design options. It is possible for designers to produce virtual apparel, accessories and other fashion items that users could buy and utilise to personalise their avatars (Sayem 2022; Giraldi 2023). The Metaverse helps to establish or participate in virtual marketplaces where designers can showcase and sell their virtual fashion creations (Giraldi 2023). Using blockchain technology will improve transaction security and ownership verification.

Fashion consumers could gain from the metaverse in a variety of fascinating ways. The Metaverse offers customisation options for virtual fashion items, allowing users to tailor designs to their preferences (Park and Lim 2023). This could include colour variations, fabrics, yarn, fibre, patterns and personalised branding. With Metaverse's virtual tailoring service, users can personalise the style and fit of virtual apparel according to their tastes and avatars' measurements (Periyasami and Periyasamy 2022). However, as the Metaverse develops, designers must adopt new technology and maintain curiosity and modernity to stay competitive in the ever-changing landscape (Hossain and Sadachar 2022; Sayem 2022).

The Metaverse offers consumers a dynamic, immersive and interactive platform to explore fashion items, express style and engage with like-minded communities (Park and Lim 2023). Fashion consumer can enjoy immersive AR experiences to virtually try on outfits and accessories via their smartphones. The Metaverse supports AR applications that allow users to virtually try on virtual fashion items using their devices or AR glasses. This enhances the shopping experience and helps users make informed decisions (Silva and Bonetti 2021). More opportunities and innovation will emerge over time with unlimited possibilities to engage with the virtual fashion world.

Research indicates that immersive Metaverse technologies can assist brands in creating immersive, 360-degree virtual experiences. They can also open up new avenues for showcasing a brand's collection, such as pop-up shops, online showrooms, digital fashion shows with 3D runways and new experiences between brands and consumers (Hossain and Sadachar 2022). The Metaverse offers opportunities to host virtual fashion shows and events to launch new collections, generate buzz and showcase the brand's creativity (Holden 2022). This can attract attention from users and potential collaborators.

The Metaverse can give fashion tech solutions to stakeholders by developing innovative technologies, such as AI-driven virtual stylists, personalised fashion recommendation algorithms and other tools that enhance the virtual fashion shopping experience (Holden 2022; Weiss 2022). Retailers and brands can collaborate together with influencers, celebrities and cross-integrations with well-known Metaverse platforms, games and social networks to market virtual fashion items to a larger audience and boost accessibility and awareness (Rodriguez Sanchez and Garcia-Badell 2022). Brands and retailers can set up a virtual store on the Metaverse which is much cheaper than setting up a physical store. Brands can also save on inventory costs, as they only need to create digital versions of their products. The Metaverse provides fashion brands with a new revenue stream by selling digital assets for the avatars including, clothing, accessories and shoes.

Fashion Metaverse providers have a plethora of fascinating opportunities for suppliers. To collaborate with designers and brands in developing distinctive and cutting-edge digital fashion items, suppliers can display virtual fashion and textile materials that can be licensed or sold to designers, brands or manufacturers (Casciani et al. 2022; Wächter and König 2023). Manufacturers can develop a virtual textile manufacturing facility within the Metaverse, producing digital fabrics for fashion designers and brands.

Fashion brands can also implement blockchain technology for secure transactions and authenticity verification (Holden 2022). There is an opportunity to collaborate with fashion brands and designers to co-create fashion items, leveraging expertise in materials, technical and aesthetic properties, and production operations (Gonzalez 2020). Manufacturers can offer AR fashion sampling services to designers to virtually try on before bulk production (Periyasami and Periyasamy 2022). Suppliers can offer sustainable production, materials and components to scale up demand for eco-friendly fashion products (Periyasami and Periyasamy 2022). However, to effectively capitalise on the potential of the metaverse, manufacturers need to stay abreast of the ever-changing metaverse environment and work in tandem with tech providers, brands, retailers and other relevant stakeholders.

There are also opportunities in metaverse fashion consulting and virtual fashion education. For example, providing consulting services to individuals and brands looking to establish a presence in the metaverse, and offering guidance on virtual fashion trends, branding and marketing strategies (Casciani et al. 2022; Park and Lim 2023). Educational institutions and even fashion companies can create virtual fashion design courses and workshops within the metaverse, catering to individuals interested in learning about digital fashion creation. This might facilitate the development of a knowledgeable and skilled digital fashion community.

The fashion industry has diverse supply chain operations, which have detrimental social and environmental impacts (Islam et al. 2021). The fashion business encompasses a wide range of supply chain activities that negatively affect the environment and society. According to McKinsey, the fashion industry will be accountable for 2.7 billion tons of carbon emissions annually by 2030 if such unsustainable practices persist in its business operations (Ghebreab and Heale 2023; Yoo et al. 2023). As fashion businesses are reshaped by sustainability and digitalisation, the metaverse helps to consider sustainability in virtual fashion practices, addressing concerns about the environmental and social impact of digital assets within the metaverse (Yan 2022). For instance, the metaverse lessens the effects on society and the environment at every level of the product life cycle and supply chain.

The adoption of eco-friendly materials, design, production methods and circular economy practices is improving the situation and the metaverse can contribute significantly (Periyasami and Periyasamy 2022). Allowing people to shop and virtually try on hyper-realistic digital renders of garments can help reduce the need for physical samples and reduce unsold products. This can enhance a brand's reputation and appeal to conscientious customers.

The Metaverse provides opportunities for bridging the virtual and physical worlds through real-world integration. To integrate virtual and real-world experiences, businesses could consider offering limited-edition physical products that are influenced by popular virtual fashion items (Yoo et al. 2023). The Metaverse facilitates the development of a community centred on virtual fashion businesses, retailers and designers. Through social media, virtual events and forums, there is an opportunity to engage with individuals in the metaverse and cultivate a loyal clientele (Yoo et al. 2023). To increase the brand's visibility and connect with a wider target audience, there are lots of chances for alliances and partnerships, such as working with content producers, virtual influencers and other companies in the metaverse (Periyasami and Periyasamy 2022).

2.6 Conclusion

VR/AR technologies have initially been applied in fashion businesses to engage with customers to promote the sales of physical garments. However, the advent of metaverse has offered a virtual marketplace for virtual fashion products creating new business opportunities for fashion retailers. Although a mass adoption of a fully realised metaverse is yet to be introduced, the fashion industry has already seen a wider adoption of immersive technologies, particularly in the areas of digital design, retailing, consumer and supply chain perspectives. However, building a successful fashion business in the metaverse requires a combination of creativity, adaptability and a keen understanding of the evolving digital landscape. It is critical to keep up with changes in technology, consumer preferences and metaverse trends.

References

Alcañiz M, Bigné E, Guixeres J (2019) Virtual reality in marketing: a framework, review, and research agenda. Front Psychol 10:1530
Baker J et al (2018) The internet dilemma: an exploratory study of luxury firms' usage of internet-based technologies. J Retail Consum Serv 41:37–47
Becker V, Rauchenstein F, Sörös G (2020) Connecting and controlling appliances through wearable augmented reality. Augmented Hum Res 5:1–16
Blázquez M (2014) Fashion shopping in multichannel retail: the role of technology in enhancing the customer experience. Int J Electron Commer 18(4):97–116
Boardman R, Henninger CE, Zhu A (2020) Augmented reality and virtual reality: new drivers for fashion retail? In: Technology-driven sustainability: innovation in the fashion supply chain, pp 155–172
Boyd DE, Koles B (2019) Virtual reality and its impact on B2B marketing: a value-in-use perspective. J Bus Res 100:590–598
Caboni F, Hagberg J (2019) Augmented reality in retailing: a review of features, applications and value. Int J Retail Distrib Manag 47(11):1125–1140
Casciani D, Chkanikova O, Pal R (2022) Exploring the nature of digital transformation in the fashion industry: opportunities for supply chains, business models, and sustainability-oriented innovations. Sustain Sci Pract Policy 18(1):773–795
Chapman JR, Wang JC, Wiechert K (2022) Into the spine metaverse: reflections on a future metaspine (uni-)verse. Glob Spine J 545–547
Cheng R et al (2022) Will metaverse be NextG internet? Vision, hype, and reality. IEEE Network 36(5):197–204
Chittaro L, Ranon R (2000) Virtual reality stores for 1-to-1 e-commerce
Chrimes C, Boardman R (2023) The opportunities & challenges of the metaverse for fashion brands. In: The garment economy: understanding history, developing business models, and leveraging digital technologies, pp 389–410
Chuah SH-W (2018) Why and who will adopt extended reality technology? Literature review, synthesis, and future research agenda. In: Literature review, synthesis, and future research agenda (13 Dec 2018) [preprint]
Cummings JJ, Bailenson JN (2016) How immersive is enough? A meta-analysis of the effect of immersive technology on user presence. Media Psychol 19(2):272–309
Dionisio JDN, Iii WGB, Gilbert R (2013) 3D virtual worlds and the metaverse: current status and future possibilities. ACM Comput Surv (CSUR) 45(3):1–38
Dwivedi YK et al (2021) Artificial intelligence (AI): multidisciplinary perspectives on emerging challenges, opportunities, and agenda for research, practice and policy. Int J Inf Manage 57:101994
Dwivedi YK et al (2022) Climate change and COP26: are digital technologies and information management part of the problem or the solution? An editorial reflection and call to action. Int J Inf Manag 63:102456
Ebay Press Release (2016) World's first virtual reality department store—eBay Inc.
Fashion Innovation Agency (2024) The fabric of reality—an immersive VR fashion show
Ghebreab S, Heale S (2023) Responsible fashion business in practice: sustainable concepts and cases across the fashion industry. Taylor & Francis
Giraldi L (2023) The metaverse as an opportunity for the development of fashion system design. Fashion Highlight 1:68–76
Gong L, Fast-Berglund Å, Johansson B (2021) A framework for extended reality system development in manufacturing. IEEE Access 9:24796–24813
Gonzalez P (2020) Digital fashion in the metaverse
Heckel J (2020) Virtual reality provides new tool for fashion design class, Illinois
Heller J et al (2019) Touching the untouchable: exploring multi-sensory augmented reality in the context of online retailing. J Retail 95(4):219–234

Helmold M (2023) Virtual and innovative quality management across the value chain: industry insights, case studies and best practices. Springer Nature, Berlin

Hilken T et al (2020) Seeing eye to eye: social augmented reality and shared decision making in the marketplace. J Acad Mark Sci 48:143–164

Holden L (2022) Reimaging fashion for the new real. Fashion Pract 14(3):401–404

Hossain MA, Sadachar A (2022) Investigating consumers' intent to shop at metaverse: a proposed agenda. In: International textile and apparel association annual conference proceedings. Iowa State University Digital Press

Intelligence M (2021) Extended reality market—XR industry—size & trends. Available at: https://www.mordorintelligence.com/industry-reports/extended-reality-xr-market. Accessed: 3 Feb 2024

Islam MM, Perry P, Gill S (2021) Mapping environmentally sustainable practices in textiles, apparel and fashion industries: a systematic literature review. J Fashion Mark Manag Int J 25(2):331–353

Javornik A (2016) Augmented reality: research agenda for studying the impact of its media characteristics on consumer behaviour. J Retail Consum Serv 30:252–261

Joy A et al (2022) Digital future of luxury brands: metaverse, digital fashion, and non-fungible tokens. Strateg Change 31(3):337–343

Kim S, Dey AK (2010) AR interfacing with prototype 3D applications based on user-centered interactivity. Comput Aided Des 42(5):373–386

Kim J, Forsythe S (2008) Adoption of virtual try-on technology for online apparel shopping. J Interact Mark 22(2):45–59

Ko SH, Rogers J (2021) Functional materials and devices for XR (VR/AR/MR) applications. Adv Funct Mater 2106546

Lee L-H et al (2021) All one needs to know about metaverse: a complete survey on technological singularity, virtual ecosystem, and research agenda. arXiv preprint arXiv:2110.05352 [preprint]

Loureiro SMC et al (2019) Understanding the use of virtual reality in marketing: a text mining-based review. J Bus Res 100:514–530

Makarov A (2022) Augmented reality trends of 2022: a vision of immersion. Georgia: Mobidev [preprint]

Marr B (2021a) COVID-19 and extended reality (XR). Curr Issues Tourism

Marr B (2021b) The fascinating history and evolution of extended reality (XR)—covering AR, VR And MR. Available at: https://www.forbes.com/sites/bernardmarr/2021/05/17/the-fascinating-history-and-evolution-of-extended-reality-xr--covering-ar-vr-and-mr/?sh=3e15af724bfd. Accessed: 3 Feb 2024

McLean G, Al-Nabhani K, Wilson A (2018) Developing a mobile applications customer experience model (MACE)-implications for retailers. J Bus Res 85:325–336

MIT Technology Review Insights (2023) The emergent industrial metaverse. Available online at https://assets.new.siemens.com/siemens/assets/api/uuid:260d1ead-250b-45fb-b32f-caa9924c1ddd/The-Emergent-Industrial-Metaverse.pdf. Accessed on 23/02/2024

Morimoto T et al (2022) XR (extended reality: virtual reality, augmented reality, mixed reality) technology in spine medicine: status quo and quo vadis. J Clin Med 11(2):470

Muñoz-Saavedra L, Miró-Amarante L, Domínguez-Morales M (2020) Augmented and virtual reality evolution and future tendency. Appl Sci 10(1):322

Mystakidis S (2022) Metaverse. Encyclopedia 2(1), article 1

Nanda AP, Banerjee R (2020) Binge watching: an exploration of the role of technology. Psychol Mark 37(9):1212–1230

Pantano E et al (2020) Competing during a pandemic? Retailers' ups and downs during the COVID-19 outbreak. J Bus Res 116:209–213

Paris S, Pedersen K, Zhao Q (2022) Adaptive discontinuous reception in 5G advanced for extended reality applications. In: 2022 IEEE 95th vehicular technology conference: (VTC2022-spring). IEEE, pp 1–6

Park H, Lim RE (2023) Fashion and the metaverse: clarifying the domain and establishing a research agenda. J Retail Consum Serv 74:103413

Periyasami S, Periyasamy AP (2022) Metaverse as future promising platform business model: case study on fashion value chain. Businesses 2(4):527–545
Peukert C et al (2022) Metaverse: how to approach its challenges from a BISE perspective. Bus Inf Syst Eng 64(4):401–406
Phoon S-Y et al (2017) Interactive solution approach for loop layout problem using virtual reality technology. Int J Adv Manuf Technol 89:2375–2385
Pizzi G et al (2019) Virtual reality, real reactions? Comparing consumers' perceptions and shopping orientation across physical and virtual-reality retail stores. Comput Hum Behav 96:1–12
PwC (2019) Seeing is believing: PwC. Available at: https://www.pwc.com/gx/en/industries/technology/publications/economic-impact-of-vr-ar.html. Accessed: 3 Feb 2024
PwC (2024) How UK organisations are using XR—PwC UK. Available at: https://www.pwc.co.uk/issues/technology/immersive-technologies/how-uk-organisations-use-vr-ar.html. Accessed: 3 Feb 2024
Qamar S, Anwar Z, Afzal M (2023) A systematic threat analysis and defense strategies for the metaverse and extended reality systems. Comput Secur 103127
Rauschnabel PA (2018) Virtually enhancing the real world with holograms: an exploration of expected gratifications of using augmented reality smart glasses. Psychol Mark 35(8):557–572
Rauschnabel PA, He J, Ro YK (2018) Antecedents to the adoption of augmented reality smart glasses: a closer look at privacy risks. J Bus Res 92:374–384
Rauschnabel PA, Felix R, Hinsch C (2019) Augmented reality marketing: how mobile AR-apps can improve brands through inspiration. J Retail Consum Serv 49:43–53
Reiners D et al (2021) The combination of artificial intelligence and extended reality: a systematic review. Front Virtual Reality 2:721933
Rodriguez Sanchez M, Garcia-Badell G (2022) Dressing the metaverse. The digital strategies of fashion brands in the virtual universe. In: International fashion and design congress. Springer, Berlin, pp 387–397
Roggeveen AL, Grewal D, Schweiger EB (2020) The DAST framework for retail atmospherics: the impact of in-and out-of-store retail journey touchpoints on the customer experience. J Retail 96(1):128–137
Sarakatsanos O et al (2021) A VR application for the virtual fitting of fashion garments on avatars. In: 2021 IEEE international symposium on mixed and augmented reality adjunct (ISMAR-adjunct). IEEE, pp 40–45
Sarakatsanos O, Papazoglou-Chalikias A, Boikou M, Chatzilari E, Jauk M, Hafliger U, Nikolopoulos S, Kompatsiaris I (2024) VR designer: enhancing fashion showcases through immersive virtual garment fitting. Virtual Reality 28(2):70
Sayem ASM (2022) Digital fashion innovations for the real world and metaverse. Int J Fashion Des Technol Educ 139–141
Scholz J, Duffy K (2018) We ARe at home: how augmented reality reshapes mobile marketing and consumer-brand relationships. J Retail Consum Serv 44:11–23
Silva ES, Bonetti F (2021) Digital humans in fashion: will consumers interact? J Retail Consum Serv 60:102430
Stephenson N (1994) Snow crash. Penguin, UK
Wächter A-K, König L-F (2023) Increasing brand equity in the metaverse: from the perspective of luxury fashion brands
Wang H, Ning H, Lin Y, Wang W, Dhelim S, Farha F, Ding J, Daneshmand M (2023) A survey on the metaverse: the state-of-the-art, technologies, applications, and challenges. IEEE Internet Things J 10(16):14671–14688
Weinberger M (2022) What is metaverse? A definition based on qualitative meta-synthesis. Future Internet 14(11):310
Weiss C (2022) Fashion retailing in the metaverse. Fashion Style Popular Culture 9(4):523–538
Wu YF, Kim EY (2022) Users' perceptions of technological features in augmented reality (AR) and virtual reality (VR) in fashion retailing: a qualitative content analysis. Mob Inf Syst

Yan R (2022) A sustainable fashion industry business model revolution based on the metaverse: practices and reciprocal processes. Highlights Bus Econ Manag 4:363–369

Yoo K et al (2023) The merchants of meta: a research agenda to understand the future of retailing in the metaverse. J Retail [preprint]

Chapter 3
Chatbots and AI in Fashion Industry

Maneesh Kumar Mishra, Rudrajeet Pal, and Rajkishore Nayak

Abstract The fashion industry, a worldwide sector that includes clothing, accessories, and beauty products, experiences ongoing changes in design, production, promotion, and sales. The complexities of supply chain management, together with the ever-changing impact of fashion events and sustainability trends, determine the dynamics of the market. The growing influence of technology, such as 3D printing, virtual reality, and blockchain, has a profound effect on the future of the sector, promoting sustainability and ethical norms. Chatbots play a crucial role in driving digital innovation and transforming the fashion industry. This research explores the diverse and complex effects of chatbots in the fashion business. By utilizing natural language processing (NLP) and machine learning algorithms, chatbots improve consumer experiences by providing personalized interactions, including customized product suggestions, order tracking, and efficient support. With the increasing popularity of conversational chatbots, their usage is expanding beyond the fashion industry to impact the fields of education and customer service. Advanced deep learning models, including RNN, Seq2Seq, LSTM, BERT, and GPT, when combined with different training techniques, highlight their ability to adapt. Within the fashion industry, chatbots fulfill various functions, ranging from offering fashion guidance to streamlining online transactions. An illustrative example is the triumph of ChatGPT, showcasing the extensive range of uses for chatbots. The study emphasizes the widespread implementation of AI, computer vision, and machine vision in retail

Chatbots in the Fashion Industry: A Comprehensive Exploration of Technological Integration, Consumer Engagement, and Ethical Considerations

M. K. Mishra (✉)
Université Paris 8 | Vincennes-Saint-Denis, 93200 Paris, France
e-mail: maneesh.mishra@univ-paris8.fr

R. Pal
Swedish School of Textiles, University of Borås, Borås, Sweden
e-mail: rudrajeet.pal@hb.se

R. Nayak
School of Communication & Design, RMIT University, Ho Chi Minh, Vietnam
e-mail: rajkishore.nayak@rmit.edu.vn

R. Nayak et al. (eds.), *Use of Digital and Advanced Technologies in the Fashion Supply Chain*, Springer Series in Fashion Business,
https://doi.org/10.1007/978-981-97-7528-6_3

operations on a global scale. The study highlights the importance of doing thorough testing, utilizing platforms such as Chattest, to assess the functionality of chatbots and guarantee realistic interactions like those of humans.

Keywords Chatbots · Artificial intelligence (AI) · Machine learning algorithms · Natural language processing (NLP) · E-commerce · Fashion industry · Supply chain management

3.1 Introduction

The fashion industry, a worldwide domain, covers all aspects of apparel, accessory, and cosmetics product development, manufacture, marketing, and retailing. The process of design culminates in the production phase, where materials are acquired and garments are constructed. Marketing and promotional activities, carried out through fashion shows and online campaigns, help spread information about products (Nikvand et al. 2018). Retailers play a crucial role as mediators connecting the fashion industry with consumers. The complexities of supply chain management regulate the smooth movement of products. Fashion events and trend analysis, which highlight the industry's shifting dynamics, have an impact on the market's relevance. There is a growing emphasis on sustainability and ethical standards (Shi and Lewis 2020).

The rapid growth of technology in the fashion business has profoundly transformed multiple aspects of the industry. Technological breakthroughs such as 3D printing and virtual reality have transformed the design and prototype processes, hastening product development (Mishra et al. 2022; Ricci et al. 2023). E-commerce platforms utilize advanced algorithms and artificial intelligence (AI) to improve tailored shopping experiences, thereby impacting consumer behavior and preferences. Additionally, cutting-edge technologies make it simpler to incorporate sustainable practices, allowing the fashion industry to address environmental issues. Implementing blockchain technology in supply chain management improves transparency, traceability, and the sourcing of ethically produced goods. With the ongoing advancement of technology, its influence on the fashion sector is set to increase, significantly impacting the future of the business (Hananto et al. 2021).

Chatbots, which are designed to mimic human conversations, are transforming the fashion business through efficient and personalized interactions. By employing natural language processing (NLP) and machine learning algorithms, they provide prompt assistance, customized product recommendations, and order tracking, emphasizing the influence of digital innovation on enhancing client experiences (Abdulla et al. 2022).

Conversational chatbots have gained popularity over the last several years. These computer programs employ NLP techniques, such as ChatGPT (https://openai.com/blog/chatgpt), to imitate conversations with humans. They are utilized to help teachers and students in a variety of scenarios, such as informal entertainment, customer service, and education (Pawlik et al. 2022; Cui et al. 2017; https://www.statista.com/statistics/1400301/ai-mv-and-cv-use-retail/). These chatbots are built utilizing various advanced deep learning models, such as RNN, Seq2Seq, LSTM, BERT, and GPT. In addition, they employ many training methodologies, such as reinforcement learning and transfer learning, to optimize the efficiency of NLP algorithms and chatbots (Ghazvininejad et al. 2018; Devlin et al. 2019; Hollander et al. 2022; Liu et al. 2022; Lee and Yeo 2022; Song et al. 2022; Pawlik et al. 2022; Cui et al. 2017). Chatbots can be categorized as either casual and open-domain or specialized and fact-based. A notable example that has become well recognized is the success of ChatGPT, which attracted much interest and stimulated researchers to develop other ideas related to chatbot applications (https://openai.com/blog/chatgpt). Retail companies worldwide employ AI. According to a poll conducted in 2023 in the United States and the EMEA region, approximately 40 percent of retail directors reported utilizing AI, computer vision (CV), and machine vision (MV) for specific operations and departments (https://www.statista.com/statistics/1400301/ai-mv-and-cv-use-retail/).

Chatbots are becoming increasingly important in a variety of areas, including fashion shopping, education, and customer support. They offer flexible and convenient learning opportunities, catering to busy schedules (Bonetti and Perry 2017). The study emphasizes the importance of thorough testing before deployment and evaluating chatbot performance based on its resemblance to human interaction. Chattest, a comprehensive platform, is used to assess the quality, relevance, comprehensiveness, accuracy, and contextual appropriateness of responses (Vijayaraghavan et al. 2020). The dominance of retrieval-based dialogue systems in real-world chatbots and assistants highlights their potential and economic worth (Dokukina and Gumanova 2020; Dokukina and Gumanova 2020; Li et al. 2021; Adamopoulou and Moussiades 2020).

Chatbots are computer programs that replicate human-user conversations, usually via text or voice interactions. In the fashion industry, chatbots play various roles such as providing personalized styling advice, recommending products based on user preferences, answering customer queries, facilitating online purchases, and enhancing customer service experiences. They can also assist in guiding users through the shopping process, providing fashion tips, and offering real-time assistance with outfit selection. Their ability to engage with customers in a conversational manner and provide tailored recommendations makes them valuable assets for fashion brands seeking to enhance their online retail experiences (Goti et al. 2023).

Chatbots and virtual assistants in the fashion industry play a crucial role in providing seamless customer service, handling inquiries, providing product suggestions, and guiding shoppers in their buying process, around the clock. They are essential for enhancing customer experience and engagement, ensuring continuous support for customers (Rathore 2019).

Chatbots in the fashion industry are empowered to instantly provide users with information, perform functions in online stores such as searching for goods and displaying products, and are expected to take on more functions due to advancements in AI and machine learning. The paper emphasizes their relevance in the context of the wide popularity of instant messaging systems and the development of alternative ways of interaction with Internet shops (Husak et al. 2020).

Chatbots play a crucial role in the fashion industry by serving as the first point of contact for consumers, providing efficient customer service, and contributing to the overall brand experience (Kull et al. 2021).

Chatbots are used in the fashion industry to manage online interactions with consumers, particularly in the context of customer service experiences, and are integrated within social network organizational accounts as Customer Relationships Management (CRM) tools. They help automate and aggregate human data to understand consumer behavior and optimize procedures and activities. Additionally, chatbots have the capability to mimic human behavior and record contact history for future reference (Murtarelli et al. 2021).

Chatbots in the fashion industry serve as AI-enabled service agents that engage in natural conversations with consumers to provide individualized information. They play a crucial role in interacting with customers throughout the entire customer journey, including tasks such as product research, comparison, purchasing, order tracking, and managing rewards and loyalty points (Selamat and Windasari 2021).

Chatbots in the fashion industry aim to provide a natural and informative way for customers to fulfill their fashion needs by generating substantive responses in both textual and visual modalities, enriched with fashion domain knowledge (Liao et al. 2018).

The chapter on "Chatbots in the Fashion Industry" provides a comprehensive educational resource on the evolving role of chatbots in the fashion sector and the impact of AI. It uses practical case examples to stimulate critical thinking on technology issues, user experience dynamics, and ethical aspects. The chapter serves professional interests by offering insights into industry processes and the convergence of technology and fashion (Castagna et al. 2022). It encourages readers to contemplate the changing technology landscape and its potential effects on the professional domain, while also addressing future trends and challenges (Kooli 2023).

3.2 The Evolution of Chatbots

Alan Turing released his work "Computing Machinery and Intelligence" in 1950, which addresses the topic "Can Machines Think?" and introduces the Turing Test for estimating and evaluating machine intelligence simulations. The Turing Test is an AI evaluation tool used to determine if a computer is capable of human-like thinking or not (The Turing test—50 years of Turing test). ELIZA is widely regarded as the first creation in the realm of Chatbots, devised by Joseph Weizenbaum in 1966 at the MIT AI Laboratory. Weizenbaum created ELIZA to emulate the conduct of a Rogerian Psychotherapist, which is a form of psychotherapy devised by psychologist Carl Rogers.

ELIZA is the inaugural program with the ability to make an effort at the Turing Test (Loeb 2021). In 1972, Kenneth Colby developed PARRY, a program that can be described as ELIZA with a distinct attitude, following the creation of ELIZA. It uses more sophisticated techniques to simulate a person with paranoid schizophrenia in a manner similar to Weizenbaum's (https://phrasee.co/news/parry-the-a-i-chatterbot-from-1972/) approach. During the 1970s, the Turing Test was employed to assess its performance, and it achieved an accurate identification rate of approximately 48%.

Initially, the first Chatbots operated by recognizing keywords from user inputs and then using predetermined rules to convert those phrases into corresponding responses. In the event that the keywords are not detected, the system responds by providing a generic response that was used in a previous session. These Chatbots employed pattern matching and parsing techniques to provide the illusion of natural communication and intelligence for the interrogators. These basic models, with little contextual understanding, successfully passed the Turing Test, which sparked debates. This results in minor modifications that enhance the Turing Test.

The term "chatterbot" was first mentioned in the 1990s, namely in 1991. During this time, several early chatbots were created, including TINY-MUD, Dr. Sbaitso, and ALICE. In addition, the paper authored by Adamopoulou et al. provides a comprehensive account of the notable progress made in chatbot technology since about 2001. This includes the creation of SmarterChild and the emergence of personal voice assistants such as Siri, IBM Watson, Google Assistant, Microsoft Cortana, and Amazon Alexa (Liao et al. 2018).

In early 2016, a significant advancement in AI Technology happened, which greatly transformed the manner in which individuals interact with manufacturers. Social media platforms facilitated the development of chatbots by developers to enable clients to carry out specific daily tasks within their messaging applications. In 2016, there were 34,000 chatbots that were utilized in various industries such as Marketing, Fashion, Support Systems, Healthcare, Entertainment, Education, and Cultural Heritage (https://chatbotsmagazine.com/a-visual-history-of-chatbots-8bf3b31dbfb2). A multitude of text-based chatbots with distinct functionalities were created for widely used messaging platforms, industrial applications, and academic investigations (Dale 2016). Furthermore, the advent of the Internet of Things (IoT) ushered in a new era of interconnected intelligent devices, with the integration of chatbots enhancing communication among them (Adamopoulou and Moussiades 2020).

The earliest use of chatbots and AI in the fashion industry can be traced back to the 2000s, with the application of AI in the color and textile industry (Adamopoulou and Moussiades 2020). This laid the foundation for the use of AI in fashion, particularly in analysis, prediction, and communication of fashion trends (Hollander et al. 2022; Vashisht and Mittar 2019) The development of AI chatbots, which simulate natural language conversations, has further enhanced the use of AI in the industry (Singh and Thakur 2020).

The "early use of chatbots in the fashion industry" in Husak et al. (2020) involves the development and implementation of a chatbot integrated with NLP to provide users with fashion recommendations through a web application. The system is designed to interact with users on the Telegram messenger platform and aims to demonstrate and analyze the functionality of chatbots in the fashion industry. The use of NLP has increased the level of recognition of the user's language, and the system is constructed to be expandable for future functionality and test cases.

3.3 Applications of AI and Chatbots in Fashion Industry

3.3.1 AI

The introduction of AI in the fashion business is transforming several facets of the sector. AI technologies are transforming various aspects of the industry, including design, production, supply chain management, and customer experiences (Fig. 3.1). AI algorithms are equipping designers with intelligent tools for analyzing trends, generating patterns, and providing style suggestions, thereby boosting creativity and efficiency in the design process. A chatbot is created to mechanize specific tasks, but Conversational AI, in a broader sense, seeks to replicate human interactions in a more advanced manner. Presently, AI is employed in various significant domains (AI applications in Fashion as shown in Fig. 3.1).

3.3.1.1 Production and Supply Chain

Product Design and Development

AI can produce novel ideas by analyzing trends, user preferences, and historical data. It can aid designers in generating novel styles, patterns, and silhouettes, resulting in

Fig. 3.1 AI applications in fashion

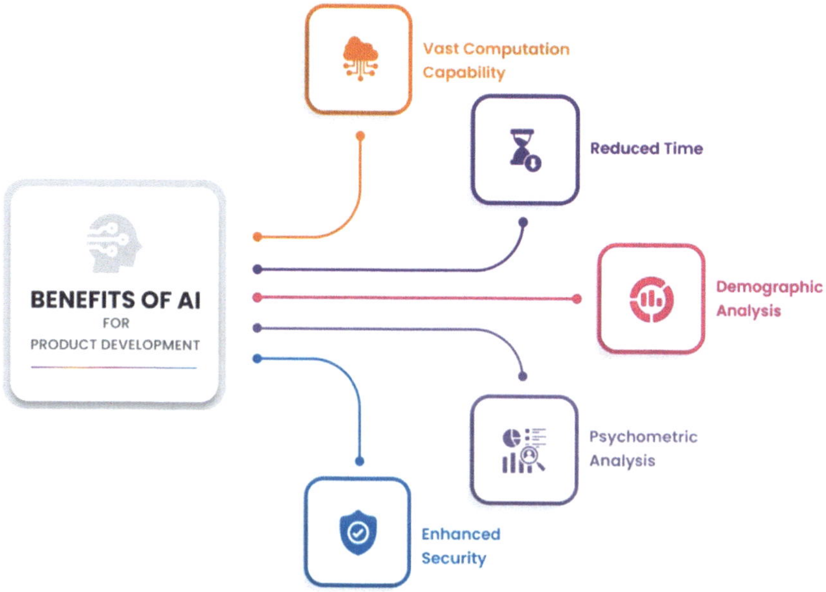

Fig. 3.2 Benefits of AI in fashion product development

improved creativity and efficiency in the design process (Guo et al. 2011). Nike has incorporated AI into their product design process by leveraging algorithms and computational design tools. AI is utilized to create and enhance different design options, enabling quick development and improvement. This allows Nike to investigate novel design concepts and expand the limits of innovation in athletic clothing (Fig. 3.2).

Supply Chain Optimization

AI may assist in improving the garment supply chain by enhancing forecasting accuracy, demand planning, and inventory management (Mohammadi and Kalhor 2021b). Machine learning algorithms utilize historical data, market patterns, and external factors to forecast demand, mitigate stockouts, and decrease surplus inventory (Fig. 3.3). Zara, a store known for its quick production and turnover of trendy items, use AI algorithms to predict customer demand, analyze sales trends, and improve the management of available stock (Yeo et al. 2022). Zara utilizes AI to make precise forecasts about fashion trends and adapt its production and distribution processes appropriately. This strategic approach minimizes the likelihood of having excess inventory or insufficient stock. Additional instances that operate on a comparable framework include Amazon, Adidas, and H&M.

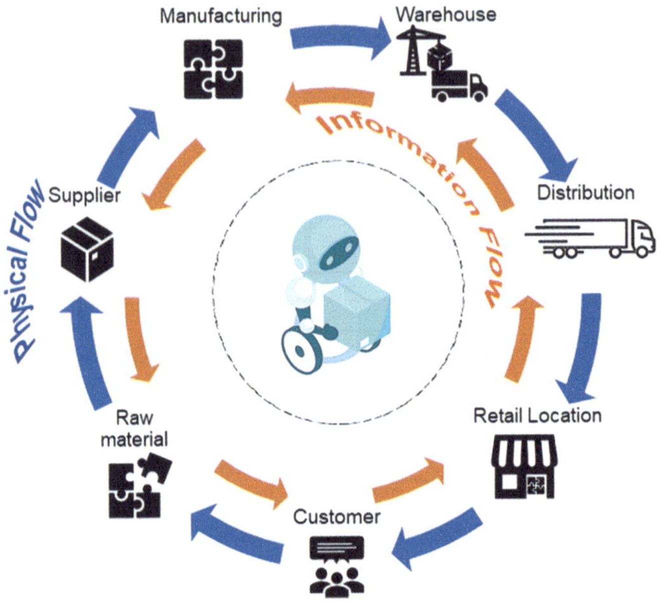

Fig. 3.3 Use of AI in supply chain optimization

Quality Control and Defect Detection

AI-based CV systems can automatically detect faults, irregularities, and inconsistencies in textiles, patterns, and stitching. This technology will facilitate effective quality control procedures, minimize human fallibility, and guarantee uniform product quality (Mohammadi and Kalhor 2021b). Stitch Fix, an Internet-based service for personalized fashion advice, uses AI algorithms to evaluate the caliber of clothing articles. Their utilization of CV technology enables them to examine apparel photographs and identify any flaws or discrepancies in stitching, color, pattern, or overall quality. This measure guarantees that customers are provided with top-notch merchandise.

Demand Forecasting and Inventory Management

AI algorithms can reliably forecast demand by analyzing enormous amounts of data, such as past sales data, market trends, social media sentiment, and weather patterns (Yeo et al. 2022). This greatly assists clothes businesses and merchants in optimizing their inventory levels, minimizing instances of stockouts, and reducing situations of overstock. ASOS, an e-commerce fashion vendor, use AI algorithms for predicting demand and managing inventories (Guo et al. 2011). They utilize machine learning methodologies to examine client data, browsing patterns, and purchase records in order to forecast trends and foresee the demand for various clothing goods. This enables them to optimize their inventory levels and assure timely availability of the appropriate products.

Sustainability and Material Innovation

AI plays an important role in improving sustainability in the garment business by optimizing material utilization, decreasing waste, and fostering material innovation (Yeo et al. 2022). AI algorithms may analyze data to uncover sustainable sourcing possibilities, environmentally friendly materials, and efficient production procedures. Bolt Threads, a startup specializing in materials innovation, employs AI to create sustainable and environmentally friendly materials. They utilize AI algorithms to analyze the molecular composition of naturally occurring proteins and generate novel materials with favorable characteristics. Their primary product, Micro-silk, is an artificial spider silk produced through the application of AI-powered biotechnology (Guo et al. 2011).

3.3.1.2 Fashion Retail

Personalized Shopping Assistance

Chatbots have revolutionized the retail experience by providing personalized shopping assistance to customers. Through advanced algorithms and NLP, chatbots analyze user preferences, browsing history, and purchase patterns to offer tailored product recommendations (Fig. 3.4). H&M, a global fast-fashion giant, has successfully implemented a chatbot to provide a personalized shopping experience (Rese et al. 2020). The chatbot engages users in natural language conversations, asking about their style preferences, preferred occasions, and budget constraints.

Leveraging advanced NLP algorithms, the chatbot analyzes responses to recommend clothing items that align with the user's individual taste and requirements. This personalized approach has significantly enhanced user engagement and conversion rates for H&M (Ashktorab et al. 2019).

Virtual Try-On and Personalization

Innovative applications of chatbots in fashion retail include the integration of virtual try-on experiences (Fig. 3.5). Brands like Sephora and Ray-Ban have leveraged chatbots equipped with augmented reality (AR) technology to enable customers to virtually try on makeup or sunglasses. This immersive experience allows users to visualize how products will look before making a purchase, enhancing the online shopping experience (Chen 2022).

Sephora's chatbot incorporates AR technology, allowing users to virtually try on makeup products. By accessing the user's device camera, the chatbot overlays virtual makeup products onto the user's face, providing a realistic preview. This interactive and immersive experience has not only increased user engagement but

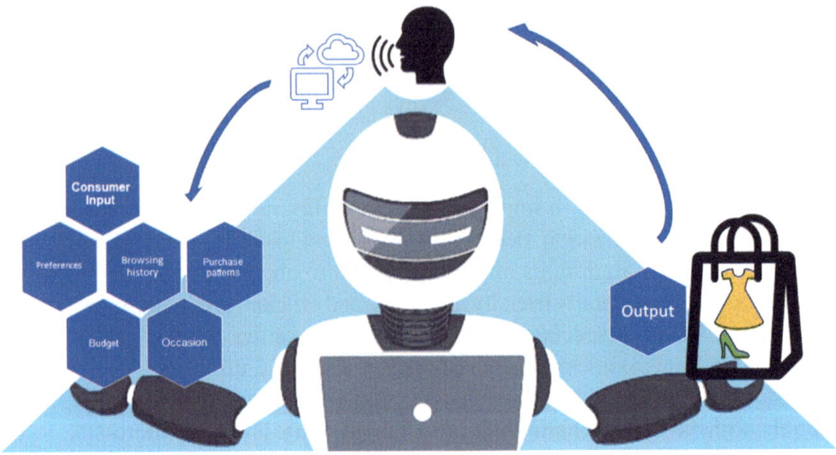

Fig. 3.4 Personalize shopping assistant

Fig. 3.5 Virtual try-on

has also contributed to a notable boost in online sales for Sephora (Behera et al. 2021).

Moreover, customers may use virtual try-on technology to see how clothes would appear on them before physically trying them on (Guo et al. 2011). Through the utilization of CV and machine learning, AI algorithms possess the capability to analyze body dimensions and suggest suitable sizes for individualized shopping experiences. Gap has integrated virtual try-on technology into their website and mobile app. Customers have the option to choose a piece of clothing and utilize the camera on their device to visualize how it would appear on themselves in a virtual manner. This feature enables consumers to visually assess the fit and appearance of the apparel on their own physique prior to completing a purchase (Mohammadi and Kalhor 2021b).

Order Tracking and Updates

Chatbots play a crucial role in providing real-time order tracking and updates, ensuring transparency in the purchase process. Zara, a global fashion retailer, utilizes a chatbot to keep customers informed about their orders. Customers can inquire about the status of their shipments, expected delivery times, and any issues related to shipping. This proactive approach enhances customer satisfaction and builds trust (Behera et al. 2021).

3.3.1.3 Customer Service

Instant Customer Support

Chatbots excel at delivering instant customer support and handling a myriad of queries efficiently. ASOS, a popular online fashion retailer, employs a chatbot for instant customer support. This chatbot addresses inquiries related to sizing, returns, and order tracking, providing quick and accurate responses. The immediacy of chatbot interactions contributes to a positive customer service experience (Yadav and Sondhi 2023).

Returns and Refunds

Handling returns and refunds can be a complex process, but chatbots streamline this aspect of customer service. Nordstrom, known for its commitment to exceptional customer service, has successfully implemented a chatbot to streamline the returns and refunds process. The chatbot guides customers through the steps of initiating a return, collecting necessary information, and providing details about the refund process. This automated approach has not only reduced the workload on customer service representatives but has also expedited the resolution of customer queries, resulting in higher customer satisfaction levels (Akhtar et al. 2019).

Size Recommendations

Chatbots play a pivotal role in addressing sizing concerns, a common issue in online fashion retail. Uniqlo, a global apparel brand, uses a chatbot to assist customers in determining the right size for their clothing items. By collecting information about the customer's body measurements and style preferences, the chatbot provides accurate size recommendations, reducing the likelihood of returns due to sizing issues (Mohammadi and Kalhor 2021b).

3.3.1.4 Marketing

Fashion marketing using chatbots and AI include employing automated conversational tools and artificial intelligence to enhance consumer interactions, customize shopping experiences, and hone marketing strategies. AI studies customer trends, preferences, and behavior; chatbots, on the other hand, provide real-time customer support, make product recommendations, and simplify online buying (Fig. 3.6).

Promotional Campaigns and Discounts

Chatbots are powerful tools for executing marketing campaigns and promoting discounts. Victoria's Secret, a renowned lingerie retailer, utilizes a chatbot to send personalized promotions to customers. By engaging users in conversations, the chatbot understands their preferences and recommends products or promotions accordingly. This targeted approach contributes to increased customer engagement and drives sales (Rathore 2019).

Style Advice and Fashion Tips

Fashion brands leverage chatbots to provide style advice and fashion tips, creating a personalized and interactive shopping experience. Burberry, a luxury fashion brand, has implemented a chatbot to provide style advice and fashion tips. The chatbot engages users in conversations about fashion trends, asking about their preferences and occasions. Based on user responses, the chatbot suggests outfit combinations, showcases new arrivals, and provides personalized styling tips. This interactive and informative approach has not only influenced purchasing decisions but has also contributed to building brand loyalty among Burberry's discerning customer base (Vashisht and Mittar 2019).

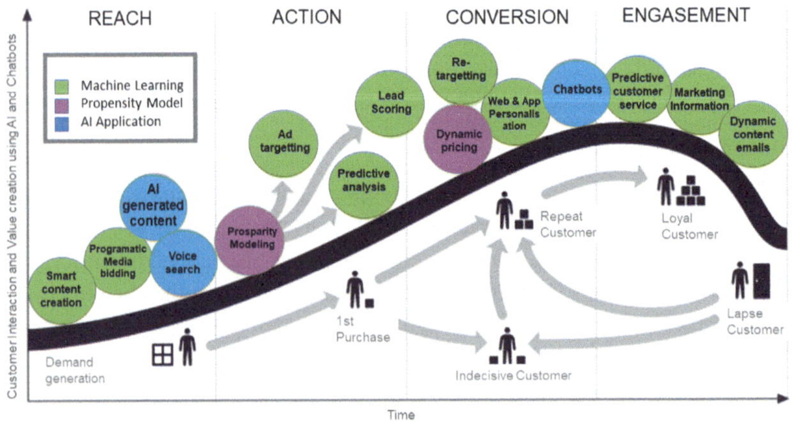

Fig. 3.6 Use of AI and chatbots in fashion marketing and retail

Social Media Integration

Chatbots seamlessly integrate with social media platforms, extending the brand's presence and engagement. Fashion brands leverage chatbots on platforms like Facebook Messenger and WhatsApp to interact with customers. Tommy Hilfiger, an iconic fashion brand, has integrated a chatbot with Facebook Messenger. This chatbot allows users to browse collections, receive styling tips, and make purchases directly within the chat interface (Siedlikowski et al. 2021).

3.3.2 *Chatbots*

Chatbots may be classified into several types based on their underlying technology and usefulness. There are two main sorts of chatbots: rule-based chatbots and AI-powered chatbots. Furthermore, there exist various categories of chatbots, each possessing distinct attributes (Fig. 3.7).

Here is a summary:

3.3.2.1 Rule-Based Chatbots

Rule-based chatbots employ established rules and decision trees to generate replies based on keywords or patterns in user input. Their benefits stem from their straightforwardness, which simplifies the process of designing and installing them. Additionally, they provide developers with exact authority over the bot's actions and ensure consistent and predictable answers. Nevertheless, these chatbots encounter constraints such as limited adaptability in dealing with complex or unforeseen inquiries, and scalability challenges may emerge as the quantity of rules increases. For example, let's assume the implementation of a virtual stylist assistant with this

Fig. 3.7 Chatbots in fashion

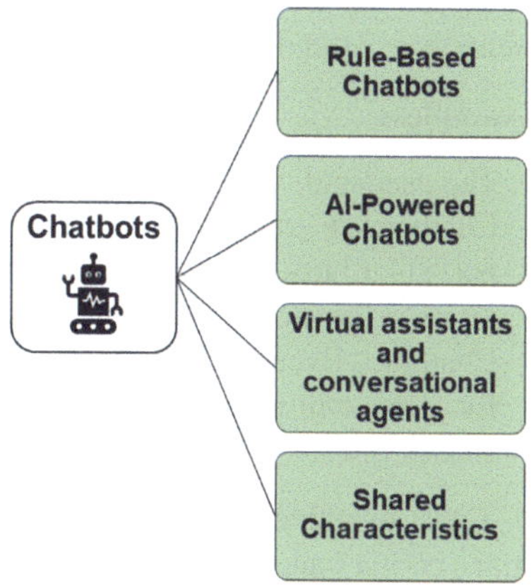

methodology (Ricci et al. 2023). The implementation entails developing a chatbot that operates on a set of predetermined criteria. The chatbot interacts with users by asking them questions about their style preferences, situations, and preferred clothing items. Based on the user's responses, the chatbot generates recommendations for outfits using the specified rules. Decision trees are thereafter utilized to direct the conversation and provide customized recommendations (Binkis et al. 2021).

Examples:

- The user said, "I have a party this weekend."
- Chatbot: "Excellent!" What kind of gathering is it? (For example, informal or formal)
- User: "It's an informal gathering."
- Chatbot: "Understood!" What do you think of a fashionable pair of trousers and a fashionable top? Additionally, you may contemplate including accessories such as earrings to enhance your appearance with a stylish flair.

3.3.2.2 AI-Powered Chatbots

AI-powered chatbots employ AI and machine learning to understand and respond to user inputs, constantly learning and improving performance through data analysis. The benefits of these systems include their ability to handle a wide range of queries, including those that are not expressly coded, their capacity for ongoing learning and adjustment depending on user interactions and data, and their enhanced understanding of context and intent through NLP (Rane et al. 2022). Nevertheless, these chatbots have limits, including their reliance on the quality and quantity of training data for optimal performance, as well as the heightened complexity involved in establishing and maintaining AI models. For example, let's suppose the development of an AI-driven chatbot, such as a personalized fashion advisor, that utilizes NLP and machine learning. The process entails instructing the chatbot using a wide-ranging collection of data that includes fashion preferences, trends, and user interactions. Advanced algorithms are then employed to scrutinize user input, comprehend style preferences, and offer tailored fashion suggestions (Sidlauskiene et al. 2023).

Examples:

- The user said, "I need an outfit for a summer wedding."
- Chatbot: "Certainly!" Could you elucidate your favored aesthetic and any particular hues that appeal to you?
- User: "I like bohemian styles and prefer pastel colors."
- Chatbot: "Excellent selection!" Considering your preferences, I suggest opting for a loose-fitting dress adorned with a pattern of delicate flowers in soft, light shades. It enhances the bohemian atmosphere and is ideal for a summer wedding.

These examples demonstrate how rule-based chatbots may navigate predetermined courses and provide suggestions based on specific rules. Conversely, chatbots powered by AI have the ability to comprehend intricate human preferences, providing tailored recommendations through the process of assimilating diverse sets of data.

In the fashion business, combining both approaches can increase the user experience. For example, a chatbot that operates based on predefined rules can effectively manage simple inquiries, whereas an AI-driven component can effectively handle intricate demands, according to individual preferences and changing fashion trends.

3.3.2.3 Virtual Assistants and Conversational Agents

"Virtual assistants" and "conversational agents" can encompass a range of functionalities, and their classification may depend on the underlying technology and capabilities. In general, both rule-based and AI-powered chatbots can be considered as types of virtual assistants and conversational agents, depending on their design and functionality (Rane et al. 2022).

Virtual assistants are primarily task-oriented, with specialized duties such as creating reminders, sending messages, and delivering weather updates. These digital assistants are generally created to aid users in certain tasks and are often integrated into gadgets or applications, improving the overall user experience. Siri, Google Assistant, and Amazon Alexa are prominent virtual assistants that are extensively used in smartphones, smart speakers, and other devices (Sidlauskiene et al. 2023).

Conversational agents, in contrast, participate in more extensive and contextually aware dialogues. These agents are specifically designed for in-depth conversations and have the capacity to address a broad spectrum of subjects while providing more advanced responses to user input. By integrating context awareness, individuals are able to comprehend and retain the surrounding circumstances of a conversation, leading to enhanced natural and cohesive interactions. These chatbots are used in various fields including customer service and data retrieval, doing exceptionally well in situations that include intricate and ever-changing interactions. Illustrations encompass chatbots integrated into websites, bots designed for customer care, and virtual customer assistants.

3.3.2.4 Shared Characteristics

Virtual assistants and conversational agents share similarities, such as using NLP to understand and reply to user input in a way similar to human communication. Their objective is to improve user engagement by facilitating intuitive and user-friendly communication through natural language, hence removing the necessity for explicit commands or interfaces. Furthermore, both categories of systems largely depend on AI algorithms and machine learning techniques, guaranteeing ongoing enhancement in performance and adjustment to user preferences as time progresses (Sidlauskiene et al. 2023).

To sum up, while virtual assistants specialize in specific tasks and personal assistance, conversational agents are designed for broader and more dynamic interactions across various domains. The distinction lies in their scope and the complexity of conversations they are capable of handling (https://doi.org/10.5281/SJIS.775985).

3.4 User Experience and Interaction

In recent years, the fashion industry has gone through a dramatic digital transformation, with technology playing a critical role in redefining how businesses interact with customers. An important element of this change is the incorporation of chatbots into different online platforms, with the goal of improving user experience and increasing consumer interaction. This article examines the influence of chatbots on user experience in the fashion business, with a specific focus on assessing conversational interfaces and their role in the sector.

3.4.1 Using Conversational Interfaces to Increase Personalization

Chatbots in the fashion industry have emerged as potent instruments for delivering tailored experiences to users. Through the utilization of AI and machine learning algorithms, these conversational interfaces have the capability to examine user preferences, browsing history, and purchasing patterns (Hasal et al. 2021). By utilizing data analysis, chatbots are able to provide personalized suggestions by recommending clothing items that match an individual's specific style preferences. Consequently, users experience an increased level of personalization, which cultivates a more profound bond with the brand.

3.4.2 Seamless Consumer Involvement and Assistance

The fashion industry has been transformed by conversational interfaces, leading to seamless client engagement and assistance in customer service. Chatbots with NLP capabilities can engage in live discussions, handling client inquiries and offering help with product details, sizing, and order tracking. The promptness of this communication enhances a smooth and effective customer experience, as users are no longer required to explore intricate websites or endure delays in receiving traditional customer service responses (Agarwal et al. 2022).

3.4.3 Driving Sales Through Conversational Agent

The implementation of chatbots has enabled the advancement of conversational commerce in the fashion industry, leading to increased sales. Users have the ability to navigate, investigate, and even complete transactions immediately within the chat interface. Conversational interfaces function as virtual shopping assistants, providing guidance to users as they navigate the product catalog, offering suggestions on styling, and smoothing the checkout process (Sidlauskiene et al. 2023). This efficient method of online buying not only improves the overall user experience but also has the potential to increase sales by minimizing obstacles in the purchasing process.

3.4.4 Data Generation and Customer Insight

Chatbots play a crucial role in gathering data and generating customer insights for fashion firms. They provide vital information about client preferences, trends, and comments. By engaging with users, chatbots acquire vital data that may be utilized to inform the development of products, marketing campaigns, and inventory management (Sidlauskiene et al. 2023). The perpetual learning powers of chatbots empower fashion firms to remain responsive to evolving consumer tastes, ultimately enhancing decision-making processes with greater knowledge and insight.

3.4.5 Alleviating Decision Fatigue and Improving User Convenience

The excessive availability of options in the fashion industry frequently results in decision fatigue among customers. Conversational interfaces tackle this difficulty by functioning as personalized shopping assistants, refining options according to user preferences, and directing them towards appropriate selections. The simplification of decision-making processes improves user convenience and promotes a more pleasant and effective buying experience (Cheng and Jiang 2020).

In summary, the incorporation of chatbots into the fashion industry has had a significant and far-reaching effect on the user experience, fundamentally transforming the manner in which consumers engage with brands on the Internet. Chatbots have become crucial elements in the contemporary fashion industry due to their ability to offer individualized advice, facilitate smooth client contact, and drive contextual commerce (Rhim et al. 2022). With the continuous advancement of technology, chatbots are increasingly playing a crucial role in determining the future of the fashion business by significantly contributing to data collection and providing valuable customer insights. As fashion firms increasingly focus on user-centric methods, the deliberate integration of chatbots is expected to continue playing a crucial role in improving user experiences in the digital domain (Cheng and Jiang 2020).

3.5 Challenges and Limitations

While chatbots have become significant tools in the fashion business, allowing for more personalized and engaging online shopping experiences, they are not without issues. This chapter examines the challenges encountered by chatbots in the fashion industry, with a specific focus on language comprehension, user confidence, and privacy issues. Gaining comprehension and effectively tackling these obstacles is vital for guaranteeing the ongoing triumph and reception of chatbots in transforming the online fashion retail domain (Cheng and Jiang 2020).

3.5.1 Difficulties in Language Comprehension

A major obstacle encountered by chatbots in the fashion sector is attaining a precise and nuanced comprehension of language. NLP is the technological foundation that enables chatbots to understand and react to human language, although it is not infallible. Chatbots face difficulties in accurately interpreting user queries in fashion-related chats due to the subjective and context-dependent nature of the language used (Choi et al. 2021).

When fashion fans talk about their tastes or ask for product recommendations, they may utilize various terms, slang, or cultural allusions. For example, a consumer may use terms such as "edgy," "vintage," or "boho-chic" to describe their style, and a chatbot must accurately understand and interpret these descriptions within the appropriate fashion context. To attain a proficient degree of language comprehension, continuous improvement and training of NLP models are necessary to adapt to ever-changing language patterns and user expressions (Patel et al. 2021).

In order to address difficulties in comprehending language, it is crucial to continuously monitor and enhance NLP algorithms. Consistent updates and adjustments informed by user feedback might improve the chatbot's capacity to understand and respond adeptly to the varied terminology employed in fashion-related discussions.

3.5.2 Establishing User Confidence

Establishing and upholding user confidence is a crucial element for the triumph of chatbots in the fashion sector. Users require assurance that the chatbot comprehends their preferences, upholds their privacy, and delivers dependable recommendations.

Trust is frequently eroded when chatbots fail to accurately comprehend user intent or when issues around privacy emerge (Cheng and Jiang 2020).

In order to cultivate trust, chatbots must provide clear and open communication regarding their skills and constraints. Users should receive comprehensive information regarding the data gathered, its intended purposes, and the robust security measures implemented to safeguard their personal information. Transparent and succinct privacy policies, readily available inside the chatbot interface, instill confidence in users regarding the confidentiality and responsible handling of their data (Hasal et al. 2021).

Furthermore, it is essential for chatbots to possess mechanisms that can swiftly rectify errors and misconceptions. The system should adapt and learn from the conversation when a user provides feedback or corrects the chatbot's knowledge. This iterative learning method facilitates the development of a chatbot that becomes increasingly dependable and credible as time progresses (Patel et al. 2021).

Engaging with fashion experts and integrating their expertise into the development process might further improve the chatbot's capacity to effectively comprehend and cater to user preferences. Given the dynamic nature of the fashion sector and its susceptibility to trends, it is imperative for chatbots to remain up-to-date and adapt to the constantly evolving environment (Agarwal et al. 2022).

3.5.3 Issues Regarding the Protection of Personal Information

Privacy problems pose a substantial obstacle for chatbots in the fashion industry, as customers rely on them for sensitive information such as style preferences, sizes, and occasionally payment details. Customers are becoming more concerned regarding the use of their data, particularly in response to prominent data breaches and privacy scandals (Thomas et al. 2022).

In order to mitigate privacy issues, developers must incorporate stringent security protocols to safeguard user data from unauthorized intrusion. Encryption mechanisms, robust data storage techniques, and strict compliance with industry standards for data protection are fundamental elements of a reliable chatbot system (Li et al. 2023).

Granting people autonomy over their data is an additional pivotal element in tackling privacy apprehensions. Chatbots ought to offer users the ability to oversee and erase their stored data, granting them a sense of self-governance and authority. It is essential to provide clear consent processes that inform users about the data being gathered and allow them to decide whether to participate in specific functionalities.

Whenever feasible, anonymizing or aggregating data can also enhance privacy safeguards. Chatbots can mitigate the risk of potential data breaches by reducing the storage and processing of personally identifiable information.

Although chatbots have made notable progress in the fashion business, they still face some hurdles. Obstacles such as language comprehension, user confidence, and privacy anxieties need to be resolved in order to guarantee the ongoing prosperity and acceptance of chatbots in the realm of online fashion shopping (Li et al. 2023).

To overcome these issues, it is crucial to continuously enhance the capabilities of NLP, ensure transparent communication on data usage, and implement strong privacy measures. By actively resolving these concerns, developers and organizations may construct chatbots that not only transform the online shopping experience but also prioritize user confidence and confidentiality, cultivating a lasting connection between customers and virtual fashion assistants (Li et al. 2023; Hasal et al. 2021).

3.6 Conclusion

The evolution of chatbots in AI has been impressive, from early models such as ELIZA and PARRY to today's sophisticated systems utilized in a variety of businesses. Alan Turing's pioneering work in 1950 raised the issue of machine intelligence, prompting the development of the Turing Test, a criterion for evaluating AI's ability to mimic human reasoning.

The first chatbot, ELIZA, was built in 1966 to simulate a Rogerian psychotherapist, followed by PARRY in 1972 to impersonate a paranoid schizophrenic. These early chatbots interacted with humans by pattern matching and keyword recognition, and despite their limited contextual awareness, they passed the Turing Test.

The phrase "chatterbot" first appeared in the 1990s, with the release of early versions such as TINY-MUD and ALICE. Since 2001, chatbot technology has advanced significantly, resulting in the development of personal voice assistants like Siri, IBM Watson, and Alexa. By 2016, chatbots have spread across multiple businesses, altering client relationships, particularly on social media platforms.

AI and chatbots have altered the fashion industry's design, manufacturing, supply chain management, and customer experience. AI algorithms monitor trends and user preferences to improve creativity and efficiency, whereas chatbots provide tailored shopping assistance, virtual try-ons, and real-time customer care. These technologies improve inventory management, demand forecasting, and sustainability by minimizing waste and encouraging material innovation. AI enhances design processes, estimates demand, and controls inventories, resulting in greater efficiency and less waste. Leading brands, such as Nike, Zara, H&M, and ASOS, use these technologies to stay competitive and sensitive to market changes.

Despite their progress, chatbots continue to encounter issues in language comprehension, user trust, and privacy. Continuous progress in NLP algorithms, transparent data handling, and strong security mechanisms are critical to addressing these issues. As technology advances, chatbots are likely to play an increasingly crucial role in improving user experiences and encouraging innovation across a variety of industries.

3.7 Future Trends and Innovations

3.7.1 Future Implications and Guidelines for Ethical Deployment

With the continuous advancement of chatbot technology in the fashion industry, it is crucial to thoroughly analyze the future consequences and ethical issues for the responsible implementation of these intelligent systems. With the growing integration of chatbots equipped with enhanced NLP and AR in fashion firms, there are various ethical concerns that need to be addressed and studied by scholars.

3.7.2 Ethical Considerations of Advanced NLP

The advancements in NLP give rise to ethical concerns about privacy, permission, and the handling of user data. As chatbots improve their ability to comprehend and address user inquiries, the risk of unintentionally accessing confidential data rises. Research in this field could focus on creating strong privacy protections and consent processes to guarantee secure and ethically sound user interactions with chatbots (Silvestri 2020).

Furthermore, ensuring the ethical utilization of consumer data is of utmost importance. Gaining insight into how fashion firms can utilize NLP to create tailored experiences while upholding user privacy is a vital component of ethical technology implementation. This research has the potential to contribute to the development of ethical norms and standards for the application of Natural Language Processing in the fashion industry (Patel et al. 2021).

3.7.3 Societal Consequences of Augmented Reality (AR) Integration

The incorporation of AR technology into chatbots to facilitate virtual try-ons and improve visual experiences gives rise to societal concerns pertaining to body image, beauty norms, and the possibility of fostering unrealistic expectations. An academic inquiry in this field could entail examining the psychological impacts of AR-powered virtual try-ons on consumer self-perception and body image (Ricci et al. 2023). Moreover, research should prioritize the reduction of potential adverse societal consequences by creating AR experiences that foster inclusiveness and variety. It is important to take ethical issues into account to make sure that AR technologies do not strengthen harmful stereotypes or contribute to practices that exclude certain groups in the fashion business (Agarwal et al. 2022).

3.7.4 *Examining and Mitigating Bias and Ensuring Fairness in Recommendations*

With the growing dependence of chatbots on sophisticated algorithms for tailored recommendations, the problem of bias in decision-making processes becomes more noticeable. An ethical investigation should focus on developing techniques to detect and correct biases in chatbot algorithms, guaranteeing impartial and comprehensive suggestions for users from diverse demographic backgrounds. This may entail creating frameworks to examine and alleviate biases in fashion chatbots, with the aim of fostering fair and impartial user interactions (Mohammadi and Kalhor 2021a).

3.7.5 *Enabling Users with Understandable AI*

Transparency of AI decision-making is another crucial factor to consider when ethically using chatbots in the fashion industry. As chatbots become increasingly advanced, the capability to provide a clear explanation for recommendations becomes essential in order to establish user trust. Explorations in explainable AI can enhance the advancement of models that offer lucid and comprehensible explanations for the judgments made by fashion chatbots, enabling consumers to make well-informed choices (Liao et al. 2018).

3.7.6 *Striking a Balance Between Innovation and Responsible Implementation*

Although chatbot technology has the ability to greatly improve the fashion retail experience, it is crucial to carefully consider the ethical implications of these innovations. Researchers have the opportunity to investigate frameworks that provide guidance for the responsible implementation of chatbots, taking into account variables such as the welfare of users, the impact on society, and environmental sustainability (Kooli 2023). Ultimately, it is crucial to actively confront the ethical consequences linked to the enhanced integration of NLP and AR as chatbot technology advances in the fashion industry. This academic chapter emphasizes the significance of continuous study in establishing ethical norms, privacy protections, and inclusive practices to guarantee that chatbot technologies have a good impact on the fashion business, while giving priority to the well-being of users and societal values. The discussion about the future direction of chatbot technology in the ever-changing fashion retail industry should prioritize ethical considerations (Murtarelli et al. 2021).

References

Abdulla H, Eltahir AM, Alwahaishi S, Saghair K, Platos J, Snasel V (2022) Chatbots development using natural language processing: a review. In: 2022 26th International conference on circuits, systems, communications and computers (CSCC), pp 122–128. https://doi.org/10.1109/CSCC55931.2022.00030

Adamopoulou E, Moussiades L (2020) Chatbots: history, technology, and applications. Mach Learn Appl 2:100006. https://doi.org/10.1016/j.mlwa.2020.100006

Agarwal S, Agarwal B, Gupta R (2022) Chatbots and virtual assistants: a bibliometric analysis. Library Hi Tech 40(4):1013–1030. https://doi.org/10.1108/LHT-09-2021-0330

Akhtar M, Neidhardt J, Werthner H (2019) The potential of chatbots: analysis of chatbot conversations. In: Conference on business informatics, vol 1, pp 397–404, July 2019. https://doi.org/10.1109/CBI.2019.00052

Ashktorab Z, Jain M, Vera Liao Q, Weisz JD (2019) Resilient chatbots: repair strategy preferences for conversational breakdowns. In: International conference on human factors in computing systems, May 2019. https://doi.org/10.1145/3290605.3300484

Behera RK, Bala PK, Ray A (2021) Cognitive chatbot for personalised contextual customer service: behind the scene and beyond the hype. Inf Syst Front. https://doi.org/10.1007/S10796-021-10168-Y

Binkis M, Kubiliūnas R, Sturienė R, Dulinskienė T, Blažauskas T, Jakštienė V (2021) Rule-based chatbot integration into software engineering course. In: International conference on information and software technologies, vol 1486 CCIS, pp 367–377. https://doi.org/10.1007/978-3-030-88304-1_29

Bonetti F, Perry P (2017) A review of consumer-facing digital technologies across different types of fashion store formats. In: Advanced fashion technology and operations management. IGI Global, pp 137–163. https://doi.org/10.4018/978-1-5225-1865-5.ch006

Castagna AC, Duarte M, Pinto DC (2022) Slow fashion or self-signaling? Sustainability in the fashion industry. Sustain Prod Consum 31:582–590. https://doi.org/10.1016/J.SPC.2022.03.024

Chen E (2022) The effect of multiple replies for natural language generation chatbots. In: CHI conference on human factors in computing systems extended abstracts. https://doi.org/10.1145/3491101.3516800

Cheng Y, Jiang H (2020) How do ai-driven chatbots impact user experience? Examining gratifications, perceived privacy risk, satisfaction, loyalty, and continued use. J Broadcast Electron Media 64(4):592–614. https://doi.org/10.1080/08838151.2020.1834296

Choi H, Kim J, Joe S, Gwon Y (2021) Evaluation of BERT and ALBERT sentence embedding performance on downstream NLP tasks. In: International conference on pattern recognition, pp 5482–5487. https://doi.org/10.1109/ICPR48806.2021.9412102

Cui L, Huang S, Wei F, Tan C, Duan C, Zhou M (2017) Superagent: a customer service chatbot for e-commerce websites. In: Proceedings of ACL 2017, system demonstrations, 2017, aclanthology.org, pp 97–102. https://doi.org/10.18653/v1/P17-4017

Dale R (2016) The return of the chatbots. Nat Lang Eng 22(5):811–817. https://doi.org/10.1017/S1351324916000243

Devlin J, Chang MW, Lee K, Toutanova K (2019) BERT: pre-training of deep bidirectional transformers for language understanding. In: NAACL HLT 2019—2019 conference of the North American chapter of the association for computational linguistics: human language technologies—proceedings of the conference, vol 1, pp 4171–4186

Dokukina I, Gumanova J (2020) The rise of chatbots-new personal assistants in foreign language learning. Procedia Comput Sci 542–546. https://doi.org/10.1016/j.procs.2020.02.212

Ghazvininejad M et al (2018) A knowledge-grounded neural conversation model. In: Proceedings of the AAAI conference on artificial intelligence, 2018, ojs.aaai.org. Accessed: 02 Feb 2024. [Online]. Available: https://ojs.aaai.org/index.php/AAAI/article/view/11977

Goti A, Querejeta-Lomas L, Almeida A, de la Puerta JG, López-de-Ipiña D (2023) Artificial intelligence in business-to-customer fashion retail: a literature review. Mathematics 11(13). (Multidisciplinary Digital Publishing Institute (MDPI), 01 July 2023). https://doi.org/10.3390/math11132943

Guo ZX, Wong WK, Leung SYS, Li M (2011) Applications of artificial intelligence in the apparel industry: a review. Text Res J 81(18):1871–1892. https://doi.org/10.1177/0040517511411968

Hananto VR, Kim S, Kovacs M, Serdult U, Kryssanov V (2021) A machine learning approach to analyze fashion styles from large collections of online customer reviews. In: 2021 6th International conference on business and industrial research (ICBIR), pp 153–158, May 2021. https://doi.org/10.1109/ICBIR52339.2021.9465830

Hasal M, Nowaková J, Ahmed Saghair K, Abdulla H, Snášel V, Ogiela L (2021) Chatbots: security, privacy, data protection, and social aspects. Concurr Comput 33(19). https://doi.org/10.1002/CPE.6426

Hollander J, Sabatini J, Graesser A (2022) How item and learner characteristics matter in intelligent tutoring systems data. In: International conference on artificial intelligence in education, 2022. Springer, Berlin, Accessed: 02 Feb 2024. [Online]. Available: https://doi.org/10.1007/978-3-031-11647-6_106

Husak V, Lozynska O, Vysotskyi A (2020) Information system for recommendation list formation of clothes style image selection according to user's needs based on NLP and chatbots

Introducing ChatGPT. Accessed: 02 Feb 2024. [Online]. Available: https://openai.com/blog/chatgpt

Kooli C (2023) Chatbots in education and research: a critical examination of ethical implications and solutions. Sustainability 15(7). https://doi.org/10.3390/SU15075614

Kull AJ, Romero M, Monahan L (2021) How may I help you? Driving brand engagement through the warmth of an initial chatbot message. J Bus Res 135:840–850. https://doi.org/10.1016/j.jbusres.2021.03.005

Lee D, Yeo S (2022) Developing an AI-based chatbot for practicing responsive teaching in mathematics. Elsevier, Amsterdam. Accessed: 02 Feb 2024. [Online]. Available: https://www.sciencedirect.com/science/article/pii/S0360131522002172

Li L, Li C, Ji D (2021) Deep context modeling for multi-turn response selection in dialogue systems. Inf Process Manag 58(1). https://doi.org/10.1016/j.ipm.2020.102415

Li J, Wu L, Qi J, Zhang Y, Wu Z, Hu S (2023) Determinants affecting consumer trust in communication with AI chatbots. J Organ End User Comput 35(1). https://doi.org/10.4018/JOEUC.328089

Liao L, Zhou Y, Ma Y, Hong R, Chua TS (2018) Knowledge-aware multimodal fashion chatbot. In: MM 2018—Proceedings of the 2018 ACM multimedia conference. Association for Computing Machinery, Inc., pp 1265–1266, Oct 2018. https://doi.org/10.1145/3240508.3241399

Liu C-C, Liao M-G, Chang C-H, Lin H-M (2022) An analysis of children' interaction with an AI chatbot and its impact on their interest in reading. Elsevier, Amsterdam. Accessed: 02 Feb 2024. [Online]. Available: https://www.sciencedirect.com/science/article/pii/S0360131522001476

Loeb Z (2021) The lamp and the lighthouse: Joseph Weizenbaum, contextualizing the critic. Interdisc Sci Rev 46(1–2):19–35. https://doi.org/10.1080/03080188.2020.1840218

Mishra MK, Abtew MA, Bruniaux P (2022) Customization of shoe last based on 3D design process with adjustable 3D ease allowance for better comfort and design. Int J Adv Manuf Technol 123(9–10):3131–3146. https://doi.org/10.1007/s00170-022-10427-5

Mohammadi SO, Kalhor A (2021a) Smart fashion: a review of AI applications in virtual try-on & fashion synthesis. https://doi.org/10.36548/JAICN.2021.4.002

Mohammadi SO, Kalhor A (2021b) Smart fashion: a review of AI applications in the fashion & apparel industry, Oct 2021. Accessed: 07 Feb 2024. [Online]. Available: https://arxiv.org/abs/2111.00905v2

Murtarelli G, Gregory A, Romenti S (2021) A conversation-based perspective for shaping ethical human–machine interactions: The particular challenge of chatbots. J Bus Res 129:927–935. https://doi.org/10.1016/j.jbusres.2020.09.018

Nikvand N, Wang Z, Farjow W, Fernando X (2018) Information distance based photoshop metric. In: Asilomar conference on signals, systems and computers, vol 2018-Oct, pp 1532–1535, July 2018. https://doi.org/10.1109/ACSSC.2018.8645090
Parry the AI chatterbot. Accessed: 01 Feb 2024. [Online]. Available: https://phrasee.co/news/parry-the-a-i-chatterbot-from-1972/
Patel A, Bhattamishra S, Goyal N (2021) Are NLP models really able to solve simple math word problems? In: NAACL-HLT 2021—2021 conference of the North American chapter of the association for computational linguistics: human language technologies, proceedings of the conference, pp 2080–2094. https://doi.org/10.18653/V1/2021.NAACL-MAIN.168
Pawlik Ł, Płaza M, Deniziak S, Boksa E (2022) A method for improving bot effectiveness by recognising implicit customer intent in contact centre conversations. Speech Commun 143:33–45. https://doi.org/10.1016/J.SPECOM.2022.07.003
Powton M (2024) A visual history of chatbots. Chatbots continue to grow in popularity…. Chatbots Magazine. Accessed: 06 Feb 2024. [Online]. Available: https://chatbotsmagazine.com/a-visual-history-of-chatbots-8bf3b31dbfb2
Rane A, Ranade C, Bandekar H, Jadhav R, Chitre V (2022) AI driven chatbot and its evolution. In: International conference on awareness science and technology, pp 170–173. https://doi.org/10.1109/ICAST55766.2022.10039515
Rathore B (2019) Fashion sustainability in the AI era: opportunities and challenges in marketing
Renaningtyas L, Dwitasari P, Ramadhani N (2023) Implementing the use of AI for analysis and prediction in the fashion industry. Sustain Creative Ind Urban City 7(1). https://doi.org/10.21625/ARCHIVE.V7I1.928
Rese A, Ganster L, Baier D (2020) Chatbots in retailers' customer communication: how to measure their acceptance? J Retail Consum Serv 56. https://doi.org/10.1016/J.JRETCONSER.2020.102176
Retailers use of AI, MV and CV 2023 | Statista. Accessed: 01 Feb 2024. [Online]. Available: https://www.statista.com/statistics/1400301/ai-mv-and-cv-use-retail/
Rhim J, Kwak M, Gong Y, Gweon G (2022) Application of humanization to survey chatbots: change in chatbot perception, interaction experience, and survey data quality. Comput Human Behav 126. https://doi.org/10.1016/J.CHB.2021.107034
Ricci M, Evangelista A, Di Roma A, Fiorentino M (2023) Immersive and desktop virtual reality in virtual fashion stores: a comparison between shopping experiences. Virtual Real 27(3):2281–2296. https://doi.org/10.1007/S10055-023-00806-Y
Selamat MA, Windasari NA (2021) Chatbot for SMEs: integrating customer and business owner perspectives. Technol Soc. https://doi.org/10.1016/J.TECHSOC.2021.101685
Shi M, Lewis VD (2020) Using artificial intelligence to analyze fashion trends. arXiv.org
Sidlauskiene J, Joye Y, Auruskeviciene V (2023) AI-based chatbots in conversational commerce and their effects on product and price perceptions. Electron Markets 33(1). https://doi.org/10.1007/S12525-023-00633-8
Siedlikowski S, Noël LP, Moynihan SA, Robin M (2021) Chloe for COVID-19: evolution of an intelligent conversational agent to address infodemic management needs during the COVID-19 pandemic. J Med Internet Res 23(9). https://doi.org/10.2196/27283
Silvestri B (2020) The future of fashion: how the quest for digitization and the use of artificial intelligence and extended reality will reshape the fashion industry after COVID-19. ZoneModa J 10(2). https://doi.org/10.6092/issn.2611-0563/11803
Singh S, Thakur HK (2020) Survey of various AI chatbots based on technology used. In: 2020 8th International conference on reliability, infocom technologies and optimization (trends and future directions) (ICRITO), pp 1074–1079, June 2020. https://doi.org/10.1109/ICRITO48877.2020.9197943
Song D, Oh E, Hong H (2022) The impact of teaching simulation using student chatbots with different attitudes on preservice teachers' efficacy. Educ Technol Soc JSTOR. Accessed: 02 Feb 2024. [Online]. Available: https://www.jstor.org/stable/48673723

The AI couturiers: redefining fashion with artificial intelligence. https://doi.org/10.5281/SJIS.775985

Turing AM (1950) I—Computing Machinery and Intelligence. Mind LIX (236) pp 433–460. https://doi.org/10.1093/mind/LIX.236.433

Thomas JH, Roopashree S, Joy JC, Abdullah Kollarath H, Siby A (2022) Deep learning: a new way of looking into fashion. In: 2022 4th International conference on advances in computing, communication control and networking (ICAC3N), pp 1592–1595. https://doi.org/10.1109/ICAC3N56670.2022.10074341

Vashisht K, Mittar S (2019) Artificial intelligence as a tool in the online fashion retail industry to communicate fashion trends. In: Fashion communication in the digital age, pp 276–282. https://doi.org/10.1007/978-3-030-15436-3_25

Vijayaraghavan V, Cooper JB, Rian Leevinson RL (2020) Algorithm inspection for chatbot performance evaluation. Procedia Comput Sci 2267–2274. https://doi.org/10.1016/j.procs.2020.04.245

Yadav A, Sondhi H (2023) Systematic literature review on sustainable marketing and artificial intelligence. In: International conference on computing for sustainable global development

Yeo SF, Tan CL, Kumar A, Tan KH, Wong JK (2022) Investigating the impact of AI-powered technologies on Instagrammers' purchase decisions in digitalization era—a study of the fashion and apparel industry. Technol Forecast Soc Change 177:121551. https://doi.org/10.1016/J.TECHFORE.2022.121551

Chapter 4
RFID Technology in Fashion Supply Chain—Recent Trends and Analysis from Developing Countries

Majo George, Phat Hung Ngo, Nhi Khac Yen Le, Han Phuong Bao Nguyen, Khue Ngoc Anh Ngo, Anna Maria Majo, Irfan Ulhaq, and Rajkishore Nayak

Abstract This paper's objective is to examine the latest Radio Frequency Identification (RFID) technologies and their potential advantages for narrowing the sustainability gaps, as well as the difficulties that they pose in Vietnam's fashion and textile supply chain. The study was based on a foundation of qualitative research including journal articles, academic research, and book chapters which can be found through online databases. The results indicated that as much as RFID is illustrated as the pivotal solution for supply chain transformation within the scope of encompassing social, economic, and environmental aspects; there are still constraints in ensuring the environmental benefits of producing RFID since certain components of the tags are either hard or non-recyclable. Furthermore, although RFID technology is employed to deter counterfeiting in the fashion supply chain, the tag itself is susceptible to cybersecurity breaches such as cloning, tracking, and disabling. Additional measures and research should be undertaken to promote the latest RFID technology and address the current issues. Implementing the ECO RFID tag and Sewed Chipless RFID tag is advised for fabricating the transformation.

M. George (✉) · I. Ulhaq
TBS, RMIT University Vietnam, Ho Chi Minh, Vietnam
e-mail: majo.george@rmit.edu.vn

I. Ulhaq
e-mail: Irfan.ulhaq@rmit.edu.vn

P. H. Ngo · N. K. Y. Le · H. P. B. Nguyen · K. N. A. Ngo
RMIT University Vietnam, Ho Chi Minh, Vietnam

A. M. Majo
Marian College Kuttikkanam, Kuttikkanam, Kerala, India

R. Nayak
SCD, RMIT University Vietnam, Ho Chi Minh, Vietnam
e-mail: rajkishore.nayak@rmit.edu.vn

R. Nayak et al. (eds.), *Use of Digital and Advanced Technologies in the Fashion Supply Chain*, Springer Series in Fashion Business,
https://doi.org/10.1007/978-981-97-7528-6_4

Keywords RFID technology · Developing country · Fashion supply chain · Sustainability · Identification

4.1 Introduction

In recent decades, Radio Frequency Identification (RFID) technology has experienced significant growth within the realm of industrial digitalization, particularly in sectors such as supply chain management, manufacturing, and asset tracking (Musa and Dabo 2016). RFID stands out as a highly promising modern technology capable of automating the identification, tracking, and tracing of various items, including those within the fashion industry's supply chain. Recent social and environmental scandals within the fashion supply chain have underscored the critical importance of traceability in safeguarding the reputations of fashion brands (Moretto et al. 2018). Consequently, there has been a notable shift toward establishing sustainable, responsible, and transparent systems within the fashion supply chain.

Technologies such as RFID, Industry 4.0, artificial intelligence, and blockchain have emerged as key enablers in enhancing transparency across social and economic dimensions. Among these technologies, RFID holds particular promise and is increasingly being embraced by major industries for functions such as inventory management, logistics, transportation, asset tracking, and object location within supply chain processes. In the fashion and textile industry, numerous fashion brands are increasingly adopting RFID technology due to its versatility across various production and distribution processes. These processes encompass yarn and fabric sourcing, garment manufacturing, inventory management, retail operations, theft prevention, and tracking product movements (Ni et al. 2011).

The integration of RFID technology offers several advantages, including reduced material usage, enhanced inventory turnover, improved stock-keeping accuracy, and more precise demand forecasting. By leveraging RFID, fashion brands can enhance productivity while concurrently lowering costs, thereby bolstering their competitiveness within the industry (Nayak et al. 2022). However, despite the considerable benefits, there is a notable scarcity of research papers addressing RFID limitations and unresolved issues, particularly concerning sustainability at the item level and the risk of product counterfeiting. Furthermore, there is a noticeable gap in research focusing on emerging RFID technologies tailored specifically for the fashion supply chain. Consequently, this study seeks to investigate recent RFID technologies and their potential sustainability benefits, as well as the associated challenges within the fashion supply chain. The findings of this research endeavor aim to provide guidance for researchers, brand managers, and fashion retailers seeking to advance sustainability objectives within Vietnam's fashion supply chain.

4.2 Literature Review

4.2.1 The Description of RFID Tag

Radio Frequency Identification (RFID) represents a sophisticated automatic identification methodology that harnesses radio and electromagnetic waves to remotely track and trace objects and living entities, obviating the necessity for visual proximity. A comprehensive system encompasses various physical components (such as active or passive tags and tag readers), alongside software components (including middleware, servers, and computer applications) (Want 2022). RFID tags, also referred to as transponders, are miniature devices employed for attachment or insertion into diverse entities, spanning from products to animals and humans alike.

Contained within each of the RFID tags is a microchip that hosts an Electronic Product Code (EPC) alongside a spectrum of product-specific data (including manufacturer details, model specifications, batch information, production year, pricing, etc.). Furthermore, these transponders are outfitted with antennas, facilitating their capability to receive and respond to radio frequency signals emitted by tag readers (also recognized as RFID transceivers or interrogators). One of the prevailing uses of this technology lies in monitoring and tracking applications (Casella et al. 2022). Across diverse sectors, including logistics, retail, construction, healthcare, fashion, and beyond, RFID has emerged as a viable alternative to conventional barcode systems. This transition is owed to RFID's capacity to furnish real-time inventory data and streamline labor-intensive processes.

4.2.2 Overview of Vietnam's Fashion and Textile Industry

The fashion and textile industry in Vietnam is a dynamic sector that plays a significant role in the nation's exports and GDP while also addressing employment concerns (Tran and Tran 2018). Due to favorable trade agreements, strategic geographic locations, and a positive economic climate, Vietnam's garment exports are consistently escalating, thereby benefiting the country's economy.

Along with the constant shift in the economic landscape, Vietnam will also have to strengthen its advantageous position in the global market; according to Dr. Nayak, Vietnam must establish its fabric manufacturing capabilities to fulfill the demand and comply with the fabric-forward rules of origin outlined in the EU-Vietnam Free Trade Agreement (EVFTA) (Hoang 2020). This situation further highlights the critical point of traceability and alignment with social, economic, and environmental aspects; Vietnamese fashion enterprises ought to focus on sustainable production frameworks, which will require investments in new technologies (Nayak et al. 2019).

4.3 Industrial Issues in Vietnam's Fashion and Textile Industry

1. **Sustainable issues in the Vietnamese fashion and textile market**

While numerous studies have examined supply chain risk assessment and management, there has been limited focus on how sustainability considerations manifest as risks within supply chain management. The triple bottom-line framework, encompassing social, economic, and environmental aspects, is commonly employed to characterize sustainable development in research (Brandenburg et al. 2014; Giannakis and Papadopoulos 2016). Therefore, this section utilizes the triple bottom-line framework to analyze the garment and textile industry in Vietnam.

The drive for shorter product lifecycles, punctual delivery, supplier streamlining, technological advancements, inventory management challenges such as buffers and stocks, and external influences like fluctuations in consumer preferences are identified as specific industry factors contributing to the growing complexity of the fashion supply chain (Irfan et al. 2020). To meet these evolving demands, both the Vietnamese and global fashion industries have embraced various supply chain architectures and philosophies, including Lean Manufacturing and Just-in-Time methodologies, as well as initiatives to streamline flow and eliminate redundancies and buffers. These adaptations have facilitated operational efficiency within global supply chains. However, while these efforts have generated significant economic benefits, they have also introduced risks within the realms of social and environmental sustainability.

The intricate nature and geographical dispersion of fashion supply chains contribute to heightened social and environmental sustainability risks and pressures (Nayak 2020). These encompass issues such as the excessive use of chemicals and water in textile manufacturing, hazardous working conditions, labor exploitation throughout the production process, carbon emissions from transportation, and the proliferation of post-consumer textile waste (Irfan et al. 2020). Particularly prevalent among these risks are unsustainable manufacturing practices, characterized by the exploitation of workers and environmental contamination during production and distribution, which are pervasive within the fashion garment industry due to the imperative to minimize costs and turnaround times (Nayak et al. 2020).

Besides, manufacturing goods in countries with lower labor costs, such as Vietnam, frequently leads to lower environmental and social standards compared to those in these as a "dumping ground" for its manufacture—where sustainable regulation is less restricted than in developed countries (Thorisdottir and Johannsdottir 2020). Hence, several multinational companies appear willing to sacrifice social-environmental values in their outsourced countries like Vietnam to prioritize the headquarters' financial gains, leading to severe social and environmental problems.

Additionally, both pre-consumer and post-consumer textile waste pose significant challenges. The phenomenon of fast fashion, often referred to as "disposable fashion," exacerbates this issue, as it entails the rapid disposal of textiles in landfills after being worn only a few times by consumers (Ngo et al. 2024).

2. **Counterfeit issues in the Vietnamese fashion and textile market**

Product forgery or counterfeiting has always been a pungent problem in the Vietnamese market, which can be found in large and developing markets, ranging from F&B, supplementary, pharmaceutical, B2B products, and, most commonly, consumer goods and luxury fashion items (OECD 2019). Unfortunately, the Vietnamese fashion market is where these products are considerably notable since it is discernible that counterfeit products of renowned brands such as Hermes, Valentino, or Dolce & Gabbana are sold in various marketplaces, even local brands are also susceptible to these infringements.

Despite the increasing popularity of RFID technology, many fashion enterprises continue to utilize barcodes and QR codes for their merchandise, due to their price differences compared to RFID technology (Tu et al. 2021). However, regarding efficiency and security, barcodes have a weakness in that they must be visible to be scanned and are more susceptible to being duplicated, many entities used to establish barcodes and QR code authentication apps for consumers, but meticulously counterfeit tags can also deceive these technologies, as such RFID is deemed more effective than barcodes in terms of preventing fraudulent (Kubáňová et al. 2022; Nayak et al. 2015; Nayak 2019).

As outlined in the previous chapter, the research into consumers' psychology of Millennials and Centennials by Marinelli and Sinatra (2023) found that buyers exhibit a high aversion toward counterfeit products, with just 15% of them being aware of the product's counterfeit nature after making a purchase. However, the research was based in Italy, where consumers exhibit different perceptions and demographical landscapes compared to Vietnam. On the other hand, research by Nguyen and Li (2022) discovered that consumers in Vietnam and developing countries consciously chose to buy forged products, since counterfeits are cheaper, and it is considered financial suicide to buy authentic items; furthermore, some segments of buyers only care about the popularity and trend without considering any authenticity.

4.3.1 RFID Benefits to Mitigate Issues in Vietnam's Fashion and Textile Industry

1. **RFID benefit in sustainable development**

Previous studies have examined the advantages of RFID technology within the framework of the three pillars of sustainability: economic, environmental, and social. From an economic perspective, RFID stands out as one of the most cost-effective approaches in the fashion industry that facilitates enhanced inventory management, operational efficiency, integration of the fashion business model, and heightened responsiveness throughout the fashion cycle, thereby diminishing the redundant resources for these tasks (Khalil et al. 2020a, b). Furthermore, the implementation of item-level tagging can yield benefits across the entire supply chain, spanning from manufacturers and logistics companies to retail outlets.

Detail-wise, RFID tags facilitate real-time access to inventory data, enhancing forecasting accuracy and, consequently, enriching the overall customer experience. In environmental terms, the adoption of RFID technology correlates positively with green performance and sustainable practices (Green et al. 2017). Improved forecasting and inventory control mechanisms translate to a reduction in product wastage (Reyes 2023). Additionally, RFID technology has the potential to minimize or eliminate stop controls, particularly within transportation and warehouse operations, leading to decreased energy consumption (Varriale et al. 2021).

Research into the social benefits of RFID technology remains sparse, previous papers with a primary focus on enhancing security and bolstering community well-being, particularly evident in applications such as prisoner control and theft reduction (Munoz-Ausecha et al. 2021). While other social impacts are intricately linked with environmental factors, previous scholarly works often intertwine these two aspects. Examples include utilizing RFID solutions to assess the carbon footprint of purchased products, employing RFID applications to examine animal behaviors (e.g., in entomology, ornithology, or farming), and implementing RFID-based solutions for enhanced traceability of food and drugs, thereby minimizing waste and mitigating health risks.

2. **RFID benefits in preventing counterfeit**

Prior research has extensively examined the role of RFID in preventing counterfeit products due to its ability to capture and transmit data. Additionally, this technology is one of the most cost-effective solutions to enhance inventory control precision and monitoring product movement, as it reduces the resources needed for these activities and mitigates the potential hazards of counterfeit, pillaging, or product loss (Tuyls and Batina 2006; Yan and Huang 2008; Cheung and Choi 2011; Tran and Hong 2015).

A well-known approach for implementing anti-counterfeiting with RFID technology involves the manufacturer storing a unique serial number, the secret key or K, for every individual tag. Additionally, the confidential key is secured on the central authentication server. During the authentication process, an RFID reader tests the legitimacy of a tag by requesting its encrypted or hashed serial key, to which the tag responds. The encrypted communication is sent to the server to be checked for validity. If the serial number is verified, the product to which the tag is affixed is confirmed authentic (Rahman and Ahamed 2012).

4.3.2 Potential Gaps of RFID in Vietnam's Fashion and Textile Industry

1. **Potential sustainable gap of RFID**

As evidenced by the previous part of the literature review, RFID technology and sustainability stand as pivotal subjects within the global fashion industry. Yet, academic research dedicated to exploring the sustainability dimensions pertaining directly to RFID tags has been notably lacking. Consequently, the emphasis of this section has been redirected toward evaluating the environmental implications of RFID tags.

Although a single RFID tag may have a minuscule chemical and physical footprint, the cumulative environmental impact becomes significant when considering the massive volume of tags deployed. As reported by IDTechEx (Das and Harrop 2009), a staggering 18 billion RFID tags were shipped worldwide in 2019, with projections indicating a growth to 55 billion tags by 2029. Therefore, the environmental consequence of a conventional RFID item-level tag warrants consideration, particularly in three key areas (Voipio et al. 2021):

(1) The carbon footprint—The environmental impact associated with the production of RFID tags, which includes assessing the various constituent components that make up an RFID tag.
(2) Chemical effluent impact—The measurement of chemical effluents and water usage during the manufacturing process can be evaluated based on their effects on eutrophication and acidification. This assessment considers emissions such as nitrogen oxides, sulfur dioxide, and chemical oxygen demand in water.
(3) Plastic waste—The quantity of plastic material produced as a fundamental component of the final RFID tag plays a crucial role in determining the tags' recyclability and contributes substantially to the accumulation of waste in landfills.

Regarding the first area, conventional tag processing entails laminating heat-stabilized polyester film and aluminum foil. Consequently, surplus aluminum is removed through a wet etching process utilizing water and chemicals, resulting in a significant volume of contaminated water waste (see Fig. 4.1).

The RAND Report offers insights into the carbon dioxide footprint linked with the conventional RFID structure, categorized into three size classifications: small (894 mm^2), medium (2219 mm^2), and large (4171 mm^2) (Voipio et al. 2021). The assessment primarily examines raw material consumption, with the largest size category showing the highest levels, as per previous dimensions. Notably, the polyester substrate and acrylate layers utilized as adhesives constitute the primary contributors to the CO_2 footprint.

Regarding recyclability, flame retardants and/or pigments incorporated into plastic components in conventionally produced RFID tags, such as potassium or bromine, could inadvertently accompany the tags into recycling/disposal processes. These additives are deemed environmentally crucial in polymer-recycling, posing challenges to the recyclability of RFID tags featuring polyester substrates. Based on the RAND Report's disclosure, a large-sized RFID tag is estimated to contain approximately 290.7 mg of polyester plastic per tag.

Therefore, various types of waste are generated throughout the lifecycle of traditional RFID tags. This acknowledgment has heightened industry practitioners' awareness, emphasizing not only the responsibility for sustainable fashion products but also for their associated components, in this case specifically RFID tags.

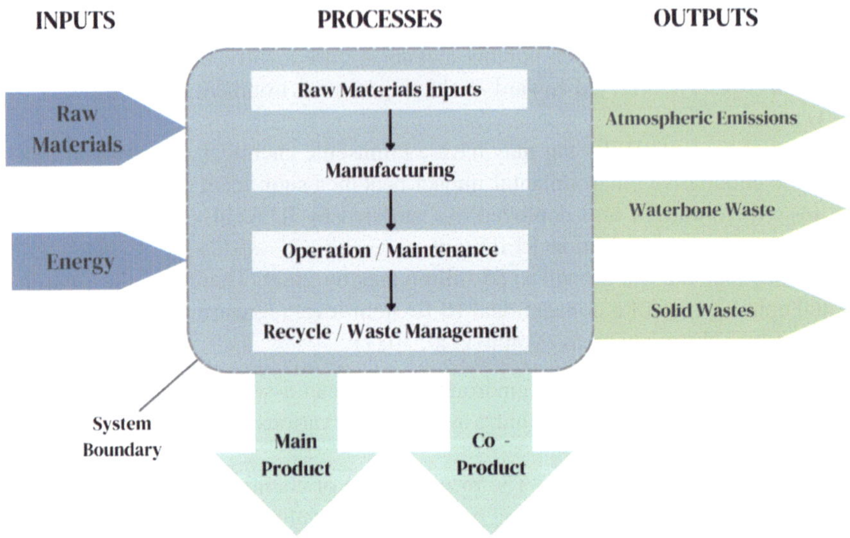

Fig. 4.1 The primary phases and typical inputs/outputs evaluated within the lifecycle of RFID tags (adapted from Voipio et al. 2021)

2. **Potential security gaps of RFID**

Mordantly, as much of a pivotal solution as RFID was narrated in terms of preventing product counterfeiting, there is a concurrent potential for counterfeiting of the very solution, as RFID is also prone to certain cyber security risks. More precisely, the duplication of the RFID affixed to the product to thwart counterfeiting (Khalil et al. 2020a). There are various methods of counterfeiting an RFID tag, including eavesdropping, cloning, encryption, and content tampering. Bagay (2020) mentioned a Denial-of-Service attack (DDoS)-based technique for impeding the ability of a reader to extract data from an RFID tag, by convulsing the signals of the tags using numerous anarchic signals in the radio air. Considerably, the latter part of this chapter will also delve into the study of RFID security risks as well as analyzing a proposed mitigation strategy established by Khalil et al. (2020a, 2020b).

Research Questions

The aforementioned section depicts a transparent overview of RFID technologies and their general benefits within the landscape of fashion and textile supply chains. Nonetheless, it is important to recognize that earlier chapters and studies in academic literature have provided insufficient information and analysis on the common and probable challenges associated with RFID technology. Accordingly, ensuing the objectives of scrutinizing the landscape of RFID implementation in Vietnam's fashion and textile sector, this chapter proposes two research questions regarding the further evaluation of sustainability pursuits and latent threats that entities might face when pursuing RFID-based solutions:

- **RQ1**: What are the potential technologies that can be applied to mitigate the RFID-gap?
- **RQ2**: What are the potential challenges when implementing the proposed RFID technologies?

4.4 Methodology

Extensive research regarding RFID technology has been conducted; however, only a small number of these studies have focused on the sustainability gaps and security problems associated with the technology, particularly in the context of the fashion and textile industry in the Vietnamese market. This paper's research was conducted using the qualitative method, by gathering and analyzing academic articles, journals, and books from various databases including Springer Link, Research Gate, IEEE, MDPI, Science Direct, and PubMed. Approximately 15 sources were retrieved from the mentioned databases, using the combination of keywords such as the following:

1. Sustainability **and** RFID **and** fashion **or** textile.
2. Sustainability **and** gaps **and** RFID **and/or** fashion or textile.
3. RFID **and** implementation **and** security risk.
4. RFID **and/or** security **and** risk **and** solutions.

After filtering out duplicates and research with unaligned objectives, 4 journals, 1 book chapter, and 1 conference paper were selected and demonstrated in the table below:

Authors and year	Type	Title	Journal/Conference/Book
Kumar et al. (2021) [A1]	Journal article	A comprehensive taxonomy of security and privacy issues in RFID	Complex & Intelligent Systems
Khattab et al. (2017) [A2]	Book chapter	RFID security threats and basic solutions	RFID Security: A Lightweight Paradigm
Nastasiu et al. (2020)	Journal article	A new method of secure authentication based on electromagnetic signatures of chipless RFID tags and machine learning approaches	Sensors
Voipio et al. (2021)	Journal article	Environmental RFID: measuring the relevance in the fashion industry	International Journal of Fashion Design, Technology, and Education
Khan et al. (2020)	Conference	A silver-coated conductive fibre HC12 sewed chipless RFID tag on cotton fabric for wearable applications	IEEE Conference

(continued)

(continued)

Authors and year	Type	Title	Journal/Conference/ Book
Ngo et al. (2024)	Journal article	Sustainability-related supply chain risks and supply chain performances: the moderating effects of dynamic supply chain management practices	Business Strategy and the Environment

Findings	
Kumar et al. (2021) [A1]	This research initially studies the foundation of RFID, which is the architecture of IoT. Then comprehensively analyzes the possible security attack of RFID under three categories: confidentiality, integrity, and availability. The authors proposed a taxonomy of defense mechanisms including public and private-key cryptography, lightweight block cipher, and schemes. However, none of them can fully demolish all the threats since developing a single strategy to deal with all forms of security breaches remains a problem in research
Khattab et al. (2017) [A2]	Analogous to A1, A2 assessed the prevailing security risks by classifying RFID security attacks into physical, communication, and overall systematic hazards given the existence of multilayer attacks, which can impact multiple layers simultaneously. Nevertheless, their remedies are founded upon tangible implementations instead of cryptographic and cipher schemes. Including Faraday cage, sleeping, or demolishing tag, however, these approaches are not universally applicable and are designed for specific applications only
Nastasiu et al. (2020)	This paper describes the creation of a neural network model that can classify RFID tags or radio frequency identification, using electromagnetic (EM) signatures for authenticating functions. A key application of chipless RFID technology is its ability to combat counterfeiting, which poses a significant danger to manufacturers. The concept involves the utilization of chipless RFID tags that possess a unique and non-reproducible fingerprint to authenticate items. The usage of EM characteristics makes it challenging to counterfeit these fingerprints. A set of eighteen tags operating in the V band (65–72 GHz) was developed and evaluated. To verify the authentication process, the 18 EM responses are analyzed and categorized using machine learning (ML) algorithms
Voipio et al. (2021)	This study was conducted to assess the significance of environmental RFID tags through a comprehensive two-stage analysis. Initially, it examined waste and emission reductions at the tag level. Subsequently, it extended these findings to the brand-owner level to gauge the overall impact on sustainability objectives. While ECO RFID tags demonstrated considerable improvements at the tag level, their broader impact was observed to be somewhat limited. Nevertheless, the research indicates that fashion companies may be compelled to integrate environmental tags into their operations, despite their relatively minor contribution to waste streams

(continued)

(continued)

Findings	
Khan et al. (2020)	This research introduces a chipless octagonal RFID tag integrated into cotton fabric and designed for wearable technology applications. Employing Frequency Selective Surface (FSS) methodology, the tag functions within the 8–18 GHz range and comprises six concentric octagonal loop resonators with a singular element. Constructed using silver-coated polyamide conductive fiber (HC12) and manufactured with a ZSK Technical Embroidery System JCZA, the tag's data encoding is validated through Radar cross-section (RCS) analysis within an anechoic chamber. Findings indicate reliable retrieval of a 4-bit codeword at distances of up to 1.8 m from the tag with 0dBm power, further supported by on-body RCS assessments, affirming its applicability for wearable technology and smart garment Internet of Things (IoT) applications
Ngo et al. (2024)	This study fills a gap in research concerning sustainability-related supply chain risks (SSCRs) within Vietnam's garment industry. Using data from 254 garment companies, the results indicate a trade-off between risk and return concerning economic hazards but not for social and environmental risks. Additionally, the study identifies the positive influence of supplier management and supply chain integration techniques in mitigating environmental risks, benefiting both businesses and the environment

4.5 Results and Discussion

In this section, the primary aim is to address two research questions, each encompassing two distinct RFID-related issues: sustainable RFID tags and counterfeit prevention. Through analysis, this report proposes and elucidates the adoption of advanced RFID technology to enhance sustainability and combat counterfeiting. Accordingly, this section explores how these RFID technologies could mitigate the issues in question, while also highlighting potential challenges in implementing these RFID innovations.

4.5.1 Potential RFID Technology

1. Sustainable RFID solution

Eco RFID Tag

Stora Enso, a leading Finnish-Swedish company specializing in forestry, pulp, packaging, and renewable materials, has recently developed an environmentally conscious RFID tag called "ECO RFID." This innovative technology adopts an additive approach, allowing for the direct printing of the antenna onto paper. ECO RFID stands out due to its elimination of plastic layers in the tag, thereby circumventing the use of chemicals typically associated with traditional etching processes

(Fig. 4.2). Additionally, the manufacturing process of ECO RFID boasts a significantly reduced carbon footprint, achieved through a less energy-intensive process. Despite these environmental improvements, ECO RFID maintains performance, reliability, and cost structures comparable to conventional RFID tags, promising similar financial and operational benefits. Moreover, with carbon tolls still under political deliberation, environmental tags like ECO RFID currently do not incur regulatory costs.

An alternative comparison between environmentally printed RFID tags and traditional polyester tags (or so-called legacy tags) sheds light on the substrate's impact during production and post-use, as well as energy consumption at the machinery level. The findings are summarized in Table 4.1, derived from a lifecycle assessment (LCA) study focusing on three sustainability emissions associated with both environmental and traditional polyester tags (Stora Enso 2020). Utilizing paper substrate in the environmental RFID tag process, coupled with reduced energy consumption during manufacturing, has a substantial effect on CO2 emissions compared to traditional

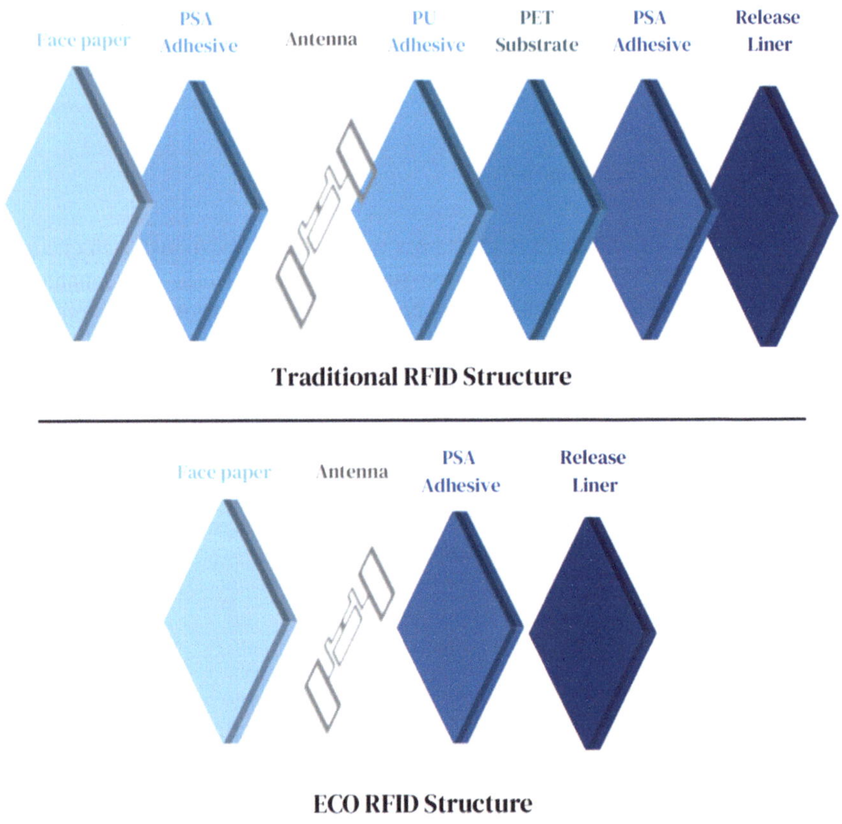

Fig. 4.2 Component comparison between traditional and ECO RFID (adapted from Voipio et al. 2021)

polyester substrates. Moreover, the elimination of water usage and effluent treatment in the antenna manufacturing process significantly contributes to eutrophication and acidification impacts.

Through advancements in component design, sustainable tags make significant strides by eliminating single-use plastics (100%), markedly reducing greenhouse gas emissions (up to 61%), and employing manufacturing methods that substantially minimize chemical waste (up to 39%) (Voipio et al. 2021). At the corporate level, with annual production volumes reaching one billion tags, environmental RFID technology yields tangible reductions in the environmental burden associated with RFID tags. To put this into perspective, these reductions translate to eliminating plastic waste equivalent to 300 football fields and greenhouse gas emissions equivalent to those of over 500 households annually.

Moreover, leveraging the printed electronics concept in the evaluated technology is expected to further enhance environmental impact by reducing logistics, particularly if printing facilities are situated near source tagging sites. Unlike traditional RFID tag manufacturing, which typically occurs in large, centralized facilities, the new generation of sustainable tag manufacturing offers increased flexibility in placement and operation.

An additional benefit of the ECO RFID tag is that customers often interpret small gestures, such as eliminating plastic straws or single-use plastic takeout cups/bottles in the fast-food industry, as meaningful indications of a company's dedication to sustainability. These actions convey a genuine commitment to environmental responsibility, thereby enhancing the company's reputation among consumers. Consequently, transitioning to ECO RFID tags in the fashion industry is expected to have a similar positive effect on customer perception and corporate reputation.

Sewed Chipless RFID Tags

If the previous technology proposed an RFID with component-collapsed tags aimed at reducing production waste, the tags may still be torn out when reaching the final customer. Consequently, the tags continue to function as single-use objects, necessitating waste management processes for their disposal, while the complexity of reverse logistics challenges of fashion finished products persists within the industry. Therefore, the introduction of sewed chipless RFID tag technology is proposed to address

Table 4.1 A comparison between sustainable and legacy tags across three domains

Impact versus tag technology	Greenhouse gas g CO_2 -eq/tag	Eutrophication 10^{-3} g PO_4 -eq/tag	Acidification 10^{-3} g SO_2 -eq/tag
Polyester tag	3.5	0.0036	0.019
Environmental ECO tag	1.4	0.0021	0.012
Difference (measure)	2.1	0.0015	0.007
Decrease (%)	60	41.67	36.84

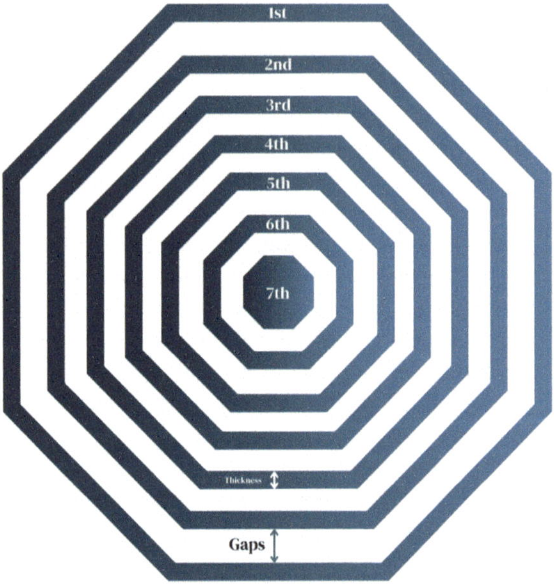

Fig. 4.3 The design of chipless RFID octagonal tag geometry (adapted from Khan et al. 2020)

the existing drawbacks of ECO RFID while upholding the principles of sustainable RFID.

The chipless RFID tag's design and simulation are rooted in an octagonal Frequency Selective Surface (FSS) unit. Employing CST MICROWAVE STUDIO, the Radar Cross Section (RCS) response of the chipless sewed octagonal RFID tag was meticulously crafted and simulated. The design encompasses a central octagon encircled by concentric octagonal rings, depicted in Fig. 4.3 (Khan et al. 2020). Each octagonal ring serves as an independent resonator, totaling six resonators altogether.

The thickness of each resonator significantly impacts the tag's radiation efficiency, while the gap between resonators influences mutual coupling. Through parameter optimization, conduction losses are minimized, and excessive mutual coupling is avoided. The octagonal rings resonate within a frequency range of 8–16 GHz, achieved by fine-tuning thickness and gap dimensions. This optimization yields a 4-bit coding capacity, accompanied by robust bit isolation and substantial 3-dB bandwidths at each resonance frequency (Khan et al. 2020).

In terms of Material and Fabrication, the octagonal chipless RFID tag was crafted utilizing a ZSK Technical Embroidery System JCZA 0109–550, achieving a resolution of 1 mm as illustrated in Fig. 4.4. Constructed from polyamide silver-coated HC12 conductive thread, the tag is sewn onto a cotton substrate measuring 25 mm × 25 mm and 90 μm thick, with a permittivity of $\varepsilon_r = 2.1$ at 8 GHz and $\varepsilon_r = 2.0$ at 18 GHz. HC12 was selected for its skin-friendly, comfortable, biocompatible, and washable attributes, rendering it suitable for smart textile applications (Khan et al. 2021). To ensure optimal conductivity and mitigate the risk of overlapping resonances that could compromise frequency resolution, meticulous attention was

Fig. 4.4 Prototype of sewed chipless RFID tags (adapted from Khan et al. 2020)

paid to the density and orientation of thread stitches per surface unit area. Moreover, maintaining minimal roughness of the sewn surface was imperative to achieve the desired surface current density. Leveraging the ZSK Technical Embroidery System facilitated resonator conductivity within the range of 104–105 S/m, resulting in a wearable tag with a total thickness of 1 mm.

This innovation represents a pivotal turning point in the RFID technology sector, holding promise for significant economic advantages. These include cost reduction in the production of individual RFID tags affixed to garments, as well as facilitating circular economy practices and enhancing reverse logistics efficiency through the permanent integration of chipless tags within the fabric (Corchia et al. 2020). By eliminating the need for separate tags, the sewed chipless RFID technology reduces material consumption and waste generated during production, thereby minimizing the environmental impact associated with traditional RFID tag manufacturing processes.

Additionally, the seamless integration of RFID functionality into clothing supports sustainable supply chain practices by promoting efficient inventory management, reducing the risk of overstocking and stockouts, and optimizing transportation and distribution processes. This not only minimizes resource consumption and greenhouse gas emissions but also enhances overall supply chain resilience and responsiveness to changing market demands. Hence, the adoption of sewed chipless RFID technology brings tangible benefits to both the environment and supply chain development, driving positive change toward a more sustainable and resilient fashion industry.

2. RFID security infiltration solution

As the use of RFID systems becomes more prevalent, there ought to be a surge in security attacks specifically aimed at these systems. These breaches will grow more sophisticated and may focus on the application system, the communication route between the tag and the reading device, or even the physical tag itself. Henceforth, studies of RFID security breaching techniques were established in the two first articles, of which [A1] categorizes these possible attacks into three main types: confidentiality, integrity, and availability, while [A2] divides them into physical, channel, and system hazards. Both articles outlined 10–15 methods each, notably, certain categories mentioned in [A1] and [A2] share the same methods; hence, this section will evaluate certain shared variables between them, as illustrated in Table 4.2. There are 9–10 attacking techniques in common between both articles; however, this chapter would only evaluate the 4 most predominant methods for conciseness.

Eavesdropping

This is classified as a passive attack, in which the adversary illicitly acquires information while it is being exchanged between the reader and the tag. The eavesdropping (shown in Fig. 4.5) adversary does not emit any signals, making the device difficult to detect, and it can function from a considerable distance. Therefore, it is significant if sensitive data are sent without cryptographic encryption.

Table 4.2 Comprehensive summary of the mentioned RFID attacking techniques (Kumar et al. 2021; Khattab et al. 2017)

	Physical threats	Channel threats	System threats
Confidentiality	Eavesdropping	Disclosure/Skimming	Tracking and tracing
Integrity	Cloning	Replay, relay (man-in middle)	Spoofing, counterfeiting
Availability	Jamming/Disabling	Covert channel or snooping/ Active jamming	Denial of service

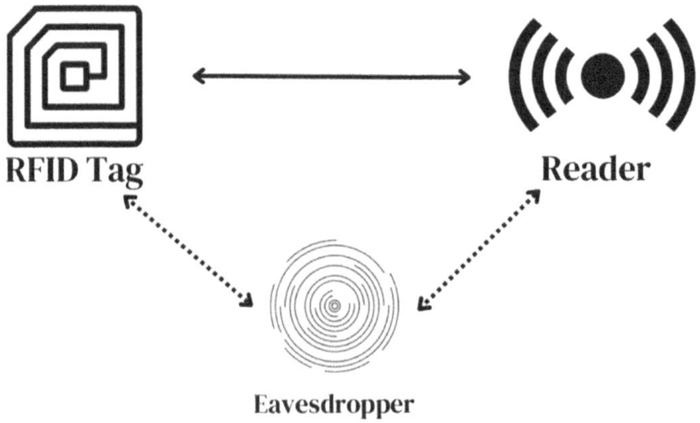

Fig. 4.5 Illustration of eavesdropping infiltration (adapted from Zhao et al. 2020)

Tracking and Tracing

Adversaries can engage in illegal tracking by gathering the signal sent by the tag at different times and places, enabling them to ascertain the tag's current location. Due to the perpetual need for RFID tags to respond to signals from other tags and readers, adversaries might exploit this vulnerability to engage in unauthorized tracing and tracking activities. Nevertheless, corporations can mitigate the risk associated with these monitoring and tracking activities by employing encryption techniques to obfuscate the values, rendering them seemingly random (Burmester and Medeiros 2007; Al-Sudani et al. 2018).

Cloning

If the attacker is successful in exposing the ID information, then this new tag will be able to function as the regular tag without being noticed. In the event that the attacker is successful, it will be simple for them to replicate the tag. There are system-level attacks that involve counterfeiting spoofing, and cloned tags are employed in these attacks. Hackers are able to retrieve data from the tag and then transfer it to another tag by intercepting the connection that takes place between the reader and the tag.

Disabling

During such attacks, the opponent exploits the wireless characteristics of RFID systems to render tags inoperable, either momentarily or permanently. The adversary achieves this by disrupting the communication between an authentic tag and the reader, causing the tag node to be unable to establish a connection with the reader. An adversary produces a signature that matches the reader's, making the tag unattainable to the reader and obstructing communication between the two parties. These acts can be accomplished by either physically obliterating the tag or by disrupting the channeling signals (Fernández-Caramés et al. 2017; Gavoni 2021).

Security RFID Solution

In the prevention of tag cloning and snooping attacks, chipless RFID tags are also proposed to be the pivotal point for authentication, and this is due to their random variability which was fabricated during the manufacturing process.

Tag discrimination is an extension of the chipless RFID concept in which each tag generates a distinct signature that is exceedingly challenging to duplicate, even with a cloned device by utilizing electromagnetic (EM) waves of radiofrequency (RF) (Ali et al. 2018). Chipless RFID technology has the ability to distinguish between two distinct tags that are influenced by comparable geometric deviations inherent in the manufacturing process. Ali et al. (2019) proposed research for the authentication efficiency of X-band chipless application (8–12 GHz), and nevertheless, it is critical to take into account the fabrication processes when handling a microstrip circuit; as the selected technology has a significant impact on the inherent irregularity in its geometrical dimensions, the inherent stochasticity can be rationalized as a result of the configuration of paper fibers (Fig. 4.6). As such, considering the application of sewed chipless RFID, it is important to evaluate the chosen yarn to determine the naturally occurring randomness for the authentication process.

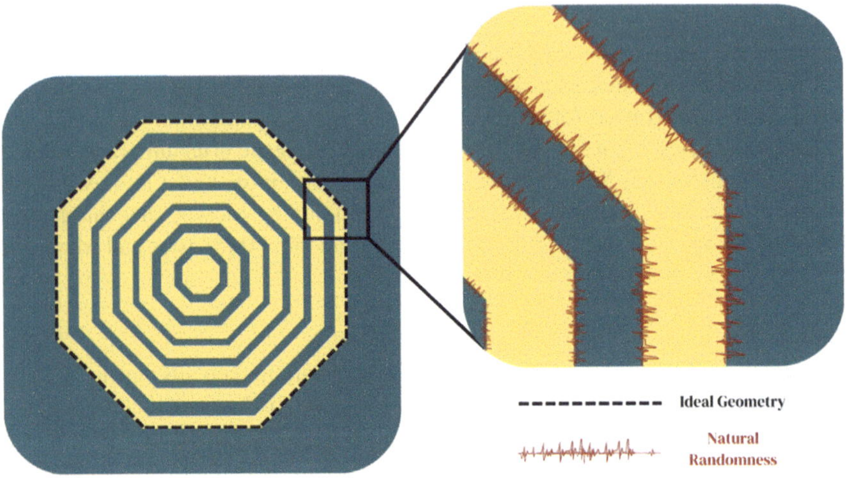

Fig. 4.6 Occurrence of natural randomness and its use for the realization process (adapted from Ali et al. 2019)

4.5.2 New Challenges of Proposed RFID Technologies

From Sustainable RFID Solution

Despite its promising sustainable benefits, the adoption of ECO RFID tags in the fashion industry hinges on whether they meet the requirements set by practitioners for RFID tags.

Firstly, the technology must demonstrate performance, ensuring reliable reading results across diverse environments. Secondly, reliability is paramount, as defective tags could lead to the loss of items within the RFID system. Thirdly, the pricing of the technology must enable its widespread use in high-volume applications. Fourthly, a comparison of pricing roadmaps is essential, considering the significant variation between older and newer technologies. While established technologies may currently offer peak efficiency, emerging innovations are still in the early stages of scalability and may require further development to achieve efficiency through market adoption and technological advancements (Voipio et al. 2021). Lastly, sustainability is a crucial consideration, as the product must support brand owners in meeting their sustainability objectives across all fronts.

As new technological innovations emerge, current studies primarily focus on analyzing the potential and promising aspects of technology adoption. However, the measurement of these requirements often remains ambiguous, leading to uncertainty regarding their practical implementation. Consequently, any fashion brand that adopts these technologies in mass production becomes a pioneer in testing these new RFID tags. This positioning can result in either becoming a leading first adopter, reaping the benefits of early adoption and innovation, or serving as a cautionary tale for other fashion businesses, highlighting potential pitfalls and challenges associated with the technology. Thus, the decision to embrace new RFID technologies carries both opportunities and risks, shaping the landscape of the fashion industry's technological evolution.

Regarding the sewed chipless RFID technology, the European Commission has emphasized the necessity for future wearable devices like this device to possess key characteristics such as shapeability, stretchability, and washability on demand (Mokhtari et al. 2020). These devices should emulate natural clothing in terms of comfort, breathability, and washability. However, despite advancements in sewed chipless RFID technology, the durability and resilience of current smart garments in washing, drying, and ironing processes are still under examination. Consequently, these garments have yet to achieve an equivalent level of robustness compared to traditional clothing.

From Security RFID Solution

The primary considerations with the implementation of chipless RFID tags pertain to financial implications and the fabrication process of the tags. Ali et al. (2019) focused exclusively on investigating the manufacturing of chipless RFID tags using chemical ink, specifically examining the natural randomness of these tags. Nevertheless, the suggested approach involves employing the framework in combination with the Sewed Chipless RFID tag mentioned previously. Therefore, it is crucial to take into consideration the readability of the tag, while utilizing polyamide silver-coated HC12 conductive thread as the base material. The device's legibility must remain consistent while it moves through the supply chain, ensuring that any extra lint from the washing, drying, and ironing processes does not alter the pattern and render the identification mechanism ineffective.

4.6 Limitation and Future Research

This paper highlights that the discussion surrounding the latest technologies is largely based on a limited number of research papers, indicating a significant gap in the existing literature. It is crucial to recognize that the suggested technologies are still in the early stages of testing and examination, signifying a considerable distance before widespread applicability in the context of Vietnam's fashion industry. Additionally, while the concept of conveying sustainability information through RFID tags is introduced, the methods for controlling and auditing this information are not addressed. The focus on successful implementations also overlooks the adoption barriers faced by the majority of Vietnamese fashion and textile businesses. As a result, no implementation strategy is provided, as the paper is confined to studying the latest RFID innovations and their associated challenges. These identified limitations present promising avenues for future research exploration.

4.7 Conclusion

Within the economic situation of Vietnam's fashion and textile industry, the scarcity of academic research focusing on RFID inherent constraints and unresolved concerns, most notably those about item-level sustainability and the potential for counterfeit merchandise. Although RFID is considered to wield extensive benefits for the organization, sustainability gaps including carbon footprint, chemical effluent, and plastic waste were also studied, as RFID contains potassium, bromine, and polyester plastic which cause recycling inefficiencies. Furthermore, despite the widespread use of RFID in preventing counterfeit fashion products, the technology itself can also be forged, or face certain cyber security risks, threatening the competitiveness of the firm and consumer satisfaction. This paper's two main research questions were resolved by investigating the mentioned problems and evaluating two new RFID alternatives, ECO RFID and Chipless RFID Octagonal Tags, not only aiming to minimize the environmental hazards throughout the tag's lifecycle but also aiding in authentication against adversaries' attacks. The results of this investigation are intended to offer recommendations for brand managers, fashion retailers, and researchers who are interested in promoting sustainability goals throughout the fashion supply chain in Vietnam.

References

Al-Sudani AR, Zhoub W, Liu B, Almansoorid A, Yang M (2018) Detecting unauthorized RFID tag carrier for secure access control to a smart building. Int J Appl Eng Res 13(1):749–760. (Research India Publications database). Accessed on 8 Apr 2024. https://www.ripublication.com/ijaer18/ijaerv13n1_103.pdf

Ali Z, Barbot N, Siragusa R, Hely D, Bernier M, Garet F, Perre E (2018) Chipless RFID tag discrimination and the performance of resemblance metrics to be used for it. In: IEEE/MTT-S international microwave symposium—IMS, pp 363–366. https://doi.org/10.1109/MWSYM.2018.8439855

Ali Z, Perret E, Barbot N, Siragusa R, Hély D, Bernier M, Garet F (2019) Detection of natural randomness by chipless RFID approach and Its application to authentication. IEEE Trans Microwave Theory Tech 67(9):3867–3881. https://doi.org/10.1109/TMTT.2019.2914102

Bagay D (2020) Information security of RFID tags. Procedia Comput Sci 169:183–186. https://doi.org/10.1016/j.procs.2020.02.133

Brandenburg M, Govindan K, Sarkis J, Seuring S (2014) Quantitative models for sustainable supply chain management: developments and directions. Eur J Oper Res 233(2):299–312

Burmester M, Medeiros B (2007) RFID security: attacks, countermeasures, and challenges. Florida State University website. Accessed on 8 Apr 2024. https://www.cs.fsu.edu/~burmeste/133.pdf

Casella G, Bigliardi B, Bottani E (2022) The evolution of RFID technology in the logistics field: a review. Procedia Comput Sci 200:1582–1592

Cheung HH, Choi SH (2011) Implementation issues in RFID-based anti-counterfeiting systems. Comput Ind 62(7):708–718. https://doi.org/10.1016/j.compind.2011.04.001

Corchia L, Monti G, De Benedetto E, Cataldo A, Angrisani L, Arpaia P, Tarricone L (2020) Fully-textile, wearable chipless tags for identification and tracking applications. Sensors 20(2):429

Das R, Harrop P (2009) RFID forecasts, players and opportunities 2009–2019. IDTechEx report

Fernández-Caramés TM, Fraga-Lamas P, Suárez- Albela M, Castedo L (2017) A methodology for evaluating security in commercial RFID systems. Radio Freq Identif. https://doi.org/10.5772/64844

Gavoni L (2021) RFID exploitation and countermeasures. Cornell University Arxiv website. Accessed on 8 Apr 2023. https://arxiv.org/pdf/2110.00094.pdf

Giannakis M, Papadopoulos T (2016) Supply chain sustainability: a risk management approach. Int J Prod Econ 171:455–470

Green KW Jr, Zelbst PJ, Sower VE, Bellah JC (2017) Impact of radio frequency identification technology on environmental sustainability. J Comput Inf Syst 57(3):269–277

Hoang H (23 June 2020) Vietnam's fashion and textile industries must become sustainable to survive. RMIT Media Release. Accessed 8 Apr 2024. https://www.rmit.edu.vn/news/all-news/2020/june/vietnam-s-fashion-and-textile-industries-must-become-sustainable

Irfan M, Wang M, Akhtar N (2020) Enabling supply chain agility through process integration and supply flexibility: evidence from the fashion industry. Asia Pacific J Mark Logistics 32(2):519–547

Khalil G, Doss R, Chowdhury M (2020a) A new secure RFID anti-counterfeiting and anti-theft scheme for merchandise. J Sens Actuator Networks 9(1):16

Khalil G, Doss R, Chowdhury M (2020b) A novel RFID-based anti-counterfeiting scheme for retail environments. IEEE Access 8:47952–47962. https://doi.org/10.1109/ACCESS.2020.2979264

Khan MUA, Raad R, Foroughi J, Theoharis PI, Liu S, Masud J (2020) A silver-coated conductive fibre HC12 sewed chipless RFID tag on cotton fabric for wearable applications. IEEE, 1728198933

Khan MUA, Raad R, Foroughi J, Raheel MS, Houshyar S (2021) An octagonal-shaped conductive HC12 & LIBERATOR-40 thread embroidered chipless RFID for general IoT applications. Sens Actuators A Phys 318:112485

Khattab A, Jeddi Z, Amini E, Bayoumi M (2017) RFID security threats and basic solutions. In: RFID security. Analog circuits and signal processing. Springer, Cham, https://doi.org/10.1007/978-3-319-47545-5_2

Kubáňová J, Kubasáková I, Čulík K, Štítik L (2022) Implementation of barcode technology to logistics processes of a company. Sustainability 14(2):790. https://doi.org/10.3390/su14020790

Kumar A, Jain AJ, Dua M (2021) A comprehensive taxonomy of security and privacy issues in RFID. Complex Intell Syst 7:1327–1347. https://doi.org/10.1007/s40747-021-00280-6

Marinelli C, Sinatra F (2023) RFID and counterfeiting: an analysis of current trends in the fashion industry. In: International conference on computational science and its applications. Accessed 8 Apr 2024. https://doi.org/10.1007/978-3-031-37123-3_32

Mokhtari F, Cheng Z, Raad R, Xi J, Foroughi J (2020) Piezofibers to smart textiles: a review on recent advances and future outlook for wearable technology. J Mater Chem A 8(19):9496–9522

Moretto A, Macchion L, Lion A, Caniato F, Danese P, Vinelli A (2018) Designing a roadmap towards a sustainable supply chain: a focus on the fashion industry. J Cleaner Prod 193:169–184

Munoz-Ausecha C, Ruiz-Rosero J, Ramirez-Gonzalez G (2021) RFID applications and security review. Computation 9(6):69

Musa A, Dabo A-AA (2016) A review of RFID in supply chain management: 2000–2015. Glob J Flex Syst Manag 17:189–228

Nastasiu D, Scripcaru R, Digulescu A, Ioana C, Amorim RDJ, Barbot N, Siragusa R, Perret E, Popescu F (2020) A new method of secure authentication based on electromagnetic signatures of chipless RFID tags and machine learning approaches. Sensors 20(21):1–18. https://doi.org/10.3390/s20216385

Nayak R (2019) Radio frequency identification (RFID) technology and application in fashion and textile supply chain. CRC Press, Boca Raton

Nayak R, Akbari M, Far SM (2019) Recent sustainable trends in Vietnam's fashion supply chain. J Cleaner Prod 225:291–303

Nayak R, Singh A, Padhye R, Wang L (2015) RFID in textile and clothing manufacturing: technology and challenges. Fashion Text 2:1–16

Nayak R (ed) (2020) Supply chain management and logistics in the global fashion sector: the sustainability challenge. Routledge, London

Nayak R, Panwar T, Nguyen LVT (2020) Sustainability in fashion and textiles: a survey from developing country. In: Sustainable technologies for fashion and textiles, pp 3–30

Nayak R, George M, Haq IU, Pham HC (2022) Sustainability benefits of RFID technology in Vietnamese fashion supply chain. Cleaner Logistics Supply Chain 5:100086

Ngo VM, Quang HT, Hoang TG, Binh ADT (2024) Sustainability-related supply chain risks and supply chain performances: the moderating effects of dynamic supply chain management practices. Bus Strategy Environ 33(2):839–857

Nguyen T, Li T (2022) The analysis of counterfeits and their impact on countries' development. Jurisprudence 64(3):55–64. https://doi.org/10.31276/VMOSTJOSSH.64(3).55-64

Ni LM, Zhang D, Souryal MR (2011) RFID-based localization and tracking technologies. IEEE Wirel Commun 18(2):45–51

OECD (2019) 'Illicit trade', trends in trade in counterfeit and pirated goods. https://doi.org/10.1787/g2g9f533-en

Rahman F, Ahamed SI (2012) Efficient detection of counterfeit products in large-scale RFID systems using batch authentication protocols. Pers Ubiquit Comput 18:177–188. https://doi.org/10.1007/s00779-012-0629-8

Reyes PM (2023) Radio frequency identification (RFID) and supply chain management. In: The Palgrave handbook of supply chain management. Springer, Berlin

Stora Enso (2020) https://www.storaenso.com/en/newsroom/news/2020/1/eco-rfid-explained--a-look-behind-the-worlds-greenes-tag

Thorisdottir TS, Johannsdottir L (2020) Corporate social responsibility influencing sustainability within the fashion industry. A systematic review. Sustainability 12(21):9167

Tran DT, Hong SJ (2015) RFID anti-counterfeiting for retailing systems. J Appl Math Phys 3(1). https://doi.org/10.4236/jamp.2015.31001

Tran TBN, Tran TPT (2018) Vietnam's textile and garment industry: an overview. J Bus IT (2):45–53. https://doi.org/10.14311/bit.2018.02.05

Tu YJ, Zhou W, Piramuthu S (2021) Critical risk considerations in auto-ID security: Barcode vs. RFID. Decis Support Syst 142. https://doi.org/10.1016/j.dss.2020.113471

Tuyls P, Batina L (2006) RFID-tags for anti-counterfeiting. In: Conference: topics in cryptology—CT-RSA 2006, USA. Accessed 8 Apr 2024. https://www.researchgate.net/publication/221208219_RFID-Tags_for_anti-counterfeiting

Varriale V, Cammarano A, Michelino F, Caputo M (2021) Sustainable supply chains with blockchain, IoT and RFID: a simulation on order management. Sustainability 13(11):6372

Voipio V, Korpela J, Elfvengren K (2021) Environmental RFID: measuring the relevance in the fashion industry. Int J Fashion Design Technol Educ 14(3):284–292

Want R (2022) RFID explained: a primer on radio frequency identification technologies. Springer Nature, Berlin

Yan B, Huang G (2008) Application of RFID and internet of things in monitoring and anti-counterfeiting for products. In: 2008 International seminar on business and information management, Wuhan. Accessed 8 Apr 2024. https://ieeexplore.ieee.org/abstract/document/5117510

Zhao B, Wang HM, Liu P (2020) Safeguarding RFID wireless communication against proactive eavesdropping. IEEE Internet Things J 7(12):11587–11600. https://doi.org/10.1109/JIOT.2020.2998789

Chapter 5
Data Analytics and Supply Chain Management: Leveraging Big Data to Optimize Production and Logistics in Fashion and Textiles

Vijay Kumar

Abstract The rapid expansion of digital solutions is transforming the landscape of the textile and fashion (T&F) industry. Advanced digitization within the T&F sector is not only altering the way the production and distribution operations are carried out, but also fostering a new paradigm of data, known as *big data* and data analytics known as *big data analytics*. This transformation is reshaping the approach of data-driven decision-making in the industry. Aligned with the recent developments, this chapter provides an overview of the characteristics of big data and data analytics, and how the T&F industry can leverage such change to create a competitive advantage.

Keywords Big data · Data analytics · Textiles and fashion · Supply chain management

5.1 Introduction

Data and data analytics are crucial assets for any organization to stay competitive. To underscore its importance, data is often termed "the new oil," indicating an essential element that ensures growth and profitability (Hartmann et al. 2016). It is considered key for obtaining insights to make business strategies, adapting to change, and making important short and long-term business decisions. The current textile and fashion (T&F) sector is a prominent example where data has become a key element in understanding customer behavior, planning and designing collections, managing inventory, forecasting trends, and forming the foundation for key decision-making processes (Acharya et al. 2018).

Data analytics enhances the ability of firms in data-driven decision-making and optimize various activities within production and supply chains. A recent report on

V. Kumar (✉)
The Swedish School of Textiles, University of Borås, Borås, Sweden
e-mail: vijay.kumar@hb.se

R. Nayak et al. (eds.), *Use of Digital and Advanced Technologies in the Fashion Supply Chain*, Springer Series in Fashion Business,
https://doi.org/10.1007/978-981-97-7528-6_5

the fashion industry reveals that data-driven store optimization led to a 10% increase in sales while data-driven supply chain optimization contributed to a noteworthy 15% reduction in inventory cost (Devillard et al. 2021). Further, the brands utilizing data-driven personalized customer e-commerce experiences have grown digital sales, ranging from 30 to 50% (Devillard et al. 2021). These examples underscore the importance of data in the current T&F industry. While the T&F industry is undergoing rapid change with the implementation of technology, so are the attributes of data and data analytics. The classic notion of data is evolving from its traditional perception of being static and structured to more dynamic and unstructured, giving rise to a new form known as *big data* (Acharya et al. 2018).

It is no longer limited to a few dimensions, attributes, or types, but represents datasets that are too complex, large, and difficult to fit in simple spreadsheets or databases, or process with traditional analysis methods. As a result, big data represents a major shift in the way the data is perceived, collected, aggregated, and analyzed to extract information. While fashion firms are known to collect, handle and utilize a range of data from day-to-day sales, stock transactions, e-commerce footprints, and more, with the advent of big data, the available sources and volume of data and limits of getting intelligent insights are exploding, which not only opening new opportunities, but also demand for new capabilities for data handling and analysis that the industry must develop. According to Devillard et al. (2021), having data systems is not new for fashion firms; however, often, their designs are inflexible and non-scalable, thus creating challenges in integrating new data sources.

Considering the abovementioned developments, this chapter provides an overview of the characteristics of big data and data analytics, and how the T&F industry can leverage such change to create a competitive advantage. Further, the chapter discusses the key risks and potential challenges in implementing big data considering the current state of T&F industry. The rest of the paper is organized as follows. Section 5.2 presents the recent transformation within T&F supply chains. The discussion in Sect. 5.3 focuses on big data and data analytics in line with the emerging nature of big data. Further, Sect. 5.4 presents an overview of key opportunities area within the T&F industry where big data can play a critical role, and Sect. 5.5 presents risks and challenges in implementing big data in the fashion industry. Finally, Sect. 5.6 presents the conclusions.

5.2 Recent Transformations in the Textile and Fashion Sector

Historically, the T&F industry has been a pioneer in technology adoption and industrial paradigm shifts (Bertola and Teunissen 2018). Tracing back to the first industrial revolution, mechanization, such as the power loom, revolutionized textile production, facilitating mass production and enhancing efficiency. This commitment to innovation has persisted through subsequent industrial revolutions. In the fourth industrial revolution, the industry witnessed the integration of technology and cyber-physical systems (Araque González et al. 2022). This transformative phase not only marked the emergence of the next generation of textiles and fashion, which not only changed the utility and meaning of fashion along with introduction of novel materials such as smart textiles, but also changed the traditional ways of conceptions, production, and distribution systems.

Traditionally considered retailer-driven, the contemporary fashion industry is witnessing a shift to a consumer-driven industry, driven by changing consumer attitudes and market trends. In the past, consumers used to be passive observers, and brands actively introduced new trends and styles, that allowed companies to forecast consumer demand and fashion trends long before the actual time of consumption (Bhardwaj and Fairhurst 2010). However, with changing consumer expectations and other emerging dynamics, the fashion industry is rapidly evolving. Customer choices are influenced by a range of factors ranging from fashion shows and runways to social media trends. In such a scenario, swiftly interpreting the trends becomes a critical requirement for production and introducing the product at the right time to create a competitive advantage (Bhardwaj and Fairhurst 2010). Further, the rising popularity of fast fashion—characterized by quick production cycles, affordable pricing, and frequency style changes—is pushing retail companies for quick responsiveness, i.e., agile production and logistics systems for producing a constant stream of updated products while keeping the overall cost low (Bhardwaj and Fairhurst 2010; Caro and Martínez-de-Albéniz 2015).

Enabled by digital technologies, digitalization of the processes and implementation of digital solutions over the different parts of the value chain made radical changes that wielded a decisive influence not only on the configuration of the supply chains but also on the dynamics of consumer interactions. For example, the application of 3D modeling allows design and development workflow, and optimization of the design and development process in a virtual environment. This allows easy collaborations among the designers, and optimization through simulations in virtual environments produces quicker results compared to physical production and testing environment (Casciani et al. 2022).

Digitalization is further transforming the conventional physical model of retailing, which encounters substantial challenges related to cost and physical space. In this context, the digital revolution within the T&F sector is transforming the business–customer interaction by replacing the limitations of physical space with limitless digital space allowing more flexibility in resource management and changing the mode of interaction (Blázquez 2014). The virtual e-commerce platforms are not only reducing the cost and other physical limitations inherent in the traditional brick-and-mortar model but also adding a new dimension to reach the end users. This transformation provides extensive capabilities for interaction, engagement, and communication with consumers, transcending the limitations imposed by the physical stores (Cao 2018).

In such a changing environment, the role of data is not only becoming critical for the functioning of the supply chains but is also essential for developing competitive strategies (Banica and Hagiu 2016). For example, the logistics and supply chain managers are now becoming increasingly reliant on data to gain visibility on material flows, inventory management, expenditures, production optimizations, and making operational and strategic decisions on organizational as well as value chain levels. Relying on traditional sources of data from ERP and transactions is not just sufficient to understand the markets and current trends. Hence brands are relying on a series of sources to make informed decisions. In this context, the growing reach of the internet and extensive application of sensors, RFIDs, software systems, and digital technologies, such as CAD and CAM in production, is changing the landscape of data collection within the production and supply chains. As a result, they are becoming enablers for a range of capabilities within the T&F sector (Ghoreishi and Happonen 2022; Pal and Jayarathne 2022).

5.3 Big Data and Its Contextualization in Supply Chain Data Analytics

5.3.1 Understanding and Defining Big Data

Within the changing industrial landscape, big data represents an evolution and paradigm shift in the collection and processing of data thanks to prolific innovations and the rapid adoption of various information and communication technologies (Acharya et al. 2018; Kitchin 2014). The widespread integration of digital technologies in industrial processes, coupled with massive scale deployment of scanners, sensors and actuators on a large scale, and adoption of digital devices such as smartphones, tablets, and computers, results in the continuous generation of data on a massive scale (Kitchin 2014). Additionally, the influx of social media platforms, websites, and blogs not only adds to the complexity of datasets by contributing unstructured data such as posts, comments, and interactions, but also contributes to the exponential growth of the data.

While having the possibility to gather such large data from different sources can provide much more information, storage, retrieval and processing of data on such a massive scale poses challenges, and often suppresses the capabilities of existing storage technologies. Hence, it calls for novel solutions that can not only handle such massive data but also process it within desirable time to extract required insights (Arunachalam et al. 2018; Yaqoob et al. 2016).

In the context of the growing volume of data, the term "big data" has become a buzzword. While it has been described several times in literature by different definitions, it is commonly characterized as large datasets that are not able to be captured, stored, or managed by traditional tools (Pathak et al. 2018). However, the definition of "large" has remained vague, because what is big today may not be attributed same tomorrow considering the rapid development in technological solutions for data storage (Arunachalam et al. 2018). Nonetheless, there is consensus in the literature that big data refers to huge, heterogeneous, and complex datasets that are formed by a combination of structured, unstructured, and semi-structured formats that cover text, sound, video, image, and more (Pathak et al. 2018).

Here, *Structured format* refers to the organized format or schema, such as rows and columns in a table, where data is stored, retrieved, and processed in an organized manner. Structured format follows a predefined set of rules for modeling data types and relationships between data. Due to an organized structure, data processing algorithms work efficiently on structured data. *Unstructured format,* on the other hand, refers to the format that does not abide by a predefined structure and data model therefore it is highly complex to arrange and convert into a structured map. Finally, *semi-structured* format is characterized by data that is irregular and incomplete and exhibits a structure that can change rapidly or unpredictably. Further, several studies explain big data with the help of different *V*s. Originally started with 3Vs i.e. *volume*, *velocity*, and *variety*, several other dimensions were added by different researchers, thus building up the big data taxonomy with different Vs (Pathak et al. 2018). A summary of the most discussed Vs is shown in Table 5.1.

As earlier mentioned, the size and type make the traditional system incapable of handling big data. While relational database management systems (RDBMS)—which are commonly used in various applications offer high-speed response and efficient retrieval of data—are usually not capable of handling unstructured and semi-structured data and offer limited scalability to handle a massive volume of data. Hence, big data is often stored in schema-free databases known as NoSQL (no structured query language) such as HBase, MongoDB and Dynamino, which act as technical enablers for the implementation of big data (Bhadani and Jothimani 2016; Pathak et al. 2018).

Table 5.1 Dimensions of big data

Dimension	Description
Volume	Refers to the massive volume of low-density, a mix of structured, semi-structured and unstructured data, gathered from a range of sources. The massive volume of data exceeds the capacity of traditional storage systems. Hence the role of big data becomes turning low-density data into information-rich insights
Velocity	Refers to the high rate and continuous data generation which may also need to be processed in real time to obtain useful information
Variety	Refers to the diversity or heterogeneity in the data formats contained in multidimensional fields and organized in both structured, unstructured, and unstructured formats and from a variety of sources such as online social networks, clickstreams, sensors, POS transactions, and industrial information systems. e.g. ERPs, PLMs, etc.
Veracity	Refers to the data quality and trustworthiness of the data as it comes from different sources
Value	Refers to insights generated from low-density data that create some useful commercial value thus facilitating reaching the goal of using such a system
Variability	Refers to the variability and complexity associated with the data due to inconsistency in the flow velocity

5.3.2 Data Analytics in Context of Big Data

Data analytics refers to the process of analyzing data to uncover trends, patterns, and correlations that provide valuable insights for a specific end-use scenario (Prema 2019). In this context, data analytics for big data, also known as *Big Data Analytics* (BDA), refers to the advanced tools and techniques that are capable of analyzing not only a high volume of data but different types of data that may be collected and analyzed in real-time (Vassakis et al. 2018). The true potential of big data is realized only when it can be used to generate useful insights that aid businesses in making informed decisions or contribute to the development of effective strategies (Gandomi and Haider 2015). Thus, BDA can be understood as advanced data analytics that works on big data to turn large low-density datasets into meaningful insights and acquire intelligence from data. Hence, BDA becomes a combined approach for data management on a large scale, combined with advanced analytics tools and techniques.

According to Pathak et al. (2018), the historical developments in analytics have happened in three epochs, namely *Analytics 1.0* up until the mid-1990s with the era of traditional analytics involving business intelligence, enterprise data, and data marts, which primarily focused on descriptive information based on historical data. This is followed by *Analytics 2.0,* which has emerged with internet-based services like Amazon and Google intending to analyze large datasets by having computations on distributed processing systems and have an emphasis on predictions, i.e., identifying the likelihood of events to happen in the near future to optimize or plan processes and operations accordingly. The third epoch termed *Analytics 3.0* focuses on utilizing Analytics 1.0 and Analytics 2.0 and advancing with the automatization of processes of decision-making while incorporating optimization to make it *smart analytics.*

A similar evolution is presented by Arunachalam et al. (2018) with development from basic statistical techniques in the 1970s followed by developments in data mining techniques and the emergence of business intelligence (BI) (1.0 and 2.0) in the 2000s that primarily aims at business decision making. Further, witnessing the growth of internet and web-based systems, BI 3.0 or what is also termed as BDA has emerged in post 2010s, that focuses on scalability and aggregation of complex data that are difficult to handle by BI 2.0. Hence, Arunachalam et al. (2018) describe BDA as an updated and upgraded form of BI2.0, where RFIDs, sensors, and IoT act as key enablers for smart analytics.

Further, BDA relies on updated methods and tools which are not only capable of processing large datasets in batches or real-time for continuous analysis, but also handle unstructured data such as images, videos, text, and more. Thus, the key enablers for BDA include natural language processing, deep learning, artificial intelligence, machine learning, optimization, visualization, etc. (Bhadani and Jothimani 2016; Pathak et al. 2018). These tools and techniques primarily discover hidden patterns, find unknown correlations, and extract meaningful information from a data stream through operations such as aggregations, regression, clustering, etc. Further, based on the aim or application, BDA is divided into the following four categories (Vassakis et al. 2018).

Descriptive analytics involves the generation of insights from past events, uncovering patterns in events or data, and identifying correlations between various determinants. This helps in creating descriptive maps, visualizations, dashboards and reports, providing summaries, and presenting key metrics of the data. Descriptive analytics enables organizations to make their data interpretable and understandable.

Diagnostic analytics involves the development of understanding through root-cause analysis from historical data. Its primary goal is to answer questions like "why it happened?" (Husamaldin and Saeed 2019). This form of analytics enables the organization to understand the relationships between variables and facilitates learning on how these variables can influence future outcomes.

Predictive analytics aims at forecasting and providing an estimation of a future result. This aims at reducing uncertainty by identifying what is likely to happen by examining past trends and employing various simulations and data mining techniques. With predictive analytics, firms aim to identify the possibility of opportunities or future risks and plan mitigation strategies. Thus, it aims to answer questions like "what will happen?".

Prescriptive analytics aims at what should happen and how to influence the outcome. It is the most advanced stage of analytics that aims to develop the capabilities of firms for optimal decisions. It guides the companies with "what-if" analysis by combining the predictions, compliance rules, and business constraints to develop different likely outcomes and help the companies take actions to meet desired objectives (Soltanpoor and Sellis 2016).

Based on the above discussion, a schematic view of big data and BDA along with their enables is presented in Fig. 5.1, where the components in the bottommost layer act as enablers for data analytics, big data storage and processing capabilities. Further integration of big data and data analytics gives rise to BDA, which further results in different types of BDA applications based on the end use.

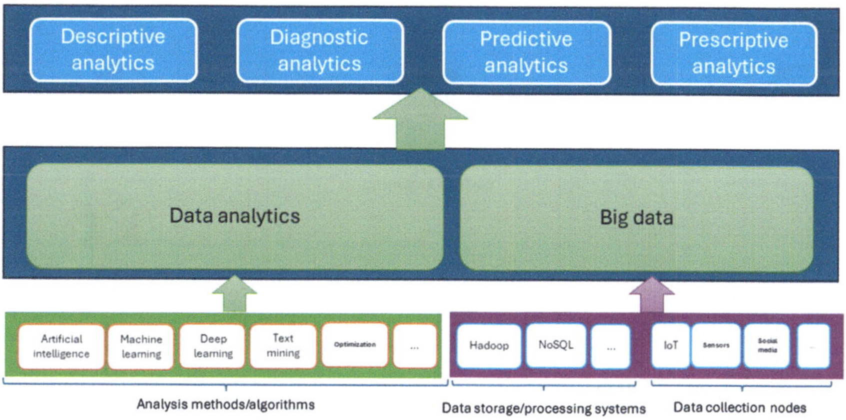

Fig. 5.1 Integrated view of big data analytics (BDA)

5.4 Leveraging Big Data in the T&F Sector

Although the T&F sector traditionally leaned on intuition and creativity to guide design, buying, and merchandising decisions, the evolving landscape shaped by the internet and social media is ushering in a new era that is paving the way for big data (Silva et al. 2020). Currently led by major players (e.g. H&M and Zara (Silva et al. 2020; Zaki et al. 2017)), the industry is undergoing a digital transition, right from manufacturing to retail, reshaping the landscape of production, distribution, and consumer interaction. The transition is not only transforming these individual stages or components but also helping to create an integrated ecosystem where insights from data are translated into tangible outputs or guiding action plans. As shown in Fig. 5.2, with the help of BDA, this ecosystem relies on multidimensional inputs, ranging from supply chain transactional data such as supply flow, point-of-sale (POS) data at retailers, etc., to individual customer data such as purchasing history, personal preferences, social media interactions, etc. Additionally, it encompasses overall market analysis gathered from the internet, social media, market-oriented research, etc. This helps to generate insights into several areas ranging from strategic decision-making to day-to-day operational planning. The following subsections provide an overview of key areas within the T&F supply chains where BDA can play a critical role.

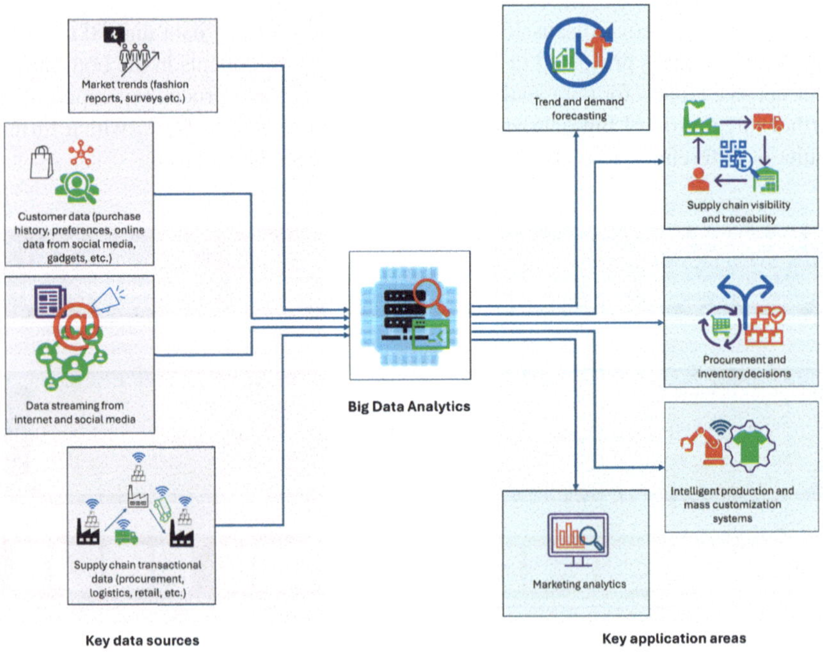

Fig. 5.2 Key sources of data and application areas for big data analytics (BDA) in the textile and fashion (T&F) sector

5.4.1 Trend and Demand Forecasting

Discovering and developing trends is a lifetime event of the T&F industry, where early capitalizing the fashion trends is key to staying ahead in the competition (Chang et al. 2021). Generally, predicting trend and demand forecasting is carried out through a subjective analysis that combines artistic viewpoints with predictive algorithms for time-series analysis of historical sales, often alongwise the close observation of fashion weeks (DuBreuil and Lu 2020). However, this approach faces challenges as well as high risk due to high subjectivity of designers and trend observers, as assessment based on subjective judgements and limited historical data may not fully capture or represent the dynamic changes occurring in the market in advance (DuBreuil and Lu 2020; Tehrani and Ahrens 2016).

Further, beyond fashion weeks, online social media is becoming increasingly influential in shaping the trends (Xue et al. 2023). Therefore, while it becomes essential to assess information from diverse sources, the classical forecasting algorithms are inadequate to handle such diverse and unstructured data (Giri and Chen 2022). In this context, the role of BDA becomes particularly pertinent for the fashion industry to analyze the stream of data from multiple sources and identify the trends. Several studies (cf. DuBreuil and Lu (2020), Giri and Chen (2022)) emphasized on the ability of BDA to target upcoming trends and allow companies to forecast customer needs with greater accuracy. While BDA on historical purchase behavior can offer valuable insights into market dynamics (Thomassey and Zeng 2018), it can allow brands to understand the purchasing behavior of individuals thus allowing the creation of personalized services.

Many brands are reported to invest in leveraging BDA to comprehend global trends in real-time and integrate this information into their operations (Devillard et al. 2021). An example of this is the fast-fashion brand Zara, which uses BDA to understand consumer demand and subsequently translate it into tangible design and personalized services (Silva et al. 2020). In addition, there are a growing number of tools and services such as WGSN and EDITED, which offer BDA-based analysis for fashion and retail brands on current trends and demands (DuBreuil and Lu 2020).

5.4.2 Supply Chain Visibility and Traceability

The T&F supply chains are often global and characterized as complex networks of stakeholders; therefore, the visibility of suppliers and the supply chain are important for uninterrupted functioning (Ahmed and MacCarthy, 2021). Although having a leading role, not all actors within the fashion supply chain are directly monitored by the lead firms. This creates the risks of non-compliance, such as not being able to ensure safe working conditions, or other unauthorized sub-contracting to non-compliant third parties (Brun et al. 2020). One notable example of this is the collapse of the Rana Plaza factory complex in Bangladesh, which exposed suboptimal working conditions within the garment industry and opaque supply chains as many lead firms denied knowing that their production was being carried out within the complex (Avins 2015).

The lack of transparency not only poses the risk of regulatory non-compliance to the lead firms but also exposes them to reputation damage and scrutiny from the consumers who associate fashion products with brand names (Amatulli et al. 2020). As the T&F supply chains are global and fragmented, and monitoring them calls for applications of advanced technologies capable of real-time collecting, monitoring and analyzing comprehensive data coming from suppliers, supply chains, online social media, blogs, and more. In such a scenario, the role of BDA becomes crucial for the brands. The BDA allows for combining and generating insights from different sources thus allows creating a comprehensive visibility of the supply chain.

Further having real-time visibility allows the companies to identify deviations within the supply chain or the potential upcoming risks, thus allowing them to take proactive actions (Singh and Singh 2019). In this context, Blekanov et al. (2019) highlight the application of BDA to identify potential risks through sentiment analysis of social media data, which can potentially be used to proactively tackle negative publicity. Further, Hader et al. (2022) demonstrate the implementation of big data with blockchain to establish supply chain traceability. This integration facilitates accurate sharing among the stakeholders, fostering trust and visibility within the supply chain. Additionally, it enables precise tracing of the root of deviations, ensuring more transparency in the supply chain.

5.4.3 Procurement and Inventory Decisions

The fashion industry is typically characterized by a short lifecycle and a huge variety of products coupled with high impulse buying behavior from the customers, making the demand highly fluctuating (Bruce and Daly 2011). Further, lengthy and rigid supply procedures make timely decisions on procurement and maintaining sufficient inventory crucial (Wen et al. 2019). Considering the global nature of the supply chain, advanced systems are required that can analyze and process the data in the real-time demand, current inventory levels, any identified bottlenecks, ongoing or possible disruptions on the supplier or logistics end, and extract valuable insights to help the companies in making quick planning decisions on procurements and maintaining sufficient inventories (Madhani 2015; Sardar and Lee 2015).

In this context, BDA finds applications in T&F supply chains, which allows the combining of internal data from a firm and its suppliers, and external data such as information on natural calamities or fluctuating currency rates. This integration can further enable automated reporting of key performance indicators and potential bottlenecks and accordingly suggest recommendations for early identification of threats as well as opportunities, and planning for procurement strategies (Handfield et al. 2019; Heidari 2018). Further, in terms of inventory management, with real-time data on sales, fashion brands can identify the fast-selling collections thus allowing reordering and refilling of the stock on time and stopping the production of items with low sales. The fashion brand Zara is a well-known example of utilizing big data for refilling the inventory with new production in a short time by closely monitoring the POS data for the fast-selling items and accordingly make procurement and production orders to the suppliers to reduce the overall time (Analytics India Magazine 2020).

5.4.4 Intelligent Production and Mass Customization Systems

Over the past few decades, the textile manufacturing sector has seen a significant transition in the implementation of technology to enhance its efficiency. This transition is further continued with the implementation of digital solutions from robots, advanced sensors and actuators, embedded software, IoT, and artificial intelligence to cyber-physical systems giving rise to a new industrial revolution, also known as Industry 4.0 (I4.0). This is further translated for the T&F sector as Textile Industry 4.0. I4.0 aims to develop autonomous intelligent machines and smart digital networks that facilitate machine-machine interactions, thus creating an autonomous environment (also termed as *smart factories*) capable of making decisions. As the backbone of I4.0 is the ability to make decisions by means of collected data through IoT, sensors, and more, the capability to analyze such diverse data is one of the foremost requirements for it, where the role of BDA becomes critical.

BDA allows aggregating and analyzing a large amount of data in real-time; thus, it enables the factory floor visibility of manufacturing assets, balancing the production lines, and providing insights on predictive maintenance to reduce downtime. Moreover, in the T&F sector, mass customization has gained prominence as a concept aimed at delivering customized apparel to consumers. Several studies (e.g., Bradlow et al. 2017; Shim and Taylor 2019) have highlighted that BDA can play a critical role in understanding customer needs and preferences by analyzing past consumption behavior combined with data from other sources such as interaction on social media to provide recommendation for customization during design or production. Further, Ji and Jiang (2020) demonstrate customization techniques driven by big data and machine learning, leveraging user data such as dressing habits and other personal preferences to identify the optimal combination of mix-and-match clothing choices. Further the authors explore generative learning for garment customization that can be used by the designer for customization. Furthermore, Zhao et al. (2021) highlight the increasing reliance of designers on big data to identify if the specific design meets the customer needs, thus emphasizing the role of BDA in mass customization.

5.4.5 Marketing Analytics

In the T&F sector, marketing plays an important role in shaping brand perception, driving product visibility, and influencing consumer preferences. These factors collectively contribute to the overall success of a firm. Marketing helps in converting consumer insights into market advantage. Nowadays, brands gather customer data from various channels to make crucial decisions regarding marketing activities (Arnett 2020). These activities include identifying suitable products for specific customer or market segments, selecting suitable marketing channels for interaction with customers, determining effective advertisement strategy, and implementing targeted promotions or discounts for select customer segments to name a few (Amado et al. 2018; Arnett 2020). Thanks to expanding digital traces of customers over the internet, online social media, mobile applications, blogs, and more, the potential to gather vast amounts of data has expanded significantly. Given the premise of increasing the volume of diverse data, BDA can play prominent role in combining data from different streams, not only creating overall insights into the data but also creating customer-specific profiling for personalized marketing (Chandra et al. 2022; Khade 2016).

5.5 Risks and Challenges in Implementing Big Data Analytics in Textile and Fashion Sector

While data analytics and big data bring a lot of potential for the current T&F industry, numerous challenges must be thoughtfully considered for the successful implementation and exploitation of such methods and technologies.

First and foremost, the implementation of data analytics, especially in the context of big data, encounters ethical and legal concerns related to data collection and use. Big data has proven its capability to generate intelligent insights from large-scale datasets and data streams collected and combined from various sources. Companies often rely on customer-specific data such as their shopping behavior, social media interactions, and similar, to create profiles for personalized services or identify broad trends and create intelligent insights. In this context, privacy is a big concern while implementing such data-driven services where BDA may be turned into a tool for mass surveillance if not properly handled (Howe III and Elenberg 2020).

In addition, the collection or handling of customer's data often faces challenges due to regulations such as European GDPR, which not only hinders the free use of data but also imposes stringent requirements on data protection and privacy (Madsen et al. 2020). While these regulations provide a framework that ensures that data is collected and handled properly, their compliance not only incurs additional costs for the companies but also increases the exposure to legal risk in case of lapses, such as data breaches, unintended use of data, etc. This further turns into challenges for adopting or implementing data-driven services. Another associated challenge, according to Nguyen and Tran (2023), is linked to the security vulnerabilities of big data systems. These vulnerabilities may expose the companies to larger cyber-attacks, and therefore, implementing such a system can increase the exposure of risks for the companies. Hence, it is important that the ethical, legal, and security risks are thoughtfully assessed before implementation of BDA.

The fashion industry is commonly recognized to heavily rely on subjectivity, creativity, and intuition for different aspects of the business including developing new designs, trends, etc. Here, BDA represents a paradigm shift for the industry which aims to leverage data-driven insights and shift from traditionally subjective and intuitive processes. However, relying too much on data brings new questions and concerns to the practitioners regarding the potential loss of creativity and its impact on the creative ability of the brands (Kenny 2018; Silva et al. 2020, 2019). At the same time, if the top management does not identify, or consider data-driven practices not compatible with their innovation approach or values, it might become a barrier to harnessing the potential of big data in the fashion supply chain.

Further, for the implementation of BDA, companies need to enhance technological capabilities as the traditional approaches of data handling or processing are just not sufficient for big data processing. This includes investment in data warehouses, distributed computing systems, software solutions, and a continuous investment in their management and maintenance (Chen and Zhang 2014). As explained earlier, the evolution of big data is rapid, requiring companies to be prepared for infrastructure upgrades and skillset enhancements to efficiently exploit BDA (Kache and Seuring 2017; Vassakis et al. 2018). As a result, investing in such systems may be a challenge for organizations, especially in the scenario of limited profit and long breakeven times (Kache and Seuring 2017).

It becomes even more difficult when the implementation requires the agreement of supply chain stakeholders. As T&F supply chains consist of a network of actors dealing with various operations and activities, the proper exploitation of big data to tackle the supply chain challenge requires agreement and synchronous actions on data collection and sharing by the supply chain stakeholders. In this context, getting agreed on investment and implementing compatible technological solutions may be a challenge in adopting big data practices. Furthermore, some segments of the fashion supply chain predominantly rely on manual operations with limited technology integration. In such cases, the implementation of infrastructure for big data may be very difficult to achieve.

A lack of high-quality data and the ability to exploit existing data is another challenge for the fashion industry in implementing BDA. A survey of 350 retailers and brand manufacturers reveals that only 16% of the retailers consider themselves experts in terms of understanding the data they are handling or harnessing (BIRA 2018). Further, according to DalleMule and Davenport (2017), less than 1% of unstructured data is analyzed overall across the industries, leaving a substantial volume of data untapped. This underscores the impact of multiple barriers in implementing BDA, a situation that is also pertinent to the fashion sector. First, it connects with a lack of skillsets among T&F professionals in understanding the data and data analytics. While the field of Big Data and data analytics is specialized and demands core expertise, it cannot be considered exclusively for experts outside of the T&F industry.

For a proper harnessing of the potential of big data and data analytics, the core expertise of the application area needs to drive the definition of the problem statement, attributes, potential solutions, etc. These aspects should then be translated into a framework of data-driven solutions, which can be implemented through BDA. Hence, there is a requirement for investment in human capital, essential to upgrade existing professionals, especially experts within the field of T&F, fostering the development of fundamental skills in statistics, data mining, visualization, machine learning, and similar domains. Silva et al. (2020) further propose data science subjects within fashion curriculums to ensure that fashion graduates are well-versed in data techniques to collaborate with BDA experts.

5.6 Conclusions

This chapter highlights the importance of data analytics in the context of big data in tackling the challenges of T&F supply chains. Data analytics, in the context of big data, signified a paradigm shift for the fashion industry, which aims to create intelligent insights from different sources of data. While fashion supply chains are global where visibility on operations, logistics, and geopolitical events become a critical aspect for efficient functioning, fashion is itself a social phenomenon that refers to the prevailing styles and trends shaped by various factors such as societal influence, cultural beliefs, and individual preferences. Here, a comprehensive visibility of how people respond to these styles and trends becomes a key to understanding customer needs and capturing emerging fashion trends. In such a scenario, big data and BDA bring tremendous potential for the fashion industry for trend forecasting, monitoring customer preferences and feedback, and developing personalized services and offers, to name a few.

While there is a common agreement on the benefits of implementing BDA, its exploitation is still at a nascent stage in the fashion industry (Sinke 2021). Among others, one important challenge for the fashion sector to exploit BDA is collaboration among the industry practitioners and big data experts, and collaboration among the stakeholders to implement data-oriented infrastructure that supports big data practices. As fashion supply chains are highly global and fragmented in nature, supply chain collaboration becomes a key for implementing such solutions. Nonetheless, big fashion brands like Zara and H&M have already paved their ways to exploit BDA for monitoring customer preferences and supply chains, facilitating the swift production of a variety of items (Madsen et al. 2020; Silva et al. 2020). Further, according to Anita Balchandani et al. (2022), fashion companies are expected to double the investment on investment in technology by 2030, which is expected to accelerate the exploitation of big data.

References

Acharya A, Singh SK, Pereira V, Singh P (2018) Big data, knowledge co-creation and decision making in fashion industry. Int J Inf Manag 42:90–101

Ahmed WA, MacCarthy BL (2021) Blockchain-enabled supply chain traceability in the textile and apparel supply chain: a case study of the fiber producer, Lenzing. Sustainability 13:10496

Amado A, Cortez P, Rita P, Moro S (2018) Research trends on big data in marketing: a text mining and topic modeling based literature analysis. Eur Res Manag Bus Econ 24:1–7

Amatulli C, De Angelis M, Pino G, Guido G (2020) An investigation of unsustainable luxury: how guilt drives negative word-of-mouth. Int J Res Mark 37:821–836

Analytics India Magazine (2020) How Zara uses big data analytics to excel in its game? Analytics India Magazine

Anita B, Berg A, Harreis H, Hurtado M, Altable CS, Roberts R, Petersens SA, Amed I (2022) State of Fashion Technology Report 2022. McKinsey & Company

Araque González G, Suárez Hernández A, Gómez Vásquez M, Vélez Uribe J, Bernal Avellaneda A (2022) Sustainable manufacturing in the fourth industrial revolution: a big data application proposal in the textile industry. J Ind Eng Manag 15:614–636

Arnett G (2020) What fashion retailers know about you. Vogue Business

Arunachalam D, Kumar N, Kawalek JP (2018) Understanding big data analytics capabilities in supply chain management: unravelling the issues, challenges and implications for practice. Transp Res Part E Logist Transp Rev 114:416–436

Avins J (2015) The way to start a real fashion revolution: put Bangladesh's invisible garment factories on a map. QUARTZ

Banica L, Hagiu A (2016) Using big data analytics to improve decision-making in apparel supply chains. In: Information systems for the fashion and apparel industry. Elsevier, pp 63–95

Bertola P, Teunissen J (2018) Fashion 4.0. Innovating fashion industry through digital transformation. Res J Text Appar 22:352–369

Bhadani AK, Jothimani D (2016) Big data: challenges, opportunities, and realities. Eff Big Data Manag Oppor Implement 1–24

Bhardwaj V, Fairhurst A (2010) Fast fashion: response to changes in the fashion industry. Int Rev Retail Distrib Consum Res 20:165–173

BIRA (2018) How to use retail analytics to delight customers and increase sales. British Independent Retailers Association

Blázquez M (2014) Fashion shopping in multichannel retail: the role of technology in enhancing the customer experience. Int J Electron Commer 18:97–116. https://doi.org/10.2753/JEC1086-4415180404

Blekanov I, Krylatov A, Ivanov D, Bubnova Y (2019) Big data analysis in social networks for managing risks in clothing industry. IFAC-Pap 52:1710–1714

Bradlow ET, Gangwar M, Kopalle P, Voleti S (2017) The role of big data and predictive analytics in retailing. J Retail 93:79–95

Bruce M, Daly L (2011) Adding value: challenges for UK apparel supply chain management—a review. Prod Plan Control 22:210–220

Brun A, Karaosman H, Barresi T (2020) Supply chain collaboration for transparency. Sustainability 12:4429

Cao H (2018) The growth of e-commerce and its impact on the fast fashion retailers.

Caro F, Martínez-de-Albéniz V (2015) Fast fashion: business model overview and research opportunities. In: Agrawal N, Smith SA (eds) Retail supply chain management, international series in operations research & management science. Springer US, Boston, MA, pp 237–264. https://doi.org/10.1007/978-1-4899-7562-1_9

Casciani D, Chkanikova O, Pal R (2022) Exploring the nature of digital transformation in the fashion industry: opportunities for supply chains, business models, and sustainability-oriented innovations. Sustain Sci Pract Policy 18:773–795. https://doi.org/10.1080/15487733.2022.2125640

Chandra S, Verma S, Lim WM, Kumar S, Donthu N (2022) Personalization in personalized marketing: trends and ways forward. Psychol Mark 39:1529–1562. https://doi.org/10.1002/mar.21670

Chang AA, Cynthia, Devita, Ramadhan, JF, Adnan ZKS, Kanigoro B, Irwansyah E (2021) Fashion trend forecasting using machine learning techniques: a review. In: Silhavy R, Silhavy P, Prokopova Z (eds) Data science and intelligent systems, lecture notes in networks and systems. Springer International Publishing, Cham, pp 34–44. https://doi.org/10.1007/978-3-030-90321-3_5

Chen CP, Zhang C-Y (2014) Data-intensive applications, challenges, techniques and technologies: a survey on big data. Inf Sci 275:314–347

DalleMule L, Davenport TH (2017) What's your data strategy. Harv Bus Rev 95:112–121

Devillard S, Harreis H, Landry N, Altable CS (2021) Jumpstarting value creation with data and analytics in fashion and luxury. McKinsey & Company

DuBreuil M, Lu S (2020) Traditional vs. big-data fashion trend forecasting: an examination using WGSN and EDITED. Int J Fash Des Technol Educ 13:68–77. https://doi.org/10.1080/17543266.2020.1732482

Gandomi A, Haider M (2015) Beyond the hype: big data concepts, methods, and analytics. Int J Inf Manag 35:137–144

Ghoreishi M, Happonen A (2022) The case of fabric and textile industry: the emerging role of digitalization, internet-of-things and industry 4.0 for circularity. In: Yang X-S, Sherratt S, Dey N, Joshi A (eds) Proceedings of sixth international congress on information and communication technology, lecture notes in networks and systems. Springer Singapore, Singapore, pp 189–200. https://doi.org/10.1007/978-981-16-1781-2_18

Giri C, Chen Y (2022) Deep learning for demand forecasting in the fashion and apparel retail industry. Forecasting 4:565–581

Hader M, Tchoffa D, El Mhamedi A, Ghodous P, Dolgui A, Abouabdellah A (2022) Applying integrated Blockchain and Big Data technologies to improve supply chain traceability and information sharing in the textile sector. J Ind Inf Integr 28:100345

Handfield R, Jeong S, Choi T (2019) Emerging procurement technology: data analytics and cognitive analytics. Int J Phys Distrib Logist Manag 49:972–1002

Hartmann PM, Zaki M, Feldmann N, Neely A (2016) Capturing value from big data—a taxonomy of data-driven business models used by start-up firms. Int J Oper Prod Manag 36:1382–1406

Heidari A (2018) Exploration of big data in procurement-benefits and challenges

Howe EG III, Elenberg F (2020) Ethical challenges posed by big data. Innov Clin Neurosci 17:24

Husamaldin L, Saeed N (2019) Big data analytics correlation taxonomy. Information 11:17

Ji Y, Jiang G (2020) Garment customization big data–processing and analysis in optimization design. J Eng Fibers Fabr 15:155892502092540. https://doi.org/10.1177/1558925020925405

Kache F, Seuring S (2017) Challenges and opportunities of digital information at the intersection of big data analytics and supply chain management. Int J Oper Prod Manag 37:10–36

Kenny B (2018) Could big data replace the creative director at the gap? Forbes

Khade AA (2016) Performing customer behavior analysis using big data analytics. Procedia Comput Sci 79:986–992

Kitchin R (2014) Big Data, new epistemologies and paradigm shifts. Big Data Soc 1:205395171452848. https://doi.org/10.1177/2053951714528481

Madhani PM (2015) Enhancing customer lifetime value in fast fashion retailing with RFID initiatives. Int J Bus Glob 15:205. https://doi.org/10.1504/IJBG.2015.071171

Madsen DØ, Silva ES, Hassani H (2020) The application of big data in fashion retailing: a narrative review. Int J Manag Concepts Philos 13:247. https://doi.org/10.1504/IJMCP.2020.112160

Nguyen MT, Tran MH (2023) Privacy and security implications of big data applications in consumer behavior analysis for fashion retail. J Empir Soc Sci Stud 7:82–98

Pal R, Jayarathne A (2022) Digitalization in the textiles and clothing sector. In: The digital supply chain. Elsevier, pp 255–271

Pathak AR, Pandey M, Rautaray S (2018) Construing the big data based on taxonomy, analytics and approaches. Iran J Comput Sci 1:237–259. https://doi.org/10.1007/s42044-018-0024-3
Prema A (2019) A study to renovate image data using data analytics methodologies. In: Kumar R, Wiil UK (eds) Recent advances in computational intelligence, studies in computational intelligence. Springer International Publishing, Cham, pp 163–171. https://doi.org/10.1007/978-3-030-12500-4_10
Sardar S, Lee YH (2015) Analysis of product complexity considering disruption cost in fast fashion supply chain. Math Probl Eng 2015
Shim JP, Taylor R (2019) Purchase-based analytics and big data for actionable insights. IT Prof 21:48–56
Silva ES, Hassani H, Madsen DØ (2020) Big data in fashion: transforming the retail sector. J Bus Strategy 41:21–27
Silva ES, Hassani H, Madsen DØ, Gee L (2019) Googling fashion: forecasting fashion consumer behaviour using google trends. Soc Sci 8:111
Singh NP, Singh S (2019) Building supply chain risk resilience: role of big data analytics in supply chain disruption mitigation. Benchmarking Int J 26:2318–2342
Sinke F (2021) The fashion of big data analytics. University of Amsterdam
Soltanpoor R, Sellis T (2016) Prescriptive analytics for big data. In: Cheema MA, Zhang W, Chang L (eds) Databases theory and applications, lecture notes in computer science. Springer International Publishing, Cham, pp 245–256. https://doi.org/10.1007/978-3-319-46922-5_19
Tehrani AF, Ahrens D (2016) Improved forecasting and purchasing of fashion products based on the use of big data techniques. In: Bogaschewsky R, Eßig M, Lasch R, Stölzle W (eds) Supply management research. Springer Fachmedien Wiesbaden, Wiesbaden, pp 293–312. https://doi.org/10.1007/978-3-658-08809-5_13
Thomassey S, Zeng X (2018) Introduction: artificial intelligence for fashion industry in the big data era. In: Thomassey S, Zeng X (eds) Artificial intelligence for fashion industry in the big data era. Springer Series in Fashion Business. Springer Singapore, Singapore, pp 1–6. https://doi.org/10.1007/978-981-13-0080-6_1
Vassakis K, Petrakis E, Kopanakis I (2018) Big data analytics: applications, prospects and challenges. In: Skourletopoulos G, Mastorakis G, Mavromoustakis CX, Dobre C, Pallis E (Eds) Mobile big data, lecture notes on data engineering and communications technologies. Springer International Publishing, Cham pp. 3–20. https://doi.org/10.1007/978-3-319-67925-9_1
Wen X, Choi T-M, Chung S-H (2019) Fashion retail supply chain management: a review of operational models. Int J Prod Econ 207:34–55
Xue Z, Li Q, Zeng X (2023) Social media user behavior analysis applied to the fashion and apparel industry in the big data era. J Retail Consum Serv 72:103299
Yaqoob I, Hashem IAT, Gani A, Mokhtar S, Ahmed E, Anuar NB, Vasilakos AV (2016) Big data: from beginning to future. Int J Inf Manag 36:1231–1247
Zaki M, Friedrich TM, Theodoulidis B, Shapira P (2017) Big data ecosystem in Re-distributed Manufacturing (RdM) past and future. Cranfield University
Zhao L, Liu S, Zhao X (2021) Big data and digital design models for fashion design. J Eng Fibers Fabr 16:155892502110190. https://doi.org/10.1177/15589250211019023

Chapter 6
Application of AI and Robotics in Fashion Manufacturing and Supply Chain

Manoj Kumar Paras

Abstract The fashion industry is going through a massive transformation due to recent advancements such as Industry 4.0 mainly propelled by technological interventions like artificial intelligence (AI) and robotics. This chapter explores the application of AI and robotics in the fashion industry focusing on its manufacturing and supply chain operations. It attempts to shed light on contemporary technologies, deliberates their potential benefits, figures out challenges, presents successful case studies, and proposes future research avenues. Fashion businesses may increase customer satisfaction and gain a competitive edge by leveraging AI and robotics to improve productivity, performance, and agility throughout the production process and supply chain. Further, it helps to drive sustainability in the fashion businesses by unlocking new horizons in the fashion industry.

Keywords Artificial intelligence · Robotics · Fashion · Manufacturing · Supply chain · Automation · Machine learning · Computer vision · Sustainability

6.1 Introduction

The fashion industry presents an intriguing and dynamic intersection of creativity, business, and cultural expression. In the fashion industry, high-end designer labels and mass-market stores can be thought of as the two extremes of a continuum. This requires an interplay between various intermediaries who collaborate in different ways to convert designs into reality and finally, make it accessible to the customers. Superficially, it may look fascinating; however, the fashion industry is grappling with a lot of challenges (e.g., Nayak et al. 2020; Hofmann et al. 2022; John and Mishra 2023). Globalization has led to the extension of supply chains across continents making them susceptible to disruptions and elevating concerns about ethical

M. K. Paras (✉)
National Institute of Fashion Technology, Patna 800001, India
e-mail: manoj.paras@nift.ac.in

R. Nayak et al. (eds.), *Use of Digital and Advanced Technologies in the Fashion Supply Chain*, Springer Series in Fashion Business,
https://doi.org/10.1007/978-981-97-7528-6_6

conduct, transparency and resilience. With the resource constraints and rising production costs, delivering the products at competitive prices has increased the burden on the decision-makers. Other concerns like carbon emission, high water consumption, water pollution, landfills, child labour and many more add to the complexity and severity. The technological revolution has transformed how consumers behave and respond. This has resulted in fast-paced alterations in marketing strategies. Thus, there are two options either to adapt to these changes or exit the market. The players in the fashion industry are striving hard to mitigate these challenges by focusing on inclusivity, equity, agility and sustainability throughout their operations. In traversing these complexities and responding to the challenges, the fashion industry continues to evolve, innovate, and collaborate.

Artificial intelligence (AI) and robotics popularly known as transformative technologies are altering industries across the globe, and the fashion industry is no exception (Jin and Shin 2021). Before delving into the application of AI and Robotics in the fashion industry, it is imperative to understand the basic notion of AI and robotics. Artificial intelligence (AI) is the technology that allows computers to simulate human intellectual processes. This allows the machines to carry out tasks like learning, problem-solving, and decision-making that require human intelligence. Overall, AI acts as a computational agent acting intelligently towards achieving any goal-directed behaviour (Davenport 2018). Structured data, unstructured data, pre-processes, main processes, knowledge base, and information are the main building blocks of AI. Problem-solving, reasoning and machine learning are the main processes (Paschen et al. 2019; Mohiuddin Babu et al. 2022).

Robotics can be employed to automate the process to reduce and simplify human intervention (Jiménez Schlegl and Čubrić 2018; Barkova 2020; Salahuddin and Lee 2022). Robots are effectively used in the designing, construction, and operations. The benefits of using robots can be understood as "When compared to traditional machines, robots offer a much higher degree of flexibility as they are not constrained to follow fixed trajectories but can switch easily between tasks, even including tool changes, and can be reprogrammed in an equally straightforward way. Compared to human workers, robots are more reliable (in general) as for repeatability and precision, they are less prone to errors, need no rest nor vacancies (besides occasional maintenance), and can work in hazardous or arduous conditions." (Jiménez Schlegl and Čubrić 2018, p 1).

AI and robotics are expected to improve efficiency, precision, scalability, adaptability, and sustainability in the fashion industry across the supply chain and manufacturing processes. Fashion firms are transforming their design, production, and consumer delivery methods with the help of these technologies. Automated sewing, cutting processes, predictive analytics and personalised marketing are some of the examples of transformation. The fashion industry is set to enter a new era of intelligent, sustainable, and socially conscious fashion. This is because AI and robotics are opening up new areas for innovation and competition. Robotics are simplifying traditional manufacturing processes by automating tasks such as cutting, sewing, and assembly, whereas AI ensures optimal performance and product quality through predictive maintenance and quality control systems. AI-driven design optimization and virtual prototyping are simplifying the product design and development cycle thus reducing time-to-market (Luce 2018; Giri et al. 2019; Mohiuddin Babu et al. 2022). AI algorithms based on machine learning can analyse vast amounts of data to forecast demand, optimize inventory levels, and streamline logistics operations for the supply chain. Robotics has the potential to automate warehouse tasks, accelerating order fulfilment and improving accuracy (Dash et al. 2019). Thus, integration of artificial intelligence (AI) and robotics in fashion manufacturing and supply chain operations is addressing business complexity.

6.2 Background

AI and robotics are bringing innovation and improving efficiency shaping in the fashion industry. AI technologies such as machine learning algorithms and computer vision capabilities are enabling fashion companies to analyse vast amounts of data, thus facilitating trend forecasting and personalized product recommendations. The creative process of the fashion industry has been modified by AI-driven design optimization and virtual prototyping. This simplifies the iteration of the prototyping and sampling process. Robotics can automate repetitive tasks such as cutting, sewing, and assembly, resulting in higher precision, consistency, and speed in manufacturing. Collaborative robots (cobots) can work along with human workers to enhance productivity and safety in the industrial environment. The integration of AI and robotics brings new possibilities for creativity, efficiency, and sustainability in fashion. This drives the fashion industry towards intelligent manufacturing and supply chain management.

6.2.1 AI and Robotics in Fashion

AI and robotics applications have the potential to automate the sewing, cutting, and assembly processes of fashion manufacturing. AI-driven technology also brings design optimization and quality control. There are multiple challenges in adopting these technologies in the fashion industry (Salahuddin and Lee 2022). Robotics are enhancing the efficiency and agility of fashion supply chain management. The application may be in warehouse automation, order fulfilment, and logistics optimization. However, there are challenges related to the integration and scalability of these technologies (Salahuddin and Lee 2022). AI and robotics can also promote sustainability in fashion manufacturing. This could be done by automated processes for waste reduction, resource optimization, and eco-friendly material selection. There is also social and ethical significance (for example transparency) of adopting these technologies that can help in achieving sustainable practices in the fashion industry (Barkova 2020). Figure 6.1 demonstrates the application of AI and robotics technology in fashion.

Fig. 6.1 Application of AI and robotics in fashion

The applications of AI and robotics across various segments such as product design, manufacturing processes, and supply chain management in the fashion industry. There is an increasing trend in the adoption of AI and robotics in fashion manufacturing and supply chain operations. Technologies are adopted in areas such as predictive analytics, collaborative robotics, and blockchain-enabled traceability. However, there are key challenges such as data privacy, regulatory compliance, and workforce readiness, providing recommendations for overcoming these barriers. The application of AI and robotics in fashion manufacturing and supply chain management holds great potential. The fundamental concepts such as machine learning, natural language processing, and computer vision have their specific applications in trend analysis, product recommendation systems, and virtual fitting rooms. The principles of robotics hold application potential in various production processes such as automated sewing, cutting, and assembly, and evaluate their impact on efficiency, quality, and flexibility in garment production.

Giri et al. (2019) examine the fundamentals of AI and robotics in fashion design and manufacturing. They categorize existing research based on AI techniques (e.g., machine learning, deep learning) and robotics applications (e.g., industrial robots, collaborative robots) and identifies key trends, challenges, and opportunities for future research. Salahuddin and Lee (2022) provide an in-depth analysis of its applications in the fashion industry. They cover the fundamental concepts such as image recognition, object detection, and image segmentation, and discuss their role in trend analysis, visual search, and virtual try-on systems. The recent advances in AI and robotics focus on sustainable fashion manufacturing. It discusses the fundamental principles such as predictive analytics, collaborative robotics, and circular economy principles, and examines their application in reducing waste, improving resource efficiency, and enhancing transparency in the fashion supply chain (Barkova 2020). The fundamentals of AI and robotics provide a solid foundation for application and practice in the fashion industry.

6.2.2 Artificial Intelligence

AI techniques such as machine learning, computer vision, and natural language processing are fundamental pillars of artificial intelligence. These pillars serve unique purposes in solving complex problems. Machine learning involves algorithms that enable systems to learn from data and make predictions or decisions without being explicitly programmed. It encompasses various approaches that include supervised and unsupervised learning. During supervised learning, the models are trained on labelled data, while unsupervised learning seeks patterns in unlabelled data. In reinforcement learning, agents learn through trial and error interactions with an environment.

Computer vision focuses on enabling machines to interpret and understand visuals such as images and videos. It involves tasks such as image classification, object detection, and image segmentation. These often utilise deep learning techniques like convolutional neural networks (CNNs) to extract features and make sense of visual data. Natural language processing (NLP) on the other hand deals with the interaction between computers and human language. It enables machines to understand, interpret, and generate human language. This facilitates tasks such as text classification, sentiment analysis, and machine translation. These AI techniques have the potential to revolutionize industries, enhance productivity, and create new opportunities for innovation and growth.

Domingos (2012) provides a concise overview of machine learning fundamentals, including key concepts such as supervised learning, unsupervised learning, and reinforcement learning. He discusses common algorithms and techniques used in machine learning and highlights practical considerations and pitfalls to avoid. LeCun et al. (2015) offer an in-depth exploration of deep learning, a subset of machine learning that focuses on neural networks with multiple layers. They discuss the theoretical foundations of deep learning, architectures such as convolutional neural networks (CNNs) and recurrent neural networks (RNNs), and applications in areas such as image recognition and natural language processing.

Szeliski (2010) provides a thorough introduction to computer vision, covering fundamental concepts, algorithms, and applications. Szeliski discusses topics such as image formation, feature extraction, object recognition, and 3D reconstruction, offering both theoretical insights and practical implementation guidelines.

Krizhevsky et al. (2012) introduces AlexNet, a deep convolutional neural network architecture that achieved breakthrough performance in the ImageNet large-scale visual recognition challenge. This provides an overview of CNNs and demonstrates their effectiveness in image classification tasks.

Natural language processing covers a wide range of topics such as text preprocessing, language modelling, syntactic analysis, and machine translation. It provides both theoretical foundations and practical techniques for processing and understanding human language. Transformer model, a novel architecture based solely on self-attention mechanisms, which revolutionized the field of natural language processing. Transformer architecture is effective for various NLP tasks, including machine translation and language modelling (Vaswani et al. 2017). The core AI techniques of machine learning, computer vision, and natural language processing, provide a solid foundation for industrial applications.

6.2.3 Robotic Technologies

Robotic technologies comprised of industrial robots and collaborative robots (cobots). These represent a transformative force in various industries, including manufacturing, healthcare, and logistics. Industrial robots are automated machines designed to perform tasks with precision, speed, and reliability in controlled environments such as factories. They are equipped with specialized arms and end-effectors capable of handling diverse materials and performing tasks like welding, assembly, and packaging. These robots operate automatically by following programmed instructions and executing repetitive tasks with high efficiency. In contrast, collaborative robots or cobots are designed to work alongside human operators. This augments human capabilities and enhances productivity and safety in industrial environments. Cobots feature advanced sensors and safety mechanisms that enable them to interact safely with humans. This allows close collaboration and flexible task allocation. They excel in applications such as pick-and-place operations, assembly line tasks, and small-batch manufacturing. Together, industrial robots and cobots offer complementary solutions for automating a wide range of tasks, driving efficiency, innovation, and competitiveness across industries. Their versatility and adaptability make them indispensable tools in the era of smart manufacturing and Industry 4.0 that empower businesses to streamline operations, optimize workflows, and meet the evolving demands of fast changing fashion business.

Industrial robotics function is based upon various concepts such as robot kinematics, dynamics, control systems, and programming languages. The design, operation, and applications of industrial robots can be made for various manufacturing processes such as welding, material handling, and assembly. (Groover 2019). The design principles, safety features, and industrial applications play a significant role in collaborative robots. This enables human–robot collaboration, such as force and tactile sensing, as well as challenges and opportunities for integrating cobots into diverse manufacturing environments. The industrial robot has various applications across industries, including automotive, electronics, and aerospace. The technological advancements shape the industrial robotics industry. The role of robots is crucial for enhancing productivity and competitiveness (Barkova 2020).

Guglielmelli et al. (2018) examine the design principles and safety standards governing collaborative robots in different application domains. They discuss risk assessment methodologies, safety features such as proximity sensors and speed monitoring, and regulatory frameworks for ensuring safe human–robot interaction. Gao and Helu (2020) provide an overview of industrial robotics technologies and their potential impact on manufacturing operations. They discuss challenges such as cost, complexity, and interoperability, as well as strategies for successful implementation, including workforce training, system integration, and performance evaluation. Thus, robotic technologies such as industrial robots and collaborative robots hold great future prospects.

6.3 Applications in Fashion Manufacturing

The integration of artificial intelligence (AI) and robotics in fashion manufacturing is revolutionizing the industry by streamlining processes, enhancing efficiency, and driving innovation. In garment production, robotics automate labour-intensive tasks such as cutting, sewing, and assembly, leading to increased precision, consistency, and speed while reducing production time and costs. AI algorithms analyse vast amounts of data to optimize manufacturing processes, predict demand, and improve product quality. Computer vision technology enables automated quality control and defect detection, ensuring that only flawless products reach consumers. Furthermore, AI-driven design optimization and virtual prototyping accelerate the product development cycle, allowing for rapid iteration and customization.

Collaborative robots (cobots) work alongside human workers, augmenting their capabilities and improving safety in dynamic manufacturing environments. By leveraging AI and robotics, fashion manufacturers can achieve greater agility, sustainability, and competitiveness, paving the way for a smarter, more efficient future in fashion manufacturing. The robotics principle can be integrated into fashion design, particularly focusing on robotic sewing and embroidery techniques for mass customization. There might be certain challenges in implementing robotic systems for flexible and personalized garment production (Salahuddin and Lee 2022). There is great potential for the application of artificial intelligence in optimizing design processes for sustainable fashion manufacturing. The AI-driven approaches are useful for material selection, pattern optimization, and waste reduction. Thus, AI has the potential to improve resource efficiency and environmental sustainability (Salahuddin and Lee 2022). Figure 6.2 demonstrates the application of AI and robotics technology in fashion manufacturing.

Computer vision technology applications can be made in quality control and defect detection in apparel manufacturing. Computer vision techniques, such as image processing and machine learning, are effective in ensuring product quality

Fig. 6.2 Application of AI and robotics in fashion manufacturing

and consistency (Luce 2018). Collaborative robotics play a crucial role in fashion manufacturing, with applications such as pick-and-place operations, assembly, and logistics. There are various benefits of cobots in improving flexibility, efficiency, and worker safety in garment production facilities. The use of machine learning techniques can be made for demand forecasting in fashion retail. The various machine learning algorithms can be used in predicting sales trends and inventory requirements. There is potential to optimize supply chain management and inventory control in the fashion industry. Thus, there are various applications of AI and robotics in fashion manufacturing, and some of the applications are listed as follows.

6.3.1 Automated Operations and Assembly

Salahuddin and Lee (2022) provide an overview of advanced automated sewing systems, discussing technologies such as computer-controlled sewing machines, robotic sewing cells, and vision-guided sewing processes. They explore their applications in industries such as apparel manufacturing, automotive upholstery, and aerospace textiles, highlighting the benefits of automation in improving productivity, quality, and flexibility. Smith and Johnson focus on automated cutting systems;

this review examines various cutting technologies and their applications in industrial manufacturing processes. It discusses techniques such as laser cutting, waterjet cutting, and plasma cutting, evaluating their performance in terms of precision, speed, and cost-effectiveness. The article also addresses challenges and future directions in automated cutting technology.

Salahuddin and Lee (2022) provide insights into automated assembly systems, covering technologies such as robotic assembly cells, flexible assembly lines, and collaborative robots (cobots). They discuss their applications in industries such as electronics manufacturing, automotive assembly, and consumer goods production, examining factors such as productivity, reliability, and adaptability. Li and Zhang focus on vision-guided robotic assembly; this research article explores the integration of computer vision technology with robotic systems to improve assembly processes. It discusses techniques such as 3D object recognition, pose estimation, and motion planning, and evaluates their effectiveness in achieving accurate and efficient assembly tasks. The article also discusses challenges and future research directions in vision-guided robotic assembly. Park and Kim (2019) provide an overview of robot-assisted flexible manufacturing systems, examining their design principles, components, and applications. It discusses the integration of robots with CNC machines, conveyors, and other manufacturing equipment to create agile and adaptable production systems. The article also explores case studies and industrial examples of robot-assisted flexible manufacturing in various sectors. The technologies, applications, and advancements lead to automated sewing, cutting, and assembly processes.

6.3.2 AI-Driven Design Optimization

The application of artificial intelligence can optimise design processes for sustainable fashion manufacturing. AI-driven approaches for material selection, pattern optimization, and waste reduction have the potential to improve resource efficiency and environmental sustainability in the fashion industry (Salahuddin and Lee 2022). The AI applications can also simulate and evaluate fashion products. Technologies such as 3D modelling, simulation software, and virtual reality (VR) are effective in reducing time, cost, and environmental impact. AI-driven generative design techniques can also be applied in fashion. Generative design algorithms such as genetic algorithms, neural networks, and evolutionary may be used in generating innovative and optimized designs across various fashion product categories (Barkova 2020). The genetic algorithm can also be used in optimizing the re-design process in the reverse supply chain of fashion (Paras et al. 2023).

Virtual prototyping techniques are extensively used for apparel product development. 2D and 3D CAD (computer-aided design), virtual fitting simulations, and digital twins are being used to streamline the design process, sampling process, improving fit accuracy, and enhancing customer satisfaction (Giri et al. 2019). Luce (2018) investigates the use of AI-driven design optimization techniques in fashion retail. Approaches such as predictive analytics, recommendation systems, and personalized styling algorithms applications can be used in enhancing product assortment planning, inventory management, and customer engagement in the fashion industry. AI-driven design optimization and virtual prototyping in the fashion industry are improving design creativity, efficiency, and sustainability.

6.3.3 Robotics for Quality Control

The applications of robotics and automation technologies in textile and apparel industries may be efficiently used in quality control, predictive maintenance, and process optimization. The robotic systems may also be used for fabric inspection, defect detection, and sewing automation to improve product quality and production efficiency (Salahuddin and Lee 2022). The use of computer vision and machine learning techniques can be made for the development of automated inspection systems for fabric defects, seam quality, and garment finishing. Thus, effectiveness in ensuring product quality and consistency in the fashion industry can be achieved (Luce 2018). The use of robotics and IoT (Internet of Things) technologies can be made for predictive maintenance techniques in textile and apparel manufacturing. Approaches such as condition monitoring, failure prediction, and maintenance schedules can be used to reduce downtime, extend equipment lifespan, and optimise maintenance costs (Barkova 2020).

Giri et al. (2019) also examine the application of robotics and artificial intelligence in the textile industry, including quality control and predictive maintenance. They discuss robotic systems for fabric inspection, yarn handling, and sewing automation, as well as AI-driven approaches for defect detection, anomaly detection, and predictive maintenance, highlighting their potential to enhance productivity and competitiveness in textile manufacturing. Park and Kim (2019) provide insights into recent advances in robotics and automation technologies in fashion manufacturing. They discuss robotic systems for quality control, defect detection, and predictive maintenance, as well as emerging trends such as collaborative robots and AI-driven automation, offering a comprehensive overview of the state-of-the-art in robotic applications in the fashion industry. The use of robotics for quality control and predictive maintenance in fashion manufacturing may enhance product quality, production efficiency, and equipment reliability.

6.4 Applications in Fashion Supply Chain

The integration of artificial intelligence (AI) and robotics in the fashion supply chain is transforming traditional practices and enhancing efficiency through innovation. AI algorithms analyse vast amounts of data, including consumer preferences, market trends, and inventory levels, to optimize various aspects of the supply chain. Predictive analytics enable accurate demand forecasting that helps retailers and manufacturers to anticipate customer needs and align production accordingly. Thus, reducing excess inventory and minimizing stockouts. Robotics streamline warehouse operations through automated picking, packing, and sorting processes. Hence, this will help in increasing productivity and order accuracy along with reducing labor costs and fulfilment times.

Collaborative robots (cobots) work alongside human workers in distribution centres to enhance efficiency and flexibility in handling tasks such as order fulfilment and inventory management. AI-powered supply chain visibility solutions provide real-time insights into inventory movements, shipment tracking, and production status, thus enabling better decision-making and proactive risk management. Companies can achieve greater agility, responsiveness, and sustainability by leveraging the power of AI and robotics in the fashion supply chain, ultimately delivering superior products and experiences to customers along with optimizing operational costs and resources. Figure 6.3 demonstrates the application of robotics technology in fashion supply chain.

Fig. 6.3 Application of robotics in fashion supply chain

Chen and Ngai provide insights into the application of artificial intelligence in fashion retailing, including its role in supply chain management. They discuss AI-driven approaches such as demand forecasting, inventory optimization, and personalized recommendation systems, highlighting their potential to enhance efficiency and customer satisfaction in the fashion supply chain. Barkova (2020) examines their applications in fashion supply chain management. His study discusses robotic systems for warehouse automation, order fulfilment, and logistics optimization, and evaluates their impact on operational efficiency, cost reduction, and customer service improvement in the fashion industry. The AI techniques such as machine learning, natural language processing, and computer vision are being used for demand forecasting, inventory management, and production planning (Luce 2018).

The robotics applications are effectively used for fashion logistics. The robotic systems can be exploited for order picking, sorting, and transportation in warehouses and distribution centres. This has a positive impact on order fulfilment speed, accuracy, and cost-effectiveness in the fashion supply chain (Barkova 2020). The integration of AI and robotics can also be used in fashion supply chain management. AI-driven approaches can be used for demand forecasting, inventory optimization, and logistics planning, whereas robotic systems for warehouse automation, order fulfilment, and last-mile delivery. The synergistic effects of AI and robotics can be used to enhance supply chain efficiency and responsiveness (Salahuddin and Lee 2022). The applications of AI and robotics in the fashion supply chain lead to operational efficiency, customer satisfaction, and competitiveness in the fashion industry as follows:

6.4.1 AI-Driven Demand Forecasting

In the fast-paced and ever-evolving fashion industry, AI-driven demand forecasting and inventory optimization have become indispensable tools for retailers and manufacturers alike. By harnessing the power of advanced machine learning algorithms and data analytics, AI systems can analyse vast amounts of historical sales data, market trends, and customer behaviour patterns to generate highly accurate demand forecasts. These forecasts take into account various factors such as seasonality, fashion trends, and promotional activities, enabling fashion companies to anticipate shifts in consumer demand and adjust their inventory levels accordingly. Additionally, AI-driven demand forecasting allows businesses to optimize their production schedules, procurement strategies, and supply chain logistics, resulting in reduced inventory holding costs and minimized stockouts. Furthermore, AI plays a crucial role in inventory optimization by dynamically adjusting stock levels based on real-time demand signals, ensuring that fashion companies can meet customer demand while minimizing excess inventory and markdowns. Overall, AI-driven demand forecasting and inventory optimization empower fashion businesses to make data-driven decisions, improve operational efficiency, and enhance customer satisfaction in today's competitive market landscape.

Demand forecasting and inventory optimization in fashion retail can be optimized with the application of AI and machine learning techniques. The demand forecasting and inventory optimization models may also improve operational efficiency and customer service in the fashion industry. The implementation of AI-driven demand forecasting is extensively used in fashion retail. The adoption of machine learning algorithms, data analytics techniques, and real-time data integration improves forecast accuracy, optimizes inventory levels, and enhances supply chain efficiency (Salahuddin and Lee 2022). The application of machine learning techniques for inventory management is widely used in fashion retail. The demand forecasting models and inventory optimization strategies have a positive impact on reducing stockouts, overstock, and inventory holding costs in the fashion supply chain (Luce 2018).

AI-driven inventory optimization in fashion supply chain management uses machine learning algorithms for demand forecasting, inventory replenishment, and order allocation, and evaluates their effectiveness in improving operational efficiency and reducing costs (LeCun et al. 2015). Giri et al. (2019) also explores the applications of artificial intelligence in fashion supply chain management for demand forecasting and inventory optimization. AI techniques such as machine learning, deep learning, and natural language processing are being exploited to improve supply chain performance and customer satisfaction in the fashion industry. AI-driven demand forecasting and inventory optimization in the fashion industry may benefit by improving supply chain efficiency, reducing costs, and enhancing customer satisfaction.

6.4.2 Robotics for Warehouse Automation

In the dynamic and rapidly evolving landscape of the fashion industry, robotics plays a pivotal role in optimizing warehouse operations, streamlining order fulfilment processes, and enhancing logistics efficiency. Robotics solutions for warehouse automation enable fashion companies to handle the complexities of modern supply chains with precision and agility. Automated guided vehicles (AGVs) and autonomous mobile robots (AMRs) navigate warehouse floors to transport goods efficiently, reducing manual labour and improving order accuracy. Robotic arms equipped with advanced vision systems are deployed for tasks such as picking, packing, and sorting, enabling faster order processing and reducing fulfilment times. Collaborative robots (cobots) work alongside human operators to handle tasks such as garment folding and packaging. Moreover, robotics technologies are utilized for logistics optimization, enabling real-time tracking and monitoring of inventory, shipments, and delivery routes. For order fulfilment and logistics optimization, fashion companies can achieve higher operational efficiency, and reduce costs, by using robotics for warehouse automation. This will meet the growing demands of consumers in an increasingly competitive market landscape.

The role of robotics and automation technologies in fashion supply chain management is significant. The robotic systems for warehouse automation, order fulfilment, and logistics optimization positively impact operational efficiency and customer service in the fashion industry (Barkova 2020). Robots are also implemented for warehouse automation technologies in a fashion retail and supply chain. The adoption of robotic systems for order picking, packing, and sorting enhances effectiveness in improving order accuracy, reducing fulfilment times, and enhancing customer satisfaction (Salahuddin and Lee 2022).

The robotic solutions have the potential to improve the efficiency and accuracy of fashion warehouses. The robotic picking systems, automated storage and retrieval systems, and autonomous mobile robot applications are optimizing order processing and reducing labour costs (Barkova 2020). Luce (2018) provides an overview of robotics applications for logistics optimization in fashion retail. The robotic solutions for inventory management, warehouse layout optimization, and last-mile delivery have an impact on reducing lead times, improving inventory accuracy, and enhancing supply chain visibility. Park and Kim (2019) also investigate the implementation of collaborative robotics in fashion warehousing operations. The deployment of cobots for tasks such as garment handling, inventory counting, and order consolidation is improving operational flexibility and worker productivity. The application of robotics for warehouse automation, order fulfilment, and logistics optimization in the fashion industry can improve supply chain efficiency and customer service.

6.4.3 Blockchain-Enabled Transparency

Blockchain technology has emerged as a game-changer in the fashion industry. This offers unprecedented levels of traceability and transparency throughout the supply chain. Fashion companies can establish immutable records of each stage in the production process, from sourcing raw materials to delivering finished products by leveraging blockchain-enabled platforms. This technology allows for the creation of transparent and tamper-proof records that are accessible to all stakeholders, thus ensuring authenticity and ethical sourcing practices. Consumers can verify the origin of materials, authenticate product provenance, and track the environmental and social impact of their purchases in real-time. Blockchain enables fashion brands to build trust with consumers and drive demand for ethically produced and sustainable products. Blockchain-enabled traceability helps to solve the problem of counterfeit goods to safeguard brand integrity and consumer confidence. Blockchain technology has the potential to revolutionize the fashion industry by fostering greater accountability, sustainability, and trust across the entire supply chain.

There are numerous advantages of implementing blockchain technology for sustainable supply chain management in the fashion industry. The potential benefits of blockchain-enabled traceability and transparency in promoting ethical sourcing, reducing counterfeiting, and enhancing sustainability practices cannot be ignored (Jin and Shin 2021). Recently, the applications of blockchain technology have increased in the fashion industry. The use of blockchain for product authentication, supply chain traceability, and transparent marketing has the potential to enhance consumer trust and brand integrity (Salahuddin and Lee 2022). Blockchain enables traceability in fashion supply chains. Blockchain applications for product provenance tracking, anti-counterfeiting measures, and ethical sourcing verification have enhanced supply chain transparency and sustainability (Luce 2018).

Salahuddin and Lee (2022) examine the implementation of blockchain-based traceability in fashion retail. The adoption of blockchain technology for product authentication, supply chain transparency, and consumer engagement is also enhancing brand trust and customer loyalty. Barkova (2020) presents case studies on enhancing supply chain transparency in the fashion industry using blockchain technology. The implementation of blockchain-enabled traceability solutions for materials sourcing and production tracking is improving supply chain visibility and sustainability. The blockchain-enabled traceability and transparency in the fashion industry have potential benefits for promoting ethical sourcing, reducing counterfeiting, and enhancing sustainability practices.

6.5 Limitation

Artificial intelligence (AI), robotics and the integration of artificial intelligence (AI) and robotics in fashion manufacturing and supply chain management have the potential to revolutionize the industry. These technologies can help to enhance efficiency, precision, and innovation in the processes. Despite various benefits, several significant limitations demotivate the application of technologies (Mohiuddin Babu et al. 2022). These limitations can be categorized into technological, organizational, economic, societal, and regulatory challenges that must be addressed to fully exploit the benefits of AI and robotics in the fashion industry.

6.5.1 Technological Limitations

The availability and quality of data is one of the main technological challenges. The vast amounts of high-quality data are one of the prerequisites for the AI system to work effectively. The data are mostly fragmented, inconsistent, or incomplete, posing significant barriers to AI implementation in the fashion industry. This is mainly because the number of production processes and stages in the supply chain of fashion are relatively high in comparison to the other industry. Thus, collecting accurate data across various stages (from raw material procurement to final product delivery) of the supply chain is difficult (Dash et al. 2019). This lack of reliable data can severely limit the performance and accuracy of AI models.

The complexity of AI models presents another technological challenge. Advanced AI techniques require substantial computational resources and specialized expertise to develop, implement, and maintain. These models are often difficult to interpret, making it challenging for stakeholders to understand and trust the AI-generated insights. This complexity can impede the broader adoption of AI technologies, especially in an industry where transparency and trust are crucial.

Integrating AI and robotics with existing traditional systems in fashion manufacturing also poses significant difficulties. Many current manufacturing processes and supply chain operations are not designed to accommodate advanced AI and robotic technologies. This necessitates substantial modifications and updates to existing systems, which can be both technically challenging and costly. The integration process can disrupt ongoing operations, leading to downtime and productivity losses.

6.5.2 Organizational Limitations

The skill gap and training requirements for organizations hold another barrier. The successful implementation of AI and robotics requires a workforce with knowledge of technology such as data science, machine learning, robotics, and related fields. There is often shortage of such specialized skills within the fashion industry. Bridging this skill gap necessitates substantial investment in training and upskilling existing employees or hiring new talent which will be time-consuming and expensive (Luce 2018).

Change management also emerges as a critical organizational challenge. Resistance to change from employees and management can be another reason for the non-adoption of AI and robotics. This resistance is due to fears of job loss, disruption of established workflows, and non-clarity about the benefits of new technologies. Overcoming these resistances requires effective change management strategies that include clear communication of the benefits. There should be adequate support and training for the employee of the organizations.

6.5.3 Economic Limitations

The implementation of AI and robotics needs high initial investment costs. Thus acquisition of AI and robotic technologies involves substantial financial expenditure that could be expensive for small and medium-sized enterprises (SMEs). These expenditures include the costs of hardware, software, infrastructure, and training. The return on investment (ROI) for AI and robotics projects may not be immediately apparent hence making it difficult to justify the expenditure (Mohiuddin Babu et al. 2022).

Additionally, the ongoing maintenance costs of AI and robotics systems are another economic burden. These systems require continuous maintenance, updates, and support to function effectively. Unexpected technical bugs or system failures may also require the involvement of financial resources of companies. The long-term economic implications of these ongoing costs may be significant for smaller companies with limited budgets.

6.5.4 Societal Limitations

The impact of AI and robotics on employment is a major concern. The automation of tasks traditionally performed by humans can lead to job loss which leads to unemployment. In the fashion industry, many jobs involve manual labour. The shift towards automation can have profound social and economic consequences. Addressing these impacts requires comprehensive strategies for workforce retraining and reskilling (Luce 2018).

Ethical and privacy concerns also arise with the use of AI in fashion supply chains. The collection and analysis of large amounts of data raise significant privacy issues regarding the protection of sensitive information. Ethical considerations related to AI decision-making processes (such as bias and fairness) need to be addressed to ensure that AI systems are transparent and equitable. Failing to address these ethical and privacy concerns can lead to loss of trust in AI technologies and hinder their adoption.

6.5.5 Regulatory and Compliance Issues

Regulatory and compliance issues present other significant challenges. Ensuring that AI and robotics systems comply with relevant industry regulations and standards can be complicated and time-consuming. The fashion industry operates globally and has different regulations and standards across different regions. Navigating this regulatory landscape requires significant effort and resources. Legal and liability issues related to the deployment of AI and robotics need to be clearly addressed to mitigate risks and ensure accountability (Dash et al. 2019).

6.6 Conclusion

Recommendations for future research and industry practice. This research provides a comprehensive understanding of the application of AI and robotics in fashion manufacturing and supply chain operations. AI and robotics technologies are improving efficiency, agility, and sustainability. However, cost, complexity, ethical implications, and technical limitations are the main challenges for the implementation of technology. Predictive analytics, collaborative robotics, and AI-enabled customization are some of the emerging applications of AI and robotics in the fashion industry. While AI and robotics offer substantial potential to transform fashion manufacturing and supply chain management, various critical limitations may slow down their widespread adoption. Addressing these technological, organizational, economic, societal, and regulatory challenges is important for unlocking the full benefits of these advanced technologies. The fashion industry can better leverage AI and robotics to drive innovation, efficiency, and sustainability. In the future, research can be undertaken to address challenges and advance AI and robotics in fashion manufacturing and supply chain.

References

Barkova NY (2020) Application of robotic technology in the fashion industry. Vestnik universiteta 2:85–91

Dash R, McMurtrey M Rebman C, Kar UK (2019) Application of artificial intelligence in automation of supply chain management. J Strateg Innovation Sustain 14(3)

Davenport TH (2018) The AI advantage: how to put the artificial intelligence. MIT Press

Domingos P (2012) A few useful things to know about machine learning. Commun ACM 55(10):78–87

Giri C, Jain S, Zeng X, Bruniaux P (2019) A detailed review of artificial intelligence applied in the fashion and apparel industry. IEEE Access 7:95376–95396

Hofmann KH, Jacob A, Pizzingrilli M (2022) Overcoming growth challenges of sustainable ventures in the fashion industry: a multinational exploration. Sustainability 14(16):10275

Jin BE, Shin DC (2021) The power of 4th industrial revolution in the fashion industry: what, why, and how has the industry changed? Fashion Text 8(1):31

Jiménez Schlegl P, Čubrić G (2018) Robots in the textile and fashion industries: facts and prospectives. https://digital.csic.es/handle/10261/180026. Accessed on 20 June 2014

John EP, Mishra U (2023) A sustainable three-layer circular economic model with controllable waste, emission, and wastewater from the textile and fashion industry. J Cleaner Production 388:135642

Krizhevsky A, Sutskever I, Hinton GE (2012) Imagenet classification with deep convolutional neural networks. Adv Neural Inf Proc Syst 25

LeCun Y, Bengio Y, Hinton G (2015) Deep learning. Nature 521(7553):436–444. https://doi.org/10.1038/nature14539

Luce L (2018) Artificial intelligence for fashion: how AI is revolutionizing the fashion industry. Apress

Mohiuddin Babu M, Akter S, Rahman M, Billah MM, Hack-Polay D (2022) The role of artificial intelligence in shaping the future of Agile fashion industry. Prod Plann Control 33(6):490–506

Nayak R, Panwar T, Nguyen LVT (2020) Sustainability in fashion and textiles: a survey from developing country. Sustain Technol Fashion Text 1(1):3–30

Park J, Kim Y (2019) Robot-assisted flexible manufacturing systems: a review. Robot Comp-Integr Manuf

Paras MK, Wang L, Pal R, Ekwall D (2023) A sustainable model based on genetic algorithm for garment redesign process. J Fashion Mark Manage Int J 27(5):870–887

Paschen J, Kietzmann J, Kietzmann TC (2019) Artificial intelligence (AI) and its implications for market knowledge in B2B marketing. J Bus Ind Mark 34(7):1410–1419

Salahuddin M, Lee YA (2022) Automation with robotics in garment manufacturing. Leading edge technologies in fashion innovation: product design and development process from materials to the end products to consumers. Springer International Publishing, Cham, pp 75–94

Szeliski R (2010) Computer vision: algorithms and applications. Springer

Vaswani A et al. (2017) Attention is all you need. Adv Neural Inf Proc Syst 30:5998–6008

Chapter 7
The Advancement of Computer-Aided Design and Computer-Aided Manufacturing in the Fashion Apparel Industry: Toward a Sustainable Development

Loan Thi Cam Bui, Hang Thi Thu Nguyen, Luu Thanh Do, Thuc Van Huynh, Thang Duc Ta, and An Thi Binh Duong

Abstract The fashion apparel business has a transient nature regarding product lifecycles, which requires the adoption of adaptable production cycles to accommodate the constantly evolving customer preferences. The labour-intensive production and escalating sustainability concerns catalyse industrial advancements. The industrial landscape is undergoing significant transformations due to the implementation of industrial 4.0 technologies, specifically computer-aided design (CAD) and computer-aided manufacturing (CAM). CAD software facilitates the fabrication of intricate digital garment models, augmenting fashion designers' capabilities. The

---

L. T. C. Bui · T. V. Huynh
Faculty of Garment Technology and Fashion Design, Industrial University of Ho Chi Minh City, Ho Chi Minh City, Vietnam
e-mail: buithicamloan@iuh.edu.vn

T. V. Huynh
e-mail: huynhvanthuc@iuh.edu.vn

H. T. T. Nguyen
School of Industrial Management, Ho Chi Minh City University of Technology, Ho Chi Minh City, Vietnam
e-mail: ntthang@hcmut.edu.vn

L. T. Do
Faculty of Business Administration, Van Lang University, Ho Chi Minh City, Vietnam
e-mail: luu.dt@vlu.edu.vn

T. D. Ta
The Business School, RMIT International University, Ho Chi Minh City, Vietnam
e-mail: s3926783@rmit.edu.vn

A. T. B. Duong (✉)
CIRTech Institute, HUTECH University, 475 Dien Bien Phu, Binh Thanh, Ho Chi Minh City, Vietnam
e-mail: dtb.an@hutech.edu.vn

R. Nayak et al. (eds.), *Use of Digital and Advanced Technologies in the Fashion Supply Chain*, Springer Series in Fashion Business,
https://doi.org/10.1007/978-981-97-7528-6_7

capacity to swiftly produce prototypes enables the investigation and execution of inventive concepts. Consequently, the design process becomes more efficient, leading to faster product launches. Moreover, CAD effectively incorporates CAM technologies, automating cutting and sewing operations. This serves to reduce errors and enhance manufacturing efficiency. The convergence of CAD and CAM technologies is fostering a more sustainable approach to apparel production. Firstly, CAD-CAM optimises material utilisation by enabling precise digital garment creation. This reduces fabric waste generated during the cutting process. Secondly, by automating production processes and minimising human error, CAD-CAM decreases overall production waste. Hence, the collective impact of these factors reduces the ecological impact in the context of garment production. Nevertheless, deploying CAD-CAM systems presents several challenges. One notable obstacle is the substantial initial capital commitment necessary for the acquisition of software, hardware, and complete people training initiatives. Additionally, the effective operation of these systems requires specialised knowledge, potentially aggravating pre-existing skill deficiencies within the business. Finally, ensuring seamless integration between CAD-CAM software suites is crucial to avoid data disruptions and workflow inefficiencies. Remarkably, CAD-CAM technologies are transforming fashion apparel manufacturing by increasing efficiency, elevating product quality, and fostering a more sustainable production method. As the industry embraces these groundbreaking advancements, finding a vital equilibrium between automation and the invaluable worth of human innovation is paramount.

Keywords Fashion apparel · CAD-CAM · Industry 4.0 · Automation · Advanced technologies · Sustainability

7.1 Introduction

The development of advanced technologies and Industrial 4.0 has drastically changed the production process of many industries following the trend of automation. Factories have become more flexible than ever in adapting to the complex and turbulent modern market (Hozdić 2015). The fashion apparel supply chain is characterised by short product life cycles, high volatility, and low predictability of the demand market, linked to market trends (Christopher et al. 2004). Besides, fashion apparel manufacturing is also labour-intensive (Gereffi and Frederick 2010; Nayak and Padhye 2018a). The process of producing fashion and apparel products has to be carried out in many stages in different countries, and the lead time from the concept design stage until the goods are on the shelf is at least 45 days; some orders can take from 3 to 4 months (Gereffi and Frederick 2010; Frederick 2010). The pressure of high requirements on garment quality and increased consumer awareness has led to the use of automated tools and equipment during garment manufacturing in recent years. Furthermore, the remarkable progress of technologies artificial intelligence (AI) in various fields in recent times presses the application of AI in all the stages of garment manufacturing, such as preproduction, production, and postproduction, involves processes such as conceptualisation, design development, PPC (production planning and control), spreading, cutting, bundling, sewing, pressing, and packaging (Nayak and Padhye 2018b). Applying innovative design, development, and production technology will reduce sample development time and shorten production time to bring products to market as quickly as possible. Another facet of applying innovative technologies in the fashion apparel industry is the sustainable development trend because the fashion apparel industry has been criticised for being one of the most polluting industries in the world (Nagurney and Yu 2012; Peleg Mizrachi and Tal 2022; Hofmann et al. 2022). In fashion apparel manufacturing, AI can be applied in all the stages of pre-production, production, and postproduction. It involves processes such as conceptualisation, design development, production planning and control (PPC), spreading, cutting, bundling, sewing, pressing, and packaging (Mohiuddin Babu et al. 2022).

This chapter focuses on the use of advanced technologies such as CAD-CAM in the development of fashion apparel products and in the process of production.

7.2 The Advanced CAD in the Design and Development of Fashion Apparel Products

Technology innovation is a key player in the product design and development process in the current digital transformation age. In the textiles and fashion apparel sectors, product innovation occurs at three levels: materials, styles, and product development (Nayak and Padhye 2018b).

The fashion apparel market always faces high competition and the constant need to "refresh" product ranges due to fashion trends and seasons of the year. On segments of the Apparel Global Value Chain, R&D and design get the highest value upstream of the chain (Fig. 7.1) (Frederick 2010). Furthermore, the quick response approach and semi-planned production are driven by real-time data collected from directly operated retail channels. Not only was the fashion apparel industry, using data analytics and forecasting, able to break the traditional fashion cycle into 8 + collections per year, but it also incorporated design content developed by high-end fashion and presented months before their production into its products (Bhardwaj and Fairhurst 2010). So, fashion design plays an important role in the creation of new products by converting ideas into patterns and sketches that are used by manufacturers to make fashion garments (Gereffi and Memedovic 2003).

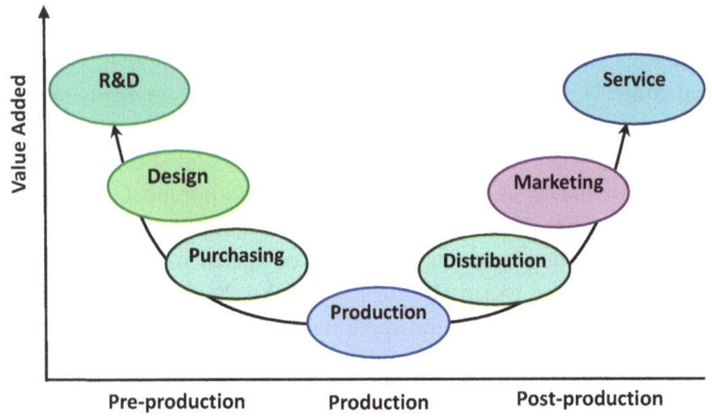

Fig. 7.1 Curve of value-added stages in the apparel global value chain. *Source* Gereffi and Frederick (2010)

7.2.1 The Use of 3D Scanner in Body Measurements

7.2.1.1 Techniques of 3D Body Scanner

In the fashion and apparel industry, measurements play a significant role in designing and producing mass-customised styles in retail stores to fix the majority of consumers. Traditionally, body dimensions may be measured using tools such as callipers and tape. The results are recorded on a paper measure. 3D body scanning is an advanced technology that can automatically extract the measurements of the body dimensions from the obtained data. That is a noncontact technique that captures the whole human body dimensions over 360 degrees. Then, appropriate software can convert these data into accurate body dimensions (Daanen et al. 2018; Bartol et al. 2021; Istook and Hwang 2001). Technologies used commercially for the digital measurement of the human body can be divided into five different groups (D'Apuzzo 2007):

(a) Laser scanning,
(b) Projection of white light patterns,
(c) Combination modelling and image processing,
(d) Digital manual measurement,
(e) Technologies based on other active sensors.

At present, the three most common 3D scanning technologies that are used for body measurement are passive stereo, structured light, and time-of-flight. Each technology has its own advantages and disadvantages for body measurement (Bartol et al. 2021):

Table 7.1 Compare the three 3D scanning technologies as mentioned above

Technology	Accuracy	Sensitivity to lighting	Difficulty with occluded objects	Cost
Passive stereo	Relatively inexpensive and accurate	Sensitive to changes in lighting	Can have difficulty with occluded objects	Relatively inexpensive
Structured Light	More accurate than passive stereo	Less sensitive to changes in lighting	Can have difficulty with shiny or reflective objects	More expensive
Time-of-flight	Very accurate	Not sensitive to changes in lighting	Can work with a variety of objects	More expensive

Source Bartol et al. (2021)

- Passive stereo uses two cameras to capture a scene from slightly different angles. The difference in the images from the two cameras is then used to calculate the depth of each point in the scene. This technology is relatively inexpensive and accurate, but it can be sensitive to changes in lighting and can have difficulty with occluded objects.
- Structured light projects a pattern of light onto the object being scanned. The camera then captures the deformed pattern, which is used to calculate the depth of each point in the scene. This technology is more accurate than passive stereo and is less sensitive to changes in lighting, but it can be more expensive and can have difficulty with shiny or reflective objects.
- Time-of-flight measures the time it takes for a pulse of light to travel from the scanner to the object and back. The time difference is then used to calculate the distance to each point in the scene. This technology is fully accurate and can work with a variety of objects, but it can be more expensive than other technologies (Table 7.1).

7.2.1.2 Process of 3D Scanning

The process of body measurement can be described in five stages (Fig. 7.2): preparation, scanning, feature extraction, model fitting, and measurement extraction. The first two stages are the acquisition stages, and the latter three are the processing stages. In the acquisition stage, the subjects are prepared, and the data in the form of 3D point clouds, depth maps, or 2D images are obtained. There are two acquisition protocols—static and dynamic. In the processing stage, the collected input is used for body measurement. Body measurement can be done directly on the given inputs, but usually, the features are extracted first, and the body model is fitted based on these features or the inputs (Bartol et al. 2021).

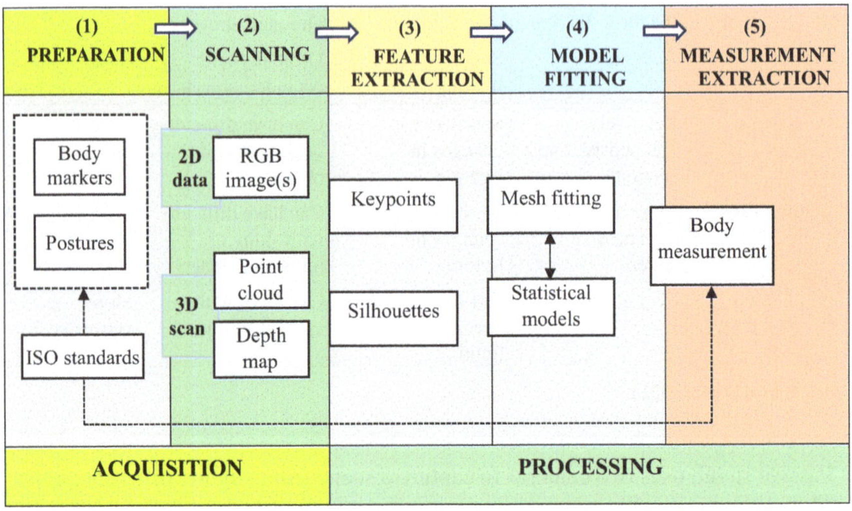

Fig. 7.2 The body measurement processing. *Source* Bartol et al. (2021)

7.2.1.3 Advantages and Disadvantages of 3D Scanning

The 3D body scanning system is not only a valuable tool for capturing and analysing body size and shape but also has a critical role in enabling retailers to rapidly collect 3D data on consumers to provide individualised and specified sizing. Besides, it serves to change the focus of the provision of fashion apparel products from mass production to mass customisation. In conjunction with advanced design, production processes and the integration of related software, body scanners will allow consumers to benefit from a modern form of custom tailoring. The relationship between body measurement and other factors changes with changing lifestyles, leisure patterns, dietary habits and growing population diversity. The result is that the association between garment sizes and body measurements also changes all the time. So, regular sizing surveys and measurement series have to be performed to provide a scientific foundation for these and to further provide information on the necessary size segments and their geographical market shares (Apeagyei 2010).

Advantages of 3D Scanning:

3D scanning offers several advantages over traditional methods of body measurement, including:

- Speed: 3D scanning can be completed much faster than manual measurement, which can be time-consuming and labour-intensive.
- Convenience: 3D scanning is a non-contact measurement technique, which means that it does not require the subject to be undressed or to remove any clothing or accessories.

- Accuracy: 3D scanning can provide highly accurate measurements of body dimensions, which can be important for applications such as garment design and medical diagnostics.
- Repeatability: 3D scans can be repeated with a high degree of repeatability, which is important for applications where accurate measurements are required over time.

Disadvantages of 3D Scanning:

3D scanning also has some disadvantages compared to traditional methods, including:

- Cost: 3D scanners can be expensive, which may limit their adoption in some applications.
- Complexity: 3D scanning data can be complex to process, which requires specialised software and expertise.
- Sensor limitations: The accuracy of 3D scans can be limited by the capabilities of the 3D scanner and the environment in which the scan is taken.

7.2.2 3D Virtual (3D Digital Simulation) in Development and Fitting Sample

7.2.2.1 Methods of 3D Virtual in Development and Fitting Clothing Sample

Competition in the global market pressures the fashion apparel industry to produce more collections in shorter lead times. This has led to the use of advanced technologies, such as 3D virtual technology, to support the process of developing new styles that are more popular (Liu et al. 2010; Kamal 2015). 3D virtual simulation systems allow fashion designers to simulate new styles of clothes and minimise the physical sampling (Choi 2022). The 3D dynamic fashion design is a digital fashion garment with transformable styles and animated colours or textile patterns that visibly change from the garments' underlying colours or patterns and even details to others and then return to the initial condition after a period of time. It is simulated and animated with 3D moving visualisations in a virtual space, and it demonstrates the potential of transformable digital expressions and aesthetics, as well as technologies programmed to this effect (Choi 2022). Normally, approaches to performing 3D virtual follow in two ways: from "3D to 2D" and "2D to 3D".

The process of creating a 3D virtual garment traditionally starts with the design of 2D patterns. These patterns are draped around a 3D human body and then assembled together, where garment simulation is used to generate the final 3D shape. The simulation of cloth is commonly based on physical models. Interactive garment modelling methods allow for instant 3D feedback in response to changes in garment patterns using a real-time physics-based simulation (Umetani et al. 2011). The basic design process can be shown as a conceptual idea: 2D sketch—2D pattern—3D toile—design/pattern alteration—sample (McQuillan 2020). However, the process of creating a 3D garment from 2D patterns is time-consuming, and several iterations are needed until the designer is satisfied with the results. Using this approach requires tailoring skills and experience to tune the parameters in the physical simulation (Zhang et al. 2018).

Sketch-based design methods provide an improved process of 3D garment design, which automatically creates a 3D garment model from user-sketched 2D silhouettes of the garment. Through 2D sketches, a feature template for creating a 3D garment is defined based on the features of a human model and the profiles of the 3D garment (Wang et al. 2003; Decaudin et al. 2006; Robson et al. 2011). Turquin et al. (2007) have combined tailoring, dressing, and physical plausibility into a single step to create a visually pleasing mesh suitable for later complex simulation or skinning approaches (Turquin et al. 2007). This technique allows the users to sketch garment contours directly onto a 3D human model; then, a 3D garment surface is generated by computing the distance field around the human body (Zhang et al. 2018). Based on the sketching system, Decaudin et al. (2006) drew the contour and seam lines on the garment surface and modified the sketched surface to make it piecewise developable, then unfolded 3D panels into 2D patterns (Decaudin et al. 2006). Bartle et al. (2016) proposed a physics-driven pattern adjustment method for 3-D garment editing, which allows designers to directly apply the changes in 3D space and create the 2D patterns that replicate this envisioned target geometry when lifted into 3D via a physical draping simulation. This method has reduced the laborious and knowledge-intensive manual 2D edits and allows users to effortlessly mix existing garment designs as well as adjust for garment length and fit by using a physical draping simulation (Bartle et al. 2016).

Some integrated methods, such as Fang et al. (2008), have proposed a clothing design process which covers both the "3D to 2D" and "2D to 3D" approaches. They demonstrated not only the creation of 3D upper body garment designs on a virtual mannequin made from body scan data but also illustrated the 2D flattening of patterns from 3D designs and the visualisation of virtual outerwear clothing with different textures, but without considering the material properties (Fang and Ding 2008; Fang et al. 2008). The research of Zhang et al. (2018) has proposed a technique that is able to design 3D garments and 2D patterns efficiently and accurately in four steps: 3D modelling, pattern development, garment simulation, and grading. Firstly, by using editable control curves, a sketch-based modelling method is proposed to design a 3D garment. Secondly, 2D patterns are developed by flattening 3D surface patches; a nice 3D garment is formed directly based on the information of sewing relations and correspondence between 3D surfaces and 2D patterns. Lastly, garment templates are introduced to realise the automatic design-preserving transfer of garments between human bodies with different sizes and shapes (Zhang et al. 2018). Liu et al. (2019) suggested a body-dimension-based associate design method to integrate fashion sketch drawing and pattern making in three stages. First, the dimensions of fashion sketches were accorded so that fashion sketches and their corresponding patterns could be associated with human body dimensions. Then, in the height and width directions, mathematical models were constructed considering fashion sketches, their corresponding patterns and human body dimensions. Finally, a software application based on the proposed method was developed to generate jean fashion sketches and their corresponding patterns rapidly and automatically. This indicates that the work of fashion designers and pattern makers will be integrated together with the help of associate designers in the future (Liu et al. 2019).

A key attribute of the development of digital 3D software for fashion has been accuracy and application as a replacement for at least part of the prototyping process. Most 3D software now allows for the pattern to be visualised in 3D, and its pattern exported for use in production. The advantages are seen in various ways in the fashion apparel industry (McQuillan 2020).

The advantages of 3D simulation, as mentioned above, show that technology innovation plays an important role in the product design and development process in the current digital transformation. Nowadays, numerous companies have already turned to 3D virtualisation of products to reduce the time and cost of product design and development and to minimise the physical sampling (Lee 2022). Meanwhile, the digital design process, using 3D virtual simulation systems, can transform the traditional process from 2D drawing to repeated modifications of 2D pattern making and 3D toiling simply into iterative interplays between 2D patterns and 3D simulations within the 3D software in a more sustainable way (McQuillan 2020).

7.2.2.2 Methods to Evaluate Fitting Sample

In the whole process, from fashion design to manufacturing and sales of fashion apparel products, garment fit evaluation is one of the biggest bottlenecks for this industry. In the design stage, designers and pattern makers have to evaluate garment fit for garment product optimisation. In the process of garment manufacturing, designers need to check whether the garment fits (Liu et al. 2017a). In the retail segment, garment fit is the issue that consumers care about most. Currently, consumers tend to buy fashion garments online; due to the bottleneck, how to evaluate garment fit prevents the development of clothing e-business; makers need to evaluate garment fit for garment product optimisation (Kim and Damhorst 2010). For the above reasons, the development of garment fit prediction models is useful. Liu et al. (2017a, b) have proposed a naïve Bayes-based model to evaluate garment fit. The inputs of the proposed model are digital clothing pressures of different body parts generated from 3D garment CAD software, while the output is the predicted result of garment fit (fit or unfit). To construct and train the proposed model, data on digital clothing pressures and garment real fit were collected for input and output learning data, respectively. By learning from these data, the proposed model can predict garment fit rapidly and automatically without any real try-on; therefore, it can be applied to remote garment fit evaluation in the context of the e-shopping (Liu et al. 2017b). In addition, by using the decision tree C4.5 algorithm and based on a mathematical relationship model between clothing fit levels and indexes reflecting the clothing fit levels, Liu et al. (2023) have suggested intelligent, fit evaluation technology to predict clothing fit. After learning from the collected data, the proposed model can predict clothing fit accurately. Next, the proposed models have validated the prediction accuracy by using K-fold cross-validation. Finally, two applications of the proposed model for clothing product development and online shopping are presented. Results show that this method has high prediction accuracy and less requirement for the number of learning samples and can predict clothing fit automatically and rapidly without a real try-on (Liu et al. 2023).

These techniques and methods are useful when combined with CAD systems to strengthen designers' understanding of the demand and satisfy consumers.

7.2.3 Intelligent Apparel CAD Systems

Nowadays, various CAD software is used in the garment industry for patternmaking, digitising, grading, and marker planning for production. The CAD software supports achieving high productivity and improved quality (Nayak and Padhye 2018b) and is a factor in reducing lead time for preparing production. In using CAD systems, designing virtual garments may be accomplished by approaches such as "2D to 3D" and "3D to 2D". The first refers to draping flat digital pattern pieces on a virtual mannequin, and the second indicates the development of clothing design on a realistic body and subsequent flattening into 2D pattern pieces. Several CAD systems for fashion apparel visualisation in space from flat patterns have already been introduced into the fashion apparel industry since the 1990s (Liu et al. 2010). From then on, these applications were constantly upgraded and improved to integrate with AI technology.

7.2.3.1 Parametric Design

Parametric design is a new frontier emerging during CAD that has transformed the fashion industry by directly applying artificial intelligence design by using mathematical algorithms and user-defined parameters to generate garment designs (Jeong et al. 2021; Cheng and Cheng 2012). In the adoption of parametric, designers only set parameters like fabric properties, desired silhouette, and functional requirements on the application. The software then uses these parameters to automatically generate a multitude of potential designs, each with its own unique properties and variations. Parametric design can be a powerful tool for sustainable fashion by optimising material usage and minimising waste, allowing designers to create garments with a smaller environmental footprint (Jeong et al. 2021). For instance, Architectonics is a testament to the transformative power of parametric design in fashion, offering a glimpse into a future where technology and creativity seamlessly blend to redefine the possibilities of couture. Iris van Herpen is renowned for her avant-garde creations; she has integrated parametric design into her collections, creating garments that respond to light and movement (Iris van Herpen's 2023).

The Future of Parametric Design in Fashion: Parametric design is important for the future of fashion. As technology and software tools continue to evolve, we can expect to see:

- More user-friendly software: Making parametric design accessible to a wider range of designers will be crucial for wider adoption.
- Advanced material integration: Exploring how parametric design can work with new and innovative materials will enable even more creative possibilities.
- Closed-loop production systems: Integrating parametric design with 3D printing and advanced manufacturing could pave the way for a more sustainable and efficient fashion ecosystem.

While still in its early stages, parametric design is an exciting development that has the potential to revolutionise the fashion industry. It offers a glimpse into a future where creativity and technology collide, giving birth to fashion garments that are not just beautiful and functional but also unique, sustainable, and truly personalised.

7.2.3.2 Combination of Artificial Intelligence on CAD Systems

AI-integrated CAD (combining apparel CAD and graphic algorithm) can be used to explore apparel designs. For example, fashion brand Tommy Hilfiger developed a project named Reimagine Retail, where they made a strategic collaboration with IBM and The Fashion Institute of Technology (FIT) Infor Design. The primary objective of this collaboration is to develop a more customer-focused and modern design by capitalising on deep learning techniques. The tools were various images, which included 15,000 product images of the fashion retailer, 0.6 million publicly available images, and 0.1 million fabric patterns (Mohiuddin Babu et al. 2022). In addition, it is based on 3D digital simulation and a series of machine learning techniques, including radial basis function artificial neural network (RBF ANN), genetic algorithms (GA), probabilistic neural network (PNN), and support vector regression (SVR). Wang et al. have put forward a new design approach for customised garments towards sustainable fashion. The proposed approach can be applied to various classical 3D garment software, promoting the implementation level of garment e-MC for different fashion brand companies (Wang et al. 2023). The proposed design method, as well as the process for customised garments, is mainly supported by five design knowledge models:

1. Estimation Human Body Dimensions
2. Generation Model of Design Solution
3. Evaluation Model of Design Solution
4. Prediction Model of Garment Fitness
5. Adjustment Model of Design Solution.

It can generate and recommend the most relevant design solution for consumers. Meanwhile, the proposed associate adjustment mechanism for garment patterns can dramatically reduce the difficulties of garment pattern-making without reducing the quality of garment patterns. More importantly, it is also able to generate personalised garment production patterns that can effectively enhance the linkage of fashion design and garment manufacturing, which is quite critical in garment e-mass customisation (e-MC) towards sustainable fashion (Wang et al. 2023).

At present, product development in the fashion apparel industry has been assisted by various fashion design software, namely CLO3D, MarvelousDesigner, Browzwear (with V-stitcher, Lotta, Stylezone), Optitex, TUKA3D, Lectra (Modaris 3D), Style 3D, PatternMaker, etc. Some specific features of these applications:

- CLO 3D: This industry-standard software lets designers craft realistic 3D garments, complete with draping, textures, and even movement simulations. Imagine virtual fashion shows before a single stitch is sewn. Furthermore, CLO3D utilises AI algorithms to simulate the drape, flow, and behaviour of various fabrics accurately based on their real-world properties. This allows designers to see how their garments will move and behave on the body with incredible realism, saving time and resources compared to traditional trial-and-error methods (Huang and Huang 2022; Features 2023).
- VStitcher: This application seamlessly integrates with 3D body scanners, allowing for highly accurate virtual try-ons on individual avatars for personalised fit analysis and customisation. Another feature is material simulation advancements, which continuously refine material simulations, capturing the unique properties and behaviour of various fabrics with even greater accuracy. In addition, VStitcher™ utilises AI algorithms to predict fit based on body measurements and garment specifications, minimising the need for physical prototypes and fit adjustments (Vstitcher 2023).
- Marvellous Designer: This powerful tool focuses on creating realistic garment movement and draping. Think of clothes dancing across the screen, helping designers perfect flow and fit (Designer 2023).
- PatternMaker: This software uses AI to optimise pattern layouts, minimising fabric waste and ensuring efficient production. Think of a digital tailor expertly cutting the perfect pieces from your fabric (PatternMaker 2023).

7.2.3.3 Examples in 3D Virtual Development Sample by Using CLO3D

1. *From 2 to 3D*:

Steps to perform virtual sample from 2D to 3D

(1) Conceptual about a new style (Fig. 7.3a)
(2) Select the avatar and adjust the measurement alignment with a size that requires the concept (Fig. 7.3b).
(3) Design detailed 2D pattern components of the new style based on the measurement from sample size. This step can be performed directly on a 2D screen from CLO3D or by any 2D pattern design applications like Gerber Accumark, Lectra, Obitex, etc. (Fig. 7.4a).
(4) Drap pattern around the body (Fig. 7.4b)
(5) Assemble the sample (Fig. 7.5a) to finish the new style (Fig. 7.5b)

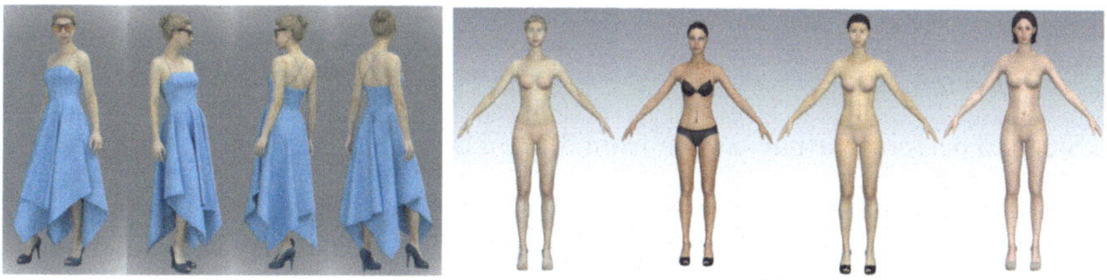

(a) (b)

Fig. 7.3 **a** Concept for a new garment style, and **b** selection of an avatar and adjustment of the measurement aligned with a size as per the concept

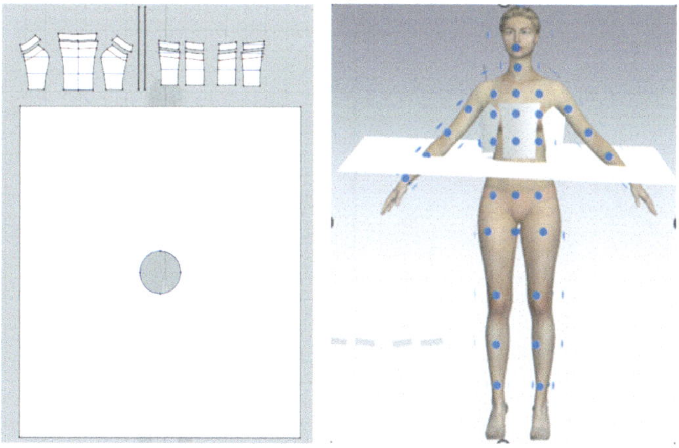

(a) (b)

Fig. 7.4 **a** Detailed 2D pattern components of the new style, **b** draped pattern around the body

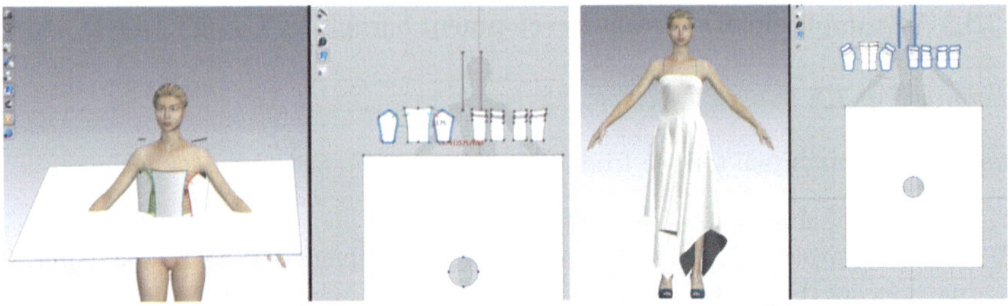

(a) (b)

Fig. 7.5 Assembling the sample, and **b** Final new style in an avatar

(6) Select fabric from the library following the new style requirement (composition, colour, decorations, etc.) (Fig. 7.6)
(7) Select the appropriate pose from the pose's library to fix the sample (Fig. 7.7).
(8) Choose accessories like shoes, glasses, belts, etc., or change the colour to finish the new sample (Fig. 7.8).

2. *From 3 to 2D*:

Steps to perform virtual sample from 3D to 2D

(1) Conceptual about a new style (Fig. 7.9)
(2) Select the avatar and adjust the measurement alignment with a size that requires the concept (like the second step from 2 to 3D, Fig. 7.3b).
(3) Design detailed components of the 2D pattern directly on the avatar of the CLO3D application for the top of the dress (Fig. 7.10a). In the 2D screen, all the pieces will appear (Fig. 7.10b).

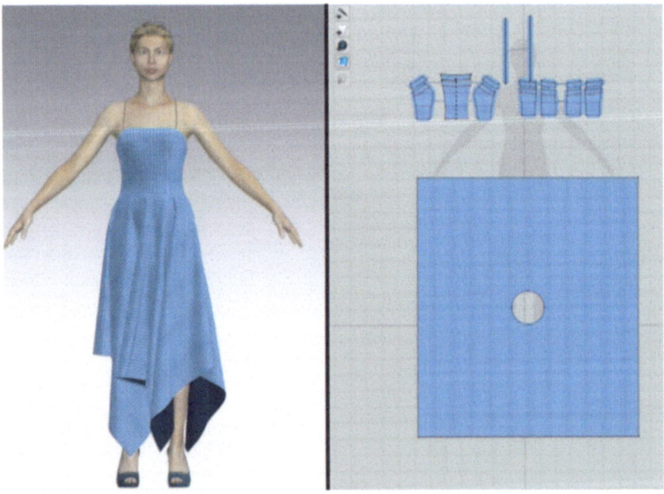

Fig. 7.6 Fabric selection from the library

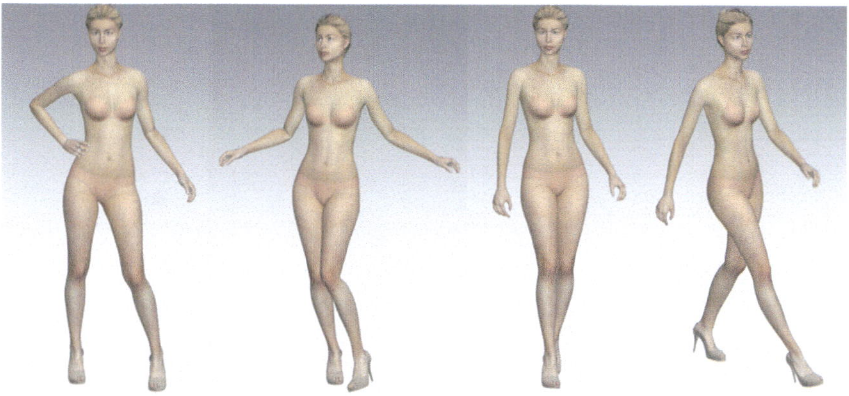

Fig. 7.7 Selection of the appropriate pose

Fig. 7.8 Selection of accessories

Fig. 7.9 Conceptualization of a new style

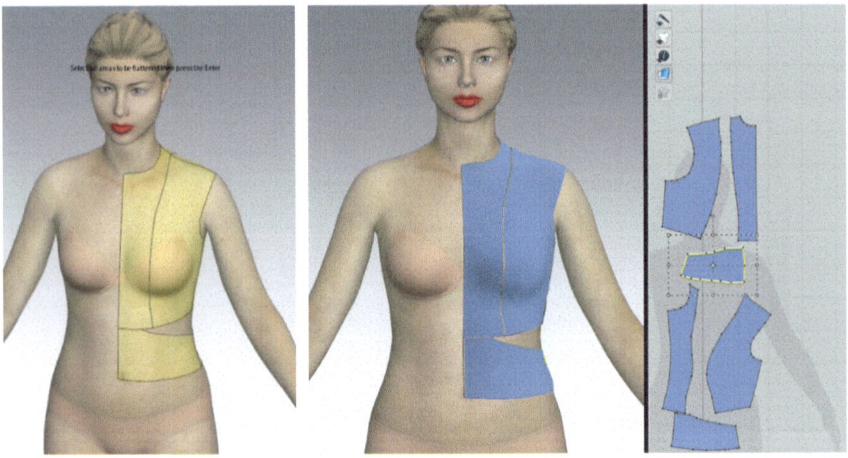

(a) (b)

Fig. 7.10 **a** Application of 2D pattern directly on the avatar of the CLO3D, **b** appearance of the pattern pieces in the 2D screen

For the bottom of the dress, the bottom of this style does not fit into the avatar; the pattern designers have to base on their experience to design this part on the 2D screen of the CLO3D application.

(4) Revise and add a seam to finish these pieces on the 2D screen (Fig. 7.11a).

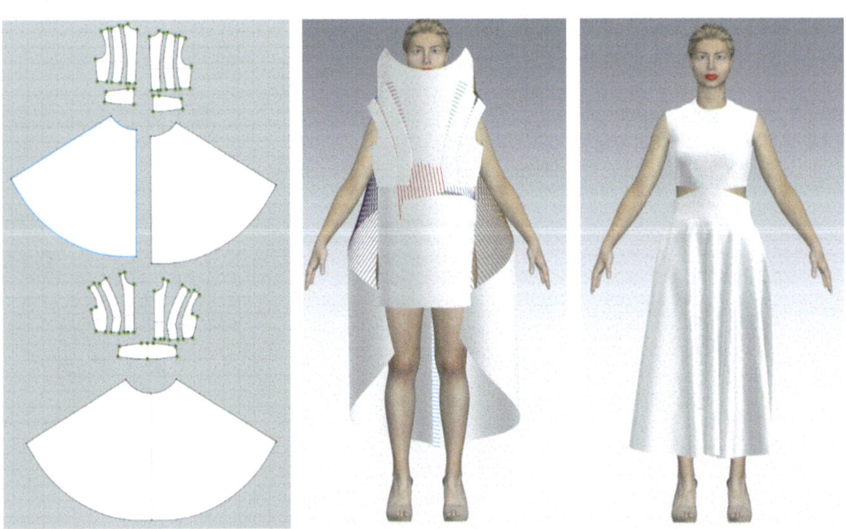

(a) (b) (c)

Fig. 7.11 **a** Revise and add a seam to finish these pieces on the 2D screen; **b** assemble the sample to make the new style, and **c** finishing the new style

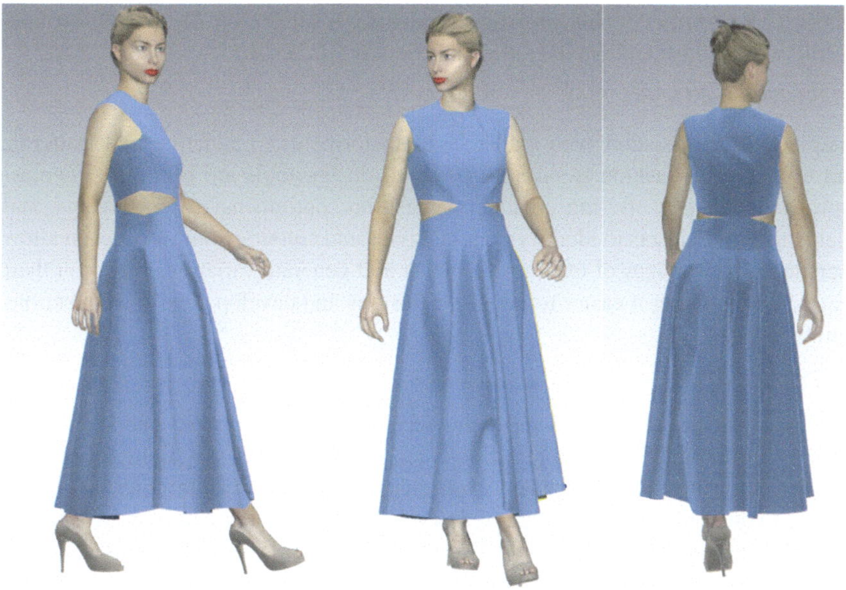

Fig. 7.12 Selection of the appropriate pose and accessories

(5) Assemble the sample (Fig. 7.11b) to finish the new style (Fig. 7.11c).
(6) Select the appropriate pose and choose accessories (like shoes, glasses, belts, etc.) or change the colour to finish the new style (Fig. 7.12).

7.2.3.4 The Future Trend in Design Fashion System

Fashion apparel design applications are undergoing a radical transformation propelled by advanced technologies. From AI-driven design tools to 3D virtual prototyping and sustainable materials, the industry is embracing innovation at a rapid pace. However, with these advancements come challenges of complex software, upskilling the workforce, and addressing ethical concerns in technology implementation. The quest for sustainability is a driving force, pushing designers to explore eco-friendly materials and circular design processes. Embracing these trends and overcoming associated challenges is pivotal for the fashion industry's evolution (Saul Maslavi and Forbes 2023).

1. *3D Design and Virtual Prototyping*:

At present, 3D design software allows designers to create realistic garments in a virtual environment, complete with draping, textures, and even simulations of movement. This enables them to visualise designs more accurately, experiment with different ideas faster, and identify potential fit issues before physical samples are even produced. Virtual prototyping takes things a step further, allowing designers to virtually "try on" their creations on digital models or even themselves through augmented reality (AR) headsets. This provides invaluable feedback on fit, proportion, and overall wearability (Goldstein et al. 2009; Baukh 2022).

2. *AI-Powered Design Tools*:

Imagine an AI assistant who can help brainstorm ideas, generate new patterns, and even predict fashion trends! AI-powered design tools are becoming increasingly sophisticated, offering creative suggestions, optimising pattern layouts, and analysing vast datasets to identify popular styles and colours. Some tools even allow users to upload images of existing garments and generate variations based on their preferences, making it easier to iterate on designs and develop cohesive collections (Smith 2022).

3. *Personalised Design and Customisation*:

Thanks to advanced technologies, the days of mass-produced, one-size-fits-all clothing are fading. Design applications incorporate features that allow for personalised sizing, fit adjustments, and even custom printing or embroidery. Imagine ordering a dress that's perfectly tailored to your body measurements or designing a T-shirt with your own unique artwork. This level of customisation is becoming increasingly accessible, empowering consumers to express their individuality through their clothing choices (Huang and Huang 2022).

4. *Sustainable Design and Material Sourcing*:

The fashion industry is facing growing pressure to become more eco-friendly. Design applications incorporate tools that help designers choose sustainable materials, track the environmental impact of their choices, and minimise waste throughout the production process (Fan and Chang 2023; Rissanen and McQuillan 2023).

7.3 Advanced CAM System in Fashion Apparel Manufacture

In fashion apparel manufacture, the major steps in garment manufacturing can be categorised into three groups such as (Nayak and Padhye 2015):

1. *Preproduction processes*, which cover product planning, sample development, designing, approvals, raw material sourcing (including steps selection and procurement of trims, threads, and accessories), preproduction meetings, and production scheduling. These preproduction processes ensure that garment manufacturing is performed on time so that the final garments are delivered within the lead time.
2. *Production processes* include fabric inspection, fabric spreading, cutting, bundling, and sewing. Fabrics are spread on flat tables and cut by tools such as knife cutters, laser cutters, or water-jet cutters. The cut components are separated, bundled and fixed with bundle tickets and moved to the sewing operation. Different workers perform a number of sewing operations to finish the garment.

3. *Postproduction processes* involve thread trimming, ressing, inspection, folding, packaging, and shipment. Once the garments are manufactured, loose threads are trimmed, garments are pressed and inspected for quality, and packed and transported to the retail stores by the manufacturer's own logistic network or any third-party logistic providers. The consumers purchase their favourite clothes from the retail stores.

Applying new technologies to the process of garment production contributes to a substantial increase in productivity and quality of work. Consequently, the apparel industry is being transformed from a traditional, labour-intensive industry into a highly automated and computer-aided industry (Nayak et al. 2018).

7.3.1 Automation in Inspection Fabric

Fabric is one of the most important factors affecting the cost and quality of apparel and fashion products. Therefore, inspection of the quality of fabric to detect, mark, classify, and evaluate defects to eliminate defective fabric parts before assembling to finish products helps to improve productivity. Testing is also important in order to control the manufacturing process and save costs. There are additional reasons, such as customer relations, reputation, employee satisfaction, and sales (Wong 2008; Hu 2008). During the process, each fabric roll is inspected carefully to identify faults in the fabric, which are inconsistencies in colour, irregularities in the print, defects in the yarn, stains, or any kind of damage in fabric construction. Fabric testing methods are classified by research and divided into seven main groups (Hanbay et al. 2016):

(1) ***Structural approaches***: Consider texture as a composition of textural primitives. Texture analysis is performed by obtaining the texture features and inferring their replacement rules. Structural texture analysis contains two sequential stages: detection of basic fabric textures and modelling of the overall fabric texture pattern.
(2) ***Statistical approaches***: use first-order statistics and second-order statistics to extract textural features in texture classification. Most of the methods used in this approach include a co-occurrence matrix, histogram features, auto-correlation function, and mathematical morphology approaches.
(3) ***Spectral approaches***: They intend primarily to remove the basics of image texture and then generalise the basics of this texture with the spatial layout rules. These approaches require a high degrce of periodicity. As subtitles of spectral approaches, the wavelet transform, Fourier transform, Gabor transform, and filtering methods are examined.
(4) ***Model-based approaches***: based on the construction of an image model. With the help of the built model, the identification of the texture, as well as texture synthesis, is carried out. This technique is suitable for fabric images which may have surface changes due to defects such as yarn breakage and needle breakage.

(5) ***Learning approaches***: use techniques such as neural networks, fuzzy systems, and support vector machines to learn complex non-linear input–output relationships.
(6) ***Hybrid approaches***: combine two or more techniques to carry out defect detection more effectively. The main objective here is to minimise the computational complexity and increase the rate of defect detection.
(7) ***Comparison studies***: compare different studies and offer the most suitable methods according to the type of fabric and defect among methods.

There are three main levels of technology available for fabric inspection: basic, intermediate, and advanced. Basic-level technology includes manual fabric inspection. This involves a human inspector visually inspecting the fabric for defects. This method is time-consuming and prone to errors, as it is difficult for a human inspector to spot all defects, especially in large batches of fabric. Intermediate-level technology includes semi-automatic fabric inspection machines. These machines use cameras to scan the fabric for defects. The images are then displayed on a screen for a human inspector to review. This method is faster and more accurate than manual inspection, but it is still prone to errors, as the human inspector may miss some defects. Advanced-level technology includes a fully automated fabric inspection system. These machines use cameras and artificial intelligence to automatically identify and classify defects (Hanbay et al. 2016; Ngan et al. 2011; Rahman 2021; Vilumsone-Nemes 2018). Fabric faults can also be determined during the automated spreading process in a manner similar to that of manual spreading processes. During this process, faults are identified visually by a spreading operator. Using a joystick and laser beam, the operator marks the fault and determines its position on a ply and also on the marker on the screen (Vilumsone-Nemes 2018; Automated and System-F 2023).

The work of inspectors is very tedious and consumes time and cost. To reduce the cost and time wastage, an automatic fabric inspection is required. The approach of automation inspection for recognising fabric defects in the textile industry helps minimise production costs and time, minimising production cost and time. The Fabric inspection system first acquires high-quality and vibration-free images of the fabric. Then, the acquired images are subjected to a defect segmentation algorithm. The output of the processed image is used as an input to the artificial neural network (ANN), which uses a backpropagation algorithm to calculate the weighted factors and generates the desired classification of defects as an output. The output of the processed image is used as an input to the artificial neural network (ANN), which uses a backpropagation algorithm to calculate the weighted factors and generates the desired classification of defects as an output (Nayak and Padhye 2018a, 2018b).

Here are some of the benefits of using advanced fabric inspection technology:

- *Increased accuracy:* Automated fabric inspection machines are more accurate than manual inspection, as they are less likely to miss defects.
- *Increased speed:* Automated fabric inspection machines can inspect fabric much faster than human inspectors, which can lead to significant productivity gains.

- *Reduced costs:* While automated fabric inspection machines are more expensive to purchase than manual inspection equipment, they can save money in the long run by reducing the number of defective garments produced.
- *Improved quality:* Automated fabric inspection machines can help to improve the quality of garments by identifying and correcting defects early on.

The best level of technology for fabric inspection depends on the specific needs of the garment manufacturer. For small manufacturers with limited budgets, manual inspection may be the only option. However, larger manufacturers with higher production volumes can benefit from investing in semi-automatic or fully automated fabric inspection machines. Overall, advanced fabric inspection technology offers a number of benefits for garment manufacturers. It can help to improve accuracy, speed, and quality while also reducing costs.

Recently, various automatic inspection systems have been delivered by manufacturing companies. The Shelton WebSpector high-speed inspection system uses artificial intelligence machine learning together with the state-of-the-art machine vision and optical hardware to achieve unparalleled defect detection in demanding applications, with deep learning techniques used to accurately deliver real-time classification and grading. This system is made up of 4 components that together deliver an automatic solution to achieve the ultimate inspection and small roll-making department that ensures maximum profit from each batch, virtually eliminates customer claims, and provides consistent data for process improvement (Shelton Vision: Visual Inspection Systems 2023). Suntech AI Automated Camera Inspection System-F can be applied to various kinds of fabric inspection machines. It is suitable for a wide range of fabrics, from tension-sensitive lycra fabrics to stable woven. The fabric will be detected with the camera inspection system, and fabric information will be recorded synchronously by the software and the computer, truly realising the 24-h unmanned testing (Suntech 2022) (Figs. 7.13 and 7.14).

Future trends in inspection fabric: Fabric defect detection is important for ensuring the quality and value of textile products, as well as reducing waste and cost. Fabric

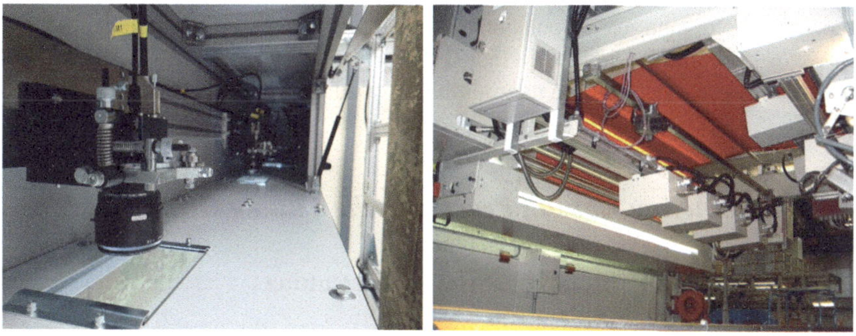

Fig. 7.13 The Shelton WebSpector machine vision system offers a sophisticated platform for automated defect detection of over 97%. *Source* Shelton Vision: Visual Inspection Systems (2023)

Fig. 7.14 The suntech AI automated camera inspection system-F. *Source* Automated and System-F (2023)

defect detection technology is the application of various methods and tools to automate and improve the accuracy and efficiency of fabric defect detection (Rasheed et al. 2020). In the future, fabric defect detection technology will be more advanced and intelligent, using artificial intelligence, machine learning, computer vision, and deep learning to analyse and process fabric images and videos (Rasheed et al. 2020; Machinery 2023). AI's deep learning algorithms, trained on vast datasets, see beyond the human eye, spotting even the subtlest flaws with superhuman accuracy. This revolution goes beyond mere flaw detection. Imagine AI predicting flaws before they appear, optimising production and minimising waste. Real-time detection is also on the horizon, ensuring flawless fabrics emerge effortlessly. But this revolution needs trust and collaboration (Shi et al. 2023). Transparency and human guidance help shape AI development for responsible innovation. By embracing AI's potential, we can weave a future for the textile industry where quality reigns, waste minimises, and sustainability becomes the natural fibre of production.

7.3.2 Automation Cutting Process in the Cutting Department

7.3.2.1 Automatic Relaxation Fabrics Before Cutting

Fabric relaxation is a critical step in the apparel and fashion industry to ensure optimal performance and appearance of various fabrics, especially for stretch and knit fabrics with elastane content. The objective of fabric relaxation is to keep the fabric's dimensional stability after cutting. Before cutting, the fabric must be loosened to stabilise the shrinkage so that the product manufacturing process can ensure quality. When the fabric is "rolled up", it stretches beyond its normal dimensions (Jayawardana et al. 2016). The time for relaxation fabric depends on the fabric's nature and customer requirements. Some methods for fabric relaxation are used, such as compressive relaxation, heat set relaxation, and sponging relaxation (Jayawardana et al. 2016). In this stage, the fabric sheet is layered one above another, maintaining pre-defined maker length and correct ply tension. Fabric is layered up to a certain height to avoid cutting quality problems.

The use of normal or manual methods of fabric relaxation takes a period of time ranging from 6 to 24 h. The new model machines, which integrate fabric relaxing machines with the AI-automated visual inspection system, represent a leap forward in production automation. This seamless combination allows for fabric rolls to be effortlessly fed into fabric-cutting machines, creating a fully automated production process. These machines allow the cutting of fabric immediately after relaxation, eliminating the tedious laying time. This dramatic reduction in waiting time translates to faster production cycles and quicker order fulfilment so that the factories can achieve meticulous fabric inspection, precise tension release, and seamless cutting, reducing labour costs, minimising errors, and delivering a level of efficiency that is unmatched by Fabric Relaxing (2023).

7.3.2.2 Automatic Spreading Fabric

In fashion and apparel products, fabric is generally the most significant factor in cost, which accounts for 60–70% of the total cost for basic-styled (Rathinamoorthy and Surjit 2018). Therefore, the support of automation in the cutting process, such as automated spreading machines, significantly reduces the workload of the spreading operator and increases work productivity. Besides, automated marker-making methods to match material patterns significantly improve the processing of garments from intricate pattern fabrics, and automated cutting systems are the most effective means of cutting garments. They ensure sufficiently high quality and accuracy, as well as very high productivity for both low-ply and high-ply cutting processes (Vilumsone-Nemes 2018).

The principle of an automatic fabric spreading machine is that fabric is loaded onto the machine and then checked manually for creases or wrinkles. The machine then automatically lays the fabric down in layers, cutting it off at the end with parameters such as length, width, and ply counts, which can be entered into the liquid crystal display touch screen according to the marker plan that is prepared by the model and pattern department. The machine automatically spreads the fabric for the number of plies and stops when the number of plies has been completed. Furthermore, the machine has the provision to slow down when it approaches both ends and takes care of the alignment of the fabric grain line with the support of sensors as well (Nayak and Padhye 2015; Vilumsone-Nemes 2018; Serkan and Öndoğan 2012).

Main parts and the function of automatic fabric spreading machine (Vilumsone-Nemes 2018):

(1) *Fabric Spreader Truck:* ensures the transportation of a fabric roll above a spreading table in the lengthways and transverse directions.
(2) *Fabric Feed System:* rolls material from a fabric setting bar or a special cradle and moves it to the spreading table. This system is synchronised to the speed of the spreader, ensures fabric tension control to provide tension-free spreading, automatically adjusts the feeding speed and measures the length of fabric.
(3) *Automatic Cutting Device:* moves together with the spreader truck. When the lay of fabric is fully spread, a round knife automatically moves across the table and cuts it off.
(4) *End-catcher*: drives and controls the spreading process using a special belt with metal denticles fixed to one side of the spreading table. The encoder system counts the number of denticles and recalculates them in the distance (meters, inches) from the start point. This defines the placement coordinates of the spreader truck on the spreading table at a given moment. A spread can be started and finished at any point on the spreading table. Semiautomated machines have a special mechanical stopping device, which stops the machine by friction at the end of a ply.
(5) *Encoder System*: counts the number of denticles and recalculates them in the distance from the start point.
(6) *Operator Stand Panel:* allows the operator to ride alongside the table during the spreading process
(7) *Interactive Control Panel:* sets up parameters and programs the spreading process.

The spreading process may be performed semiautomated with the operator's support to smooth the surface of the lay, identify faults in the spread fabric, and decide whether to leave faults in the spread or cut them out. And fully automated modes without the operator. This method is used for special materials which are easily spread. The operator sets the parameters according to the length of the lay (dependent on the length of the marker), the spreading speed, the fabric tension, etc. The spreading machine automatically performs the following operations: lays the fabric with the length requirement, cuts the material at the end of every ply, counts the number of plies, and stops after laying the required number of plies (Vilumsone-Nemes 2018).

7.3.2.3 Automatic Cutting Fabric System

Automated cutting systems are used to process a wide variety of materials. Although there are differences in the cutting tools and materials to be cut, the work principles and main parts involved in the automated cutting process are similar (Vilumsone-Nemes 2018). In general, a full set of modern automated cutting systems specifically includes (Fig. 7.15) automatic fabric loaders, automatic fabric spreading machines, automatic labelling machines, conveyor systems and automatic cutting machines. This system is driven by several smart software CAD solutions such as marker-making software, pattern design software, digital cutting room software, and cut planning software (for instance, COPS from Cosma Technology) (ITALY CT 2021) (Fig. 7.16).

1. ***Automatic Fabric Loader***: This unit eliminates the manual handling of heavy fabric rolls. It uses suction cups or grippers to grab the fabric roll and automatically feed it into the spreading machine. This reduces the risk of injuries and saves time compared to manual loading.
2. ***Automatic Spreading Machine***: This machine evenly spreads the fabric onto a large table in layers. Various spreading machines with different speeds and capabilities, like the Venus series from COSMA, offer high-speed spreading and the smart series for heavier materials. The machine can handle single-ply fabrics or stacks of fabric, depending on the model.
3. ***The automatic Labeling Machine***: is an automated system that reads the files (i.e., ISO, PLT from Cosma Postmaster 20 Labeling Machine) from the marker, prints labels, and places them on the top layer. The self-adhesive labels (barcodes) or RFID that replace large marker paper used for identification purposes; the labelling machine provides marker information, the start point of the marker, dimensional checks width and length, checks the alignment of the fabric before cutting and helps for the continuous cutting process. This task is used for bundle identification, improves productivity, reduces time and labour, eliminates errors and the costs involved in manual operation, and saves on paper costs; it is environmentally friendly.

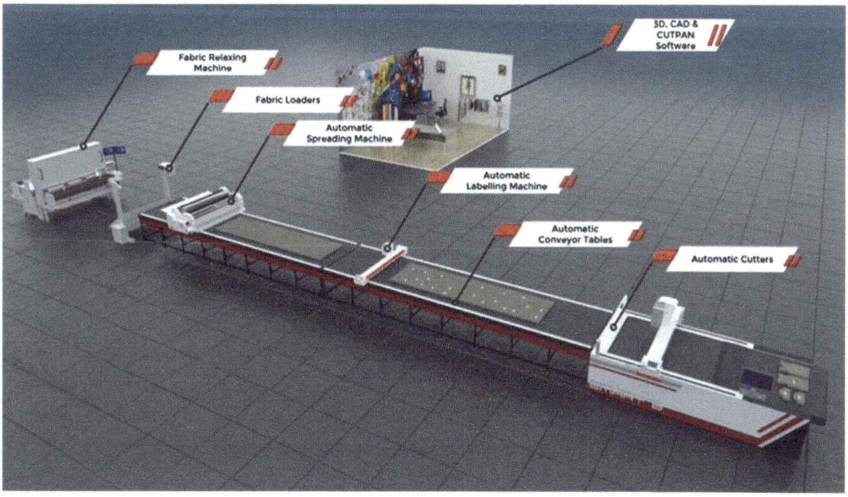

Fig. 7.15 A simulation in automatic cutting fabric system from cosma technology. *Source* ITALY CT (2021)

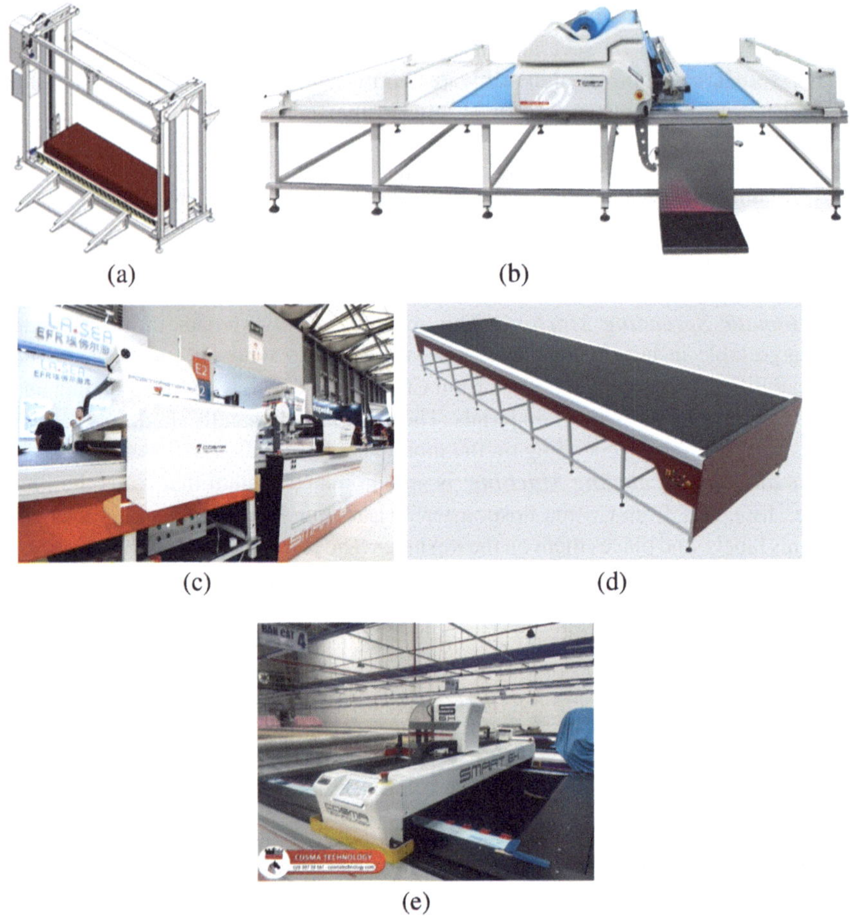

Fig. 7.16 The system of an automatic cutting fabric: **a** automatic fabric loader; **b** automatic spreading machine; **c** automatic labelling machine; **d** conveyor system; **e** auto cutting machine. *Source* (ITALY CT 2021)

4. ***Conveyor System***: Once cut, the fabric pieces are automatically transferred to a conveyor belt for sorting and bundling. This eliminates manual handling and further streamlines the process.
5. ***The auto-cutting machine***: is the heart of the system, and it uses a high-powered laser or oscillating knife to cut the fabric according to the pre-programmed patterns. Several models of cutting machines are used for various needs, like for high-speed cutting of light to medium-weight fabrics and for heavy materials like denim and leather. The auto-cutting machine can handle intricate shapes and curves with high precision, minimising waste and maximising fabric utilisation.
6. ***Software and Control System***: The entire cutting line is controlled by COSMA's user-friendly software. The software allows users to upload patterns, manage

cutting orders, and monitor the machine's performance. The intuitive interface makes it easy for operators to learn and use the system.

In addition, several other computer-controlled cutting devices, such as laser, ultrasound, plasma, or waterjet, are employed to increase productivity in the cutting room. Some cutting methods are used to cut the components made of technical textiles based on specific requirements like sponges, leathers, etc. (Vilumsone-Nemes 2018).

7.3.2.4 Advanced Technology in Fusing and Numbering Making

1. *Advanced Technology in Fusing*

The fusing of interlinings is a key process in fashion apparel manufacturing. Where interlinings are the accessories used between two layers of fabric to keep the different components of apparel in a desired shape and improve the aesthetics and performance in production. Fusing technology is a process in which cut components are fused with interlinings, which are coated with thermoplastic resin by the application of heat and pressure over a short time (Vilumsone-Nemes 2018; Sarkar et al. 2023).

Based on the working processes of fusing, there are two groups: discontinuous work process (flat) fusing presses and continuous work process fusing presses. Discontinuous fusing presses work sequentially and separately from other fusing processes. They are less productive and are suitable for small and medium production units. Continuous fusing presses enable an ongoing process by moving the components on a conveyor belt. They offer a higher level of productivity, are more energy efficient, and can ensure fusing without material shrinkage and fading. In continuous fusing, the pressing operation relies on a conveyor belt that moves continuously. It helps to carry the base fabric along with its interlining materials inside and outside the heating chamber. Figure 7.17 shows the schematic diagram of a continuous fusing press (Vilumsone-Nemes 2018).

(1) loading and feed (lower) conveyer belt,
(2) upper conveyer belt,

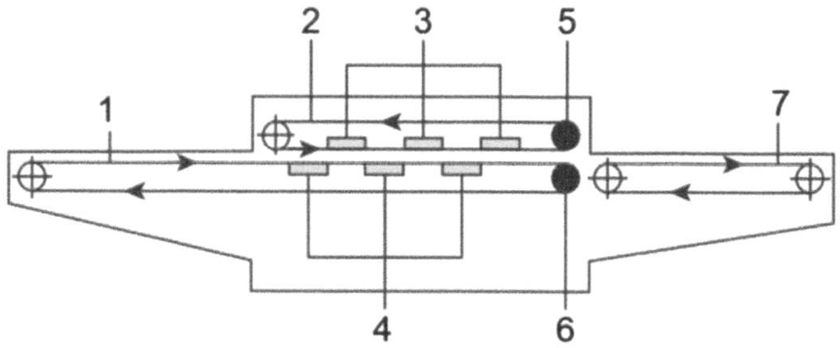

Fig. 7.17 The schema of a continuous fusing press with components. *Source* (Vilumsone-Nemes 2018)

(3) upper heating zone,
(4) lower heating zone,
(5, 6) pressure rolls, and
(6) exit conveyor belt.

The functions of the fusing machine components:

(1) and (2) surfaces of work for moving the materials,
(3) and (4): chambers for heating which heat the materials,
(5) and (6): press the materials, and
(7) a cooling system that cools down the fused components.

The fusing press device is developed by using various additional equipment, such as:

(a) Feeding conveyors, consisting of several belts for loading, which are placed on the front side of a press for creating ergonomic places of work and enhancing productivity;
(b) Collection stackers, which stack fused components and require fewer workers;
(c) The return belts return the materials that are fused to the front press side when only a single worker is available. (Sarkar et al. 2023)

A big problem during fusing is fabric shrinkage. In this process, high heat damages fabrics and makes them shrink unevenly. This wastes material and requires extra cutting steps. Modern fusing machines are solving this problem. They have long heating chambers that raise the temperature slowly and multiple heating zones to adjust heat for different fabric parts. This minimises shrinkage and allows for better fabric use (Vilumsone-Nemes 2018; Sarkar et al. 2023). The MP 2S Fusing Machine by MAICA is an example of a high-tech solution (MAICA 2023). It offers features like:

- Pre-fixing system to avoid fabric movement due to static electricity.
- Touch screen for easy temperature control and resistance adjustment.
- Unloading device for automated stacking of fused components, reducing manual labour.
- Patented conveyor cleaning system for specific materials.
- Significantly reduced need for manpower (1 operator for 4000 parts daily).

The EPA 740 Front Placket Fusing Press is another example which is designed to give shirts a perfect form after the front placket has been stitched with the technical specifications (Akin et al. 2018):

- A double ironing table allows for high-capacity pressing.
- The heat and timing can be adjusted depending on the material being pressed.
- High-vacuum lower mould and vacuum systems help to create a strong bond between the fabric and the interlining.
- Specially designed resistors and an upper pressing head ensure even heat distribution across the pressing area.

- PLC controlled, ensuring precise operation. Digital display and production reports are easy to use and provide hourly and daily production reports.
- Smart fault notification systems help identify and troubleshoot any problems with the machine.

At present, the practices for fusing use human operators to perform fabric pick-up, alignment, and manipulation tasks to feed the combined materials into a fusing machine. The development of a robotic system with an electro-adhesion robot gripper containing actuated pins prevents human operators from performing these repeated and laborious tasks in an uncomfortable manufacturing environment. This robotic system can reliably pick up fabric pieces, place them without wrinkles, align them using machine vision, and feed the combined bundle through the conveyor belt into the fusing machine. The actuated pins interlaced with the electrodes on the gripper can detach the fabric from the gripper with residual charges and slide the bundle onto the conveyor belt without affecting the fabric alignment. The electro-adhesion force depends on the applied voltage, fabric material property, and humidity (He et al. 2022). Furthermore, kaizen on the robotic arms is used as a support device to manipulate fabrics, minimising damage and enabling precise control. This innovative approach promises reduced labour costs, improved efficiency, and high-quality garment production, especially for delicate materials (Figs. 7.18, 7.19 and 7.20).

2. Automatic *in numbering making*

Numbering making on the components after cutting fabric helps to eliminate any confusion when joining it in different colour shades for a garment. In general, the numbering is done manually or using a special hand-held numbering device (a sticker gun) with small labels (Vilumsone-Nemes 2015). This is quite a tedious job, and it takes a lot of time and extensive labour. Nowadays, with automatic numbering

Fig. 7.18 MP 2S fusing machine by M.A.I.C.A (*Source* MAICA 2023)

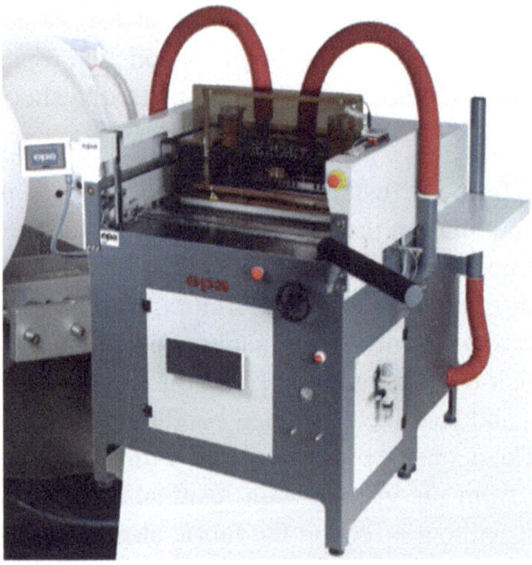

Fig. 7.19 Front placket fusing press by Epa Akin

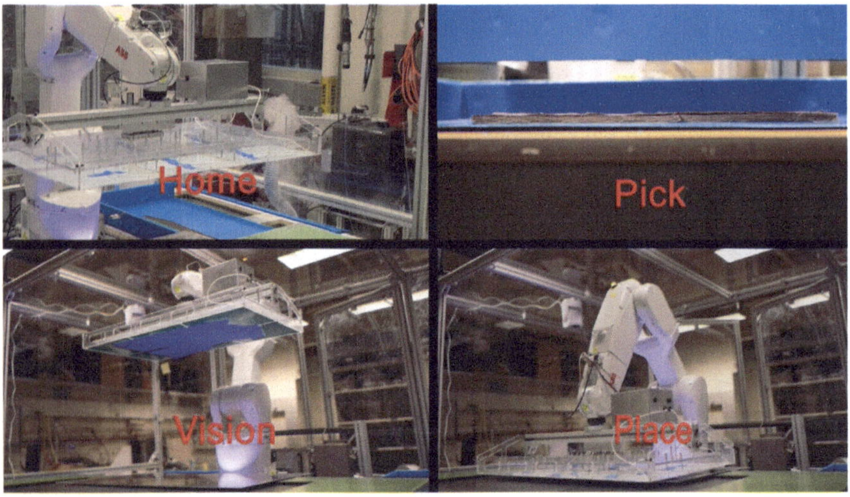

Fig. 7.20 Automated fabric fusing process through robotic electro-adhesion gripper, developed at Rensselaer Polytechnic Institute and demonstrated at Hickey Freeman Factory

marking, a worker can operate multiple machines simultaneously at a speed of around 70 pieces per minute, depending on the fabric. This machine automatically counts numbers continuously, accurately, and quickly and adjusts numbers, suitable for both thick and thin materials. Besides, it has an in-built laser lamp for fabric positioning, and the digital touchscreen display makes it user-friendly. Automatic ink filling is suitable for many different types of ink (TPET 2023).

7.3.2.5 Future Trends in Apparel Cutting Technology

Automated cutting systems have emerged as a game-changer in manufacturing. By using robotic machines, these systems utilise advanced technology to cut fabric or other materials accurately based on pre-programmed patterns, significantly reducing material waste and improving production speed. Automated spreaders utilise AI algorithms to optimise fabric placement, minimising waste and maximising efficiency. Automated cutting systems enable precise and efficient cutting, leading to higher productivity and cost savings. Besides, *integration by AI-powered Pattern Matching and self-optimising cutting Systems* can analyse fabric patterns and automatically adjust them for different garment sizes and types, reducing errors and material waste. Cutting machines equipped with AI can learn from past data and adjust cutting parameters in real time, ensuring optimal fabric utilisation and minimising errors. Furthermore, software that analyses garment patterns and suggests ways to minimise fabric waste promotes a more sustainable approach to cutting. Cutting technologies are also adapting to handle recycled and upcycled materials, contributing to a circular economy and sustainability focus in the apparel industry (Vilumsone-Nemes 2018; Services FAF 2023; Xu et al. 2018; Taifa et al. 2021).

7.3.3 Advanced Technologies in Apparel Production System

In the fashion apparel manufacturing process, sewing is the most important stage in fashion apparel joining technology, which takes 85% of all joining methods. Until now, sewing has been dependent on highly skilled labour for manual operations and takes 35–40% of the total cost. Under the pressure of fast fashion trends and the rapidly increasing labour costs in many developing countries, the apparel manufacturing industry is impulsive in striving for sewing automation to reduce labour costs, increase productivity and quality, and provide the shortest lead time (Sarkar et al. 2023; Gries and Lutz 2018). Sewing is also a complex section since it deals with a large number of various operations, relevant operators, and machines (Vilumsone-Nemes 2018). Automation in the sewing process and industrial robots that can handle the fabric during sewing operations have recently been developed (Lu et al. 2010).

7.3.3.1 Types of Production Systems

The production system is the framework within which the production activities take place. A production system consists of attributes such as human labour, machines, or tools with the function of transforming inputs into desired and predicted outputs (Jacobs and Chase 2018). In the apparel industry, the production system is defined as "an integration of material handling, production processes, personnel and equipment" (Kincade and Kanakadurga 2013). Four types of production systems are commonly used in the apparel industry: bundle system (BS), progressive bundle system (PBS), unit production system (UPS), and modular production system (MPS) (Kincade and Kanakadurga 2013; Oliver et al. 1994; Bailey 1993). The bundle system and PBS are categorised into mass production, and UPS and modular systems are categorised into flexible specialisation (Bailey 1993). The research of Kanakadurga (1994) has proposed five attributes of the production systems: worwflow, method of retrieval between workstations, work in progress (WIP) inventory, number of tasks per operator, and interaction between workers. The production systems in the apparel industry are classified into three categories: bundle system, PBS, and modular system (Kanakadurga 1994). The main objective of any production system is to achieve the minimum possible total production time. This leads to a reduction in in-process inventory and its cost. The subassembly system reduces temporary storage time to zero by combining temporary storage time with transportation time (Sarkar et al. 2023).

7.3.3.2 Advanced Technologies in Sewing

In apparel manufacturing, the process of assembly to make garment products involves two sub-functions—handling of material and joining of fabric components. A significant amount of time and labour is spent in material handling, such as lifting, moving, mounting, repositioning, and re-orientating cut or semi-finished fabric components. It is important to handle seams precisely and gently in an economical and efficient way to ensure requirement quality, minimising human intervention and preventing potential human mistakes during manufacturing (Lutz et al. 2018). In commercially available workstations, loading is typically manual, while sewing and unloading processes may be automated. So, industrial robots that can handle fabric during sewing activities are being built to minimise labour-intensive. The process of forming seams in these automatic machines is similar to that of previous sewing machines. Many types of sewing stitches, such as overlock stitch, double chain stitch, double lock stitch, etc. can be formed by robotic sewing machines (Sarkar et al. 2023; Jana et al. 2018). Advanced technologies in sewing may be summarised into six groups:

1. ***Automated Bobbin Changes*** Picture a scenario where manual bobbin changes no longer cause frustrating downtime. The automated system is established by two conjugated principles: checking the existing bobbin thread amount and then altering it with a loaded bobbin after the pre-fixed remaining thread amount is achieved. Automated bobbin changers, such as Kinoshita's magazine-fed system, come to the rescue by pre-loading bobbins for up to 2.5 h of uninterrupted stitching. This not only enhances efficiency but also eases the workload on operators, creating a win–win situation (Sarkar et al. 2023; Jana et al. 2018).
2. ***Modular sewing*** machines have increased flexibility; users can adapt their machines to new needs by swapping modules instead of buying entirely new machines. It is also simpler to repair by replacing faulty modules to reduce downtime. Machines like Vetron by Xi'an Typical can transform between different configurations (e.g., flatbed to longarm) (Sarkar et al. 2023).

3. ***Convertibility*** of bed, feed, and stitch types has been a long-requested feature in sewing tables. For a long time, Juki and Brother's double-needle lock stitch machines had the option of switching between needle feed and drop feed. Bed types were altered customarily from raised to flat in the case of lengthy overlocking seams. Convertibility from bar tack to button stitching is another feature that sewing companies have recently introduced. Simply changing the presser foot and activating the built-in software, a bar tack machine may be converted to a button sewing machine without modifying any internal components (Fashinza 2023; Somani 2023).
4. ***Robotic Seamstresses***: Beyond basic tasks, robots like Juki's automated machines excel in specialised functions with consistent accuracy. These dedicated machines handle tasks like button attaching, bartacks, and buttonholes flawlessly, eliminating issues such as uneven buttons or inconsistent seams. Automation reaches a new level of detail with these robotic artisans. A sewing machine with a USB port is also a new technology which enables the easy transfer of settings such as stitch length and stitching speed to other machines. Apart from that, the USB drive enables quick pattern copying and software upgrades (Sarkar et al. 2023; Fashinza 2023; Somani 2023).
5. ***Sewbots***: Software Automation's Sewbots represent the forefront of sewing automation. These intelligent machines, equipped with advanced vision systems and agile robotic arms, can see, analyse, and manipulate fabric with exceptional precision. Whether tracking individual threads at the needle or delicately managing intricate patterns, the potential applications seem limitless (Sarkar et al. 2023; Fashinza 2023; Resources 2018).

   The use of sustainable fashion is more popular in many countries the world. Robotics is making its way into the barely automated textile industry and opening up a new chapter for an entire sector (Fischer 2022; https://www.kuka.com/en-de/industries/solutions-database/2022/06/robotextile_small-robotics-in-textile-production).
6. ***The vision sewing system***, integrated with an industrial camera look (capture image), processes the captured image at the split of a second and directs mechanical actions by transferring it to the electronic programmable sewing machine. The whole process requires no high skill sets but much less time. The key benefits of a vision system include a consistent sewing speed for multiple patch sewing, automatic sewing of patterns, improved/less handling of the garment or fabric, and no operator sewing skills (Somani 2023; Pooja 2023) along with offset patterns, which allows the pattern to be made inside or away from the perimeter edge (Corp 2018).

Brother is one of the pioneered manufactures in producing Vision Sewing System. This system normally use for sewing patches, appliques, letters and numbers to fabrics and garments with automated precision. It is simple to operate. First, place the fabric and the object to be applied (patch, label, etc.) onto the machine and the integrated digital camera takes a photo of the set up. The system then analyses the image and defines the perimeter of the applied item. Using preset stitch specifications, the system then automatically generates a stitch pattern and proceeds to create a sew pattern along the edge of the object. The user can select specific stitch types such as straight or zigzag before the operation begins. Other specifications such as stitch pitch (length), width and over-sew can also be preset ahead of time, along with offset patterns, which allows the pattern to be made inside or away from the perimeter edge (Figs. 7.21 and 7.22).

Furthermore, the research of Ku et al. (2023) has developed an automated sewing system by integrating a custom-built sewing machine with a machine vision system, which does not need any interventions or assistance from the human operator. All the components were systematically connected through the ROS (Robot Operating System). This system plays an essential role in achieving smart manufacturing in the future of fashion apparel industry (Ku et al. 2023).

With the support of automatic sewing machines, sewbots, and advanced technologies in production, fashion and apparel manufacturers achieve higher productivity, better and more consistent product quality and less dependence on the labour force.

Fig. 7.21 Small robots from KUKA impress with compact design, long reach and precision. *Source* (https://www.kuka.com/en-de/industries/solutions-database/2022/06/robotextile_small-robotics-in-textile-production)

Fig. 7.22 Brother vision sewing system BAS-326G-VGSM. *Source* Corp (2018)

7.3.3.3 Advanced Technologies in Pressing and Packing Process

Pressing and finishing are the last segments in final fashion apparel products for customers, which are the important steps to enhance the aesthetics of the product before going to the customers. Pressing is done to remove any unwanted creases and wrinkles in the garment, to apply creases in the desired locations as needed, and to shape different or whole parts of a garment so that it is attractive when the customer purchases it. A better way of presenting the purchased garment to the customers helps in brand recognition (Sarkar et al. 2023).

Modern pressing machines often include features such as automatic steam generation, temperature control, and fabric-specific settings. These advancements ensure that the pressing process is gentle on the fabrics while providing the necessary heat and pressure for a crisp finish. Although there have been several technical advancements in the pressing technology, the number of automation tools is limited. A number of advanced technologies, such as pressing robots, tunnel finishing, jacket finishers, shirt finishers, pants finishers, shirt press, etc., have been commercially available. However, operations in loading or removing the garment into the buck, smoothing, and shaping still employ workers. For the successful automation of the whole garment manufacturing process, it is vital to make significant improvements in pressing.

Furthermore, automatic garment packing is also getting a tech makeover. Robotic systems can now grab, fold, and pack garments efficiently (Bernier 2021). Smart packaging materials are on the rise, boasting features like anti-wrinkle coatings,

RFID tracking tags, and even self-sealing mechanisms. Vision recognition systems help robots "see" different garments and pack them accordingly. 3D printing allows for customised packaging that perfectly fits each item, reducing waste. Finally, sustainability is a major focus, with eco-friendly options like recycled paper boxes, biodegradable plastics, and dissolvable films gaining traction. These innovations transform garment packing into a faster, more efficient, and greener process (Singh and Nijhar 2018; https://www.sportcasuals.com/news/sustainable-apparel-packaging#:~:text=Apparel%20brands%20are%20exploring%20a,shells%2C%20and%20seaweed%20for%20garments).

7.4 Conclusion

The evolution of industrial 4.0, particularly Computer-Aided Design (CAD) and Computer-Aided Manufacturing (CAM) has significantly shaped the landscape in fashion apparel manufacturing, leading to a transformative era marked by productiveness, efficiency, and sustainability. The use of CAD in the design process enables fashion designers to create intricate and detailed digital representations of garments. This expedites the design phase and facilitates rapid prototyping, allowing for quick iterations and exploration of innovative designs. The synergy between CAD and CAM ensures a seamless transition from digital concepts to physical garments during manufacturing. CAM systems, characterised by automation, are vital in guiding cutting, sewing, and other production processes, reducing faults and increasing efficiency. The impact of CAD-CAM technologies on fashion apparel manufacturing enhances production efficiency and overall garment quality through CAD-CAM integration. The transformative influence of these technologies is minimising errors and streamlining workflows. Additionally, the customisation and flexibility aspects of CAD-CAM systems in fashion production emphasise their role in reshaping traditional manufacturing processes to adapt to the dynamic demands of the industry. As the fashion industry embraces technological advancements, integrating CAD-CAM technologies has proven instrumental in fostering sustainability and innovation. These technologies contribute to more efficiency, minimise manufacturing process errors, and empower designers to push the boundaries of creativity. The challenges of implementing model CAD-CAM technologies are, first, a costly entry; implementing complex systems requires hefty upfront investments in software, hardware, and training. Next, the skill gap is another thing: operating these systems requires specialised expertise, potentially widening the industry's skill gap. And last, the integration problem is another challenge: Different systems may not play nice together, leading to data hiccups and workflow disruptions. Finding the right blend between machine efficiency and human creativity is also crucial.

References

3D C: Features (2023) https://clo3d.com/en/clo/features. Accessed
Apeagyei PR (2010) Application of 3D body scanning technology to human measurement for clothing Fit. Int J Digital Content Technol Appl 4(7):58–68
Bartle A, Sheffer A, Kim VG, Kaufman DM, Vining N, Berthouzoz F (2016) Physics-driven pattern adjustment for direct 3D garment editing. ACM Trans Graph 35(4):50:1–:11
Bailey T (1993) Organizational innovation in the apparel industry. Ind Relat: A J Econ Soc 32(1):30–48
Baukh O (2022) What is 3D fashion design and how does it impact the future of fashion? https://techpacker.com/blog/design/what-is-3d-fashion-design/#which-3d-software-is-best-for-fashion-design. Accessed on 2 Dec 2023
Bartol K, Bojanić D, Petković T, Pribanić T (2021) A review of body measurement using 3D scanning. IEEE Access 9:67281–67301
Bhardwaj V, Fairhurst A (2010) Fast fashion: response to changes in the fashion industry. Int Rev Retail Distrib Consum Res 20(1):165–173
Bernier C (2021) Packaging robots: maximizing throughput through automation. https://howtorobot.com/expert-insight/packaging-robots. Accessed on Dec 2023
Cheng W, Cheng ZL (2012) Applications of CAD in the modern garment industry. Appl Mech Mater 152:1505–1508
Choi K-H (2022) 3D dynamic fashion design development using digital technology and its potential in online platforms. Fashion Text 9(1):9
Christopher M, Lowson R, Peck H (2004) Creating agile supply chains in the fashion industry. Int J Retail Distrib Manage 32(8):367–376
Corp. BI: vision sewing system (2018). https://www.brother-usa.com/-/media/brother/product-catalog-media/documents/2018/10/10/14/11/vision-sewing-brochure---web.pdf. Accessed Dec 2023
Daanen HA, Psikuta A (2018) 3D body scanning. In: Nayak R, Padhye R (eds) Automation in garment manufacturing. Elsevier, pp 237–252
D'Apuzzo N (2007) 3D body scanning technology for fashion and apparel industry. In: Beraldin J-A, Remondino F, Shortis MR (eds) Videometrics IX: SPIE, pp 203–214
Decaudin P, Julius D, Wither J, Boissieux L, Sheffer A, Cani MP (2006) Virtual garments: a fully geometric approach for clothing design. Computer Graphics Forum: Wiley Online Library, pp 625–34.
Designer M (2023) Newfeature. https://www.marvelousdesigner.com/learn/newfeature. Accessed
Epa Akin, Front Placket Fusing Press (2018). https://www.epaakin.com/shirt-machines/epa-740/front-placket-fusing-press. Accessed on 24 Dec 2023
Fabric Relaxing machine: best solution for efficient fabric relaxing (2023). Accessed on 8 Nov 2023
Fan K-K, Chang Y-T (2023) Exploring the key elements of sustainable design from a social responsibility perspective: a case study of fast fashion consumers' evaluation of green projects. Sustainability 15(2):995
Fang JJ, Ding Y (2008) Expert-based customized pattern-making automation: Part I. Basic patterns. Int J Clothing Sci Technol 20(1):26–40
Fang JJ, Ding Y, Huang SC (2008) Expert-based customized pattern-making automation: Part II. Dart design. Int J Clothing Sci Technol 20(1):41–56
Fashinza: 5 advanced technologies for sewing seamless garments. https://fashinza.com/manufacturing/industry-4-0/5-advanced-technologies-for-sewing-seamless-garments/. Accessed on 4 Dec 2023
Fischer T (2022) Textile turning point: robotics for the apparel industry. https://www.kuka.com/en-de/company/iimagazine/2022/robotics-for-the-apparel-industry. Accessed on Dec 2023
Frederick SE (2010) Development and application of a value chain research approach to understand and evaluate internal and external factors and relationships affecting economic competitiveness in the textile value chain. North Carolina State University

Gereffi G, Frederick S (2010) The global apparel value chain, trade and the crisis: challenges and opportunities for developing countries. World Bank Policy Research Working Paper Series
Gereffi G, Memedovic O (2003) The global apparel value chain: what prospects for upgrading by developing countries. United Nations Industrial Development Organization Vienna
Goldstein Y, Robinet P, Kartsounis G-A, Kartsouni F-F, Lentziou Z, Georgiou H et al (2009) Virtual prototyping: from concept to 3D design and prototyping in hours. In: Transforming clothing production into a demand-driven, knowledge-based, high-tech industry: the leapfrog paradigm, pp 95–139
Gries T, Lutz V (2018) Application of robotics in garment manufacturing. In: Nayak R, Padhye (eds) Automation in garment manufacturing. Elsevier, pp 179–197
Hanbay K, Talu MF, Özgüven ÖF (2016) Fabric defect detection systems and methods—a systematic literature review. Optik 127(24):11960–11973
He H, Saunders G, Wen JT (2022) Robotic fabric fusing using a novel electroadhesion gripper. In: 2022 IEEE 18th international conference on automation science and engineering (CASE), IEEE, pp 2407–2414
Hofmann KH, Jacob A, Pizzingrilli M (2022) Overcoming growth challenges of sustainable ventures in the fashion industry: a multinational exploration. Sustainability 14(16):10275
Hozdić E (2015) Smart factory for industry 4.0: a review. Int J Mod Manuf Technol 7(1):28–35
Hu J (2008) Fabric testing. Woodhead Publishing Limited and CRC Press LLC
Huang S, Huang L (2022) CLO3D-based 3D virtual fitting technology of down jacket and simulation research on dynamic effect of cloth. Wirel Commun Mob Comput 2022
International SSC: sustainable packaging solutions in apparel. https://www.sportcasuals.com/news/sustainable-apparel-packaging#:~:text=Apparel%20brands%20are%20exploring%20a,shells%2C%20and%20seaweed%20for%20garments. Accessed on Dec 2023
Iris van Herpen's new collection, inspired by aquatic architecture and bionic innovations (2023). https://parametric-architecture.com/iris-van-herpens-new-collection-inspired-by-aquatic-architecture-and-bionic-innovations/. Accessed on 3 Dec 2023
Istook CL, Hwang SJ (2001) 3D body scanning systems with application to the apparel industry. J Fashion Mark Manage Int J 5(2):120–132
ITALY CT: fully automatic fabric cutting machine (2021). https://cosmatechnology.com/about-us. Accessed on 2 Dec 2023
Jacobs FR, Chase RB (2018) Operations and supply chain management. McGraw-Hill
Jana P (2018) Automation in sewing technology. In: Nayak R, Padhye R (eds) Automation in garment manufacturing. Elsevier, pp 199–236
Jayawardana T, Fernando E, Wijesena G, Kuruppu R (2016) Development an effective quick fabric relaxation machine. Int J Eng Trends Technol 42(6):310–318
Jeong J, Park H, Lee Y, Kang J, Chun J (2021) Developing parametric design fashion products using 3D printing technology. Fashion Text 8:1–25
Kanakadurga K (1994) A comparative study of the flexibility of three types of apparel production systems to variations in collar designs. Virginia Polytechnic Institute and State University
Kamal M (2015) Developing a conceptual model for restructuring apparel sampling development process using virtual reality technology. Int Des J 5(2):415–423
Kincade DH, Kanakadurga KS (2013) An empirical investigation of apparel production systems and product line groups through the use of collar designs. J Text Apparel Technol Manage 8(1)
Kim H, Damhorst ML (2010) The relationship of body-related self-discrepancy to body dissatisfaction, apparel involvement, concerns with fit and size of garments, and purchase intentions in online apparel shopping. Cloth Text Res J 28(4):239–254
Ku S, Choi H, Kim H-Y, Park Y-L (2023) Automated sewing system enabled by machine vision for smart garment manufacturing. IEEE Robot Autom Lett 8(9):5680–5687
Lee Y-A (2022) Trends of emerging technologies in the fashion product design and development process. Leading edge technologies in fashion innovation: product design development process from materials to the end products to consumers. 1–16

Liu K, Zeng X, Tao X, Bruniaux P (2019) Associate design of fashion sketch and pattern. IEEE Access 7:48830–48837

Liu K, Wang J, Hong Y (2017a) Wearing comfort analysis from aspect of numerical garment pressure using 3D virtual-reality and data mining technology. Int J Clothing Sci Technol 29(2):166–179

Liu K, Zeng X, Bruniaux P, Wang J, Kamalha E, Tao X (2017b) Fit evaluation of virtual garment try-on by learning from digital pressure data. Knowl-Based Syst 133:174–182

Liu K, Zhu C, Tao X, Bruniaux P, Zeng X, Wang J (2023) A novel evaluation technique for human body perception of clothing fit. Multimedia Tools Appl 1–13

Liu Y-J, Zhang D-L, Yuen MM-F (2010) A survey on CAD methods in 3D garment design. Comput Ind 61(6):576–93

Lu J-M, Wang M-JJ, Chen C-W, Wu J-H (2010) The development of an intelligent system for customized clothing making. Expert Syst Appl 37(1):799–803

Lutz V, Früh H-C, Gries T, Klingele J (2018) Automation in material handling. In: Nayak R, Padhye R (eds) Automation in garment manufacturing. Elsevier, pp 165–177

Machinery ST: unveiling the untold: a comprehensive journey into the world of AI visual inspection (2023). https://www.linkedin.com/pulse/unveiling-untold-comprehensive-journey/. Accessed on 29 Nov 2023

M.A.I.C.A, MP 2S Fusing machine (2023). https://www.maicaitalia.com/en/product/mp-2s/. Accessed on 24 Dec 2023

McQuillan H (2020) Digital 3D design as a tool for augmenting zero-waste fashion design practice. Int J Fashion Des Technol Educ 13(1):89–100

Mohiuddin Babu M, Akter S, Rahman M, Billah MM, Hack-Polay D (2022) The role of artificial intelligence in shaping the future of Agile fashion industry. Prod Plann Control 1–15

Nayak R, Padhye R (2015) Garment manufacturing technology. Elsevier

Nayak R, Padhye R (2018) Introduction to automation in garment manufacturing. In: Nayak R, Padhye R (eds) Automation in garment manufacturing. Elsevier, pp 1–27

Nayak R, Padhye R (2018) Automation in garment manufacturing. The Textile Institute Book Series. Woodhead publishing

Nayak R, Padhye R (2018) Artificial intelligence and its application in the apparel industry. Automation in garment manufacturing. Elsevier, pp 109–38

Ngan HY, Pang GK, Yung NH (2011) Automated fabric defect detection—a review. Image Vis Comput 29(7):442–458

Nagurney A, Yu M (2012) Sustainable fashion supply chain management under oligopolistic competition and brand differentiation. Int J Product Econ 135:532–540

Oliver BA, Kincade DH, Albrecht D (1994) Comparison of apparel production systems: a simulation. Cloth Text Res J 12(4):45–50

PatternMaker: Programs (2023). https://www.patternmakerusa.com/programs/. Accessed

Peleg Mizrachi M, Tal A (2022) Sustainable fashion—rationale and policies. Encyclopedia 2(2):1154–1167

Pooja P (2023) Tshe top technology trends in apparel manufacturing (2023). https://reads.alibaba.com/the-top-technology-trends-in-apparel-manufacturing/. Accessed on 06 Dec 2023

Rahman MM (2021) Applications of the digital technologies in textile and fashion manufacturing industry. Technium: Rom J Appl Sci Technol 3(1):114–27

Rasheed A, Zafar B, Rasheed A, Ali N, Sajid M, Dar SH et al (2020) Fabric defect detection using computer vision techniques: a comprehensive review. Math Probl Eng 2020:1–24

Rathinamoorthy R, Surjit R (2018) Apparel merchandising. CRC Press

Resources A (2018) 10 Popular sewing technology trends. https://apparelresources.com/technology-news/manufacturing-tech/10-popular-sewing-technology-trends/. Accessed on 3 Dec 2023

Rissanen T, McQuillan H (2023) Zero waste fashion design. Bloomsbury Publishing

Robson C, Maharik R, Sheffer A, Carr N (2011) Context-aware garment modeling from sketches. Comput Graph 35(3):604–613

robotextile MFFaCo: Textile (r)evolution (2022). https://www.kuka.com/en-de/industries/solutions-database/2022/06/robotextile_small-robotics-in-textile-production. Accessed on Dec 2023

Sarkar J, Rifat NM, Sakib-Uz-Zaman M, Al Faruque MA, Prottoy ZH (2023) Advanced technology in apparel manufacturing. In: Rahman MM, Mashud M, Rahman MM (eds) Advanced technology in textiles: fibre to apparel. Springer, pp 177–231
Saul Maslavi FCM, forbes business council: the future of fashion: exploring how artificial intelligence is transforming the market (2023). https://www.forbes.com/sites/forbesbusinesscouncil/2023/02/10/the-future-of-fashion-exploring-how-artificial-intelligence-is-transforming-the-market/?sh=6fda991a2764. Accessed 28 Nov 2023
Serkan B, Öndoğan Z (2012) An investigation on the cutting parameters for various types of fabrics. Text Apparel 22(1):52–57
Services FAF: the top garment manufacturing trends in 2023: a comprehensive guide (2023). https://www.linkedin.com/pulse/top-garment-manufacturing-trends-2023-comprehensive. Accessed on 1 Dec 2023
Shelton vision: visual inspection systems (2023). https://www.sheltonvision.co.uk/visual-inspection-systems/. Accessed on 5 Nov 2023
Shi L, Song J, Gao Y, Cheng G, Hao B (2023) YOLO-GFD: a fast and accurate fabric defect detection model. In: 2023 4th International conference on big data, artificial intelligence and Internet of Things engineering (ICBAIE). IEEE, pp 229–233
Singh A, Nijhar K (2018) Recent developments in the garment supply chain. In: Nayak R, Padyye R (eds) Automation in garment manufacturing, pp 377–96
Smith MS (2022) AI-generated fashion is next wave of DIY design. https://spectrum.ieee.org/dall-e-fashion-design. Accessed on 2 Dec 2023
Somani V (2023) 10 technology trends defining the future of textile and garment manufacturing. worldfashionexchange.com. Accessed on 6 Dec 2023
Suntech AI Automated Camera Inspection System-F (2023). https://www.suntech-machine.com/product/st-aci-automatic-camera-inspection-system-152.html. Accessed on 25 Nov 2023
Suntech: the application of AI in fabric inspection—the inevitable trend (2022). https://www.suntech-machine.com/events/the-application-of-ai-in-fabric-inspection-532.html. Accessed on 28 Nov 2023
Taifa IW, Twaha I, Mwakibambo MA (2021) Critical analysis of material consumption and cost reduction techniques for the apparel cutting processes. Tanzania J Sci 47(5):1689–1700
TPET, Automatic Marking Machine TP-8901 (2023). https://www.youtube.com/watch?v=3w-OJe-dnzw. Accessed on 25 Dec 2023
Turquin E, Wither J, Boissieux L, Cani M-P, Hughes JF (2007) A sketch-based interface for clothing virtual characters. IEEE Comput Graph Appl 27(1):72–81
Umetani N, Kaufman DM, Igarashi T, Grinspun E (2011) Sensitive couture for interactive garment modeling and editing. Trans Graph 30(4):90
Vilumsone-Nemes I (2015) Fabric spreading and cutting. In: Padhye R, Nayak R (eds) Garment manufacturing technology. Elsevier, pp 221–246
Vilumsone-Nemes I (2018) Automation in spreading and cutting. Automation in garment manufacturing. Elsevier, pp 139–164
Vstitcher: the industry's leading 3D fashion design and development software (2023). https://browzwear.com/products/v-stitcher. Accessed
Wang CC, Wang Y, Yuen MM (2003) Feature based 3D garment design through 2D sketches. Comput Aided Des 35(7):659–672
Wang Z, Tao X, Zeng X, Xing Y, Xu Z, Bruniaux P (2023) Design of customized garments towards sustainable fashion using 3D digital simulation and machine learning-supported human-product interactions. Int J Comput Intell Syst 16(1):16

Wong WK, Leung SJIJoPE (2008) Genetic optimization of fabric utilization in apparel manufacturing. 114(1):376–387

Xu Y, Thomassey S, Zeng X (2018) AI for apparel manufacturing in big data era: a focus on cutting and sewing. In: Thomassey S, Zeng X (eds) Artificial intelligence for fashion industry in the big data era, pp 125–151

Zhang D, Liu Y, Wang J, Li J (2018) An integrated method of 3D garment design. J Text Inst 109(12):1595–1605

Loan Thi Cam Bui is a lecturer in faculty of Garment Technology and Fashion Design, Industrial University of Ho Chi Minh City, Vietnam. She has 22 years of experience in teaching, 28 year working and researching in fashion apparel industry, with research interests including not limited in apparel industry but also in supply chain management, risk management, quality management, sustainability, etc. She has published many papers in related areas in quality academic journals. At present, she is a Ph.D Student at School of Industrial Management—Ho Chi Minh City University of Technology, Ho Chi Minh City, Vietnam with the research's field on in supply chain management and supply chain risk management.

Hang Thi Thu Nguyen has dedicated 33 years to teaching at the University of Technology (UT), Vietnam National University, Ho Chi Minh City (VNU-HCM), and 31 years at the School of Industrial Management (SIM). Her expertise focusses on Production Systems, Production Management, and Technology Management. Holding a Master's degree in Business Administration from AIT, Thailand, and a Doctor's degree in Business Administration also from UT, VNU-HCM, Dr. Hang has a remarkable track record of 27 published articles in domestic journals. She has actively participated in and led numerous research projects in supply chain management, technology management, and related fields.

Luu Thanh Do completed his Ph.D. in Industrial Engineering and Management at the Asian Institute of Technology (AIT) in Thailand. He is a scholarship recipient from the Vietnamese government for his degree of Mechanical Engineer at Ho Chi Minh City University of Technology (Vietnam), from the Belgian government for his master degree in Manufacturing Systems Engineering at the AIT, and from the DAAD (Deutscher Akademischer Austauschdienst, Germany) for his Ph.D. His present research interests are in the area of application of advanced technologies and optimization techniques to manufacturing systems.

Thang Duc Ta is an undergraduate student specializing in Logistics and Supply Chain Management at the Business School, RMIT International University, Vietnam. Thang was one out of four students with the highest Advanced English score in the school's entrance exam for gifted students. So far, he has achieved many prizes in the Advanced English field, ranging from small-scale to higher-scale competitions. He successfully accomplished the first and second prizes for school and provincial excellent contests for gifted students for three years during high school. Apart from being an excellent member of the National English Excellent team, he earned the prestigious silver medal for the Traditional Olympic 30/4 organized for high schools for gifted students in the southern part of Vietnam. His research interests include but are not limited to supply chain risk management, quality, and supply chain management. He has participated in several research papers for academic conferences such as the RMIT International Conference on Business Innovation, the International Conference on Quality Engineering and Management (Portugal), and the 2nd International Conference on Advanced Technology and Sustainable Development.

An Thi Binh Duong is a member of CIRTech Institute, HUTECH University, Ho Chi Minh City, Vietnam. She conducted doctoral research at the Graduate School of Culture and Information Science, Doshisha University, Kyoto, Japan under a Research Fellowship for Young Scientists of Japan Society for the Promotion of Science (JSPS). She is also serving as Supply chain manager at Nipro Sales Vietnam Co. Ltd.—a Japanese leading medical device manufacturer. Her research interests include supply chain risk management, quality and supply chain management, statistics, and data science. She has published on these topics in high-quality academic journals such as Engineering, Construction and Architectural Management, Construction Management and Economics, International Journal of Quality & Reliability Management, International Journal of Productivity and Performance Management, Behaviormetrika, Smart Innovation, Systems, and Technologies, Operations Management Research, Journal of Enterprise Information Management, Business Strategy and Environment, etc. She has also conducted some research projects on these topics in (1) Graduate School of Culture and Information Science, Doshisha University, Kyoto, Japan, (2) the Systems and Production Department, University of Minho, Portugal, (3) RMIT International University, Vietnam, etc.

Chapter 8
The Internet of Things (IoT) Revolution: Transforming the Fashion Supply Chain

Scott Douglas McDonald

Fashion has to do with ideas, the way we live, what is happening.
Coco Chanel, founder of Chanel

Abstract The fashion industry is undergoing a significant transformation propelled by the integration of Internet of Things (IoT) technologies into its supply chain processes. This chapter looks into the multifaceted impact of IoT on various stages of the fashion supply chain, from design and production to distribution and retail. By leveraging IoT devices such as RFID tags, sensors, and smart devices, fashion companies are enhancing visibility, traceability, and efficiency throughout the supply chain network. At the design and production stage, IoT-enabled systems facilitate real-time monitoring of inventory levels, production progress, and quality control, leading to optimized manufacturing processes and reduced lead times. Furthermore, IoT applications enable proactive maintenance of machinery, ensuring uninterrupted production cycles and minimizing downtime. In the distribution and logistics arena, IoT-driven solutions enable accurate tracking of shipments, allowing for timely delivery and improved inventory management. Real-time data generated by IoT devices enable predictive analytics, enabling fashion companies to anticipate demand fluctuations and optimize inventory levels across different sales channels. Moreover, IoT technologies are revolutionizing the retail experience by enabling personalized customer interactions, inventory visibility, and seamless omnichannel integration. Through the deployment of smart fitting rooms, interactive displays, and mobile applications, fashion retailers can enhance customer engagement and drive sales. This chapter provides a comprehensive overview of the transformative role of IoT in the fashion supply chain and discusses the opportunities and challenges associated with its adoption. By embracing IoT technologies, fashion companies can achieve greater transparency, agility, and sustainability across their supply chain operations, thereby gaining a competitive edge in today's dynamic market landscape.

S. D. McDonald (✉)
The Business School, RMIT University Vietnam, 702 Nguyen Van Linh, Tan Phong, District 7, TPHCM, Ho Chi Minh City, Vietnam
e-mail: scott.mcdonald@rmit.edu.vn

R. Nayak et al. (eds.), *Use of Digital and Advanced Technologies in the Fashion Supply Chain*, Springer Series in Fashion Business,
https://doi.org/10.1007/978-981-97-7528-6_8

Keywords RFID · Sensors · Inventory management · Logistics · Retail transformation

8.1 Introduction

The Internet of Things (IoT) is a system of interconnected devices that are used to collect, store, and communicate information automatically. IoT represents a paradigm-shifting technological innovation that can be found in various sectors, profoundly impacting the way we perceive, interact with, and adapt to the digital world (Khan et al. 2022). IoT combines the interconnectivity between physical objects and digital systems, creating a dynamic ecosystem wherein objects communicate, collect, analyze, and share data without human intervention. This transformative phenomenon has gained traction across industries, and one of its prominent domains of application is the fashion industry, which has witnessed a remarkable change owing to the inclusion of IoT technologies (Akram et al. 2022). In fashion supply chain, IoT can be applied to optimize fashion supply chain, inventory tracking, efficient inventory management and reduced stock out situations. Further, IoT can be integrated into clothing and accessories along with sensors, to collect and exchange information related to human biological functions with nearby devices.

This discussion clearly explains the IoT's significance in the fashion industry context and forecasts its transformative potential, even more so in developing countries. The relationship between IoT and fashion is symbolic of a broader industrial and technological revolution, whose impact is poised to go beyond geographical boundaries, bridging the gap between developed and developing nations (Saha 2022). The application of IoT in various industries is in continuous rise due to several benefits. Figure 8.1 shows the IoT applications, especially the connected objects between 2018 and 2025 (Source: Statista).

8.1.1 The Genesis of IoT

The idea of IoT goes back to the late twentieth century when technological advancements, including the increased use of microelectronics, wireless communication, and sensor technologies, began to converge. In 1999, Kevin Ashton, known for establishing global RFID standards, introduced the term "Internet of Things" and presented its conceptual framework in a groundbreaking paper. Interestingly, during the same year, MIT professor Neil Gershenfeld released his book "When Things Start to Think," although the two works were unrelated (Ashton 2009). They both envisaged a world in which everyday objects are given digital identities, interconnected through a ubiquitous network, and capable of exchanging information without human intervention. The combination of these enabling technologies created a paradigm

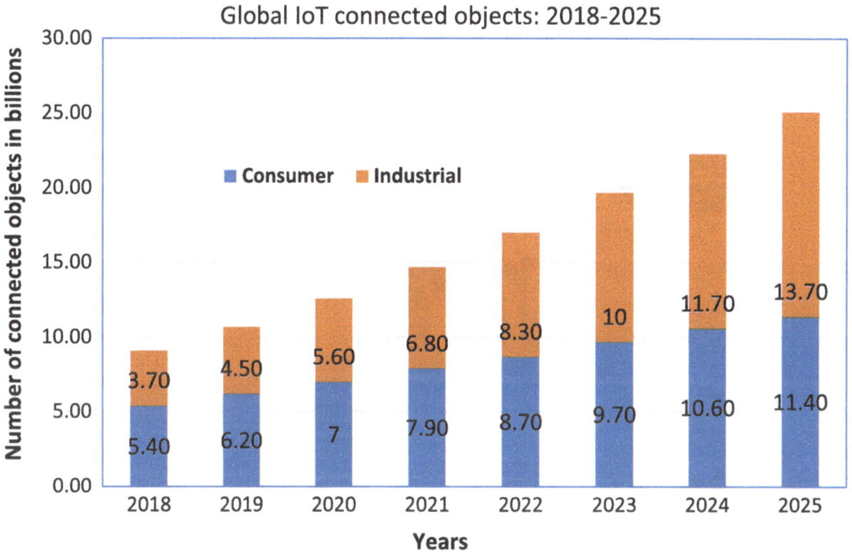

Fig. 8.1 IoT connected with systems and devices. *Source* https://www.statista.com/statistics/976079/number-of-iot-connected-objects-worldwide-by-type/

where the physical and digital realms converged, pushing traditional boundaries, and launching the IoT phenomenon (Madakam et al. 2015).

8.1.2 IoT in the Fashion Industry Supply Chain

IoT is revolutionizing the fashion industry supply chain by seamlessly connecting every aspect of production, distribution, and retail. By integrating smart sensors, RFID technology, and real-time data analytics, IoT allows for better transparency, efficiency, and sustainability, ushering in a new era of innovation and accountability in the fashion supply chain. The following areas identify the individual ways that IoT in the supply chain of the fashion industry influences it by exploring its diverse features, attributes, influence, advantages, and evolving trends in no particular order of importance. Figure 8.2 shows IoT during the fashion logistics activities.

8.1.2.1 Supply Chain Optimization

IoT-enabled sensors and RFID tags have revolutionized supply chain management in the fashion industry, enabling better transparency, traceability, and real-time inventory monitoring. This option allows manufacturers to optimize production, reduce overstock, and minimize waste (Majeed and Rupasinghe 2017).

Fig. 8.2 IoT during the fashion logistics activities

In the fashion industry, IoT optimizes supply chain operations in various ways.

8.1.2.2 Smart Inventory Management

This could be applied to a retailer or a warehouse to optimize the handling, tracking, and replenishment of inventory. In such an industry where trends are constantly changing, and consumer preferences are highly volatile, smart inventory management plays a crucial role in ensuring that the right products are available at the right time and in the right quantities.

8.1.2.3 Scenario

A fashion retailer wants to improve its inventory management practices, reducing carrying costs, minimizing stockouts, and boosting its supply chain's overall efficiency, resulting in higher profits.

8.1.2.4 IoT Solution

The retailer implements IoT-enabled RFID (Radio-Frequency Identification) tags on each clothing item. The RFID tags have sensors that can monitor various parameters, such as temperature, humidity, and movement. Additionally, smart shelves and racks in the store have RFID readers and sensors.

8.1.2.5 How It Works

Real-Time Inventory Tracking

RFID tags continuously transmit data about each garment's location within the store, the current status (on display, in the fitting room, or sold), and any physical environmental conditions it encounters (temperature or humidity). The system collects this data in real time (Tejesh and Neeraja 2018).

Automated Reordering

The system automatically updates the inventory status without human input as items are sold or moved around the store. When the stock of any individual item falls below a predefined threshold, the system triggers an automatic reorder request to the supplier or the warehouse (Karri et al. 2022).

Reduced Stockouts and Overstock

With accurate, real-time inventory data, the retailer can minimize stockouts (items being out of stock vs. customer demand) and overstock (excess inventory beyond customer demand). This optimization improves sales and reduces carrying costs (Saillaja et al. 2023).

Dynamic Pricing

IoT data can also help develop and implement "dynamic pricing" strategies. For instance, if a particular garment experiences high demand in any specific location within the store, the system can automatically adjust its price in real-time to maximize profit (Wang et al. 2021).

Supply Chain Efficiency

Beyond the store, IoT sensors can track the movement and condition of products throughout the entire supply chain. From manufacturing to distribution and transportation, various stakeholders can monitor the status of products, ensuring they reach their destinations at optimal times and conditions (Ben-Daya et al. 2019).

8.1.3 Benefits

The benefits obtained from IoT applications are shown in Fig. 8.3, which can include: improved customer experience, reduced operational costs, data-driven decision-making, and supply chain transparency. The discussions are given below.

8.1.3.1 Improved Customer Experience

Customers can rely on the availability of their desired products, reducing frustration caused by stockouts (Hoyer et al. 2020).

8.1.3.2 Reduced Operational Costs

Efficient inventory management reduces the need for excess inventory and associated carrying costs (Esmaeilian et al. 2020).

8.1.3.3 Data-Driven Decision-Making

The retailer uses data to gain valuable insights into customer preferences, product demand, and supply chain performance, enabling data-driven decision-making and forecasting (Koot et al. 2021).

8.1.3.4 Supply Chain Transparency

Enhancing increased visibility into the supply chain allows for proactive issue resolution and greater transparency for customers and other stakeholders (Astill et al. 2019).

This IoT solution in the fashion industry illustrates how real-time data, automation, and smart sensors can optimize inventory management, enhance the customer experience, and streamline supply chain operations.

Fig. 8.3 IoT benefits in fashion logistics and distribution

8.1.4 Smart Textiles

The integration of IoT into textiles has resulted in the development of smart clothing, boasting functionalities such as temperature regulation, fitness tracking, and biometric monitoring. These innovations are due to consumer demand for aesthetics and utility (Fernández-Caramés and Fraga-Lamas 2018). One example of IoT-enabled smart textiles in the fashion industry supply chain is using RFID technology integrated into garments and accessories. Some of the application areas of IoT have been shown in Fig. 8.4.

8.1.4.1 RFID-Enabled Smart Textiles

In the fashion industry, we can embed RFID tags or chips within clothing and fashion products, such as garments, shoes, or accessories. These RFID tags are connected to the internet and can communicate with various devices and systems throughout the supply chain. Various circumstances are applying this technology, which are given as follows.

8.1.4.2 Inventory Management

Retailers and fashion brands can use RFID-enabled textiles to track inventory in real time. Each garment or product receives a tag with an RFID chip, and as these items

Fig. 8.4 Some of the application areas of IoT

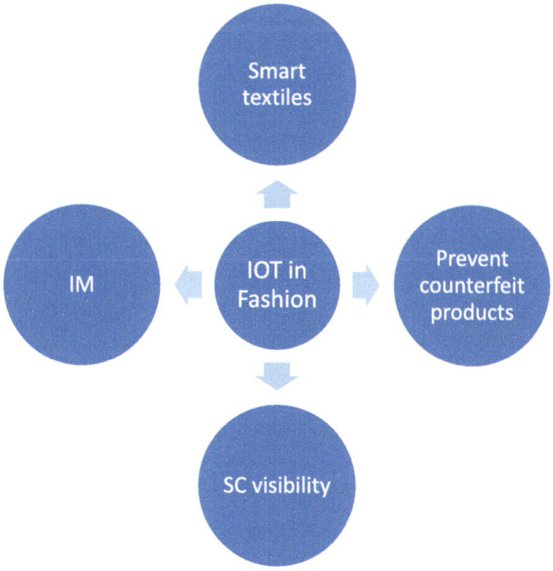

progress through the supply chain, RFID readers can automatically scan and update their status. This process reduces manual labor and improves inventory accuracy, helping companies manage stock levels more efficiently (Mostafa et al. 2019).

8.1.4.3 Supply Chain Visibility

RFID technology provides visibility into the entire supply chain, from manufacturing to distribution and retail. Brands and manufacturers can monitor the movement of their products, which is especially beneficial for international shipping and customs clearance (Moshood et al. 2021).

8.1.4.4 Anti-counterfeiting Measures

Smart textiles with RFID tags can verify product authenticity. Consumers can use their smartphones to scan the RFID tag on a garment, confirming its origin and authenticity. This incentive helps combat counterfeit products in the fashion industry (Chin et al. 2021).

8.1.4.5 Customer Engagement

Brands can engage consumers by offering interactive experiences through RFID-enabled textiles. For example, customers can scan a garment's RFID tag to access information about the product's materials, manufacturing process, or care instructions. This effort enhances the shopping experience and builds brand loyalty (Hoyer et al. 2020).

8.1.4.6 Smart Fitting Rooms

Some retailers implement smart fitting rooms with RFID technology. When a customer brings items into the fitting room, RFID sensors detect the tagged garments and display additional product information on a touchscreen, such as available sizes and colors. Customers can also directly request different sizes or styles from retail staff through the interface (Mashayekhy et al. 2022).

8.1.4.7 Supply Chain Efficiency

RFID technology can improve the efficiency of the entire fashion supply chain. For instance, it can help automate the receiving and sorting of goods at distribution centers, reducing handling time and errors (Ben-Daya et al. 2019). Overall, IoT smart textiles with RFID technology offer numerous advantages regarding supply chain visibility, inventory management, and customer engagement within the fashion industry. These innovations are helping fashion brands and retailers streamline their operations, reduce costs, and provide better experiences to consumers.

8.1.5 Customer Engagement

IoT facilitates personalized customer experiences through interactive retail environments, wherein smart mirrors, RFID-enabled apparel, and augmented reality applications converge to enhance the shopping experience. Data analytics from IoT devices allow brands to tailor their marketing strategies and product offerings (Hoyer et al. 2020). In the fashion industry, companies can leverage IoT technology to create innovative customer engagement experiences. An example is the use of smart mirrors in retail stores. How it works.

8.1.5.1 Smart Mirrors for Personalized Shopping

Imagine a customer walking into a fashion boutique equipped with smart mirrors. These mirrors have embedded IoT sensors and technology. How they engage customers.

Virtual Try-On

Customers can select clothing items from the store's collection and virtually 'try them on' using the smart mirror. The mirror uses augmented reality (AR) technology to superimpose the selected clothing items onto the customer's reflection, allowing them to see how the outfit would look on them without physically trying it on (Attaran 2020).

Style Recommendations

The smart mirror can analyze the customer's body shape and the clothing they've tried on. Based on this information and the store's inventory, it can recommend complementary items or accessories to suggest a new look. For example, if a customer tries on a dress, the mirror might suggest matching shoes or jewelry (Akram et al. 2022).

Inventory Availability

The store's inventory management system connects to the mirror in real time. If a customer selects a clothing item not available in their size or color, the mirror can suggest alternatives or check if the item is available at nearby stores (De Vass et al. 2021).

Virtual Stylist Assistance

Customers can request assistance from virtual stylists through the smart mirror. A live chat or video call feature lets customers get personalized fashion advice, ask questions about the products, or request different sizes or colors from nearby staff (Rathore 2019).

Mobile Integration

Customers can sync the mirror with their smartphones. They can save their favorite looks, access their shopping history, and receive notifications about promotions or new arrivals based on their preferences (Subramanian et al. 2021).

Feedback and Reviews

After trying on an outfit, customers can provide feedback and reviews directly through the smart mirror interface, helping other shoppers make informed decisions based on common trends (Pasi et al. 2020).

Convenient Checkout

Customers can complete the transaction directly through the smart mirror if they decide to purchase. The mirror connects to the store's payment system, allowing for a seamless and convenient checkout process (De Vass et al. 2021). This IoT-powered smart mirror enhances the customer's in-store shopping experience by providing personalized recommendations and convenience and collecting valuable data for the retailer. Retailers can analyze customer interactions and preferences gathered through the smart mirror to fine-tune their inventory, marketing strategies, and customer engagement efforts (Hoyer et al. 2020). IoT technology in the form of smart fitting rooms shows how the fashion industry can use technology to engage customers, create a more efficient supply chain, and provide a personalized and enjoyable shopping experience.

8.1.6 *Transformative Potential in Developing Countries*

IoT offers great promise for the fashion industry in several developing countries, offering opportunities for economic growth, sustainability, and increased competitiveness on the global stage (López et al. 2022).

8.1.6.1 Sustainable Manufacturing

IoT technologies enable more efficient use of resources and waste reduction, falling in line with the sustainable development goals of many nations. Developing countries can use IoT to reduce the environmental impact of their fashion production processes, thereby appealing to environmentally conscious consumers (Stulga et al. 2022). An example of IoT sustainable manufacturing in the fashion industry supply chain is the implementation of "Smart Textile Factories" (Fig. 8.5). These factories use IoT technology to improve efficiency, reduce waste, and minimize the environmental impact of clothing production. How it works.

Energy Management

The application of IoT helps in managing consumption of electricity in various operations.

IoT Sensors

IoT sensors in smart textile factories constantly monitor energy consumption in real-time. These sensors collect data on electricity, water, and gas usage throughout manufacturing (Akram et al. 2022).

Fig. 8.5 IoT for improved efficiency

Energy Optimization

AI and machine learning algorithms analyze data to identify patterns and opportunities for energy optimization. For example, they can suggest the most energy-efficient production schedules or adjust machine settings for optimal performance (Manavalan and Jayakrishna 2019).

Waste Reduction

The use of IoT infrastructure along with RFID technology for reducing the creation of waste and management of waste such as recycling rather than landfilling.

Inventory Tracking

Companies use RFID tags and sensors to track raw materials and work-in-progress items throughout the factory. This activity ensures better inventory management and reduces overproduction and material waste (Tejesh and Neeraja 2018).

Quality Control

IoT-connected cameras and sensors inspect textiles for defects during production. Faulty items are identified and removed from the process early, reducing the production of defective goods (Pal 2020).

Sustainable Sourcing

This involves sourcing of sustainable materials, sustainable transportation, waste management and reducing environmental pollution.

Supply Chain Transparency

IoT devices are employed to trace the origins of raw materials, such as cotton or synthetic fibers. This transparency allows fashion brands to ensure their materials come from sustainable and ethical sources (Hauschild and Coll 2023).

Water and Chemical Management

IoT applications can help to monitor the amount of water and chemical applications mainly in chemical processing in addition to other important areas.

IoT Water Sensors

Sensors monitor water usage and wastewater quality. If issues are detected, the system can shut down or adjust processes to prevent water pollution or other violations (Piramuthu 2022).

Chemical Usage

Sensors also track the usage of chemicals and dyes, ensuring they apply them in the right quantities and according to eco-friendly or legal standards (Wang et al. 2020).

Worker Safety and Well-Being

It relates to the IoT applications for the occupational health and safety (OH&S) issues of employees and society.

Wearable IoT Devices

Factory workers may wear wearable IoT devices that monitor their health and safety. These devices can track factors like temperature, humidity, and air quality, ensuring a safe and comfortable working environment (Venkatesh et al. 2020).

Predictive Maintenance

This relates to IoT applications for predictive maintenance.

Machine Health Monitoring

IoT sensors are installed on machinery to monitor their health and performance. Data analytics predict when equipment will likely fail, allowing preventive maintenance to reduce downtime and extend machine lifespan (Pal 2020).

Sustainable Packaging

The use of sustainable packaging can also be monitored by IoT.

Smart Packaging

IoT technology can be integrated into the packaging to monitor its environmental impact. For example, sensors can track how often a package opens, enabling brands to optimize packaging designs for reuse or recycling (Fernandez et al. 2018).

Consumer Engagement

IoT application for keeping consumer records to improve consumer satisfaction.

QR Codes and NFC Tags

IoT-enabled tags and clothing labels allow consumers to access information about the garment's production process, materials, and sustainability credentials. This transparency can influence purchasing decisions and promote sustainable fashion (Heim and Hopper 2022).

Implementing IoT in this manner makes fashion manufacturing more sustainable and matches consumers' increasing demand for environmentally conscious products. It can help fashion brands reduce their ecological footprint, improve operational efficiency, and contribute to a more sustainable fashion industry supply chain.

8.1.7 Accessible Market Expansion

IoT-powered e-commerce platforms offer a cost-effective means for fashion entrepreneurs in developing countries to access global markets, reducing traditional barriers to entry. This market access democratization can potentially invigorate local fashion industries (Chen 2019).

One example of IoT-driven market expansion in the fashion industry supply chain is using smart RFID tags and sensors to enhance retail store inventory management and customer experiences. How this works.

8.1.7.1 Scenario

A clothing retailer aims to expand its market presence and improve its supply chain efficiency using IoT technology.

8.1.7.2 IoT Implementation

The network of devices is implemented in the facilities.

Smart RFID Tags

The retailer attaches RFID tags to each clothing item. These tags contain unique identification information (Nayak et al. 2022).

Inventory Tracking

Strategically place RFID readers and sensors throughout the store, stockrooms, and along the supply chain. These readers continuously scan RFID tags and update the inventory database in real-time (Tejesh and Neeraja 2018).

Real-Time Inventory Visibility

With IoT technology, the retailer gains real-time visibility into their inventory. They precisely track the quantity of each product in stock, the location of items, and when stock levels are depleted (Lee 2021).

Market Expansion and Improved Supply Chain

The use of IoT can help us to penetrate new markets in addition to improving supply chin efficiency.

Enhanced Customer Experience

The customer experience can be improved by satisfying their needs whenever possible by style and product suggestions.

Inventory Availability

Customers can use a store app or website to check the availability of specific items in real-time. This app reduces the chances of disappointment when an item they want is out of stock (De Vass et al. 2021).

Personalized Recommendations

Businesses can use IoT data to offer personalized product recommendations to customers based on their preferences and the items they've interacted with in the store or online (Hoyer et al. 2020).

Supply Chain Efficiency

Improvement of overall supply chain efficiency can be obtained by the use of IoT.

Inventory Optimization

IoT technology helps the retailer optimize inventory levels. They can reduce overstocking and stockouts, minimizing storage costs and lost sales (Yerpude and Singhal 2018).

Demand Forecasting

You can use real-time RFID tags and sensor data for more accurate demand forecasting. This allows the retailer to plan production and procurement more efficiently (Seyedan and Mafakheri 2020).

Loss Prevention

IoT helps prevent theft and shrinkage by monitoring items moving through the supply chain and alerting staff to irregularities in the system (Pal 2020).

Expansion into E-commerce

The IoT integration can expand the market share of e-commerce.

Omnichannel Retailing

With real-time inventory data, the retailer can seamlessly integrate their physical and online stores. Customers can buy items online and pick them up in-store, or vice versa, improving the overall shopping experience (Princes and So 2021).

Global Market Reach

With a well-optimized supply chain and accurate inventory information, the retailer can confidently expand its market reach by offering its products to customers in other regions or countries through e-commerce (Chen 2019).

Sustainability Initiatives

IoT applications can also support the drive to achieve the triple bottom line (TBL) of sustainability, which involves people, planet, and profit.

Reduced Waste

Accurate inventory data reduces the chances of unsold items ending as waste. Such data aligns with sustainability goals by reducing the environmental impact of excess production and waste disposal (Alves et al. 2022).

By implementing IoT technology in this way, the fashion retailer can expand its market reach, improve supply chain efficiency, and provide a more satisfying shopping experience for customers, all of which contribute to the growth and success of the business in the competitive fashion industry (Ben-Daya, Hassini, and Bahroun 2019).

8.1.8 Skill Development

The adoption of IoT technologies in fashion necessitates a skilled workforce. Developing countries can use IoT as a directive for skill development programs, developing a technologically knowledgeable labor force poised for participation in the global digital economy (Dash et al. 2019). IoT skill development has become increasingly important for optimizing various processes and improving overall efficiency in the fashion industry supply chain. An example of how the fashion industry can apply IoT skills has been shown in Fig. 8.6.

8.1.8.1 Inventory Management and RFID Integration

It has been well established that IoT applications can improve inventory management.

Scenario

A fashion brand produces and distributes clothing to multiple retail stores and e-commerce platforms. They face challenges in tracking inventory accurately, resulting in stockouts, overstock situations, and a lack of real-time visibility into product availability.

Fig. 8.6 IoT applications for skill development

IoT Skill Development

The fashion brand invests in IoT skill development for its supply chain team to implement RFID technology (Dash et al. 2019).

Application

RFID tags are attached to each garment, and RFID readers are installed in warehouses, distribution centers, and retail stores (Nayak et al. 2022). Supply chain professionals with IoT skills set up the system to track each item's movement automatically. The team develops the following skills.

RFID System Integration

IoT-trained personnel integrates RFID data into the brand's inventory management software, ensuring seamless data flow and real-time updates (Tan and Sidhu 2022).

Data Analytics

They use data analytics skills to analyze RFID-generated data, providing insights into demand patterns, stock levels, and supply chain performance (Pal 2020).

Predictive Maintenance

IoT skills enable them to implement predictive maintenance for RFID readers and equipment, ensuring uninterrupted tracking capabilities (Chang et al. 2021).

8.1.8.2 Benefits

Real-Time Inventory Visibility

The IoT-enabled RFID system offers real-time visibility into inventory levels, allowing the brand to monitor stock levels accurately (Lee 2021).

Reduced Stockouts and Overstocks

With accurate inventory data, the brand can optimize its stock levels, reducing stockouts and overstock situations. This result leads to better customer satisfaction and cost savings (Saillaja et al. 2023).

Efficient Replenishment

IoT skills help in automating replenishment processes. When stock levels reach predefined thresholds, the system can trigger reorder requests, ensuring timely restocking (Francisco and Swanson 2018).

Improved Demand Forecasting

Data analytics skills enable the supply chain team to analyze historical data and make more accurate demand forecasts, helping with production planning (Seyedan and Mafakheri 2020).

Enhanced Loss Prevention

RFID technology helps reduce theft and shrinkage, as it can trigger alerts when unauthorized item movements are detected (Pal 2020).

By developing IoT skills and implementing RFID technology in its supply chain, this fashion brand improves inventory management, enhances customer satisfaction, and optimizes operational efficiency, ultimately benefiting its bottom line and competitiveness in the market (Nayak et al. 2022).

The advent of the Internet of Things marks a pivotal moment in the evolution of the global fashion industry. As it combines with the fashion world, IoT promises to change the industry's modus operandi significantly. For developing countries, this presents an opportunity to leapfrog into a new era of fashion production and consumption, narrowing the global technological divide and developing sustainable growth. This discussion sets the stage for a comprehensive examination of the multi-faceted dimensions of IoT's transformative impact on the fashion industry (Ahmad et al. 2020).

8.2 Fundamentals of IoT in the Fashion Supply Chain: A Global Perspective

8.2.1 Introduction

The Internet of Things (IoT) is an interdisciplinary paradigm that has gained acceptance in supply chain management, offering opportunities for efficiency, transparency, and sustainability (Khan et al. 2022). IoT comprises a network of interconnected physical objects embedded with sensors, actuators, and communication capabilities, facilitating the seamless exchange of data, and enabling real-time decision-making. In the fashion supply chain realm, a complex and dynamic ecosystem marked by diverse stakeholders and rapidly changing consumer preferences, IoT presents a transformative force with global implications (Ahmad et al. 2020). This section investigates the fundamentals of IoT and clarifies its applications in the global fashion supply chain.

8.2.2 Fundamentals of IoT

8.2.2.1 Sensing and Data Collection

At the heart of IoT lies the capability to sense and collect data from the physical world. Sensors and actuators embedded in objects or products gather information about various parameters such as location, temperature, humidity, etc. This data is then transmitted to a central system for analysis and decision-making (Plageras et al. 2018).

IoT sensing and data collection can greatly benefit the fashion industry supply chain. An example.

Smart Inventory Management and RFID Tags

In the fashion industry, brands and retailers efficiently track large volumes of clothing items throughout the supply chain. IoT technology can help streamline this process.

Scenario

Let's consider a high-end fashion retailer that wants to improve its inventory management and enhance customer experience. They decided to implement IoT solutions.

IoT Implementation

RFID Tags

Each clothing item has an RFID tag equipped with unique identifiers that can be read wirelessly. These tags are attached to clothing items at the manufacturing stage (Nayak et al. 2022).

Sensors and RFID Readers

Strategically place sensors and RFID readers throughout the supply chain in warehouses, distribution centers, and retail stores. These devices can scan RFID tags on clothing items and collect data (Nayak et al. 2022).

Real-Time Tracking

As the clothing items move through the supply chain, the RFID tags are scanned at various points, providing real-time location and status information. This method lets the company know precisely where each item is at any given time (Akram et al. 2022).

Data Analytics

The centralized system or cloud-based platform sends the collected data. Businesses use data analytics tools to process information. These tools can generate insights into inventory levels, stock movement, and product demand (Pal 2020).

Benefits

Inventory Accuracy

The retailer can maintain accurate, real-time inventory records with RFID and IoT sensors. These tools reduce the risk of overstocking or understocking products, optimizing supply chain efficiency (Caro and Sadr 2019).

Reduced Shrinkage

RFID tags can help prevent theft and reduce shrinkage by providing real-time alerts when items are moved without proper authorization (Pal 2020).

Enhanced Customer Experience

When a customer in a physical store is interested in a specific item, store employees can quickly locate it using RFID technology, improving the shopping experience, and reducing wait times (Hoyer et al. 2020).

Demand Forecasting

Data analytics can reveal consumer preferences and demand patterns, allowing the retailer to make data-driven decisions about production and inventory levels (Seyedan and Mafakheri 2020).

Supply Chain Visibility

IoT sensing and data collection provide end-to-end visibility into the supply chain, helping to identify bottlenecks, delays, and areas for improvement (Ahmed et al. 2021).

Sustainability

By optimizing inventory management and reducing waste, the fashion industry can contribute to sustainability goals by minimizing overproduction and excess inventory disposal (Prajapati et al. 2022).

IoT sensing and data collection in the fashion industry supply chain, particularly through RFID technology, offer advantages such as improved inventory management, reduced shrinkage, enhanced customer experiences, and better demand forecasting (Nayak et al. 2022). These technologies help streamline operations and contribute to a more sustainable and efficient fashion supply chain.

8.2.2.2 Connectivity

Various communication protocols interconnect IoT devices, including Wi-Fi, Bluetooth, RFID, and cellular networks. This connectivity ensures that data can be transmitted seamlessly between devices and systems, regardless of geographical location (Ding et al. 2020).

Fig. 8.7 Fundamentals of IoT applications

IoT connectivity is crucial in enhancing efficiency and transparency in the fashion industry supply chain. An example is shown in Fig. 8.7.

RFID-Enabled Inventory Management

Many fashion retailers and brands utilize RFID technology to improve inventory management and streamline the supply chain.

How It Works

RFID tags are attached to individual clothing items or product packaging at various points in the supply chain, such as manufacturing, warehousing, and distribution. These tags contain unique identification information that can be wirelessly scanned and tracked.

Benefits

Real-Time Inventory Tracking

Retailers can monitor the movement and availability of each item in real-time, helping prevent overstocking or understocking of products and ensuring that popular items are always in stock (Tejesh and Neeraja 2018).

Reduced Shrinkage

RFID can help reduce theft and loss because any unauthorized removal of items can trigger alerts (Pal 2020).

Efficient Replenishment

When inventory runs low, the system can automatically generate orders for replenishment, optimizing stock levels (Francisco and Swanson 2018).

Enhanced Customer Experience

Customers can use mobile apps or in-store kiosks to check product availability, sizes, and colors, improving their shopping experience (Hoyer et al. 2020).

Supply Chain Visibility

Brands and manufacturers can track products from the factory to the store shelves, enhancing supply chain visibility and traceability (Ahmed et al. 2021).

Seasonal Rotation

For seasonal fashion, RFID can help ensure that older items are sold before newer ones, reducing the need for clearance sales (Tan and Sidhu 2022).

Example

A high-end fashion retailer uses RFID tags on all clothing items. When a customer selects a piece of clothing, RFID sensors detect the item's removal from the rack and update the inventory in real-time. The system can trigger a restocking request if the item is not purchased. Additionally, customers can use the retailer's mobile app to check if specific sizes or colors are available in-store, increasing convenience and sales. This IoT-powered inventory management system helps the retailer maintain better control over its supply chain, reduce costs, and provide customers with a more satisfying shopping experience.

8.2.2.3 Data Analytics and Processing

The sheer volume of data IoT devices generate necessitates sophisticated analytics and processing capabilities. Advanced algorithms and machine learning techniques extract meaningful insights from the data, enabling predictive and prescriptive analysis (Abd Rahman et al. 2021).

IoT data analytics and processing play a crucial role in enhancing the efficiency and transparency of the fashion industry supply chain. An example.

RFID-Based Inventory Management and Demand Forecasting

Many companies in the fashion industry have adopted IoT technologies like RFID to monitor their products' journey from manufacturing to retail stores. How it works.

RFID Tags

Each fashion item, such as clothing or an accessory, is equipped with an RFID tag. These tags contain unique identifiers that can be wirelessly scanned and tracked (Nayak et al. 2022).

Tracking in Real-Time

As these items move through the supply chain, RFID readers placed at various checkpoints (e.g., production facilities, warehouses, and distribution centers) automatically record the movement of each item in real-time, including when it leaves the factory, arrives at a distribution center, or is stocked on a retail shelf (Tejesh and Neeraja 2018).

Data Collection

The RFID system collects vast amounts of data, including item location, time, and quantity, and sends it to a centralized database or cloud platform (Chan, Lau, and Fan 2018).

Analytics and Processing

IoT data analytics platforms process this data to extract valuable insights. Here are a few ways this data can be analyzed and utilized.

Inventory Management

Retailers can monitor their inventory levels in real-time, reducing the risk of overstocking or understocking, ensuring that popular items are always available, and minimizing losses due to excess inventory (Mostafa et al. 2019).

Demand Forecasting

Fashion companies can make more accurate demand forecasts by analyzing historical data and real-time sales trends, helping to optimize production schedules and reduce the likelihood of overproduction or stockouts (Seyedan and Mafakheri 2020).

Supply Chain Efficiency

IoT data can identify bottlenecks or delays in the supply chain. For instance, if items spend too much time in a particular distribution center, adjustments can be made to streamline the process (Ben-Daya et al. 2019).

Product Authentication

Companies can use RFID tags for product authentication and counterfeit prevention. Retailers and customers can verify the authenticity of luxury fashion items using smartphones or in-store scanners (Alves et al. 2022).

Customer Insights

Companies can use IoT data to gather customer insights. For instance, retailers can track which items customers are trying on most often, which can inform future inventory decisions (Pal 2020).

Automated Actions

Automated actions can be triggered based on the insights gained from the IoT data analytics. For instance, when inventory levels reach a certain threshold, businesses can automatically initiate reorders or adjust production schedules to meet changing demand (Chen 2019).

By implementing IoT data analytics and processing in this manner, the fashion industry can significantly improve its supply chain management, reduce operational costs, minimize waste, and better respond to changing customer preferences, ultimately enhancing the overall efficiency and sustainability of the industry (Abd Rahman et al. 2021).

8.2.2.4 Real-Time Decision-Making

IoT enables real-time decision-making, which is particularly valuable in the context of supply chain management, where quick responses to disruptions, demand fluctuations, and quality issues are essential by providing instant access to data (Syafrudin et al. 2018). IoT (Internet of Things) technology can enable real-time decision-making to improve efficiency and responsiveness in the fashion industry supply chain. An example is given in Fig. 8.8.

Inventory Management and Demand Forecasting

Suppose a fashion retailer utilizes IoT devices such as RFID tags and sensors on clothing items and shelves within their stores and warehouses. These IoT devices continuously collect data on inventory levels, customer foot traffic, and even environmental conditions like temperature and humidity.

In real-time, the centralized analytics platform transmits this data and employs machine learning algorithms for analysis. How real-time decision-making using IoT can work.

Fig. 8.8 Real time decision-making to improve efficiency

Demand Forecasting

The IoT sensors actively detect which clothing items customers pick up and try on. Machine learning algorithms analyze this data to identify trends, such as which products are popular, what sizes are in demand, and how seasonal factors affect purchasing behavior (Seyedan and Mafakheri 2020).

Inventory Tracking

RFID tags on clothing items track their movement through the supply chain, from manufacturing to distribution centers to individual stores. The IoT system constantly updates inventory levels and locations, preventing stockouts or overstock situations (Tejesh and Neeraja 2018).

Optimizing Shelf Space

Sensors in the store monitor the availability of items on shelves and in the fitting rooms. If a particular product is frequently tried on but rarely purchased, the system can recommend moving it to a more prominent location to increase sales (Maïzi and Bendavid 2021).

Supply Chain Optimization

Beyond the retail store, IoT devices track the movement of clothing items in transit. Real-time data about the location and condition of shipments can trigger automatic rerouting in case of delays or damage, ensuring timely deliveries to stores (Majeed and Rupasinghe 2017).

Dynamic Pricing

IoT data, combined with external factors like local weather conditions or special events, can influence pricing strategies. For instance, if the system detects a sudden increase in demand for raincoats due to unexpected rain, it can temporarily adjust prices to maximize profit (Caro and Sadr 2019).

Reducing Waste

IoT-enabled sensors can monitor environmental conditions like temperature and humidity. If they detect unfavorable conditions that could damage clothing items, they can send alerts to take corrective actions, such as adjusting climate controls (Alves et al. 2022).

Using IoT data and real-time decision-making, the fashion retailer can respond swiftly to changing customer preferences, minimize stockouts, reduce excess inventory, optimize supply chain operations, and improve profitability. This level of data-driven decision-making is a key advantage of implementing IoT in the fashion industry supply chain (Koot et al. 2021).

8.2.3 IoT in the Fashion Supply Chain: Global Application

8.2.3.1 Supply Chain Visibility

IoT enhances supply chain visibility by tracking the movement of products from manufacturing facilities to distribution centers and retail stores. RFID tags and GPS-enabled devices allow stakeholders to monitor the location and condition of goods in real-time, reducing the risk of loss or theft (Al-Khatib 2023). Companies can use IoT technology to enhance supply chain visibility in various ways (Fig. 8.9). One example involves employing RFID tags and sensors to track and monitor clothing items throughout the supply chain. How it works.

Fig. 8.9 IoT in global fashion supply chain

RFID-Enabled Garment Tracking

Imagine a high-end fashion brand that wants to improve supply chain visibility for its luxury clothing line. The company decided to integrate IoT technology into its supply chain. Each clothing item, such as a designer dress, receives an RFID tag or sensor at the manufacturing stage. How IoT can improve supply chain visibility.

Manufacturing Stage

RFID tags are embedded or attached to each garment during production. These tags contain unique identification information for each item (Nayak et al. 2022).

Inventory Management

As the clothing items move through the supply chain, RFID readers placed at various checkpoints automatically scan and record the presence of each item. This data is then transmitted to a centralized database in real-time (Mostafa et al. 2019).

Warehouse and Distribution Centers

The company places RFID sensors in the brand's warehouses and distribution centers. As clothing items arrive, RFID technology identifies and logs them, providing accurate and up-to-date information about inventory levels (Pal 2020).

Shipping and Transportation

During transportation, the IoT system tracks the location of each item within shipping containers or pallets. Sensors can also monitor environmental conditions, such as temperature and humidity, to ensure that delicate fabrics or materials are transported under the appropriate conditions (Tan and Sidhu 2022).

Retail Stores

When the clothing items arrive at retail stores, RFID readers at the entrance or within the store can automatically update inventory levels and help store staff locate specific items quickly (Mostafa et al. 2019).

Customer Experience

Some fashion brands offer customers the option to interact with RFID tags using smartphones or dedicated apps. Customers can scan the tag to access detailed product information, view care instructions, or even learn about the item's journey from creation to the store (Hoyer et al. 2020).

Benefits of IoT Supply Chain Visibility in Fashion

Real-Time Inventory Management

The fashion brand can maintain accurate inventory records, reducing the risk of overstocking or understocking products (Mostafa et al. 2019).

Efficient Replenishment

Retailers can quickly identify which items are selling well and restock them promptly to meet customer demand (Francisco and Swanson 2018).

Reduced Loss and Theft

RFID technology helps prevent inventory shrinkage and unauthorized removal (theft) of items from stores or warehouses (Pal 2020).

Enhanced Customer Experience

Customers can access additional information about the product, its origin, and care instructions, enhancing their overall experience and trust in the brand (Hoyer et al. 2020).

Supply Chain Efficiency

Improved visibility allows for more efficient transportation and distribution, reducing costs and environmental impact (Ben-Daya et al. 2019).

IoT supply chain visibility in the fashion industry, through RFID technology, offers benefits that include accurate inventory management, improved customer experiences, and greater operational efficiency, all of which contribute to a more transparent and competitive supply chain.

8.2.3.2 Inventory Management

Efficient inventory management is critical in the fashion industry to minimize overstock and stockouts. IoT sensors can monitor inventory levels and provide automated alerts for restocking or reordering, optimizing the supply chain's performance (Mashayekhy et al. 2022).

In the fashion industry, companies can apply IoT technology to inventory management to improve efficiency, reduce costs, and enhance the overall customer experience. An example of how the fashion industry uses IoT for inventory management is shown in Fig. 8.10.

RFID-Enabled Inventory Tracking

Many fashion retailers implement RFID (radio-frequency identification) technology to track their inventory in real-time. The company equips each clothing item or accessory with an RFID tag containing a unique identifier. How it works.

Tagging Merchandise

The company tags each item in the store with an RFID tag or label, which holds a unique ID associated with that product (Nayak et al. 2022).

Fig. 8.10 IoT applications in inventory management

Reader Infrastructure

Strategically place RFID readers throughout the store, in stockrooms, and the supply chain. These readers can communicate with the RFID tags (Tan and Sidhu 2022).

Real-Time Tracking

As merchandise moves within the store, the RFID tags send signals to nearby readers. Inventory management software collects and processes this real-time data (Akram et al. 2022).

Inventory Visibility

Store staff and management can access a central inventory management system to view the real-time status of every item in the store, including information on which items are in stock, their location, and their sizes or variants (Lee 2021).

Automated Reordering

The system automatically updates inventory levels when it sells items. When the stock reaches predefined reorder points, the system can generate automated orders to replenish inventory, ensuring that popular items are never out of stock (Karri et al. 2022).

Benefits of IoT Inventory Management in Fashion

Accuracy

RFID technology significantly reduces the risk of manual errors in inventory counts. Retailers can achieve near-perfect inventory accuracy (Caro and Sadr 2019).

Efficiency

Employees spend less time on manual inventory counts, allowing them to focus on customer service and other value-added tasks (Mostafa et al. 2019).

Stock Visibility

Retailers can see the precise location of items, helping staff quickly locate products for customers and reducing the time customers spend searching for items (Lee 2021).

Preventing Stockouts and Overstock

Automated reordering ensures that items are restocked at the right time, preventing stockouts and reducing the costs associated with overstocking (Mashayekhy et al. 2022).

Loss Prevention

RFID helps deter theft and can track items that may leave the store without being purchased (Pal 2020).

Customer Experience

Customers can access product availability and location information, making their shopping experience more convenient (Hoyer et al. 2020).

Data Insights

Retailers can analyze data collected from RFID to gain insights into consumer behavior, such as which items are frequently tried on but not purchased.

Omni-Channel Integration

IoT inventory management systems can be integrated with e-commerce platforms, ensuring online shoppers can access accurate stock information (Princes and So 2021).

IoT-based inventory management in the fashion industry improves operational efficiency, enhances the customer experience, and enables retailers to adapt to changing consumer preferences quickly.

8.2.3.3 Sustainable Practices

Sustainability is a paramount concern in the fashion industry. IoT supports sustainable practices by enabling the monitoring of environmental conditions, such as temperature and humidity, during the transportation and storage of sensitive materials like

Fig. 8.11 The working of IoT for sustainable development goals

textiles and leather, ensuring compliance with sustainability standards (Manavalan and Jayakrishna 2019).

One example of IoT-sustainable practices in the fashion industry is using smart clothing and connected supply chain management systems to reduce waste and improve environmental sustainability. How it works (Fig. 8.11).

Smart Clothing for Sustainable Fashion

Companies are developing smart clothing items embedded with IoT technology to promote sustainability in the fashion industry.

Smart Fabrics

Some fashion brands use IoT-enabled fabrics to monitor and respond to environmental conditions. For instance, a smart fabric may change color or texture in response to changes in temperature or humidity, reducing the need for multiple clothing items for different weather conditions (Fernández-Caramés and Fraga-Lamas 2018).

Wearable Sensors

IoT sensors embedded in clothing can track the wearer's activity, body temperature, and other vital signs. This information can help consumers make more informed choices about their clothing and lifestyle, potentially reducing consumption and waste (Venkatesh et al. 2020).

Extended Product Life

IoT technology can monitor the condition of clothing and provide maintenance alerts. For example, sensors can detect wear and tear, prompting consumers to repair or recycle clothing instead of discarding it prematurely (Ghoreishi et al. 2020).

Connected Supply Chain Management

IoT can also be applied to improve the sustainability of fashion supply chains.

Inventory Management

RFID and IoT sensors enable real-time inventory tracking, reducing overproduction and excess inventory. This minimizes waste and lowers the environmental impact of unsold clothing (Mostafa et al. 2019).

Supply Chain Transparency

IoT technology allows brands to provide consumers with information about the origins of their clothing, including the sourcing of materials and the manufacturing process. This transparency builds consumer trust and encourages sustainable practices throughout the supply chain (Hauschild and Coll 2023).

Energy Efficiency

IoT-connected devices can help monitor and optimize energy usage in factories and warehouses, reducing the carbon footprint of the fashion industry's operations (Sadeeq and Zeebaree 2021).

Transportation Efficiency

IoT sensors can track the location and condition of clothing shipments. Businesses can use this data to optimize transportation routes and reduce emissions associated with logistics (Pal 2020).

Consumer Engagement

IoT-driven sustainability practices can also engage consumers in sustainable fashion choices.

Personalized Recommendations

The IoT sensors can gather consumer clothing preferences and behavior data via smart mirrors or online apps, allowing brands to provide customers with personalized fashion recommendations. This capability can result in consumers making more intentional and sustainable purchasing decisions (Hoyer et al. 2020).

Circular Fashion Models

IoT technology can support clothing rental and resale platforms. Sensors can ensure the quality and condition of garments, extending their lifespan and promoting a circular fashion economy (Charnley et al. 2022).

By integrating IoT technology into various aspects of the fashion industry, companies can reduce waste, improve supply chain transparency, and engage consumers in sustainable practices, benefitting the environment and aligning with the growing consumer demand for eco-friendly and socially responsible fashion choices.

8.2.3.4 Consumer Engagement

IoT technologies enhance consumer engagement through interactive retail experiences. Smart mirrors and fitting rooms equipped with IoT sensors enable customers to try on virtual outfits, receive personalized recommendations, and access product information, allowing for a more immersive and enjoyable shopping experience (Ajayi et al. 2022).

IoT technology can enhance consumer engagement and provide transparency in the fashion industry supply chain. An example.

Smart Clothing Tags and Consumer Apps

Imagine a fashion retailer using smart clothing tags with RFID or NFC (Near Field Communication) chips. Each garment contains these tags; consumers can interact with them using a dedicated smartphone app. How it works.

Product Information

Customers can use the app to scan the clothing tag when they walk into the store, instantly providing detailed information about the product, including its design, materials, care instructions, and available sizes and colors. It may also include information about the manufacturing process and sustainability practices (Ghoreishi et al. 2020).

Virtual Try-On

Using augmented reality (AR) technology within the app, customers can virtually try on the clothing without physically wearing it. They can see how different items look on them and mix and match outfits in the app (Akram et al. 2022).

Inventory and Availability

The app can check real-time inventory and store availability. If a particular size or color is not in stock in the physical store, the app can suggest alternatives or provide the option to order it online (Hoyer et al. 2022).

Sustainability and Supply Chain Transparency

The app can provide information on the garment's environmental impact for customers interested in sustainability. It can display the materials used, whether organic or sustainable, and even trace the supply chain, showing information about the source of the fabric and the location of where the garment was manufactured (Ghoreishi et al. 2020).

Personalized Recommendations

Over time, the app can gather data on the customer's preferences and style choices. Using machine learning, it can offer personalized product recommendations and notify customers of new arrivals or promotions tailored to their tastes (Hoyer et al. 2020).

Benefits

Enhanced Customer Experience

This IoT-based system provides a more engaging and informative shopping experience, helping customers make informed decisions (Hoyer et al. 2020).

Increased Sales

The retailer can increase sales and customer satisfaction by offering personalized recommendations and virtual try-on features (Hoyer et al. 2020).

Supply Chain Transparency

Customers interested in sustainability can gain insights into the supply chain and make more conscious purchasing decisions (Hauschild and Coll 2023).

Inventory Optimization

Real-time inventory data helps the retailer manage stock efficiently and avoid overstock or understock situations (Yerpude and Singhal 2018).

Data Insights

The retailer can gather valuable data on customer behavior and preferences and use this data to refine marketing strategies and inventory planning (Pal 2020).

This example shows how the fashion industry supply chain can leverage IoT technology to engage consumers, create a more interactive shopping experience, and provide transparency into the product's origin and sustainability, ultimately benefiting both the retailer and the customers.

8.2.3.5 Predictive Analytics

Fashion supply chains can leverage IoT data for predictive analytics to forecast demand and trends accurately, minimizing the risk of overproduction and waste and aligning production with consumer preferences (Fahim and Sillitti 2019). IoT predictive analytics can be a game-changer in the fashion industry supply chain, helping companies forecast demand, optimize inventory management, and enhance production efficiency (Fig. 8.12).

Smart Inventory Management

Imagine a fashion retailer that uses IoT devices such as RFID tags and sensors on clothing items and within its warehouses. These IoT devices continuously collect real-time data on each item's movement and status. How to apply it.

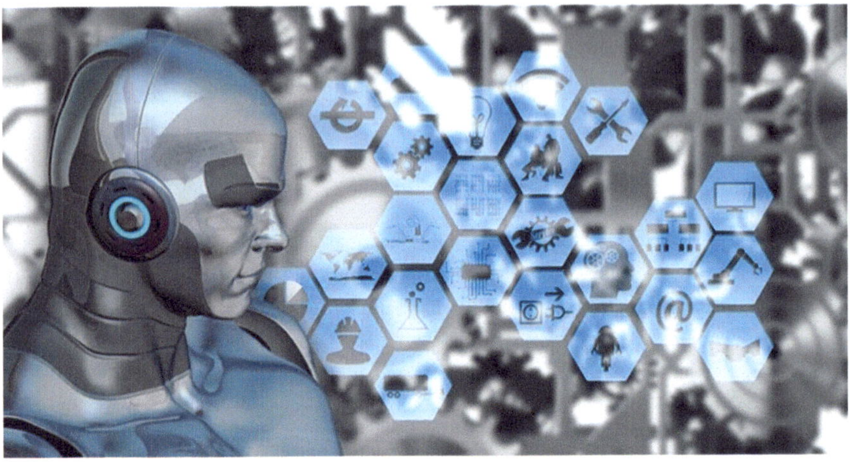

Fig. 8.12 IoT in predictive analysis

Real-Time Inventory Tracking

RFID tags and sensors provide real-time data on the location and status of each clothing item, sending this data to a centralized system (Tejesh and Neeraja 2018).

Demand Forecasting

Predictive analytics algorithms analyze historical sales data, seasonality, trends, and external factors (weather) to forecast future demand for specific clothing items. For instance, the system can predict that a certain type of winter coat will be in high demand in the upcoming months based on historical sales patterns and weather forecasts (Seyedan and Mafakheri 2020).

Optimized Replenishment

If you utilize demand forecasts and real-time inventory data, the system can automatically trigger reordering items running low in stock, ensuring that popular items are always available and reducing the risk of stockouts (Francisco and Swanson 2018).

Dynamic Pricing

Predictive analytics can also help in setting dynamic pricing strategies. For instance, if the system predicts high demand for a particular dress style in the coming weeks, the retailer can adjust the price upward to maximize profit (Wang et al. 2021).

Supply Chain Optimization

The system can predict potential supply chain disruptions, such as delays in shipping or manufacturing, by analyzing historical data and external factors, allowing the company to take proactive measures to mitigate disruptions and maintain a smooth supply chain (Majeed and Rupasinghe 2017).

Reduced Overstock

Predictive analytics can identify items likely to become overstocked or go out of season. The system can provide recommendations for markdowns or promotions to clear excess inventory before it becomes a financial burden (Saillaja et al. 2023).

Personalized Recommendations

IoT devices can also collect data on customer behavior, such as what items they try on and how long they spend in the store. Predictive analytics can use this data to make personalized product recommendations, enhancing the shopping experience and increasing sales (Hoyer et al. 2020).

Production Planning

Predictive analytics can extend to the production stage by forecasting demand for raw materials and components, optimizing production schedules, and reducing waste in the manufacturing process (Seyedan and Mafakheri 2020).

By applying IoT predictive analytics in this manner, fashion companies can achieve more efficient inventory management, reduce costs, increase customer satisfaction, and ultimately enhance their competitiveness in the market. This data-driven approach allows businesses to adapt quickly to changing market conditions and consumer preferences, which is crucial in the fast-paced fashion industry.

8.2.3.6 Ethical Sourcing and Transparency

IoT can verify the authenticity of products and materials, helping combat counterfeiting in the fashion industry. Additionally, blockchain technology, often integrated with IoT, enhances transparency by providing an immutable ledger of the product's journey from source to consumer (Radanliev et al. 2021).

How can the fashion industry supply chain use IoT to promote ethical sourcing and transparency.

Traceability of Sustainable Fabrics

Imagine a clothing brand committed to using sustainable and ethically sourced fabrics. To provide transparency to consumers and ensure the authenticity of its claims, the brand integrates IoT technology into its supply chain.

Smart Tags on Fabrics

The clothing brand attaches smart RFID tags or NFC (Near-Field Communication) chips to each fabric roll it sources. These tags contain detailed information about the fabric's origin, including the farm or factory where it was produced, its composition, and any certifications for sustainability and fair labor practices (Nayak et al. 2022).

Data Collection and Monitoring

Throughout the supply chain journey, various checkpoints, such as textile factories, warehouses, and distribution centers, strategically place IoT sensors. These sensors collect data on the fabric's movement, storage conditions (e.g., temperature and humidity), and handling procedures (Ahmed et al. 2021).

Blockchain Integration

The smart tags and IoT sensors record the data they collect on a blockchain, which is a temper-proof digital ledger. The blockchain ledger is accessible to all stakeholders involved in the supply chain, including consumers, suppliers, and auditors (Alves et al. 2022).

Consumer Transparency

Customers can use a mobile app or website to scan the smart tags on clothing items. This action gives them instant access to a detailed history of the fabric used in their garment, including its journey from source to production. They can verify the fabric's authenticity and sustainability certifications (Sunny et al. 2020).

Supply Chain Accountability

In the fashion industry, manufacturers and suppliers have incentives to adhere to ethical and sustainable practices. They know that they transparently record and make their actions and adherence to standards accessible to the public, creating accountability and encouraging responsible sourcing (Jayashri et al. 2023).

Benefits

Enhanced Trust

Consumers can trust the brand's claims about ethical sourcing and sustainability, as they can access verifiable information about the fabric's journey (Alves et al. 2022).

Ethical Sourcing

Suppliers and manufacturers are encouraged to uphold ethical and sustainable practices to maintain their reputation and business relationships (Rejeb et al. 2020).

Reduced Counterfeiting

The transparency offered by IoT and blockchain reduces the risk of counterfeit fabrics entering the supply chain (Chin et al. 2021).

Data-Driven Decision-Making

The data collected from IoT sensors can be analyzed to identify inefficiencies, optimize transportation routes, and reduce waste in the supply chain (Koot et al. 2021).

By utilizing IoT technology and blockchain integration, this fashion brand ensures ethical sourcing and transparency in its supply chain, aligning its business practices with the growing consumer demand for sustainable and ethically produced clothing.

Integrating IoT into the global fashion supply chain represents a profound transformation of traditional practices. The fundamentals of IoT, including sensor devices, connectivity, data analytics, and real-time decision-making, combine to optimize supply chain operations, enhance sustainability, and improve consumer engagement. This holistic approach to supply chain management is poised to revolutionize the fashion industry worldwide, developing efficiency, transparency, and ethical practices while catering to evolving consumer demands. As the fashion supply chain continues to evolve, the role of IoT remains central to its advancement in a rapidly changing global landscape (Rejeb et al. 2020).

8.3 Brand Leaders in the Fashion Industry Utilizing IoT in the Supply Chain

Several fashion industry companies utilize IoT technologies in their supply chains to enhance efficiency, transparency, and sustainability.

In today's fast-paced and interconnected world, technology is revolutionizing almost every aspect of our lives, and the fashion industry is no exception. The fashion supply chain, a complex web of processes that bring clothing from concept to consumer, has seen a remarkable transformation thanks to the integration of cutting-edge technologies. One of the most noteworthy advancements is the utilization of IoT technologies. IoT, a network of interconnected devices and sensors that communicate and share data, has been harnessed by numerous companies in the fashion industry to enhance their supply chain operations. We will look at a few of them as prime examples of how effective these technologies are and the impact they can have on any organization (Pal 2020).

We will uncover the innovative ways three real companies leverage IoT to improve efficiency, transparency, sustainability, and customer experiences. From real-time inventory tracking using RFID technology to responsive manufacturing based on customer preferences, IoT enables fashion brands to stay ahead in an ever-evolving industry. The fascinating world where fashion meets technology, where smart solutions are woven seamlessly into the fabric of the supply chain.

8.3.1 Let's Begin with Zara (Inditex)

Zara, one of the most well-known fast-fashion retailers, has strategically integrated IoT technologies into its supply chain operations to achieve greater efficiency, accuracy, and responsiveness. Here is an explanation of how Zara uses IoT in its supply chain, according to López et al. (2022), as shown in Fig. 8.13.

8.3.2 RFID Technology

Zara is a pioneer in the fashion industry regarding RFID adoption. They attach RFID tags to every single item of clothing in their stores. These RFID tags contain unique identifiers that can be wirelessly scanned and tracked throughout the supply chain. How Zara utilizes RFID.

Fig. 8.13 IoT applications by Zara in retailingsss

8.3.2.1 Inventory Tracking

RFID technology allows Zara to monitor the movement of items in real-time. Zara tags a product with an RFID chip as soon as it is manufactured, enabling them to know the exact location of each item within their supply chain, from production to distribution to stores.

8.3.2.2 Stock Replenishment

Zara quickly identifies when products are running low on the shelves. Staff easily locate items that need replenishment and restock them promptly, reducing out-of-stock situations and missed sales opportunities.

8.3.2.3 Inventory Accuracy

Traditional inventory counting methods are often time-consuming and prone to errors. With RFID, Zara performs inventory counts rapidly and accurately, ensuring their inventory records are always up to date minimizing discrepancies.

8.3.2.4 Streamlined Returns

RFID tags also simplify the returns process. When customers return items, the RFID technology helps Zara quickly identify the product, verify its authenticity, and restock it efficiently.

8.3.3 Real-Time Data Analytics

Zara collects data from RFID tags and IoT devices throughout its supply chain. This data is processed and analyzed in real-time to make informed decisions. Here's how Zara utilizes it.

8.3.3.1 Demand Forecasting

Zara analyzes customer buying patterns and preferences based on real-time sales data, helping them to anticipate customer demand for specific products and to adjust the production schedules, accordingly, thus reducing overproduction and excess inventory.

8.3.3.2 Inventory Optimization

By continuously monitoring inventory and sales data, Zara optimizes its stock levels in stores and warehouses, reducing storage costs and ensuring that products are readily available when customers want them.

8.3.3.3 Supply Chain Efficiency

Real-time data analytics help Zara streamline its supply chain operations. They identify bottlenecks, optimize routes, and improve overall logistics efficiency.

8.3.4 Responsive Manufacturing

Zara is renowned for its fast turnaround time in getting new fashion trends from the runway to the store shelves. IoT plays a crucial role in this process.

8.3.4.1 Quick Response (QR) System

Zara's IoT-driven QR system quickly relays customer feedback and market trends to their design and production teams, enabling Zara to design, produce, and deliver new clothing lines in a matter of weeks, compared to the months it takes traditional retailers.

8.3.4.2 Customization

Zara adapts its production based on real-time sales and customer feedback, allowing for customization and small-batch production runs of popular items.

8.3.5 Enhanced Sustainability

Zara's use of IoT also extends to sustainability efforts.

8.3.5.1 Material Traceability

IoT technologies help Zara trace the source of materials and monitor their environmental impact, allowing it to make more sustainable sourcing decisions.

8.3.5.2 Reduced Waste

Better inventory management through IoT reduces the risk of overproduction and waste, contributing to Zara's sustainability goals.

Zara's innovative use of IoT in its supply chain operations has transformed how it manages inventory, responds to customer demands, and stays ahead of fashion trends. By leveraging RFID technology and real-time data analytics, Zara has achieved greater operational efficiency, reduced costs, and improved its ability to quickly deliver fresh fashion styles to consumers.

8.3.6 Next, Let's Move on to Take a Look at Adidas

Adidas actively uses IoT technology in its supply chain to enhance efficiency, visibility, and sustainability (Fig. 8.14). While specific details and initiatives may have evolved more recently, this is a general overview of how Adidas has been utilizing IoT in its supply chain, according to Galluccio and Agrell (2022) and Wibowo et al. (2020).

8.3.6.1 Inventory Management

Adidas implemented RFID technology in its supply chain to improve inventory management. RFID tags are attached to products, enabling real-time tracking of items through the supply chain, and allowing Adidas to have a more accurate and

Fig. 8.14 IoT application by Adidas

up-to-date view of its inventory levels at various stages of production, warehousing, and distribution.

8.3.6.2 Visibility and Transparency

IoT sensors and RFID technology give Adidas greater visibility into its supply chain operations by enhancing transparency and allowing the company to monitor the location and status of products, from raw materials and components to finished goods. This visibility helps identify bottlenecks, reduce lead times, and improve supply chain efficiency.

8.3.6.3 Quality Control

Adidas uses IoT sensors to actively monitor the quality and condition of products during transportation and storage. For instance, temperature and humidity sensors ensure that sensitive materials, such as footwear with adhesives, are stored optimally to prevent damage or degradation.

8.3.6.4 Predictive Maintenance

In manufacturing facilities, Adidas uses IoT sensors to monitor the condition of machinery and equipment. This data is analyzed to predict when maintenance is needed, reducing downtime and ensuring efficient production.

8.3.6.5 Sustainability Efforts

Adidas has been actively working on sustainability initiatives. IoT plays a role in tracking and tracing sustainable materials and processes in the supply chain, enabling the company to provide consumers with more information about the environmental impact of their products.

8.3.6.6 Consumer Engagement

While primarily focused on the supply chain, Adidas also explores IoT-connected products like smart sneakers. These products provide consumers with athletic performance shoe 'wear and tear' data and even offer personalized workouts or shoe maintenance recommendations.

8.3.6.7 Supply Chain Optimization

Adidas optimizes its supply chain operations by leveraging IoT data and analytics, including demand forecasting, production planning, and logistics optimization. For instance, real-time consumer preferences and inventory level data can help adjust production schedules and distribution routes accordingly.

8.3.6.8 Counterfeit Prevention

RFID technology also helps in counterfeit prevention. Each authentic product has a unique RFID tag verified by both Adidas and consumers, helping maintain brand integrity and ensure customers are buying genuine products (Nayak et al. 2021).

It is important to note that Adidas, like many other companies in the fashion industry, is continually innovating and expanding its use of IoT technology in its supply chain to stay competitive, reduce costs, enhance sustainability, and improve customer experiences.

8.3.7 Lastly, Let's Take a Look at Levi Strauss & Co.

Levi Strauss & Co. is actively exploring and implementing IoT technologies in its supply chain operations to enhance efficiency, transparency, and sustainability (Fig. 8.15). The following is an overview of how Levi's uses IoT in its supply chain. The following is an explanation of how Levi Strauss & Co. is utilizing IoT in its supply chain, according to Dutta (2020) and Anis et al. (2022).

Fig. 8.15 IoT application by Levi's

8.3.7.1 RFID Technology for Inventory Management

Levi's uses RFID technology to track and manage inventory more effectively. RFID tags are attached to individual clothing items or shipping cartons, allowing for real-time tracking of products as they move through the supply chain (Nayak et al. 2015). The benefits of this technology include.

Improved Inventory Accuracy

RFID helps ensure that the company always has an accurate and up-to-date view of its inventory, reducing the risk of overstocking or understocking products, which can lead to cost savings and better customer service.

Enhanced Visibility

RFID enables Levi's to track the location of products in real-time, from manufacturing facilities to distribution centers and retail stores. This visibility allows for better demand forecasting and efficient restocking.

Reduced Shrinkage and Theft

RFID tags deter theft and reduce reported shrinkage in retail outlets. If someone tries to remove or tamper with an RFID tag, it triggers an alarm, helping to prevent theft.

Supply Chain Transparency

IoT technologies are instrumental in improving the transparency of Levi's supply chain. The company traces the journey of its products from the raw materials stage through production and distribution to the retail stores. This transparency is increasingly important to consumers who want to know the origins of the products they purchase and the sustainability of the supply chain.

Sustainability Initiatives

Levi's is using IoT to support its sustainability efforts. By tracking and monitoring the environmental impact of its supply chain operations, the company identifies areas where it can reduce waste, energy consumption, and water usage. IoT sensors and data analytics help pinpoint opportunities for improvement.

Quality Control

Quality control processes employ IoT devices. Levi's utilizes sensors to monitor the condition of garments during production and transportation, ensuring that products meet their quality standards and are delivered in the best possible condition to customers.

Smart Manufacturing

Levi's is exploring the use of IoT in smart manufacturing processes, involving connecting machinery and equipment in factories to collect data on production efficiency, machine health, and worker safety. By analyzing this data, Levi's optimizes its manufacturing processes and ensures a safer working environment.

Consumer Engagement

While not directly related to the supply chain, Levi's has also been experimenting with IoT-connected clothing and accessories that enhance the customer experience. For example, they've developed products like the "Levi's Commuter Jacket," which features built-in IoT technology, allowing wearers to control their smartphone and receive notifications through gestures on the jacket's sleeve.

Levi Strauss & Co. is leveraging IoT technologies in its fashion supply chain to improve inventory management, enhance transparency, support sustainability initiatives, maintain product quality, and optimize manufacturing processes. These initiatives help the company operate more efficiently and meet the evolving demands of today's fashion industry while providing a better experience for both customers and stakeholders.

8.4 Conclusion

Integrating IoT technology into the fashion industry supply chain has developed a transformative era of efficiency, transparency, and sustainability. This chapter has shared the impact of IoT on every section of the fashion supply chain, showing the changes and benefits it brings to both industry players and consumers alike. From the beginning of a garment's creation, IoT plays a part as sensors monitor and optimize conditions in textile manufacturing, ensuring the quality and consistency of materials. This level of precision continues through production, with IoT-driven processes enhancing machinery efficiency, reducing waste, and minimizing environmental impact.

The most visible change occurs in inventory management, where RFID technology offers real-time tracking and accuracy (George et al. 2023). Retailers like Levi Strauss & Co. have used this capability to avoid overstocking and understocking issues, ensuring that customers find the products they desire when they want them. IoT's influence extends beyond the factory floor and stockroom as supply chain transparency becomes the new industry standard (Hauschild and Coll 2023). Consumers increasingly demand to know the origins and ethical practices behind the products they purchase. IoT technology helps meet this expectation by providing a clear and detailed record of a garment's journey from source to shelf.

Furthermore, IoT is pivotal in advancing sustainability efforts across the fashion supply chain. By monitoring environmental impact and resource consumption, companies can identify areas for improvement and drive the industry toward more eco-conscious practices. In the age of IoT, quality control reaches unprecedented levels as sensors and data analytics ensure that garments meet stringent standards, resulting in greater customer satisfaction and loyalty (Pal 2020). Beyond supply chain optimization, IoT has even ventured into consumer engagement by introducing smart clothing and accessories. Innovations like the "Levi's Commuter Jacket" demonstrate how IoT can seamlessly merge fashion and technology, enhancing the wearer's experience while maintaining style and functionality.

As we conclude this chapter, it is evident that IoT has become an indispensable tool in the fashion industry supply chain. Its ability to enhance efficiency, transparency, sustainability, and customer engagement is a testament to the impact of technology on an age-old industry. The future promises even greater innovation and integration of IoT, paving the way for a fashion industry that is stylish but also conscientious and dynamic. The intersection of fashion and technology is worth following as it reshapes how we dress and view the industry.

References

Abd Rahman MSB, Mohamad E, Abdul Rahman AAB (2021) Development of IoT—enabled data analytics enhance decision support system for lean manufacturing process improvement. Concurrent Eng 29(3):208–220

Ahmad S, Miskon S, Alabdan R, Tlili I (2020) Towards sustainable textile and apparel industry: exploring the role of business intelligence systems in the era of industry 4.0. Sustainability 12(7):2632

Ahmed S, Kalsoom T, Ramzan N, Pervez Z, Azmat M, Zeb B, Ur Rehman M (2021) Towards supply chain visibility using internet of things: a dyadic analysis review. Sensors 21(12):4158

Ajayi S, Loureiro SMC, Langaro D (2022) Internet of things and consumer engagement on retail: state-of-the-art and future directions. EuroMed J Bus

Akram SV, Malik PK, Singh R, Gehlot A, Juyal A, Ghafoor KZ Shrestha S (2022) Implementation of digitalized technologies for fashion industry 4.0: opportunities and challenges. Sci Program

Al-Khatib AW (2023) Internet of things, big data analytics and operational performance: the mediating effect of supply chain visibility. J Manuf Technol Manage 34(1):1–24

Alves L, Ferreira Cruz E, Lopes SI, Faria PM, Rosado da Cruz AM (2022) Towards circular economy in the textiles and clothing value chain through blockchain technology and IoT: a review. Waste Manage Res 40(1):3–23

Anis M, Chawky S, Abdel Halim A (2022) Retail. Mapping innovation: the discipline of building opportunity across value chains. Springer International Publishing, Cham, pp 283–306

Ashton K (2009) That 'internet of things' thing. RFID J 22(7):97–114

Astill J, Dara RA, Campbell M, Farber JM, Fraser ED, Sharif S, Yada RY (2019) Transparency in food supply chains: a review of enabling technology solutions. Trends Food Sci Technol 91:240–247

Attaran M (2020) Digital technology enablers and their implications for supply chain management. Supply Chain Forum: Int J 21(3):158–172 Taylor & Francis

Ben-Daya M, Hassini E, Bahroun Z (2019) Internet of things and supply chain management: a literature review. Int J Prod Res 57(15–16):4719–4742

Caro F, Sadr R (2019) The internet of things (IoT) in retail: bridging supply and demand. Bus Horiz 62(1):47–54

Charnley F, Knecht F, Muenkel H, Pletosu D, Rickard V, Sambonet C, Schneider M, Zhang C (2022) Can digital technologies increase consumer acceptance of circular business models? The case of second-hand fashion Sustainability 14(8):4589

Chan CO, Lau HC, Fan Y (2018) IoT data acquisition in fashion retail application: fuzzy logic approach. In: 2018 International conference on artificial intelligence and big data (ICAIBD). IEEE, pp 52–56

Chang RI, Lee CY, Hung YH (2021) Cloud-based analytics module for predictive maintenance of the textile manufacturing process. Appl Sci 11(21):9945

Chen CL (2019). Value creation by SMEs participating in global value chains under industry 4.0 trend: case study of textile industry in Taiwan. J Glob Inf Technol Manage 22(2):120–145

Chin SH, Lu C, Ho PT, Shiao YF, Wu TJ (2021) Commodity anti-counterfeiting decision in e-commerce trade based on machine learning and internet of things. Comput Stan Interfaces 76:103504

Dash D, Farooq R, Panda JS, Sandhyavani KV (2019) Internet of things (IoT): the new paradigm of HRM and skill development in the fourth industrial revolution (Industry 4.0). IUP J Inf Technol 15(4)

De Vass T, Shee H, Miah SJ (2021) IoT in supply chain management: a narrative on retail sector sustainability. Int J Logistics Res Appl 24(6):605–624

Ding J, Nemati M, Ranaweera C, Choi J (2020) IoT connectivity technologies and applications: a survey. IEEE Access 8:67646–67673

Dutta P, Choi TM, Somani S, Butala R (2020) Blockchain technology in supply chain operations: applications, challenges, and research opportunities. Trans Res Part E: Logistics Trans Rev 142:102067
Esmaeilian B, Sarkis J, Lewis K, Behdad S (2020) Blockchain for the future of sustainable supply chain management in Industry 4.0. Resour Conserv Recycl 163:105064
Fahim M, Sillitti A (2019) Anomaly detection, analysis and prediction techniques in IoT environment: a systematic literature review. IEEE Access 7:81664–81681
Fernández-Caramés TM, Fraga-Lamas P (2018) Towards the internet of smart clothing: a review on IoT wearables and garments for creating intelligent connected e-textiles. Electronics 7(12):405
Francisco K, Swanson D (2018) The supply chain has no clothes: technology adoption of blockchain for supply chain transparency. Logistics 2(1):2
Galluccio, A. and Agrell, P.J., 2022. Industry 4.0 in Focus: the Adidas Speedfactory, Université Catholique de Louvain, pp 21–32
George M, Nayak R, UlHaq I, Pham H, Panwar T, Nguyen DA (2023) RFID technology for sustainable fashion and textile manufacturing. In: Sustainability, economics, innovation, globalisation and organisational psychology conference. Springer Nature Singapore, Singapore, pp 473–484
Ghoreishi M, Happonen A, Pynnönen M (2020) Exploring industry 4.0 technologies to enhance circularity in textile industry: role of internet of things. In: Twenty-first international working seminar on production economics, p 16
Hauschild C, Coll A (2023) The influence of technologies in increasing transparency in textile supply chains. Logistics 7(3):55
Heim H, Hopper C (2022) Dress code: the digital transformation of the circular fashion supply chain. Int J Fashion Des Technol Educ 15(2):233–244
Hoyer WD, Kroschke M, Schmitt B, Kraume K, Shankar V (2020) Transforming the customer experience through new technologies. J Interact Mark 51(1):57–71
Jayashri N, Rampur V, Gangodkar D, Abirami M, Balarengadurai C, Kumar A (2023) Improved block chain system for high secured IoT integrated supply chain. Measur Sens 25:100633
Karri A, Rao SS, Ashoka DV, Nethravathi B, Sahana V, Vishnu BV (2022) Hardware Inventory Management System Using IoT. In: 2022 4th International conference on cognitive computing and information processing (CCIP). IEEE, pp 1–4
Khan Y, Su'ud MBM, Alam MM, Ahmad SF, Ahmad AYB, Khan N (2022) Application of internet of things (IoT) in sustainable supply chain management. Sustainability 15(1):694
Koot M, Mes MR, Iacob ME (2021) A systematic literature review of supply chain decision making supported by the internet of things and big data analytics. Comput Ind Eng 154:107076
Lee YK (2021) Transformation of the innovative and sustainable supply chain with upcoming real-time fashion systems. Sustainability 13(3):1081
López T, Riedler T, Köhnen H, Fütterer M (2022) Digital value chain restructuring and labour process transformations in the fast-fashion sector: evidence from the value chains of Zara & H&M. Glob Netw 22(4):684–700
Madakam S, Lake V, Lake V, Lake V (2015) Internet of things (IoT): a literature review. J Comput Commun 3(05):164
Maïzi Y, Bendavid Y (2021) Building a digital twin for IoT smart stores: a case in retail and apparel industry. Int J Simul Process Model 16(2):147–160
Majeed AA, Rupasinghe TD (2017) Internet of things (IoT) embedded future supply chains for industry 4.0: an assessment from an erp-based fashion apparel and footwear industry. Int J Supply Chain Manage 6(1):25–40
Manavalan E, Jayakrishna K (2019) A review of internet of things (IoT) embedded sustainable supply chain for industry 4.0 requirements. Comput Ind Eng 127:925–953
Mashayekhy Y, Babaei A, Yuan XM, Xue A (2022) Impact of internet of things (IoT) on inventory management: a literature survey. Logistics 6(2):33
Moshood TD, Nawanir G, Sorooshian S, Okfalisa O (2021) Digital twins driven supply chain visibility within logistics: a new paradigm for future logistics. Appl Syst Innov 4(2):29

Mostafa N, Hamdy W, Alawady H (2019) Impacts of internet of things on supply chains: a framework for warehousing. Soc Sci 8(3):84
Nayak R, George M, Haq IU, Pham HC (2022) Sustainability benefits of RFID technology in Vietnamese fashion supply chain. Clean Logistics Supply Chain 5:100086
Nayak R, Singh A, Padhye R, Wang L (2015) RFID in textile and clothing manufacturing: technology and challenges. Fashion Tex 2:1–16
Nayak R, Majo G, Haq IU, Panwar T, Pham HH (2021). Sustainable Fashion Manufacturing in Vietnam Achieved by the Use of RFID Technology. In: American collegiate retailing association (ACRA) 2022 conference proceedings. American Collegiate Retailing Association (ACRA) 2022 Conference Proceedings, pp 113–119
Pal K (2020) Internet of things and blockchain technology in apparel manufacturing supply chain data management. Procedia Comput Sci 170:450–457
Pasi BN, Mahajan SK, Rane SB (2020) Smart supply chain management: a perspective of industry 4.0. Supply Chain Manage 29(5):3016–3030
Piramuthu S (2022) IoT, Environmental sustainability, agricultural supply chains. Procedia Comput Sci 204:811–816
Plageras AP, Psannis KE, Stergiou C, Wang H, Gupta BB (2018) Efficient IoT-based sensor big data collection-processing and analysis in smart buildings. Future Gener Comput Syst 82:349–357
Prajapati D, Chan FT, Chelladurai H, Lakshay L, Pratap S (2022) An internet of things embedded sustainable supply chain management of B2B e-commerce. Sustainability 14(9):5066
Princes E, So IG (2021) IoT based Omni-channel consumer conformity in fashion industry: do gender, age, monthly income still matter? Int J Organ Bus Excellence 4(1):9–20
Radanliev P, De Roure D, Ani U, Carvalho G (2021) The ethics of shared Covid-19 risks: an epistemological framework for ethical health technology assessment of risk in vaccine supply chain infrastructures. Health Technol 11:1083–1091
Rathore B (2019). Artificial intelligence in sustainable fashion marketing: transforming the supply chain landscape. Eduzone: Int Peer Rev/Refereed Multi J 8(2):25–38
Rejeb A, Simske S, Rejeb K, Treiblmaier H, Zailani S (2020) Internet of things research in supply chain management and logistics: a bibliometric analysis. Internet of Things 12:100318
Sadeeq MA, Zeebaree S (2021) Energy management for internet of things via distributed systems. J Appl Sci Technol Trends 2(02):59–71
Saha P, Talapatra S, Belal HM, Jackson V (2022) Unleashing the potential of the TQM and industry 4.0 to achieve sustainability performance in the context of a developing country. Glob J Flex Syst Manage 23(4):495–513
Saillaja V, Menaka M, Kumaravel V, Machap K (2023) Development of an IoT-based inventory management system for retail stores. In: 2023 International conference on sustainable computing and smart systems (ICSCSS). IEEE, pp 954–958
Seyedan M, Mafakheri F (2020) Predictive big data analytics for supply chain demand forecasting: methods, applications, and research opportunities. J Big Data 7(1):1–22
Stulga P, Whitfield RI, Love J, Evans D (2022) Towards sustainable manufacturing with industry 4.0: a framework for the textile industry. Proc Des Soc 2:283–292
Subramanian G, Thampy AS, Ugwuoke NV, Ramnani B (2021) Crypto pharmacy-digital medicine: a mobile application integrated with hybrid blockchain to tackle the issues in pharma supply chain. IEEE Open J Comput Soc 2:26–37
Sunny J, Undralla N, Pillai VM (2020) Supply chain transparency through blockchain-based traceability: an overview with demonstration. Comput Ind Eng 150:106895
Syafrudin M, Alfian G, Fitriyani NL, Rhee J (2018) Performance analysis of IoT-based sensor, big data processing, and machine learning model for real-time monitoring system in automotive manufacturing. Sensors 18(9):2946
Tan WC, Sidhu MS (2022) Review of RFID and IoT integration in supply chain management. Oper Res Perspect 9:100229
Tejesh BSS, Neeraja SJAEJ (2018) Warehouse inventory management system using IoT and open-source framework. Alexandria Eng J 57(4):3817–3823

Venkatesh VG, Kang K, Wang B, Zhong RY, Zhang A (2020) System architecture for blockchain based transparency of supply chain social sustainability. Robot Comput-Integrated Manuf 63:101896

Wang B, Luo W, Zhang A, Tian Z, Li Z (2020) Blockchain-enabled circular supply chain management: a system architecture for fast fashion. Comput Ind 123:103324

Wang T, Lu Y, Wang J, Dai HN, Zheng X, Jia W (2021) EIHDP: edge-intelligent hierarchical dynamic pricing based on cloud-edge-client collaboration for IoT systems. IEEE Trans Comput 70(8):1285–1298

Wibowo L, Widjajanta B, Fadillah A, Riswanto A, Aprianti V, Widjaja Y, Eka A, Sujono H, Romi M (2020) Supply chain analysis of hedonic shopping value on behavioral intention creation of multinational footwear company. Uncertain Supply Chain Manage 8(4):745–752

Yerpude S, Singhal TK (2018) Smart warehouse with internet of things supported inventory management system. Int J Pure Appl Math 118(24):1–15

Chapter 9
3D Printing and Additive Manufacturing: Recent Trends in Fashion and Textile Production

Ashish Bhardwaj

Abstract 3D printing and additive manufacturing represent revolutionary advancements in production technology, enabling the creation of complex, customized, and functional objects through layer-by-layer material deposition. This process is different from traditional subtractive manufacturing, which shapes an object by removing material. Because of the technology's adaptability to a wide range of materials—including plastics, metals, ceramics, and composites—it can be applied to a variety of industries, including consumer goods, healthcare, automotive, and aerospace. Key advantages include reduced material waste, the ability to produce intricate geometries, and the facilitation of rapid prototyping, which accelerates the product development cycle. Furthermore, 3D printing supports on-demand manufacturing, reducing inventory costs and enabling localized production, thereby minimizing supply chain disruptions. Despite its numerous benefits, challenges such as material limitations, print speed, and high initial costs remain. To overcome these obstacles and realize the full potential of additive manufacturing and 3D printing to completely transform contemporary manufacturing processes, more research and development is imperative.

Keywords 3D printing · Additive manufacturing · 3D modelling · Fashion and textile · Zero-waste manufacturing · Sustainability

9.1 Introduction

The technique of layer-by-layer building three-dimensional objects from a digital file is called additive manufacturing, or 3D printing. It makes use of a 3D printer, which can print with a wide range of materials, such as food, plastic, resin, and metal (Spahiu et al. 2016; Vanderploeg et al. 2016). 3D printing is the general term

A. Bhardwaj (✉)
FAE Department, TIT&S, Bhiwani 127021, India
e-mail: ashishbha21@gmail.com

R. Nayak et al. (eds.), *Use of Digital and Advanced Technologies in the Fashion Supply Chain*, Springer Series in Fashion Business,
https://doi.org/10.1007/978-981-97-7528-6_9

for those technologies that, based on a geometrical representation, create physical objects by successive addition of material according to the standard, ISO/ASTM52900:2015 (Additive manufacturing—General principles—Terminology). Prototypes were initially produced using 3D printing, also known as rapid prototyping. 3D printing technologies have garnered significant attention in various production domains in recent times.

The fact that it is widely used in various fields demonstrates how important it is for producing or prototyping various items. When producing complex geometries that are challenging to create with traditional industrial production methods, or when producing objects for the aviation industry or other fields without access to other production machinery, 3D printing proves to be advantageous. Many industries, including healthcare, aerospace, and infrastructure, have made extensive use of 3D printing to create intricate and personalized products. The fashion industry has shown increasing interest in 3D printing in recent times. This is a result of the inadvertent advantages of 3D printing for the fashion industry, including personalization, customization, and the ability to create intricate and unusual designs. With the increasing advancement and accessibility of 3D printing technology, it is probable that a growing number of fashion designers and brands will integrate 3D printing into their products and collections (Berman 2012).

Approximately 6% of world trade is made up of the apparel sector. The industry's massive scale and the concerning rate of waste generation make waste reduction a crucial task. Landfills receive about 11 million tons of textile waste annually in the United States alone (Kaye 2011; Gillson et al. 2004). The apparel industry can pollute the environment and uses a lot of energy and water, in addition to producing a lot of waste. The source of clothing fiber is either natural (cotton, silk, sheep, etc.) or synthetic (such as oil-based polyester), and in both cases requires significant amount of water and energy to be produced first hand. While synthetic fibers emit a variety of pollutants, including volatile organic compounds (VOCs) and acid gases, the production of cotton fiber necessitates the use of pesticides that are hazardous to both human health and the environment. Therefore, to lessen the effects of production methods on the environment, cleaner technologies are required.

Clothes are disposable items these days, and the emergence of fast fashion ideas raises environmental risks if the lifecycle of the product is not carefully managed (Claudio 2007). The world's environment and resources will be under more and more strain from the use of clothing with short lifespans and fast fashion, rendering the garment production sector unsustainable. Consequently, to lessen the industry's environmental impact and improve sustainability, it is crucial to investigate potential ways of extending the clothing lifecycle. Here, we hope to highlight the opportunities presented by the rapidly developing field of additive manufacturing technology for enhancing the sustainability of the apparel sector.

A novel production technique called additive manufacturing (AM) involves directly manufacturing digital models by adding smaller components. It is the next development in computer numeric control (CNC) machines, with the main distinction being that it uses an additive process instead of a subtractive one to construct objects (Gibson et al. 2015). Because of this, AM has unique qualities that have the power to fundamentally alter how goods are created, assembled, and delivered to consumers. With AM, products can be customized on a case-by-case basis in new business model (NBM) arrangements with more design freedom and less manufacturing waste (Kuhn and Minuzzi 2015). These advancements have the potential to redefine sustainability across several industries, including the apparel sector, if they are combined with in situ service provision.

The Evolution of 3D Printing in Fashion

In the early stages, 3D printing was mainly used for prototyping and conceptual designs in the fashion industry. Designers and manufacturers saw the potential of this technology to bring their creative visions to life with greater precision and efficiency. As technology advanced, 3D printing started being used for producing actual wearable fashion pieces. Fashion houses and independent designers began incorporating 3D printing into their design processes, resulting in unique and innovative creations. 3D printing is a form of additive manufacturing, where products are manufactured by the process of directly printing some specific types of polymers and input raw materials.

9.2 3D Printing Processes

Materials for clothing and textiles can be 3D printed using a variety of techniques. The section that follows discusses a few of the procedures.

9.2.1 Fused Deposition Modelling (FDM)

In 3D printing, fused deposition modeling, or FDM, is a well-liked additive manufacturing method. FDM, which was created by Scott Crump in the late 1980s and brought to market by Stratasys, is now one of the most extensively used 3D printing technologies because of its affordability, adaptability, and ease of use (Moreau 2019). The FDM process includes the following steps (the FDM printing is shown in Fig. 9.1).

- **Model design:** Using computer-aided design (CAD) software, a 3D model is produced.
- **Slicing:** Slicing software divides the model into thin horizontal layers and creates a G-code file that instructs the printer.
- **Printing:** A thermoplastic filament, such as PLA (polylactic acid), ABS (acrylonitrile butadiene styrene), or another polymer, is extruded from the printer's nozzle. After being heated to its melting point, the filament is extruded onto a build platform layer by layer. The substance quickly cools and solidifies, sticking to the layer underneath it.

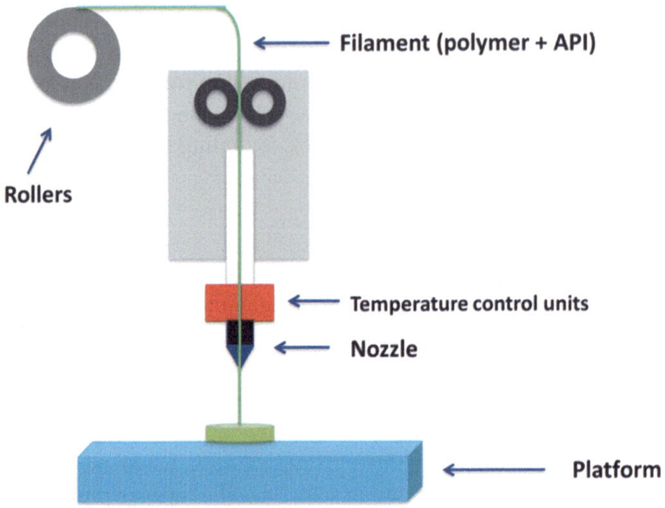

Fig. 9.1 Schematic diagram of fused deposition modelling (FDM) printing system

- **Post-Processing:** Post-processing procedures like support removal, sanding, or extra finishing might be necessary for printed parts.

Key Features and Benefits

- Accessibility and Cost: FDM printers are generally more affordable and user-friendly compared to other AM technologies.
- Material variety: Thermoplastics, composites, and even certain specialty materials with qualities like flexibility or heat resistance are among the many materials that FDM can handle (Melnikova et al. 2014).
- Strength and durability: Strong and long-lasting parts made with FDM technology are appropriate for tooling applications, functional prototypes, and end-use parts.
- Ease of use: Because of the technology's simplicity, both industrial users and enthusiasts can use it.

Applications of Fused Deposition Modelling

- Prototyping: Quick and cost-effective production of prototypes for design validation and functional testing.
- Manufacturing: Production of custom jigs, fixtures, and end-use parts.
- Education: An educational tool for teaching engineering, design, and manufacturing principles.
- Healthcare: Fabrication of custom prosthetics, anatomical models, and medical devices.
- Aerospace and Automotive: Creation of lightweight components, custom parts, and tooling.

9.2.2 *Stereolithography (SLA)*

One of the first and most popular forms of additive manufacturing, or 3D printing, is stereolithography (SLA). Charles Hull created SLA in the 1980s, and because of its accuracy and adaptability, it is still a mainstay in the fields of advanced manufacturing and rapid prototyping (Sclater 2011). Layer by layer, liquid resin is cured into hardened plastic using a laser in the Process SLA method. The schematic diagram of stereolithography printing system is shown in Fig. 9.2.

SLA process can be broken down into the following steps:

Design and Slicing

- **CAD Model Creation**: Using computer-aided design (CAD) software, the initial design is produced.
- **Slicing Software**: Layers of the CAD model are cut, usually with a thickness of 25–100 microns.

Printer Preparation

- **Resin Vat**: The vat is filled with a liquid photopolymer resin. Different resins are available for various applications, offering properties such as flexibility, durability, or high-temperature resistance.
- **Build Platform**: The platform is positioned in the vat, with a small gap between it and the surface of the resin.

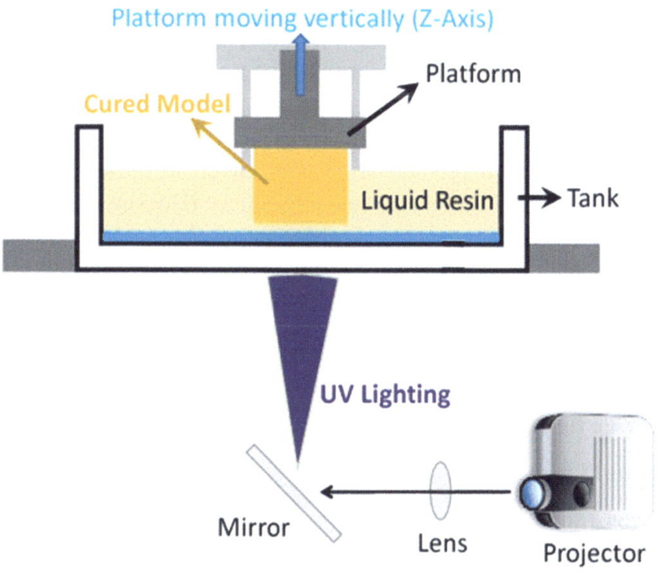

Fig. 9.2 Schematic diagram of stereolithography (SLA) printing system

Layer-vis-Layer Printing

- **Laser Exposure**: Curing and solidifying the resin where it comes into contact with it, the UV laser follows the part's cross-section on the resin's surface.
- **Layer Formation**: The build platform moves up slightly (or the resin level is adjusted) to prepare for the next layer. This process repeats for each layer.
- **Re-coating**: Some printers have a wiper mechanism to ensure a smooth resin layer before the next layer is cured.

Post-Processing

- **Part Removal**: The completed part is carefully detached from the build platform.
- **Cleaning**: The part is cleaned to remove uncured resin. This is typically done using an alcohol bath.
- **Secondary Curing**: To achieve full mechanical properties, the part is often cured further in a UV oven.
- **Finishing:** After the removal of support structures, the part's surface can be finished with sanding or another method to give it the desired look.

Advantages

- High precision: SLA is well known for its capacity to create precise, well-detailed parts with silky surface finishes, which makes it perfect for intricate features and complicated geometries.
- Material versatility: There is a large selection of resins with different qualities (like stiffness, flexibility, and biocompatibility) that can be customized for particular uses.
- Speed of Prototyping: SLA works well for rapid prototyping, allowing designers to iterate and improve their designs more quickly.

Applications of Stereolithography (SLA)

- Prototyping: used a lot in product development to create intricate prototypes that enable testing of both functionality and appearance (Hoskins 2013; Huang et al. 2013).
- Medical and health: Surgical guides, dental prosthetics, and customized medical devices all benefit from SLA's accuracy and biocompatible materials.
- Jewellery and accessories: The technology is widely used in jewellery making and other artistic endeavours due to its capacity to generate complex designs.
- Engineering: Because of its accuracy and material qualities, SLA is frequently used to create functional parts, intricate assemblies, and tooling components.

Challenges and Limitations

- Material constraints: Though more diverse than materials used in traditional manufacturing, the small range of SLA materials affects the mechanical properties of finished parts.

- Cost: Because SLA printers and resins can be expensive, some users may find SLA printing less accessible than other 3D printing technologies like Fused Deposition Modelling (FDM).
- Requirements post-processing: The need for cleaning and curing increases the process' complexity and duration.

9.2.3 Selective Laser Sintering (SLS)

One of the first and most popular additive manufacturing techniques, or 3D printing, is selective laser sintering (SLS) (Murugesan et al. 2012). Because of its accuracy and adaptability, SLS, which Charles Hull invented in the 1980s, is still a mainstay in the fields of advanced manufacturing and rapid prototyping. Layer by layer, liquid resin is cured into hardened plastic via SLS using a laser. The schematic diagram of SLS printing system has been shown in Fig. 9.3.

The process can be broken down into the following steps.

Preparation

- **Design Preparation:** Computer-aided design (CAD) software is used to create the object that will be printed.
- **Conversion:** The CAD file is used to create the Standard Tessellation Language (STL) file, which represents the surface geometry of the model.
- **Cutting and Slicing:** The STL file is split into thin horizontal layers using slicing software, and these layers are then converted into a file format that the SLS machine can read, such as G-code.

Setup

- **Powder Bed Preparation:** The SLS machine's build chamber is filled with a layer of fine powder, usually made of thermoplastics like nylon or polyamide.

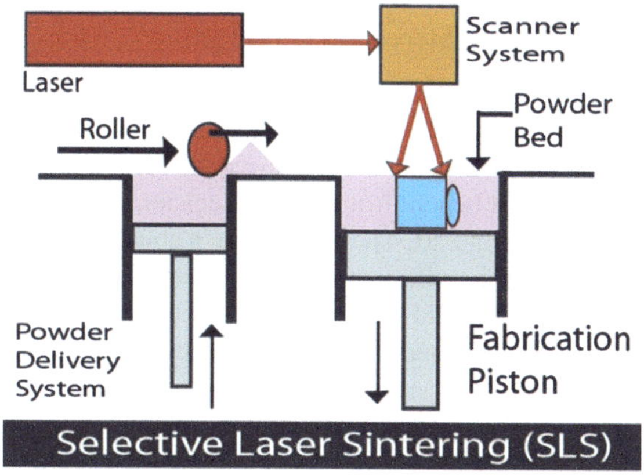

Fig. 9.3 Schematic diagram selective laser sintering (SLS) printing system

- **Preheating:** To speed up the sintering process, the powder bed is preheated to a temperature slightly below the material's melting point.

Printing

- **Laser Sintering:** Based on the model's cross-section, a strong laser scans the powder bed's surface, selectively fusing (sintering) the powder particles to create a solid layer.
- **Layer by Layer:** The build platform descends by the thickness of one layer (typically 0.1–0.15 mm) after a layer is sintered, and a fresh layer of powder is applied to the surface. This process is repeated layer by layer until the object is printed in its entirety.

Cooling

- To prevent thermal stress and deformation of the printed part, the build chamber is allowed to slowly cool after printing.

Post-Processing

- **Depowdering:** Excess powder is blown or brushed off after the printed portion is taken out of the powder bed.
- **Finishing:** To obtain the appropriate surface finish and properties, additional post-processing procedures could involve bead blasting, polishing, dying, or coating.

Advantages

- High Precision and detail: SLS is well known for producing parts with smooth surface finishes that are incredibly accurate and detailed, which makes it perfect for intricate geometries and fine features (Murugesan et al. 2012).
- Material versatility: There is a large selection of resins with different qualities (like stiffness, flexibility, and biocompatibility) that can be customized for particular uses.
- Prototyping speed: Rapid prototyping with SLS allows designers to iterate and improve their designs more quickly.

Applications of Stereolithography

- Prototyping: Used extensively for creating detailed prototypes in product development, allowing for functional and aesthetic testing.
- Medical and dental: Customized medical devices, surgical guides, and dental prosthetics benefit from SLA's precision and biocompatible materials.
- Jewellery and art: The technology's ability to produce intricate designs makes it popular in jewellery making and artistic endeavours.
- Engineering and manufacturing: Functional parts, complex assemblies, and tooling components are often created using SLS due to its accuracy and material properties.

Challenges and Limitations

- Material constraints: The mechanical properties of finished parts are impacted by the limited range of SLS materials, despite their diversity when compared to traditional manufacturing materials.
- Cost: The cost of SLS printers and resins can be high, making it less accessible for some users compared to other 3D printing technologies like Fused Deposition Modelling (FDM).
- Post-processing requirements: The necessity for cleaning and curing adds time and complexity to the overall process.

9.2.4 *Digital Light Processing (DLP)*

Overview: Digital light processing (DLP) is a sophisticated additive manufacturing technique that is highly accurate and quick in 3D printing. Because DLP can efficiently produce detailed, high-quality parts, it has found widespread application in a variety of industries. DLP was developed in the late 1980s by Dr. Larry Hornbeck of Texas Instruments (Reilly 2014). Using a digital projector, the DLP process cures photopolymer resin layer by layer to create solid objects. Figure 9.4 shows the schematic diagram of digital light processing (DLP) printing system.

The key steps in the DLP process include:

Preparation

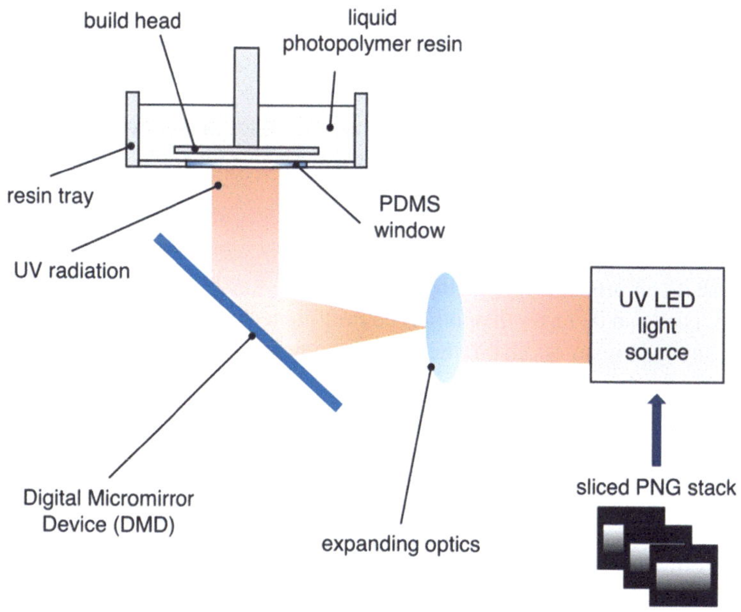

Fig. 9.4 Schematic diagram of digital light processing (DLP) printing system

- **Design:** Computer-aided design (CAD) software is used to design the object.
- **Conversion:** The model's surface geometry is described in a Standard Tessellation Language (STL) file created from the CAD file (Venuvinod and Ma 2004).
- **Slicing:** Using slicing software, the STL file is divided into thin horizontal layers to produce image files for each layer of the model.

Setup

- **Resin preparation:** A liquid photopolymer resin is selected and poured into the resin tank of the DLP printer.
- **Calibration:** The build platform is calibrated to ensure proper alignment and distance from the resin surface.

Printing

- **Layer curing:** A UV image of the model's cross-section is projected onto the resin surface using a digital light projector. The resin is selectively cured (hardened) by the light, which forms a layer by solidifying the exposed areas.
- **Layer by layer:** The build platform moves up (or the resin tank moves down) by the thickness of one layer (typically 25–100 microns) after one layer has cured. Until the entire object is printed, this process is repeated, projecting the image of each subsequent layer onto the resin.

Post-Processing

- **Cleaning:** To get rid of any uncured resin, the printed object is taken off the build platform and rinsed in isopropyl alcohol (IPA).
- **Post-curing:** To guarantee that any residual uncured resin is completely hardened and enhance the part's mechanical qualities and stability, the object is usually placed in a UV curing oven.
- **Finishing:** Sanding, painting, or coating are examples of additional steps that can be taken to achieve the desired aesthetics and surface finish.

Advantages

- High resolution and detail: DLP is perfect for intricate designs and fine features because it can produce parts with smooth surface finishes and excellent detail.
- Speed: DLP can be faster than other 3D printing technologies because it cures an entire layer of resin at once rather than tracing the outline of each layer with a laser.
- Material efficiency: The technology makes efficient use of resin, with minimal waste, as excess material can be reused for future prints.
- Versatility: A wide range of photopolymer resins with different mechanical properties and colours are available, allowing for customization based on specific application requirements.

Applications of DLP

- Dental and Medical: Customized dental models, aligners, surgical guides, and prosthetics benefit from DLP's high accuracy and biocompatible materials.

- Jewellery: The technology is popular in jewellery making for creating highly detailed and intricate designs, including custom Molds for casting.
- Consumer goods: Prototypes and end-use products, such as eyewear frames and intricate decorative items, are often produced using DLP.
- Engineering and manufacturing: Functional prototypes, small components, and intricate parts for various applications benefit from DLP's precision and material properties.

Challenges and Limitations

- Material constraints: While there are many photopolymer resins available, they may not match the mechanical properties and durability of traditional manufacturing materials like metals and certain plastics.
- Post-processing requirements: Objects printed with DLP often require thorough cleaning and additional curing, adding time and complexity to the process.
- Build size limitations: The build volumes of DLP printers are generally lower than those of other 3D printing technologies, which may restrict the size of parts that can be manufactured.
- Cost: The initial cost of DLP printers and resins can be relatively high, which may be a barrier for some users

9.2.5 *Multi-jet Fusion (MJF)*

- HP created multi-jet fusion (MJF), a cutting-edge 3D printing technology used in the additive manufacturing of plastic components. It is distinguished by its capacity to create robust, finely detailed parts with exceptional mechanical qualities (Korger et al. 2016). Here are the key aspects of MJF (Fig. 9.5).

Process Overview

By applying a layer of powdered material over the build platform, MJF uses a powder bed fusion technique. The following steps are involved in the process.

- Layer application: A thin layer of powder, typically nylon or similar thermoplastic, is spread across the build platform.
- Jetting agents: A printhead passes over the powder bed, jetting two types of agents: fusing agents and detailing agents. The fusing agent is applied where the powder needs to solidify, while the detailing agent is applied where the powder needs to remain loose or have finer details.
- Energy application: An infrared heating element passes over the bed, causing the areas with the fusing agent to solidify and fuse together while the rest remains in powder form.
- Repetition: Layer by layer, this process is repeated until the entire object is constructed.

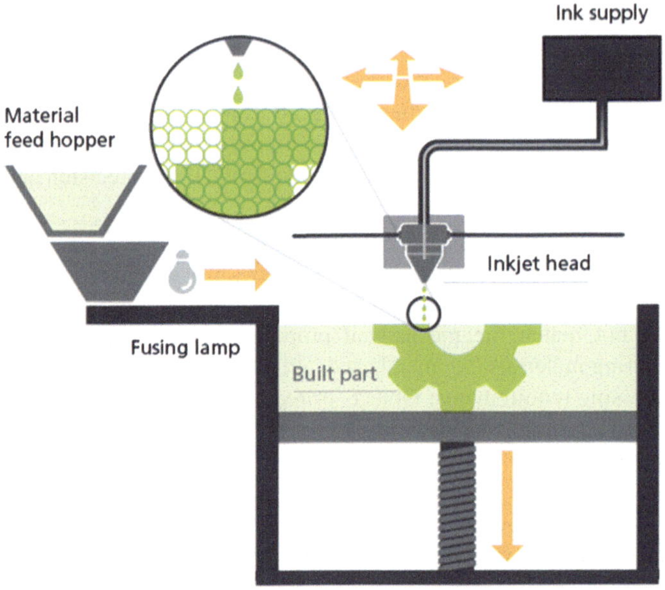

Fig. 9.5 Schematic diagram of multi-jet fusion (MJF) printing system

Advantages

- Speed: MJF can produce parts faster than many other 3D printing technologies, as it processes each layer in a single pass.
- Detail and accuracy: The use of detailing agents allows for high-resolution features and smooth surface finishes.
- Mechanical properties: Because of their superior mechanical qualities—such as their high strength and durability—the produced parts are appropriate for practical end-use applications.
- Cost-effectiveness: MJF is efficient in material usage, as the unfused powder can often be reused, reducing waste and lowering costs.
- Scalability: MJF is suitable for both prototyping and production, making it versatile for various scales of manufacturing.

Applications of MJF

Because of its adaptability and the high caliber of the parts it creates, MJF is extensively utilized in many different industries Common applications include:

- Prototyping: Rapid production of prototypes with high detail and functional properties.
- End-Use Parts: Manufacturing of functional parts, including automotive components, consumer goods, and medical devices.
- Tooling: Creation of custom tools, jigs, and fixtures for manufacturing processes.

- Customization: Production of custom, personalized items in low to medium volumes

9.2.6 Direct Ink Writing (DIW)

It is possible to precisely and carefully deposit materials to create intricate three-dimensional structures using direct ink writing (DIW), also known as robocasting. DIW is a sophisticated additive manufacturing process. In contrast to conventional 3D printing techniques, which depend on the layer-by-layer deposition of materials, DIW enables the extrusion of pastes, gels, or inks through a syringe or nozzle to produce complex geometries with customized material properties. Here are the key aspects of DIW (Fig. 9.6)

The DIW process involves the following steps

- Material Preparation: The material to be printed is combined with a viscous paste or ink, which is often composed of metal, ceramics, composites, or polymers. These materials are typically placed into a reservoir or syringe.
- Extrusion: The material is extruded through a nozzle or small aperture under controlled pressure, allowing for precise deposition onto a substrate or previous layers.
- Layer-by-layer building: The deposition process is repeated layer by layer while following a pre-established design or CAD model. Complex structures can be produced with careful manipulation of the toolpath and deposition parameters.

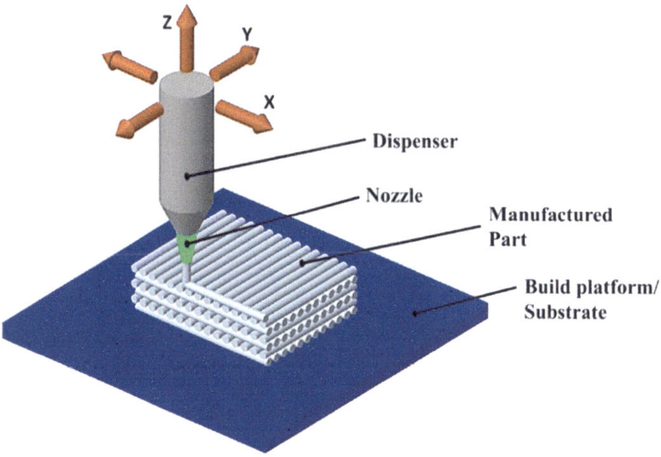

Fig. 9.6 Schematic diagram of direct ink writing (DIW) printing system

- Curing or solidification: Depending on the material used, stabilizing the printed structure between deposition layers or after printing is complete may involve the use of curing, drying, or solidification techniques.
- Post-processing: There may be a need for additional post-processing steps like sintering, annealing, or surface treatment to achieve the necessary mechanical, thermal, or electrical properties.

Advantages

- Complex geometry: Complex structures like lattices, porous scaffolds, and custom designs can be fabricated with amazing geometric resolution and fidelity thanks to DIW.
- Material versatility: Hydrogels, metals, polymers, ceramics, and bioinks are just a few of the materials that can be used in DIW to make functional parts with unique features.
- Controlled microstructure: The deposition process offers precise control over the microstructure and porosity of the printed materials for uses such as tissue engineering, filtration, and catalysis.
- Multi-material printing: With DIW, multiple materials can be extruded at the same time, enabling the construction of composite structures with graded compositions or functional gradients.
- Scalability: Large-scale structures and small-scale prototypes can be fabricated using DIW, which makes it suitable for both prototyping and scalable production.

Applications of DIW

- Biomedical engineering: Creation of organs-on-a-chip devices, implants, drug delivery systems, and tissue scaffolds.
- Electronics: printing of flexible electronic components, antennas, sensors, and conductive traces.
- Aerospace and automotive: production of heat exchangers, lightweight constructions, and intricate parts with optimal functionality.
- Energy: Manufacturing of batteries, photovoltaic systems, fuel cells, and thermal management devices.
- Art and design: Production of personalized artwork, architectural models, and ornately designed decorative items

9.2.7 Binder Jetting

Binder jetting is an additive manufacturing (AM) technique that uses powdered materials, usually sand, metal, or ceramic, to create objects layer by layer. A thin layer of powdered material is uniformly distributed over the build platform using binder jetting (Brody et al. 1989). After that, a print head applies liquid binder to the powder bed in a targeted manner, combining the particles to create the layer's desired shape. Layer by layer, this process is repeated until the object is finished (Fig. 9.7).

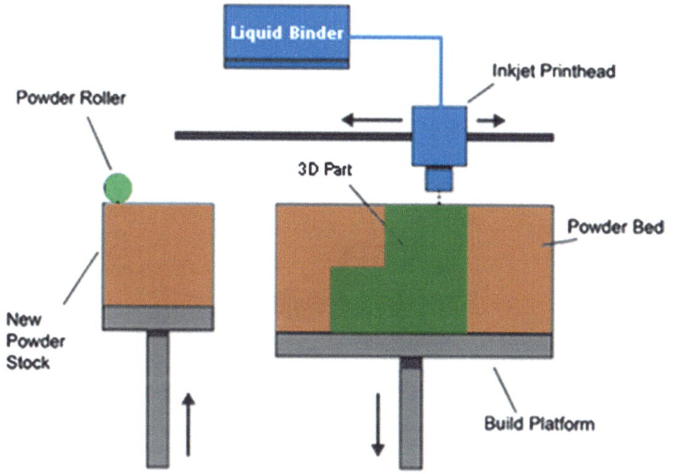

Fig. 9.7 Schematic diagram of binder jetting printing system

Speed and cost-effectiveness are two of binder jetting's main benefits, particularly when producing large or complex geometries. It also permits the use of a broad variety of materials, such as sand, ceramics, and metals like titanium, aluminum, and stainless steel.

Post-processing, such as sintering to strengthen metal parts or infiltrating with a secondary material for increased strength and density, is frequently necessary to obtain the desired properties, though. Despite this, the ability of binder jetting to produce high-quality parts with shorter lead times and costs than traditional manufacturing methods is making it more and more popular in a variety of industries, including aerospace, automotive, and healthcare.

Material Jetting

A sophisticated method of additive manufacturing called material jetting involves depositing material droplets onto a build platform to create three-dimensional objects. Material jetting uses printheads to precisely control the layer-by-layer deposition of materials like metals, polymers, or resins, much like traditional inkjet printing (Fig. 9.8).

The ability of material jetting to produce complex and intricate parts, prototypes, and models with high levels of detail and surface quality is one of its main advantages. Because of its high resolution, objects with smooth finishes and fine features can be created that frequently match or even exceed those made using conventional manufacturing techniques.

The ability to print with multiple materials at once, which enables the creation of objects with different characteristics or colors within the same build, is another advantage of material jetting. Because of its adaptability, it is especially useful in situations where functional diversity or customization is crucial.

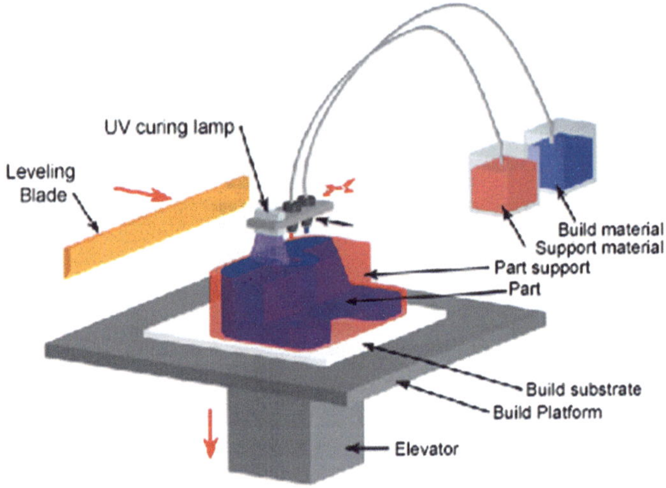

Fig. 9.8 Schematic diagram of material jetting printing system

Material jetting does, however, have certain drawbacks. In comparison to other additive manufacturing techniques, the process can be somewhat slow, and material costs could be higher—particularly for some specialized materials. In addition, post-processing actions like support removal or curing might be required to get the required surface finish and final properties.

All things considered, material jetting provides an effective way to create detailed, high-quality 3D objects using a variety of materials, which makes it an important tool in many different industries, such as consumer goods, automotive, aerospace, and healthcare. Material jetting is anticipated to develop further as technology progresses, possibly opening new avenues for additive manufacturing.

9.2.8 Electrospinning

All things considered, material jetting is a valuable tool in a wide range of industries, including consumer goods, automotive, aerospace, and healthcare, since it offers an efficient means of producing intricate, high-quality 3D objects using a variety of materials. As technology advances, material jetting is expected to advance even further, potentially creating new opportunities for additive manufacturing (Radacsi and Nuansing 2020) (Fig. 9.9).

Fundamentally, electrospinning is the process of applying an electric field to a melt or polymer solution to cause a fine material jet to extrude. Ultrafine fibers are created by the jet's complex interactions, which include stretching and solvent evaporation. These fibers can be gathered on a substrate to create non-woven mats

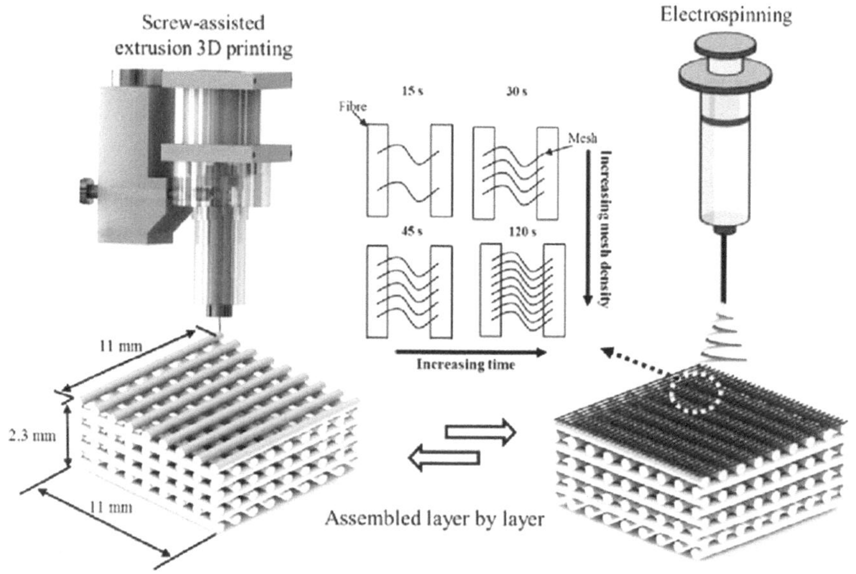

Fig. 9.9 Schematic diagram of electrospinning

or other structured forms. Comparing the method to traditional fiber production techniques, there are several advantages:

- Controlled fiber morphology: The process of electrospinning enables the precise manipulation of multiple parameters, including polymer concentration, solution viscosity, applied voltage, and the distance between the spinneret and collector, to achieve desired results in terms of fiber diameter, morphology, and alignment.
- Versatility: It works well with a broad variety of materials, such as biomolecules, ceramics, composites, and both natural and synthetic polymers. Because of its adaptability, fibers can be produced with specific uses in mind, like scaffolds for tissue engineering, filtration membranes, protective textiles, and drug delivery systems.
- High surface area: Because of their extraordinarily high surface area-to-volume ratio, electrospun fibers are perfect for applications like energy storage devices, catalyst supports, and sensors that call for improved surface interactions.
- Scalability: The process of electrospinning is easily scalable to industrial scale, providing an economical way to generate large amounts of nanofibers for use in industry.

Applications of electrospun fibres

- Biomedical engineering: Electrospun scaffolds are useful for tissue regeneration and wound healing applications because they closely resemble the structure of natural extracellular matrix. Additionally, bioactive molecules can be functionalized them to deliver drugs in a targeted manner.

- Environmental remediation: Water purification, air filtration, and oil spill cleanup can be accomplished with the help of electrospun membranes that have specific pore sizes and surface chemistries.
- Energy storage and conversion: In lithium-ion batteries, supercapacitors, and fuel cells, electrospun nanofibers function as electrodes and separators to improve energy storage capacity and device performance.

9.3 Examples of 3D Printing in Fashion

Numerous examples of clothing and accessories made with these techniques already exist. Fashion designer Danit Peleg created a line of clothing that was shown at New York Fashion Week using 3D printing. Using a 3D printer, a range of products, including dresses, jackets, and shoes, were produced for the collection. Customized eyewear is another example. A number of businesses, such as Optinvent and XYZ printing, provide 3D printed sunglasses and eyewear that can be tailored to a customer's unique preferences and face measurements (Baggaley 2018).

Apart from these instances, numerous fashion labels and trailblazers are incorporating 3D printing technology into their designs. Nike has created limited-edition items and prototypes, including a collection of shoes with 3D printing. The clothing line Continuum Fashion made a range of undergarments. These examples demonstrate 3D printing's potential in the fashion sector and suggest that in the future, an increasing number of clothing and accessories will be produced with this technology.

Benefits of 3D Printing in Fashion

3D printing benefits the fashion industry in a number of ways. First of all, it permits the personalization and customization of clothing. Designers can easily customize apparel items with 3D printing to fit each customer's unique body type and dimensions. Customization at this stage used to be costly and time-consuming to complete. Furthermore, challenging details and intricate geometries that would be challenging to obtain using traditional manufacturing techniques can be created with 3D printing. By experimenting with novel forms, styles, and textures, designers can push the boundaries of fashion arrangement.

The ability to customize and personalize products is one of the main benefits of using 3D printing in fashion. Using 3D printing, one can create one-of-a-kind items that are customized to a person's exact specifications and tastes. Customers can now further customize the style and fit of their clothing and accessories thanks to this.

The ability of 3D printing to shorten the supply chain and cut waste is another advantage for the fashion industry. Long supply chains are often involved in the conventional fashion manufacturing process, requiring the transportation of textiles and goods from one location to another before they are delivered to the customer. Conversely, local production of goods is made possible by 3D printing, which lowers the need for transportation and the resulting carbon emissions. Additionally, because complex shapes and structures that would be delicate or impossible to produce using traditional manufacturing techniques can be produced, 3D printing makes it possible to use textiles more effectively.

For fashion designers, 3D printing also increases creative freedom and design flexibility. It enables designers to create intricate and unusual structures and forms that would be difficult to realize with conventional manufacturing techniques. This may result in the production of distinctive and avant-garde fashion items. In the long run, 3D printing will help the fashion industry produce and prototype more quickly. Prototyping and sampling are often done in multiple rounds during traditional fashion production, which can be costly and time-consuming. Faster prototyping and the ability to make adjustments and improvements more quickly are made possible by 3D printing. This may shorten the time needed to launch a new product.

Design Possibilities with 3D Printing in Fashion

In the fashion industry, 3D printing offers almost endless design possibilities. Previously unachievable complex patterns, textures, and structures can now be found in clothing and accessories designed by designers. Furthermore, the range of textures and finishes can be expanded by incorporating non-traditional materials like plastics, metals, and even materials that resemble fabric thanks to 3D printing. For designers, this opens up a whole new creative realm to explore and play with.

9.4 Sustainable Practices in Fashion Through 3D Printing

The fashion industry has long faced criticism for its negative effects on the environment, which range from excessive waste to pollution and high water consumption. On the other hand, 3D printing technology presents a viable path toward more environmentally friendly business practices. The following are some ways that 3D printing supports sustainable fashion.

1. **Reduction of waste**

Because fabric must be cut and sewn, traditional fashion manufacturing processes frequently produce a significant amount of material waste. By contrast, additive manufacturing, or 3D printing, uses materials only where they are needed. This significantly lowers the quantity of waste fabric. Without having to cut away extra material, designers can make clothes that fit perfectly and use almost all the material.

2. **On-Demand production**

On-demand production or producing goods only when there is a demand for them, is made possible by 3D printing. In the fashion industry, where unsold inventory frequently ends up in landfills, this lessens the common overproduction. By matching supply to actual consumer demand, on-demand production reduces waste and the environmental impact of mass production and unsold inventory.

3. **Recycling and material innovation**

Innovative, sustainable materials as well as recycled materials can be used in fashion thanks to 3D printing. For instance, new clothes can be made using filaments derived from biodegradable or recycled plastics. Furthermore, eco-friendly bio-based materials are being experimented with by designers. This change lessens the fashion industry's dependency on virgin resources and promotes the growth of a circular economy.

4. **Energy efficiency**

It is possible that 3D printing uses less energy than conventional manufacturing techniques. 3D printing frequently combines the many steps and energy-intensive machinery used in traditional textile manufacturing into a single, efficient process. The energy efficiency of 3D printing is continuously being improved by technological advancements, making it a more and more practical option for sustainable production.

5. **Customization and longevity**

High degrees of customization are possible with 3D printing, allowing customers to receive products that are precisely matched to their preferences and measurements. People are more likely to maintain and take care of clothing that fits well and meets their unique needs when it is highly customized, which can boost customer satisfaction and extend the life of the item. Clothing that fits well decreases the possibility that it will be thrown out because it does not fit right, which lowers the amount of textile waste produced.

6. **Innovative design possibilities**

Innovative designs are now possible with 3D printing, which are not achievable with conventional manufacturing techniques. Designers can produce elaborate, complex structures and patterns that employ less material and provide novel functionalities. This invention has the potential to produce apparel that is not only more environmentally friendly but also has new fashionable and functional advantages.

9.5 Challenges and Limitations of 3D Printing in Fashion

Although 3D printing has many advantages, there are certain obstacles and restrictions in the fashion sector. The expense of technology is one of the biggest obstacles. While the cost of 3D printing has decreased recently, small-scale designers may still need to make a sizable initial investment in printers and materials. Technical limitations and problems with quality control are additional restrictions. It can be difficult to achieve the right level of detail and finish, and several iterations and adjustments may be needed during the printing process. Additionally, there are issues with intellectual property because 3D printing makes it possible for designs to be reproduced without permission and for copyright violations.

9.6 Future of 3D Printing in Fashion

The fashion industry is about to undergo a revolution thanks to the integration of 3D printing technology, which offers unmatched customization, sustainability, and innovation. These salient features illustrate the potential of 3D printing in the fashion industry:

1. **Customization and personalization**

Custom apparel and accessories can be made using 3D printing to fit each person's unique body type and preferences. This degree of personalization improves the shopping experience for customers by providing distinctive designs and well-fitting clothing. The capacity to produce one-of-a-kind items on demand will get easier and more affordable as technology advances.

2. **Sustainability**

The ability of 3D printing to cut waste is one of its main benefits in the fashion industry. Conventional manufacturing techniques frequently produce excess material and unsold inventory, which worsen the state of the environment. Conversely, 3D printing creates objects layer by layer with only the required amount of material. Sustainable practices are further supported by the capacity to recycle and reuse the materials used in 3D printing.

3. **Innovation in design**

Design opportunities made possible by 3D printing were previously unattainable through traditional techniques. By experimenting with intricate patterns, new materials, and complex geometries, designers can push the envelope of creativity. Unique, cutting-edge fashion items that stand out in the market are the result of this innovation.

4. **Rapid prototyping and production**

The fashion industry is known for its rapid trends and expediency in meeting deadlines. Rapid prototyping made possible by 3D printing enables designers to quickly iterate and improve their designs. This speed carries over to production, where 3D printers can create finished goods faster than with conventional manufacturing techniques, cutting lead times and better meeting consumer demands.

5. **Accessibility and democratization**

Fashion design and production are becoming more accessible and affordable thanks to 3D printing technology. Without a lot of infrastructure or resources, consumers, small companies, and independent designers can make their own fashion products. This change encourages diversity in fashion and empowers a wider spectrum of creators.

6. **Innovative materials**

The creation of new materials with improved qualities is one aspect of 3D printing's future in the fashion industry. Researchers are developing biodegradable and intelligent materials with the ability to adapt to changes in their surroundings by changing their color, texture, or shape. These developments will increase the use of 3D printing in the fashion industry and result in dynamic and interactive apparel.

7. **Impact on supply chain**

The supply chain for fashion could change dramatically if 3D printing becomes widely used. It lowers the need for substantial shipping and warehousing, resulting in a reduction in transportation emissions and logistics expenses by enabling localized production. The transition to manufacturing on demand has the potential to alleviate problems associated with surplus inventory and overproduction.

9.7 Conclusions

The design, development, and production of products have undergone a paradigm shift thanks to 3D printing and additive manufacturing. The aerospace, healthcare, automotive, fashion, and consumer goods industries are among the many sectors that are undergoing a revolution thanks to these technologies, which are distinguished by their capacity to produce intricate and highly customized objects layer by layer from digital models. The unparalleled customization offered by 3D printing enables the efficient and accurate production of one-of-a-kind, custom products. This adaptability is revolutionizing industries that need custom solutions, like dental products, medical implants, and customized apparel. One major benefit of additive manufacturing is the freedom to design intricate structures and complex geometries that are hard or impossible to achieve with traditional manufacturing methods. This capacity encourages creativity and allows engineers and designers to push the limits.

The ability to produce parts on demand and conduct rapid prototyping reduces development cycles and expedites time-to-market. This efficiency is especially helpful in sectors like aerospace and automotive where quickness and flexibility are essential. The long-term advantages of 3D printing technology include lower material waste, lower tooling costs, and the possibility of more effective supply chains, even though the initial investment can be substantial. These elements support increased competitiveness and overall cost savings. Notwithstanding its benefits, 3D printing has drawbacks, including material restrictions, production speed constraints, and the requirement for industry standards. These problems are being addressed by ongoing research and development, opening the door for wider adoption and more sophisticated applications.

Looking Forward

With ongoing developments in materials, technologies, and manufacturing procedures, 3D printing and additive manufacturing have a promising future. These technologies will spur more innovation, sustainability, and efficiency across a range of industries as they are more widely incorporated into manufacturing. As 3D printing and other cutting-edge technologies, like artificial intelligence and the Internet of Things, come together, new opportunities and uses will arise, confirming 3D printing's position as a key component of contemporary manufacturing.

Adopting additive manufacturing and 3D printing gives you a competitive edge and is in line with the global trend toward more flexible and sustainable production methods. These technologies will surely continue to influence manufacturing in the future as they develop, opening up new possibilities for efficiency, creativity, and environmental responsibility.

References

Baggaley K (2018) Soon you may be able to 3D print clothing in your own home. https://www.nbcnews.com/mach/science/soon-you-may-be-able-3d-print-clothing-your-own-ncna848646

Berman B (2012) 3-D printing: the new industrial revolution. Bus Horiz 55:155–162

Brody HD, Haggerty JS, Cima MJ, Flemings MC, Barns RL, Gyorgy EM, Johnson DW, Rhodes WW, Sunder WA, Laudis RA (1989) Highly textured and single crystal $Bi_2CaSr_2Cu_2O_x$ prepared by laser heated float zone crystalization. J Cryst Growth 96:225–233

Claudio L (2007) Waste couture: environmental impact of the clothing industry. Environ Health Perspect 115:A449–A454

Gibson I, Rosen D, Stucker B (2015) Additive manufacturing technologies 3D printing, rapid prototyping, and direct digital manufacturing, 2nd edn. Springer, New York, NY, USA

Gillson I, Poulton C, Balcombe K, Page S (2004) Understanding the impact of cotton subsidies on developing countries. MPRA, Munich, Germany

Hoskins S (2013) 3D printing for artists, designers and makers. Bloomsbury Publishing, London, UK

Huang SH, Liu P, Mokasdar A, Hou L (2013) Additive manufacturing and its societal impact: a literature review. Int J Adv Manuf Technol 67:1191–1203

Kaye L (2011) Textile recycling innovation challenges clothing industry. https://www.theguardian.com/sustainable-business/textile-recycling-challenges-industry. Accessed 15 June 2019

Korger M, Bergschneider J, Neuss J, Lutz M, Mahltig B, Rabe M (2016) Functionalization of textiles using 3D printing-add-on technology for textile applications testing new material combinations. Int Congr 3:1–6

Kuhn R, Minuzzi FB (2015) The 3D printing's panorama in fashion design. Mem Des 2:1–12. https://silo.tips/download/the-3d-printing-s-panorama-in-fashion-design. Accessed 21 July 2020

Melnikova R, Ehrmann A, Finsterbusch K (2014) 3D printing of textile-based structures by fused deposition modelling (FDM) with different polymer materials. IOP Conf Ser Mater Sci Eng 62:012018

Moreau C (2019) The state of 3D printing. Sculpteo, Villejuif, France

Murugesan K, Anandapandian PA, Sharma SK, Vasantha Kumar M (2012) Comparative evaluation of dimension and surface detail accuracy of models produced by three different rapid prototype techniques. J Indian Prosthodont Soc 12:16–20

Radacsi N, Nuansing W (2020) Fabrication of 3D and 4D polymer micro- and nanostructures based on electrospinning. In: 3D and 4D printing of polymer nanocomposite materials. Elsevier, Amsterdam, The Nederlands, pp 191–229

Reilly L (2014) The shift from 3D body scanned data to the physical world shapeshifting. In: Proceedings of the a conference on transformative paradigms of fashion and textile design, Auchland, New Zealand, 14–16 April 2014

Sclater N (2011) Mechanisms and mechanical devices sourcebook. McGraw-Hill, New York, NY, USA

Spahiu T, Grimmelsmann N, Ehrmann A, Shehi E, Piperi E (2016) On the possible use of 3D printing forclothing and shoe manufacture. In: Proceedings of the 7th international conference of textile, Tirana, Albania, 10–11 November 2016, pp 10–11

Vanderploeg A, Lee S-E, Mamp M (2016) The application of 3D printing technology in the fashion industry. Int J Fash Des Technol Educ 10:170–179

Venuvinod KP, Ma W (2004) Rapid prototyping: laserbased and other technologies. Springer Science and Bussiness Media, New York, NY, USA

Chapter 10
Fashioning a Transparent Future: Blockchain Applications in the Textile and Garment Supply Chain

Thinh Gia Hoang, An Duong Thi Binh, and Phuong Thi Nguyen

Abstract This chapter delves into the vital intersection of blockchain technology and traceability within the intricate world of the fashion and textile supply chain. The fashion and textile industry, a cornerstone of global trade, confronts a range of challenges, including ethical dilemmas, supply chain intricacies, and the shifting expectations of consumers who demand transparency. Blockchain technology, renowned for its decentralized and unchangeable characteristics, emerges as a pivotal solution to address these issues. It provides clear and tamper-proof records that guarantee the legitimacy of products, their traceability, and the ethical origins of the materials. Through a detailed examination of the Vietnamese textile and garment industry, this chapter vividly demonstrates the severe consequences that arise when traceability is lacking, emphasizing the pressing need for blockchain adoption. By focusing on its applications and the resulting impacts, this chapter underscores how blockchain is reshaping the fashion and textile industry, advancing transparency, accountability, and sustainability.

Keywords Blockchain technology · Traceability · Fashion industry · Textile supply chain · Transparency · Accountability

10.1 Introduction

In recent years, the fashion and textile industry has undergone a significant transformation driven by the integration of cutting-edge technologies (Behera et al. 2021). Among these, blockchain has emerged as a game-changer, revolutionizing the way

T. G. Hoang (✉) · P. T. Nguyen
International School of Business, University of Economics Ho Chi Minh City, Ho Chi Minh City, Vietnam
e-mail: giathinhhoang@gmail.com

A. D. T. Binh
CIRTech Institute, HUTECH University, Ho Chi Minh City, Vietnam

R. Nayak et al. (eds.), *Use of Digital and Advanced Technologies in the Fashion Supply Chain*, Springer Series in Fashion Business,
https://doi.org/10.1007/978-981-97-7528-6_10

the industry operates (Nguyen et al. 2021). This transformation is driven by the industry's recognition of the urgent need for transparency, accountability, and sustainability. Blockchain technology, renowned for its decentralized and immutable nature, has stepped in as a robust solution to these challenges. Blockchain's role in the fashion and textile industry is multifaceted. At its core, it offers an immutable ledger that records every transaction and change in a transparent and tamper-proof manner (Hoang et al. 2022). This foundational characteristic holds immense promise in addressing the authenticity and traceability of products. In an industry riddled with concerns about counterfeit products, blockchain provides a means to verify the origin and authenticity of goods, instilling trust among consumers and stakeholders.

One of the key applications of blockchain in the fashion and textile sector is traceability. As consumers become increasingly conscious of the products they purchase, they demand to know the journey of a product from its source to their hands (Hoang and Phan 2022). Blockchain technology allows for an unbroken trail of data, making it possible to trace a garment or textile back to its origin. This traceability is not limited to the manufacturer but extends to the raw materials used in the production process. For example, it can verify the source of the cotton used in a shirt or the origin of the dyes that color a dress. Moreover, blockchain offers a dynamic solution to ethical concerns within the industry (Agrawal et al. 2021). Consumers are increasingly concerned about the ethical practices of fashion and textile companies. They want assurance that the products they purchase are not the result of forced labor or unethical practices. Blockchain's transparent ledger can provide the necessary proof of ethical sourcing and manufacturing (Nguyen et al. 2021). It can track the labor conditions of workers, ensuring that they adhere to international labor standards and ethical guidelines.

Another fascinating aspect of blockchain in fashion is its impact on supply chain efficiency (Nguyen et al. 2023; Ngo et al. 2023). With a technology that eliminates intermediaries and streamlines processes, blockchain reduces the chances of errors, delays, and inefficiencies. Smart contracts, a feature of blockchain technology, can automate various aspects of the supply chain, such as payments, quality control, and even restocking, resulting in a more efficient and cost-effective system (Nguyen et al. 2021; Hoang and Bui 2023). Blockchain is also fostering a new level of collaboration and trust in the industry. In a traditionally competitive sector, companies are now incentivized to collaborate and share data within blockchain networks to benefit from enhanced traceability and sustainability (Agrawal et al. 2018). This newfound transparency can boost consumer trust and drive industry-wide improvements.

In summary, blockchain's presence in the fashion and textile industry is a transformative force, offering solutions to age-old challenges. It enhances transparency, traceability, authenticity, and ethical practices while streamlining supply chain processes (Agrawal et al. 2021). As consumers increasingly demand accountability and sustainability, blockchain stands as a technological ally, pushing the industry toward a more responsible and efficient future.

The convergence of blockchain and traceability represents a pivotal point of intersection within the fashion and textile supply chain. This chapter delves into this technology' indispensable role in addressing the myriad challenges inherent to the industry (Tripathi et al. 2021; Hader et al. 2022). The fashion and textile sector, while a vital economic engine, has long grappled with a host of issues, from ethical concerns to complex supply chain dynamics. Blockchain and traceability offer a beacon of hope, promising to instill transparency and accountability throughout this intricate web (Nguyen et al. 2021). With this synergy, the industry can progress towards a more sustainable, ethical, and efficient future.

The primary objectives of this chapter are twofold: to elucidate the paramount importance of blockchain and traceability in the context of the fashion and textile supply chain and to provide a comprehensive exploration of their applications and impact. We aim to achieve a nuanced understanding of how these technologies can revolutionize the industry. Furthermore, by scrutinizing a real-world case study from the Vietnamese textile and garment industry, we intend to shed light on the consequences of inadequate traceability and reinforce the urgency of finding viable solutions. Ultimately, we aim to delve into blockchain's transformative potential as a solution to the pervasive issues of traceability and accountability in the industry.

The chapter's structure mirrors the sequential unfolding of this narrative. It commences with an in-depth overview of the fashion and textile supply chain in the second section. Here, we dissect the intricate threads that comprise this industry, shedding light on its global significance and the complexities it faces, particularly in developing nations. The third section drills into the need for transparency and accountability, unraveling the intricacies of environmental, ethical, and operational challenges that this industry grapples with. Consumer demand for transparency takes center stage in the fourth section, where we explore how shifting paradigms in consumer behavior resonate through the fashion and textile landscape. The fifth section brings forth a poignant case study from the Vietnamese textile and garment industry, serving as a stark reminder of the consequences of inadequate traceability. As we progress to the sixth section, we immerse ourselves in the transformative potential of blockchain applications as a solution to these pervasive challenges. In the concluding section, we encapsulate the chapter's core insights, gazing into the future to explore emerging applications and challenges of blockchain in fashion and textile supply chain management.

10.2 Understanding the Fashion and Textile Supply Chain

10.2.1 Fashion and Textile Industry Overview

The fashion and textile industry is a multifaceted and dynamic sector that plays a vital role in the global economy. It encompasses the entire process of producing, distributing, and selling clothing, textiles, and related products (Viswaprakash and Sentamilselvan 2012). From the manufacturing of raw materials such as fibers and fabrics to the creation of fashion products, this industry is characterized by its global reach and intricate supply chain. The fashion and textile industry is of paramount importance for several reasons. Firstly, it is a significant contributor to the global economy. According to data from the World Trade Organization (WTO), the textile and apparel sector accounts for approximately 6% of the world's total merchandise exports, making it one of the most traded commodities globally (Gereffi et al. 2010). This makes it a significant source of employment and economic development in many countries.

Furthermore, the fashion and textile industry is deeply intertwined with culture and self-expression. It shapes and reflects societal norms, values, and trends. Fashion is not just about clothing; it is a form of communication, allowing individuals to express their identities and aspirations (Casciani et al. 2022). From high fashion to everyday attire, it influences how people present themselves to the world. The industry also has a substantial environmental and social footprint. It is known for its resource-intensive processes, waste generation, and labor issues. As a result, the fashion and textile sector has come under scrutiny for its environmental and ethical impact, and there is a growing demand for sustainable and responsible practices (Luque and Herrero-García 2019).

Despite its significance, the fashion and textile industry faces numerous challenges. One of the primary challenges is its susceptibility to rapidly changing consumer preferences. Trends in the fashion world evolve at a breakneck pace, requiring companies to adapt quickly. This creates pressure for frequent product turnover and, in some cases, encourages a throwaway culture that contributes to waste (Turcan et al. 2020). In addition to consumer-driven challenges, the fashion and textile industry grapples with issues related to globalization and offshoring. Many developing countries have become hubs for textile and apparel manufacturing due to lower labor costs. This has raised questions about labor conditions, worker rights, and ethical practices in these regions (Lopez-Acevedo et al., 2016). Ensuring fair and safe working conditions is a significant challenge.

Environmental concerns are also prevalent in the industry. The production of textiles and apparel is resource-intensive and often involves the use of chemicals and water. This leads to environmental degradation, pollution, and excessive waste. Sustainability and eco-friendly practices are becoming more important to address these issues. Moreover, supply chain complexity is a major challenge in the fashion and textile industry. The supply chain encompasses a vast network of processes, from sourcing raw materials and manufacturing to distribution and retail (Zhu and Pickles 2014). Coordinating these activities efficiently, while maintaining transparency and traceability, is a considerable challenge.

10.2.2 Complexities and Intricacies of the Fashion and Textile Supply Chain

The fashion and textile supply chain is a complex web of interrelated activities. It begins with the sourcing of raw materials, including fibers like cotton, wool, and synthetic materials. These materials are processed into fabrics and textiles. The fabrics are then transformed into various products, including clothing, accessories, and home textiles (Turcan et al. 2020; Casciani et al. 2022). This process involves multiple stages, including spinning, weaving, dyeing, printing, cutting, and sewing. Once the products are manufactured, they are distributed through a network of wholesalers, retailers, and e-commerce platforms. This supply chain includes a vast array of intermediaries and logistics providers, each playing a crucial role in ensuring that products reach consumers in a timely and cost-effective manner (Gereffi et al. 2010). The fashion and textile supply chain involves a multitude of key stakeholders, each contributing to the creation and distribution of fashion products:

- Raw Material Suppliers: These include cotton growers, wool producers, and manufacturers of synthetic fibers. They provide the essential starting point for the supply chain.
- Textile Manufacturers: Companies involved in spinning, weaving, and dyeing processes turn raw materials into fabrics.
- Garment Manufacturers: These companies transform fabrics into finished clothing items. This stage often takes place in countries with lower labor costs, primarily in developing countries.
- Brands and Designers: Fashion brands and designers are responsible for creating, branding, and marketing the final fashion products. They set the trends and consumer demand.
- Wholesalers and Distributors: These intermediaries purchase bulk quantities of products from manufacturers and distribute them to retailers.
- Retailers: Retailers encompass physical stores and online marketplaces. They are the interface between the products and consumers.
- Consumers: The end consumers are the ultimate stakeholders who drive demand in the fashion industry.
- Logistics and Transport Providers: These entities manage the movement of products from one stage of the supply chain to another.
- Regulatory Authorities: Governments and regulatory bodies may enforce laws and regulations related to labor, safety, and environmental standards in the industry.

The complexity of the supply chain arises from the involvement of numerous stakeholders, often spanning multiple countries. This complexity poses challenges for transparency, traceability, and accountability, which are crucial for addressing ethical and environmental concerns in the industry. Moreover, the supply chain's intricacies also make it susceptible to disruptions, such as those experienced during the COVID-19 pandemic, highlighting the need for more resilient supply chain management (Chakraborty and Biswas 2020). In developing countries, the fashion and textile industry often serves as a vital driver of economic growth and employment. However, these regions also face unique challenges related to labor conditions, environmental impact, and the need for sustainable practices (Castañeda-Navarrete et al. 2021). As the industry navigates these complexities and challenges, the adoption of innovative technologies like blockchain is emerging as a potential solution to enhance transparency and accountability, which will be discussed further in this chapter.

10.3 The Need for Transparency and Accountability for the Fashion and Textile Industry

The fashion and textile industry, particularly in developing countries, faces a multitude of challenges when it comes to transparency and accountability. These challenges stem from various aspects, including ethical, environmental, and operational concerns. One of the most pressing ethical concerns is the labor practices within the industry (Su et al. 2022). In many developing countries, the use of sweatshops, child labor, and poor working conditions has been a significant issue. Ensuring fair wages, safe working conditions, and adherence to labor laws is paramount in addressing these ethical concerns (Santos and Castanho 2022). Moreover, the industry often relies on subcontracting, which can obscure the true conditions under which garments are produced.

Environmental challenges in the industry are substantial. The production of textiles requires immense amounts of water and involves the use of various chemicals. This contributes to pollution and resource depletion (Szewczyk 2016). Furthermore, the industry generates a vast amount of waste, including textile scraps and discarded clothing. As such, sustainable and eco-friendly practices are imperative to mitigate these environmental concerns. Operational challenges also compound the industry's transparency and accountability issues. The intricacy of the global supply chain, with numerous intermediaries and subcontractors, complicates the monitoring and enforcement of ethical and environmental standards throughout the production process. This complexity makes it easier for unethical practices to go unnoticed and can hinder the traceability of products to their sources (Jia et al. 2020). Counterfeit products are often introduced into the market due to the lack of transparency, which can harm both consumers and legitimate manufacturers. The fragmented nature of the supply chain is another challenge. Different stages of production often occur in different countries, making it challenging to monitor and enforce ethical and environmental standards consistently (Luo et al. 2021). This fragmentation can lead to a lack of transparency and accountability at various stages of the production process.

In light of these challenges, addressing the ethical, environmental, and operational concerns is essential to enhance transparency and accountability in the fashion and textile industry, especially in developing countries. Innovative approaches and technologies are emerging as potential solutions to mitigate these challenges and foster a more responsible and sustainable industry (Fig. 10.1).

10.4 Consumer Demand for Transparency

The landscape of consumer expectations in the fashion and textile industry has witnessed a notable transformation in recent years, accentuating the significance of transparency and sustainability. Consumers are increasingly seeking comprehensive information about the products they purchase, specifically desiring insights into

Fig. 10.1 A view of a cotton farm in Xinjiang, a place with serious human rights concerns (*Source* Li 2021)

their origin, production processes, materials used, and associated environmental and social impacts (Bhaduri and Ha-Brookshire 2011). This shift in consumer behavior is driven by several factors.

Firstly, there is a growing awareness and education among consumers regarding the environmental and ethical challenges tied to the fashion and textile industry. This heightened awareness empowers consumers to make more informed purchasing choices based on a deeper understanding of the implications of their decisions (Modi and Zhao 2021). Secondly, consumers are demonstrating an inclination to support brands and products that align with their values. Ethical considerations, including fair labor practices and environmental sustainability, have become a driving force behind consumer preferences. Thirdly, the industry has witnessed an influx of transparency initiatives and advocacy by non-governmental organizations, activists, and extensive media coverage (Gonçalves and Silva 2021). This has served to educate consumers about the imperative need for transparency and accountability within the fashion supply chain. Additionally, the advent of the digital age has transformed access to information. Consumers now possess the ability to research brands, products, and their supply chain practices with ease, making informed choices the new norm.

The ramifications of this shift in consumer expectations extend to brand reputation and customer loyalty. Brands that proactively embrace transparency and sustainability measures stand to benefit significantly (Modi and Zhao 2021). These advantages include the enhancement of their reputation as socially responsible entities, an increase in consumer trust, augmented customer loyalty, and enhanced marketability. Conversely, brands that fail to meet consumer demands in these areas may face damage to their reputation, declining sales, and attrition of customer loyalty.

10.5 Case Study: A Traceability Problem in Vietnam Textile and Garment Industry

Vietnam's textile and garment industry is not just a crucial economic sector within the country; it's a global powerhouse. Over the last few decades, it has propelled Vietnam into the esteemed position of being the second-largest supplier in this industry worldwide. With its impressive contributions, the industry holds a pivotal role in Vietnam's economic landscape, accounting for a significant chunk of the nation's total export value, which ranges from 12 to 16%. In the first ten months of 2022, this industry's exports surged to nearly US$37.5 billion, marking a remarkable year-on-year increase of 14.5% (Nguyen and Hoang 2023a). The sector casts its net wide, exporting to 66 nations and territories, signifying its global reach. However, this meteoric growth trajectory is not without its share of challenges, and one of the most glaring is compliance with fundamental labor rights. This includes the formidable task of eliminating forced labor, a fundamental labor right recognized by international labor conventions. Despite the remarkable success of the textile and garment industry, the shadow of forced labor and human rights abuses looms large.

The U.S. Uyghur Forced Labor Prevention Act (UFLPA), enacted on December 23, 2021, marked a significant turning point in the global landscape, particularly in the textile and garment industry. This legislation emerged in response to the dire situation of Uyghurs and other persecuted minority groups in China's Xinjiang Uyghur Autonomous Region (XUAR). The UFLPA addresses allegations of forced labor and human rights abuses in Xinjiang, aiming to put an end to such practices. Its provisions are broad-reaching, and they entail strict measures:

- Prohibition of Forced Labor: The UFLPA bans the importation of goods produced entirely or partially by forced labor.
- Presumption of Forced Labor: It establishes a presumption that all goods mined, produced, or manufactured in the XUAR are products of forced labor.
- Entity Designation Authority: The UFLPA authorizes the U.S. Secretary of the Treasury to designate entities complicit in the use of forced labor in the XUAR.

The UFLPA has unleashed seismic disruptions upon Vietnam's textile and garment industry, primarily stemming from the profound deficiency in a robust traceability system capable of effectively tracking, verifying, and validating the origin of materials used in textile and garment production. This shortfall has led to an array of multifaceted challenges, causing far-reaching repercussions. Vietnam has found itself at the heart of these disturbances, experiencing unprecedented supply chain disruption. Data reported by U.S. customs up to April 3, 2023, illustrates the impact of the Act, subjecting approximately $15 million worth of apparel and footwear shipments to rigorous inspections, with over 80% of these shipments originating from Vietnam (Nguyen and Hoang 2023b). Alarmingly, merely 13% of these shipments were granted clearance for entry into the lucrative U.S. market, clearly highlighting the substantial obstacles faced by Vietnamese textile and garment enterprises. Furthermore, the consequences of the UFLPA have been exacerbated by a recent decline in demand for clothing from more affluent nations, particularly the U.S. and the European Union. Rising inflationary pressures in these regions have compelled consumers to tighten their spending, resulting in a notable reduction in demand. This decline has, in turn, led to a significant decrease in industrial output and exports from Vietnam, directly impacting major brands such as Nike, Gap, and Adidas. Beyond operational disruptions, the financial ramifications of the UFLPA have been substantial. The value of shipments from Vietnam that have been barred from entering the U.S. market has surpassed $2 million, a figure that continues to surge dramatically in the initial months of the year. This underscores the acute challenges faced by the industry and further accentuates the urgency for solutions addressing traceability and transparency in the fashion and textile supply chain (Nguyen and Hoang 2023a).

The UFLPA mandates that U.S. importers rigorously verify the absence of forced labor within their supply chains. This verification procedure holds the potential for considerable disruptions not only for U.S. importers but also for Vietnamese small and medium-sized enterprises (SMEs). These businesses may find themselves compelled to furnish compelling evidence that their products are devoid of any inputs originating from Xinjiang or produced using forced labor. This challenge is magnified by the fact that a substantial portion of Vietnam's apparel manufacturers rely heavily on China, sourcing nearly half of their input materials from this region (Nguyen and Hoang 2023b).

The impact of the UFLPA on Vietnam's textile and garment industry underlines the compelling imperative of establishing a robust traceability system or platform within the supply chain, particularly in the garment and textile sector. The need for this traceability system is paramount as it can effectively track, verify, and validate the origins of crucial materials, thereby mitigating the multifaceted challenges confronting the industry. This traceability system is not only vital for the interests of Vietnamese businesses but also resonates with the broader global stakeholders in the textile and garment sector. By ensuring the transparency and accountability of the supply chain, a traceability system aligns with international labor standards and secures the continued growth and success of the industry. To tackle this complex issue, disruptive technologies such as blockchain applications present themselves as promising solutions. The adoption of blockchain technology has the potential to revolutionize traceability in the supply chain by providing immutable, decentralized, and transparent record-keeping. This enhances accountability and guarantees the authenticity of materials used, which is essential in an industry with global reach and complex supply networks.

10.6 Blockchain Technology and Its Applications in Fashion and Textile Industry

Blockchain technology is a revolutionary advancement that has the potential to transform various industries, including the supply chain, in the pursuit of addressing transparency and accountability issues (Nguyen et al. 2021). At its core, a blockchain is a decentralized and distributed digital ledger that records transactions across a network of computers. Initially designed as the underlying technology for cryptocurrencies like Bitcoin, its applications have since expanded beyond digital currencies (Hoang et al. 2022). A blockchain is essentially a chain of blocks, where each block contains a list of transactions. These transactions are grouped together in a secure and immutable manner. What sets blockchain apart from traditional databases is its decentralized and trust less nature. It operates on a peer-to-peer network, meaning that no central authority or intermediary is needed to validate or oversee transactions (Agrawal et al. 2021). Instead, transactions are validated and recorded by a network of participants, known as nodes, who reach a consensus through a process called a consensus mechanism.

Blockchain technology is underpinned by core principles of decentralization, transparency, security, and immutability. In essence, blockchain operates through a distributed network of computers, known as nodes, where each node maintains a copy of the entire ledger. This decentralization guarantees that no single entity wields control over the network, ensuring resistance to censorship and manipulation (Hoang and Phan 2022). The process begins with users initiating transactions, which are then broadcast to the network, containing details of the sender, recipient, and the transaction amount. These transactions undergo validation by the network of nodes through a consensus mechanism such as Proof of Work (PoW), wherein nodes compete to solve intricate mathematical puzzles. Successfully solved puzzles lead to the addition of transactions into a new block. These blocks, each referencing the previous one, form a chronological chain of blocks, thereby named "blockchain." Importantly, once a block is integrated into the chain, altering or deleting its contents becomes extremely challenging due to cryptographic hashing. Each block contains a unique code or hash, derived from its contents and the previous block's hash, ensuring immutability (Agrawal et al. 2021; Nguyen et al. 2021). The decentralized nature and consensus mechanism are fundamental to the security and reliability of blockchain, as they guarantee that all nodes agree on the blockchain's state. Furthermore, blockchain can incorporate smart contracts, which are self-executing agreements with terms encoded directly into the code. These contracts automatically execute when predefined conditions are met, offering the potential to automate intricate processes within the blockchain (Fig. 10.2).

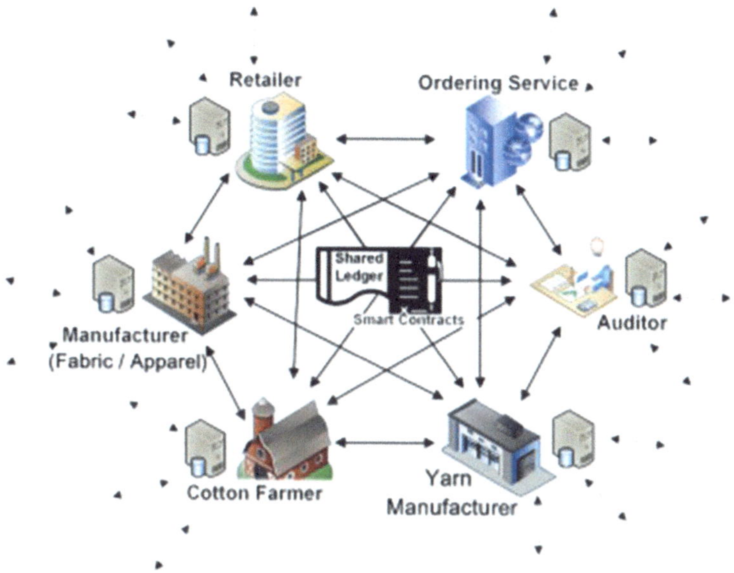

Fig. 10.2 Blockchain-based decentralized network (*Source* Agrawal et al. 2021)

10.6.1 Blockchain Applications in Supply Chain for Addressing Challenges of Transparency and Accountability

The fashion and textile industry, particularly in developing countries as exemplified in the case study discussed earlier, grapples with profound challenges pertaining to transparency and accountability within its supply chain. These challenges encompass the intricacies of the supply chain itself, the pervasive issue of counterfeit products, ethical concerns surrounding labor and environmental standards, and the imperative need for precise record-keeping and documentation (Hader et al. 2022). Blockchain technology emerges as a potent and transformative solution, offering several inherent benefits directly addressing these multifaceted issues.

Firstly, blockchain's immutability is a pivotal feature, ensuring that once data is recorded on the blockchain, it becomes indelible, safeguarding the accuracy and integrity of records detailing each product's journey through the supply chain. Brands can utilize blockchain to provide consumers with a transparent, reliable, and tamper-proof record of their products' origins, production processes, and distribution. Secondly, blockchain's decentralized nature implies the absence of a central authority or intermediary controlling information, thus cultivating trust in the supply chain by eliminating dependence on a single entity for vital information (Agrawal et al. 2021). This decentralization aligns with the industry's growing demand for transparency and independence from centralized authorities.

Moreover, blockchain's transparency serves as a linchpin, granting all participants in the supply chain access to information that can be comprehensively verified. This transparency empowers consumers to trace a product's journey, from its inception to their possession, delivering a level of insight hitherto unattainable. Additionally, the integration of smart contracts within blockchain technology introduces automation into various aspects of the supply chain, such as triggering payments to suppliers upon the fulfillment of predefined conditions, thus guaranteeing fair and timely compensation and the enforcement of ethical practices, labor standards, and environmental compliance (Agrawal et al. 2018; Hoang and Phan 2022). Finally, blockchain enhances efficiency in record-keeping and documentation, mitigating the risk of errors and inefficiencies that could plague the supply chain. This efficiency not only translates into cost savings but also enables a swifter response to issues within the supply chain, further enhancing its resilience and effectiveness.

By incorporating blockchain technology into the fashion and textile supply chain, the industry not only elevates transparency and accountability but also drives improvements in efficiency and trust among all stakeholders. This powerful integration furnishes a robust and transformative solution to the complex and pressing challenges faced by the industry, ultimately benefiting consumers, businesses, and the environment while fostering a more ethically and environmentally conscious fashion and textile sector.

10.6.2 Traceability in the Supply Chain

The concept of traceability in supply chain management refers to the ability to track and trace products or components from their source of origin to their final destination, typically the end-consumer. This process is crucial in ensuring transparency, accountability, and compliance with various standards and regulations. Traceability provides a comprehensive view of a product's journey through the supply chain, offering insights into its origins, production processes, handling, and distribution (Agrawal et al. 2018). It also enables the monitoring of factors such as quality, safety, and sustainability (Hader et al. 2022) (Fig. 10.3).

10.6.2.1 Importance of Traceability

Traceability stands as a paramount element in supply chain management, wielding substantial significance for various compelling reasons. Firstly, it plays a pivotal role in assuring product quality by enabling the early identification of quality issues or defects at multiple junctures within the supply chain. This timely discovery empowers companies to take swift corrective actions, effectively mitigating the risk of defective products infiltrating the market and reaching consumers (Ahmed and MacCarthy 2021). Furthermore, traceability assumes a crucial function in ensuring compliance and accountability, particularly in industries like fashion and textiles that are bound

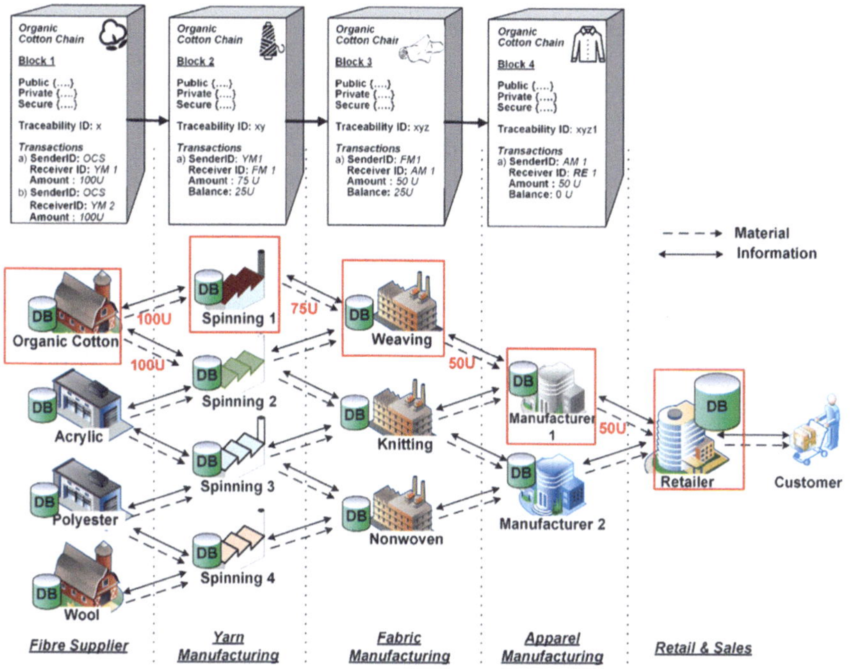

Fig. 10.3 Blockchain applications in textile supply chain (*Source* Agrawal et al. 2021)

by stringent international labor standards, environmental regulations, and ethical considerations. It serves as an indispensable mechanism for verifying that companies uphold these exacting standards and can be held answerable for their supply chain practices (Kumar et al. 2017).

In an era characterized by heightened consumer demand for transparency and ethical sourcing, traceability serves as a linchpin for instilling confidence. The ability of consumers to trace a product's journey through the supply chain not only fosters trust but also empowers them to make well-informed choices, underlining the pivotal role traceability plays in building and sustaining consumer trust (Garcia-Torres et al. 2022). Moreover, traceability emerges as a robust tool for effective crisis management. In scenarios where product recalls or supply chain disruptions materialize, it equips companies with the capability to expeditiously and efficiently identify affected products, thus minimizing the ramifications on both consumers and the brand's reputation. Beyond these considerations, traceability actively supports sustainability endeavors by meticulously tracking the environmental footprint of products (Agrawal et al. 2018). This, in turn, furnishes companies with data-driven insights to guide decisions aimed at reducing their carbon footprint and championing eco-friendly practices, thereby contributing to a more sustainable and responsible industry landscape.

10.6.2.2 Blockchain-Enabled Traceability

Blockchain technology emerges as an influential and highly effective solution for the establishment of traceability within supply chains, seamlessly aligning with its core principles of decentralization, immutability, transparency, and security. In this context, the process of creating a traceability system within the supply chain is facilitated by several key components. Initially, each facet of the supply chain, ranging from the procurement of raw materials to the various stages of production, transportation, and distribution, is meticulously recorded as individual transactions on the blockchain (Dasaklis et al. 2022). These transactions are subsequently organized into blocks and interlinked to create a coherent and chronological chain of data. The immutability characteristic of blockchain further reinforces the integrity and security of these records, ensuring that once a transaction is logged on the blockchain, it remains unaltered and impervious to tampering.

Moreover, the decentralization aspect of blockchain technology plays a pivotal role in promoting trust and credibility within the supply chain. By operating on a decentralized network, blockchain disperses control and access across all participants in the supply chain, effectively nullifying the existence of a single controlling entity (Ahmed and MacCarthy 2021). This ensures that every stakeholder involved in the supply chain has equal access to the same dataset, bolstering transparency and instilling confidence. Transparency, a foundational feature of blockchain, is a cornerstone of the traceability system. It endows all stakeholders, including consumers, with the ability to seamlessly access and rigorously verify the data enshrined within the blockchain. This open and accessible nature of blockchain data fosters trust and confidence, marking a significant departure from previous models of supply chain management. Furthermore, the integration of smart contracts within blockchain technology represents a transformative force in automating and streamlining supply chain processes. Smart contracts, which embody self-executing agreements with predefined conditions, have the capacity to revolutionize the supply chain by automating specific functions, such as the automatic triggering of payments to suppliers when predetermined criteria are met (Yang et al. 2023). This automation leads to increased efficiency and accuracy within the supply chain, making it a powerful tool for modernizing and enhancing traceability.

10.6.2.3 Examples of Successful Implementations

Blockchain technology has been effectively applied across various industries, showcasing its potential in enhancing supply chain traceability. In the food industry, companies like Walmart have harnessed blockchain to rapidly trace the origins of food products, significantly aiding in the rapid identification of sources of contamination in cases of foodborne illnesses (Tan et al. 2018). Similarly, the luxury goods sector has embraced blockchain to offer consumers a means of verifying product authenticity. By scanning a QR code on luxury items, consumers can access blockchain records that provide detailed information about the product's journey from its production to sale, assuring its genuine origin (Tan et al. 2018; Yang et al. 2023).

The mining industry, especially in the context of conflict minerals, has also embraced blockchain as a powerful tool for tracking mineral sourcing. This application ensures that minerals used in electronic devices are free from any association with conflict zones or human rights violations. Furthermore, the pharmaceutical industry utilizes blockchain to ensure the integrity of the drug supply chain, combating counterfeit medicines and verifying the maintenance of appropriate temperature conditions during transportation (Schinckus 2020). This safeguards the safety and efficacy of medicines throughout their journey from manufacturer to patient. Similarly, in the fashion and textile industry, the incorporation of blockchain-enabled traceability can empower consumers to trace the fabric's origin, understand the intricacies of the production processes, and ascertain the industry's adherence to rigorous environmental and ethical standards. This elevated level of transparency cultivates consumer trust and bolsters ethical and sustainable practices, thereby fostering the industry's compliance with international labor standards and regulatory requirements, ultimately amplifying its integrity and accountability.

By leveraging blockchain technology to establish traceability, the fashion and textile supply chain can address the challenges of transparency, authenticity, and ethical sourcing while meeting the growing demands of consumers for accountability and sustainability (Garcia-Torres et al. 2022; Nguyen et al. 2023). Blockchain offers a versatile and secure solution for the fashion and textile industry to ensure that products meet the highest standards and comply with international labor and environmental regulations. The successful implementations in other industries demonstrate the potential and benefits of incorporating blockchain into the fashion and textile supply chain to ensure its growth and success in an increasingly conscious and demanding market.

10.7 Closing Remarks

In the closing pages of this chapter, we reflect on the transformative role of blockchain technology in the fashion and textile supply chain, offering a dynamic framework for transparency and accountability. Beyond being just a technological tool, blockchain acts as a catalyst for change, aligning the industry with evolving consumer expectations, ethical standards, and regulatory demands. In these closing remarks, we highlight the profound impact of blockchain and its potential to shape a more responsible and sustainable future for the fashion and textile industry.

The integration of blockchain technology into the fashion and textile supply chain represents a pivotal step towards addressing the industry's pressing challenges while embracing a future defined by transparency, accountability, and sustainability. By leveraging blockchain's decentralized framework, immutability, and smart contract capabilities, fashion brands can instill trust among consumers, enhance efficiency within the supply chain, and uphold ethical and environmental standards. As we move forward, it is imperative for stakeholders across the industry to recognize the transformative potential of blockchain and embrace its adoption to drive positive change. Through collaborative efforts and innovative solutions, we can revolutionize the fashion and textile sector, ensuring that products meet the highest standards of quality, authenticity, and social responsibility. The successful implementations of blockchain technology in other industries serve as inspiring examples of its efficacy in enhancing traceability and fostering consumer trust (Agrawal et al. 2021; Nguyen et al. 2021). By drawing upon these lessons and leveraging blockchain's capabilities, the fashion and textile industry can position itself at the forefront of ethical and sustainable practices.

10.7.1 Key Takeaways

Recapping the essential insights of this chapter, we have navigated the intricate terrain of the fashion and textile industry, particularly in developing countries. The challenges span from ethical sourcing dilemmas and environmental sustainability concerns to operational intricacies. Simultaneously, we have explored the surging consumer demand for transparency, underlining the industry's evolving focus on ethical and sustainable consumption patterns.

The case study, which unveils the predicament of the Vietnamese fashion and textile industry, lays bare the urgent necessity of implementing a robust traceability system. The repercussions of the U.S. Uyghur Forced Labor Prevention Act (UFLPA) serve as a stark reminder of the consequences of insufficient traceability, driving home the imperative of prioritizing its establishment.

As the fashion and textile industry embraces blockchain, it enters an era where traceability and accountability are not just ideals but practical realities. Blockchain's transformative role goes beyond technology; it reshapes industry norms, aligns with consumer expectations, and positions the sector as a steward of sustainability. The future of the fashion and textile industry, entwined with blockchain, is one that stands on the principles of responsibility, ethics, and sustainability.

In this journey, the industry faces both opportunities and hurdles. The challenges posed by data privacy, interoperability, regulatory compliance, scalability, and smart contract optimization are genuine and must be met with strategic solutions. However, these challenges are eclipsed by the promise of a fashion and textile sector that stands as a shining example of how technology can usher in an era of responsible prosperity.

With blockchain as its guide, the fashion and textile industry embarks on a path of progress. It not only secures its growth and success but also contributes to a larger narrative of a conscientious global economy. The principles of transparency, accountability, and sustainability are not just aspirations; they are the building blocks of a new era in fashion and textiles. The future is in the hands of those who dare to innovate and embrace the transformative potential of blockchain, and in doing so, pave the way for a supply chain that transcends conventions and heralds a new era of conscientious and sustainable prosperity.

10.7.2 Future Studies in Blockchain Applications

As we look to the future, the fashion and textile industry stands on the brink of a profound transformation driven by blockchain applications. However, this transformation comes with a unique set of challenges that must be addressed. First and foremost, the industry must prioritize data privacy and security, especially as blockchain systems accumulate vast amounts of sensitive data. Safeguarding this information from breaches and unauthorized access becomes paramount. Furthermore, the integration of blockchain applications across a diverse array of supply chain stakeholders may introduce interoperability challenges (Dasaklis et al. 2022; Yang et al. 2023). To ensure seamless communication and data sharing, the establishment of standardized protocols and platforms is essential. Given that the industry operates within a framework of ever-evolving regulatory requirements, adapting to these standards and ensuring that blockchain applications remain compliant with both local and international laws is a complex undertaking. Additionally, the scalability of blockchain networks must be addressed, particularly as they continue to expand. Solutions are needed to handle the growing volume of transactions and data while upholding the efficiency and speed that blockchain promises (Tripathi et al. 2021; Hoang and Phan 2022). Lastly, while smart contracts offer the promise of efficiency gains, they necessitate ongoing optimization to reduce errors and streamline processes. Navigating this dynamic landscape of blockchain applications in the fashion and textile industry requires a careful balance between embracing opportunities and addressing the complexities that inevitably arise.

References

Agrawal TK, Kumar V, Pal R, Wang L, Chen Y (2021) Blockchain-based framework for supply chain traceability: a case example of textile and clothing industry. Comput Ind Eng 154:107130

Agrawal TK, Sharma A, Kumar V (2018) Blockchain-based secured traceability system for textile and clothing supply chain. In: Artificial intelligence for fashion industry in the big data era, pp 197–208

Ahmed WA, MacCarthy BL (2021) Blockchain-enabled supply chain traceability in the textile and apparel supply chain: a case study of the fiber producer, Lenzing. Sustainability 13(19):10496

Behera M, Nayak J, Banerjee S, Chakrabortty S, Tripathy SK (2021) A review on the treatment of textile industry waste effluents towards the development of efficient mitigation strategy: An integrated system design approach. J Environ Chem Eng 9(4):105277

Bhaduri G, Ha-Brookshire JE (2011) Do transparent business practices pay? Exploration of transparency and consumer purchase intention. Cloth Text Res J 29(2):135–149

Casciani D, Chkanikova O, Pal R (2022) Exploring the nature of digital transformation in the fashion industry: opportunities for supply chains, business models, and sustainability-oriented innovations. Sustain Sci Pract Policy 18(1):773–795

Castañeda-Navarrete J, Hauge J, López-Gómez C (2021) COVID-19's impacts on global value chains, as seen in the apparel industry. Dev Policy Rev 39(6):953–970

Chakraborty S, Biswas MC (2020) Impact of COVID-19 on the textile, apparel and fashion manufacturing industry supply chain: case study on a ready-made garment manufacturing industry. J Supply Chain Manage Logist Procur 3(2):181–199

Dasaklis TK, Voutsinas TG, Tsoulfas GT, Casino F (2022) A systematic literature review of blockchain-enabled supply chain traceability implementations. Sustainability 14(4):2439
Garcia-Torres S, Rey-Garcia M, Sáenz J, Seuring S (2022) Traceability and transparency for sustainable fashion-apparel supply chains. J FAshion Mark Manage 26(2):344–364
Gereffi G, Frederick S, Gereffi G (2010) The global apparel value chain, trade and the crisis: challenges and opportunities for developing countries. The World Bank, Washinton, D.C
Gonçalves A, Silva C (2021) Looking for sustainability scoring in apparel: a review on environmental footprint, social impacts and transparency. Energies 14(11):3032
Hader M, Tchoffa D, El Mhamedi A, Ghodous P, Dolgui A, Abouabdellah A (2022) Applying integrated blockchain and big data technologies to improve supply chain traceability and information sharing in the textile sector. J Ind Inf Integr 28:100345
Hoang TG, Bui ML (2023) Business intelligence and analytic (BIA) stage-of-practice in micro-, small-and medium-sized enterprises (MSMEs). J Enterp Inf Manag 36(4):1080–1104
Hoang TG, Phan TNT (2022) Cultural entrepreneurship and disruptive blockchain applications in vietnam: the status quo and the transition towards a digital economy. In: Cultural entrepreneurship: new societal trends. Springer Nature Singapore, Singapore, pp 23–38
Hoang TG, Nguyen GNT, Le DA (2022) Developments in financial technologies for achieving the sustainable development goals (SDGs): FinTech and SDGs. In: Disruptive technologies and eco-innovation for sustainable development. IGI Global, pp 1–19
Jia F, Yin S, Chen L, Chen X (2020) The circular economy in the textile and apparel industry: a systematic literature review. J Clean Prod 259:120728
Kumar V, Hallqvist C, Ekwall D (2017) Developing a framework for traceability implementation in the textile supply chain. Systems 5(2):33
Li X (2021) Western crackdown inspires Xinjiang cotton industry to rise. Global Times. https://www.globaltimes.cn/page/202403/1308177.shtml
Lopez-Acevedo G, Robertson R (eds) (2016) Stitches to riches? Apparel employment, trade, and economic development in South Asia. World Bank Publications
Luo Y, Song K, Ding X, Wu X (2021) Environmental sustainability of textiles and apparel: a review of evaluation methods. Environ Impact Assess Rev 86:106497
Luque A, Herrero-García N (2019) How corporate social (ir)responsibility in the textile sector is defined, and its impact on ethical sustainability: an analysis of 133 concepts. Corp Soc Responsib Environ Manag 26(6):1285–1306
Modi D, Zhao L (2021) Social media analysis of consumer opinion on apparel supply chain transparency. J Fashion Market Manage 25(3):465–481
Ngo VM, Quang HT, Hoang TG, Binh ADT (2023) Sustainability-related supply chain risks and supply chain performances: The moderating effects of dynamic supply chain management practices. Bus Strat Environ. https://doi.org/10.1002/bse.3512
Nguyen AH, Hoang TG, Ngo VM, Nguyen LQT, Nguyen HH (2023) Sustainability-oriented supply chain finance in Vietnam: insights from multiple case studies. Oper Manag Res 16(1):259–279
Nguyen G, Hoang T (2023a) Supply traceability: how US trade policies affect Vietnam's garment industry. Hinrich Foundation. https://www.hinrichfoundation.com/research/article/trade-and-geopolitics/trade-policies-and-vietnam-garment-industry/
Nguyen G, Hoang T (2023b) Impact of US anti-forced labor laws on Vietnam's textile industry. Hinrich Foundation. https://www.hinrichfoundation.com/research/wp/sustainable/impact-of-us-anti-forced-labor-laws-on-vietnam-textile-industry/
Nguyen LT, Hoang TG, Do LH, Ngo XT, Nguyen PH, Nguyen GD, Nguyen GN (2021) The role of blockchain technology-based social crowdfunding in advancing social value creation. Technol Forecast Soc Chang 170:120898
Santos E, Castanho RA (2022) The impact of size on the performance of transnational corporations operating in the textile industry in Portugal during the COVID-19 pandemic. Sustainability 14(2):717
Schinckus C (2020) The good, the bad and the ugly: An overview of the sustainability of blockchain technology. Energy Res Soc Sci 69:101614

Su J, Hodges NN, Wu H, Iqbal MA (2022) Coping with the COVID-19 pandemic: evidence from the apparel industry in Bangladesh and China. J Fashion Market Manage 1–19

Szewczyk M (2016) Corporate social responsibility in the textile and apparel industry: barriers and challenges. J Corp Responsib Leadership 3(4):67–81

Tan B, Yan J, Chen S, Liu X (2018) The impact of blockchain on food supply chain: the case of Walmart. In: Smart blockchain: first international conference. SmartBlock 2018, Tokyo, Japan, December 10–12, 2018, proceedings, vol 1. Springer International Publishing, pp 167–177

Tripathi G, Tripathi Nautiyal V, Ahad MA, Feroz N (2021) Blockchain technology and fashion industry-opportunities and challenges. In: Blockchain technology: applications and challenges, pp 201–220

Turcan RV, Boujarzadeh B, Dholakia N (2020) Late globalization and evolution, episodes and epochs of industries: Evidence from Danish textile and fashion industry, 1945–2015. Thunderbird Int Bus Rev 62(5):515–530

Viswaprakash V, Sentamilselvan K (2012) Globalization & trade in textile industry. Int J Market Technol 2(5):201

Yang L, Ni Y, Ng CT (2023) Blockchain-enabled traceability and producer's incentive to outsource delivery. Int J Prod Res 61(11):3811–3828

Zhu S, Pickles J (2014) Bring in, go up, go west, go out: upgrading, regionalisation and delocalisation in China's apparel production networks. J Contemp Asia 44(1):36–63

Thinh Gia Hoang (Ph.D.) is a researcher and author specializing in innovation and technology management. He currently serves as a lecturer at the International School of Business, University of Economics Ho Chi Minh City. His research focuses on innovation and technology management, sustainable business models, and disruptive technologies in business applications. He also serves as an Associate Editor for Technology Analysis & Strategic Management. He has contributed to the editorial boards of Information Systems Research in Vietnam (Springer Nature) and the SAGE Handbook of Qualitative Research in Asian Context (SAGE Publishing). He is the editor of the book Navigating the Circular Age of a Sustainable Digital Revolution (IGI Global).

An Duong Thi Binh (Ph.D.) is a member of CIRTech Institute, HUTECH University, Ho Chi Minh City, Vietnam. She conducted doctoral research at the Graduate School of Culture and Information Science, Doshisha University, Kyoto, Japan under a Research Fellowship for Young Scientists of Japan Society for the Promotion of Science (JSPS). She is also serving as Supply chain manager at Nipro Sales Vietnam Co. Ltd.—a Japanese leading medical device manufacturer. Her research interests include supply chain risk management, quality and supply chain management, statistics, and data science. She has published on these topics in high-quality academic journals such as Engineering, Construction and Architectural Management, Construction Management and Economics, International Journal of Quality & Reliability Management, International Journal of Productivity and Performance Management, Behaviormetrika, Smart Innovation, Systems, and Technologies, Operations Management Research, Journal of Enterprise Information Management, Business Strategy and Environment, etc. She has also conducted some research projects on these topics in (1) Graduate School of Culture and Information Science, Doshisha University, Kyoto, Japan, (2) the Systems and Production Department, University of Minho, Portugal, (3) RMIT International University, Vietnam, etc. More information is at http://orcid.org/0000-0003-1154-2983.

Phuong Thi Nguyen graduated with a PhD in Management from RMIT University with a HDR full scholarship. She is an academic and expert in management, currently serving as a Lecturer in the University of Economics Ho Chi Minh City (UEH), the UEH-International School of Business. With over a decade of experience in the higher education sector, Phuong has cultivated a diverse skill set encompassing international program franchise, academic research, fundraising for research projects, and teaching at both undergraduate and postgraduate levels in global institutions such as RMIT University, Birmingham City University, Leipzig University, Liverpool John Moores University, Western Sydney University, and others. She has held various management roles in higher education projects within both for-profit and non-profit sectors, including her tenure as Program Manager at the Hinrich Foundation, a non-profit organization collaborating with companies across different global supply chain sectors and providing scholarships for top-tier universities globally. Phuong's research interests span a wide array of fields, including corporate governance, strategic management, sustainability, supply chain management, and marketing, etc. For more information, please visit her profile at https://orcid.org/0000-0002-5855-8512.

Chapter 11
Smart Textiles and Wearable Technology: Opportunities and Challenges in the Production and Distribution

Saniyat Islam and Ravi Shekhar

Abstract The chapter delves into the potential opportunities presented by this innovative technology, including its potential to revolutionise various sectors such as healthcare, sports, and fashion. It also addresses the challenges faced in the production and distribution of smart garments, such as technical difficulties, high production costs, and the need for standardisation. The chapter further discusses the importance of interdisciplinary collaboration in overcoming these challenges and realising the full potential of smart textiles. It concludes by emphasising the need for further research and development in this field to ensure its sustainable growth and widespread adoption.

Keywords Smart textiles · Wearable technology · Intelligent textile · Industry 4.0 · Manufacturing and application

11.1 Introduction

In the rapidly evolving world of technology, one of the most exciting developments is the integration of digital components into textiles, creating what is known as 'smart textiles' or 'wearable technology'. These innovative products can potentially transform many sectors, from healthcare to sports and even fashion. However, the journey from concept to prototype to consumer is filled with challenges, particularly in the production and distribution of these smart garments (Zhang et al. 2023). The notion of intelligent or smart materials was first outlined by Takagi in 1990 (Takagi 1990). He described them as 'materials that react to environmental shifts under the most ideal conditions and exhibit their unique functions in response to these changes'.

S. Islam (✉)
School of Fashion and Textiles, RMIT University, Melbourne, VIC, Australia
e-mail: saniyat.islam@rmit.edu.au

R. Shekhar
School of Engineering, RMIT University, Melbourne, VIC, Australia

R. Nayak et al. (eds.), *Use of Digital and Advanced Technologies in the Fashion Supply Chain*, Springer Series in Fashion Business,
https://doi.org/10.1007/978-981-97-7528-6_11

He also made a distinct separation between structural and functional materials and intelligent materials (Takagi 1990). This chapter aims to provide a comprehensive overview of this ever-evolving field, exploring both the opportunities it presents and the obstacles it faces. Through this exploration, we hope to shed light on the future of this industry and the steps needed to ensure its sustainable growth and widespread adoption.

11.1.1 Brief History and Evolution of Smart Garments

The history of smart textiles can be traced back to the late twentieth century when researchers began exploring the possibilities of integrating electronics with fabrics. The integration of various fields such as textile technology, materials science, chemistry, physics, microelectronics, computer science, biomedicine, optics, and other technologies has paved the way for the creation of technologically sophisticated textiles and clothing made from advanced smart materials (Rijavec 2010; Liu et al. 2022). This was initially driven by the needs of specialised industries such as the military and space exploration. However, with technological advancements, smart textiles have expanded into various sectors, including healthcare, sports, fashion, automotive, and other industries (Sajovic et al. 2023).

Smart textiles and wearable technology have transformed the garment industry by integrating intelligent materials and electronic technologies into clothing. These innovations have created various opportunities and challenges in producing and distributing smart garments. Incorporating sensors, processors, communication equipment, and displays into textile-based garments has facilitated the development of smart clothing or smart garments (Sonderegger 2013; Al Mahmud et al. 2020). These garments can sense, react, or adapt behaviour to various circumstances, providing advantages such as enhanced well-being for athletes (Duarte et al. 2022) and improved muscle recovery and performance for individuals involved in physical activities (Chen et al. 2020).

The progress of wearable technology has given rise to smart textiles that can harness various forms of energy, including biomechanical, body heat, biochemical, and solar energy (Patel et al. 2012). Additionally, wearable systems equipped with sensors and data analysis techniques have been applied in rehabilitation, diagnosis, and therapy, demonstrating the versatility and potential of smart garments in the healthcare sector (Zheng et al. 2014). Furthermore, the advancement of unobtrusive sensing methods, smart textile technology, flexible-stretchable-printable electronics, and sensor fusion has laid the foundation for pervasive health information acquisition (Smith et al. 2023).

The future of smart garments lies in their capacity to transform various industries, particularly healthcare, through wearable biosensors that enable continuous monitoring of vital signs and health parameters (Lin 2022). These biosensors, coupled with advancements in human–computer interaction and flexible electronics, are propelling the evolution of wearable devices and broadening their applications (Lin

2022). Moreover, integrating wearable device technology, such as smart clothing and diverse sensors, into garments enhances human–computer interaction and enables new functionalities (Chang et al. 2021).

Challenges persist in the production and distribution of smart garments, such as ensuring the washability of the entire garment, which is essential for preserving the functionality and durability of the technology integrated into the textiles (Heikenfeld 2016). Additionally, advancements in sweat stimulation, sample collection efficiency, compact sensors, and target analytes' detection repertoire are crucial for advancing wearable chemical sensors for biomarker discovery (Sempionatto et al. 2022).

In summary, smart textiles and wearable technology have significant potential to enhance various aspects of human life, from sports performance and rehabilitation to healthcare monitoring. Overcoming usability, aesthetics, energy harvesting, and sensor integration challenges will be pivotal in unlocking the full capabilities of smart garments and ensuring their widespread adoption.

11.1.2 Smart Textiles Definition of Smart Textiles and Wearable Technology

Smart Textiles are materials that intelligently sense and respond to external stimuli or environmental conditions (Persson et al. 2018). Smart textiles, also known as electronic textiles (e-textiles) or smart fabrics, are a revolutionary development in the textile industry. They are materials enhanced with electronic components, either during manufacturing or afterwards, to provide additional functionality beyond traditional textiles (Ielo et al. 2021). These functionalities can range from simple aesthetic enhancements, such as changing colour, to more complex features, like monitoring health data or providing connectivity to other devices (Grancarić et al. 2018).

The terms 'technical textile', 'intelligent textile', 'functional material', 'functional textile', 'functional fabric', 'nano-fabric', 'electronic fabric', 'smart fibre', and 'soft circuit' are often used to discuss smart textiles (Kongahage and Foroughi 2019; Liao et al. 2015). While they can sometimes be used interchangeably with 'smart textiles', it is important to note that each term may have specific connotations or nuances depending on the context. For example, a 'functional fabric' might refer to a textile designed with a specific function, such as water-resistant or flame-retardant. Still, it might not necessarily contain electronic components. Smart textiles represent a fascinating intersection of technology and textiles, offering many opportunities for innovation and application. However, as with any emerging technology, it also presents its challenges and considerations, which we will explore in this paper.

11.2 Understanding Smart Textiles

11.2.1 Types of Smart Textiles

Smart textiles can be broadly categorised into two types: passive and active. Passive smart textiles only respond to external conditions or stimuli, such as changing colour in response to changes in temperature. On the other hand, active smart textiles can adapt and react to conditions more dynamically, often powered by an external source. They can include features like heating elements, sensors, or connectivity to other devices.

The inception of passive smart textiles can be traced back to the late twentieth century (Takagi 1990), during the era of Garment Industry 3.0, characterised by the advent of automation and computerisation. This period saw significant advancements in understanding certain materials' chemical and physical properties and their interactions with textile substrates. Researchers began to explore how these materials responded to various environmental stimuli such as abrasion, mechanical agitation, heat, and moisture. An early example of passive smart textiles is a fabric designed to release fragrance when it reaches a specific body temperature. The development of active smart textiles coincides with the early twenty-first century, marking the transition from Garment Industry 3.0 to Garment Industry 4.0, which introduced digitalisation and smart manufacturing (Akram et al. 2022). This phase involved embedding small electronic components, such as sensors, into garments to monitor bodily functions. The progress in electronics, characterised by increasingly compact, reliable, and efficient components, facilitated the integration of these technologies into specialised garments for military, aerospace, and medical applications and later into sportswear.

The current phase in smart textiles represents integrating passive smart textile attributes with digitally controlled modules, forming a sophisticated interaction between textiles and electronic systems. For instance, the fragrance-releasing textile now includes an electronic switch, enabling controlled fragrance to release independent of environmental stimuli like body heat or ambient temperature. This marks a significant advancement in the functionality and versatility of smart textiles, paving the way for innovative applications and enhanced user experiences. Such smart textiles can be categorised as ultra-smart textiles based on their performance characteristics (Canan Çelikel 2020).

In summary, the progression of smart textiles from passive to active and advanced forms reflects the broader technological evolution within the garment industry, driven by advancements in material science, electronics, and digital technologies.

11.2.2 Components and Technologies in Smart Textiles

Smart textiles incorporate various advanced components and technologies to enable enhanced functionalities. Sensors embedded in the fabric detect various physical, chemical, and biological conditions (Koncar 2018). These sensors include temperature sensors for monitoring body temperature or environmental conditions, pressure sensors for detecting pressure changes, chemical sensors for identifying specific substances or pollution levels, and biosensors for measuring physiological parameters like heart rate, glucose levels, or hydration status (Koncar 2018; Majumder et al. 2017; Oatley et al. 2021). Actuators in smart textiles allow the fabric to respond to stimuli by performing specific actions, such as thermochromic materials that change colour in response to temperature variations. These shape-memory alloys alter shape with temperature changes and piezoelectric actuators that generate movement or vibration in response to electrical signals (Koncar 2018).

Conductive fibres and yarns, made from materials such as metallic threads (e.g., silver, copper, and stainless steel), conductive polymers (e.g., polypyrene and polyaniline), or carbon-based materials (e.g., carbon nanotubes and graphene), create pathways for electrical signals and power within the textiles (Shekhar et al. 2023). Microcontrollers serve as the brains of these smart systems, processing data from sensors and controlling actuators (Nasri et al. 2021). Key features of microcontrollers include programmability for customising responses to sensor inputs, connectivity with wireless technologies like Bluetooth or Wi-Fi for data transmission and remote control, and energy efficiency essential for wearable applications (Nesenbergs and Selavo 2015). Smart textiles, including gesture recognition sensors, offer flexibility and stretchability due to technologies like screen-printing capacitive sensors on non-rigid substrates (Ferri et al. 2019).

Powering smart textiles presents challenges by integrating small, flexible batteries or employing energy harvesting techniques to capture and convert ambient energy (Krifa 2021). These methods include solar cells that harvest energy from sunlight, kinetic energy harvesters that generate power from body movements, and thermoelectric generators that convert body heat into electrical energy (Krifa 2021). Advanced data processing and connectivity solutions enhance smart textile functionality using artificial intelligence (AI) and machine learning to analyse sensor data, Internet of Things (IoT) connectivity to link textiles to broader device networks, and blockchain for secure, transparent data management (Nasri et al. 2021; Proesmans et al. 2021).

Smart materials play a crucial role, including phase-change materials (PCMs) that regulate temperature by absorbing or releasing heat, hydrogels responsive to moisture for applications like controlled drug release, and electroactive polymers (EAPs) that change size or shape when stimulated by an electric field. Integration techniques ensure durability, flexibility, and comfort, using methods such as embroidery and sewing with conductive threads, printing with conductive inks, and incorporating conductive fibres during the weaving and knitting (Ferri et al. 2019; Shekhar et al. 2023). This combination of traditional textile properties with advanced electronic functionalities results in innovative solutions for health monitoring, sports performance, military applications, and more, driving the future of wearable technology.

11.2.3 Applications of Smart Textiles in Various Industries

The sustainable development goals (SDGs) are a collection of objectives established by the United Nations to create a more prosperous and environmentally friendly world by 2030. These goals serve as a call to action for all United Nations member countries to foster prosperity while safeguarding the planet. The 17 SDGs act as catalysts for addressing global issues related to water, energy, climate, oceans, urbanisation, transport, science, and technology (Nations 2015).

Emerging digital technologies such as IoT, AI, blockchain, AR, and VR are key tools for achieving these goals. These technologies can help create smart garments and footwear that are fashionable and reliable and contribute to health and well-being. For example, IoT and AI can enhance the real-time monitoring of physical activities and health status, while blockchain can help track and trace fashion activities to create a more circular economy. AR and VR technologies (Daniel Shadrach et al. 2022) can also improve the retail experience by allowing customers to try on clothes virtually from any location (Bagarello 2016). However, it is noted that while some studies have discussed the implementation of these digital technologies in the fashion industry, there is a lack of comprehensive research addressing all these technologies under one umbrella. Integrating these technologies could significantly contribute to achieving the SDGs and transforming the fashion industry into a more sustainable sector.

Smart textiles and wearable technology are revolutionising various sectors by integrating intelligent materials and electronic technologies into clothing. A myriad of applications are possible in the digitalisation of the fashion industry, as shown in Fig. 11.1.

In the health and medical fields, smart textiles enable continuous monitoring of vital signs, controlled drug administration, and assistance with physical therapy through IoT. By embedding sensors that track parameters like heart rate, respiratory rate, body temperature, and blood pressure, these textiles provide real-time data for early detection of health issues and timely interventions. In sports and fitness, smart textiles enhance performance by monitoring metrics such as heart rate and muscle activity, optimising training, and aiding recovery. The fashion industry benefits from interactive clothing that can change colour, display messages, or respond to environmental conditions, merging technology with personal expression through blockchain and AI. Military and safety applications utilise smart textiles to monitor soldiers' health, detect hazardous substances, and enhance camouflage, improving operational security. In-home and environmental contexts, smart textiles contribute to comfort and energy efficiency through smart upholstery and light-regulating curtains. Smart textiles and clothing offer innovative solutions across diverse applications,

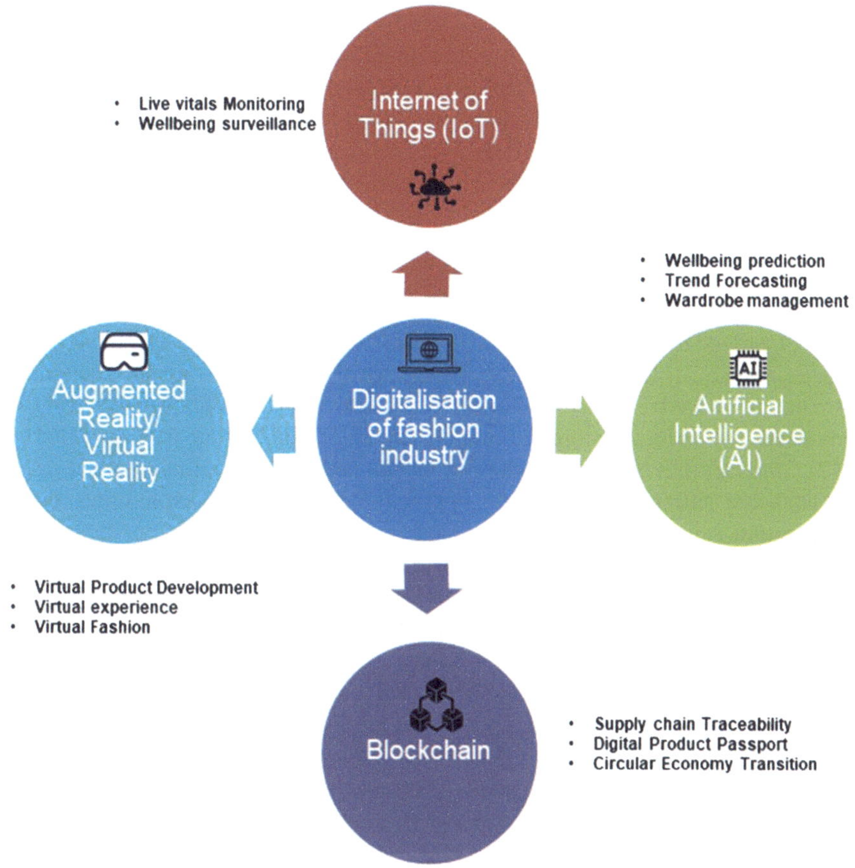

Fig. 11.1 Digitalisation of the fashion and textile industry

combining advanced electronic functionalities with traditional textile properties to transform our interactions with clothing and surroundings.

11.2.3.1 Health and Medical

Smart textiles have significantly impacted the healthcare and medical industry by introducing innovative applications that enhance patient care, monitoring, and treatment. Embedded with advanced technologies, these textiles offer various functionalities that can sense, react to, and adapt to external stimuli or conditions (Xiaopei Wu and Li 2019). The integration of smart textiles in healthcare has led to various applications, such as wearable sensors, interactive textiles, and medical garments, that can monitor vital signs, deliver medications, and provide personalised care (Ahmed et al. 2022). Another significant area where smart textiles have substantially impacted is the development of wearable sensors for healthcare monitoring. These sensors, integrated into textiles, can collect real-time data on various physiological parameters, allowing for continuous health monitoring without the need for invasive procedures (Ahmed et al. 2022). Additionally, smart textiles have been utilised to create ambulatory measurement systems for patients with cardiovascular diseases, protective GPS suits for military personnel, and bleeding sensor threads for surgical applications (Iftekhar Shuvo et al. 2021).

The incorporation of stimuli-responsive materials, such as pH-responsive chitosan hydrogels, into smart textile fabrics has enabled the development of medical textiles with enhanced functionalities. These materials can respond to changes in pH levels, making them ideal for applications like wound dressings and drug delivery systems (Chatterjee and Chi-Leung Hui 2019). Furthermore, using shape-memory polymers in smart textiles has paved the way for creating garments that can adapt to the wearer's body shape, providing customised and comfortable solutions for patients (Thakur 2017). Smart textiles have also been instrumental in advancing antimicrobial textiles for healthcare settings. By integrating antimicrobial agents into textile fibres, these smart textiles can inhibit the growth of bacteria and pathogens, reducing the risk of infections in medical environments (Selvasudha et al. 2021). Moreover, the development of smart bio-textiles, which combine biological components with textile materials, has opened up new possibilities for personalised medicine and targeted therapies (Arik 2024).

In patient care, smart textiles have been used to create interactive and stretchable sensors that can be seamlessly integrated into clothing. These sensors enable continuous monitoring of vital signs, movement, and activity levels, providing valuable data for healthcare professionals to assess patient health and well-being (Ahmed et al. 2022). Additionally, using conductive yarns and embroidered circuits in smart textiles has facilitated the development of wearable electronic devices for health monitoring and motion-sensing applications (Jung-Sim 2018). The future trends in smart textiles for healthcare indicate a shift towards more sustainable and eco-friendly materials. Researchers are exploring using biodegradable and environmentally friendly polymers in smart textiles to reduce the environmental impact of medical textiles (Karuppusamy et al. 2015). Furthermore, advancements in wireless monitoring technologies and IoT sensors are driving the development of smart textiles that can wirelessly transmit patient health data to healthcare providers, enabling remote monitoring and timely interventions (Andersen and Mihovska 2019).

Overall, the application of smart textiles in healthcare and medicine holds great promise for improving patient outcomes, enhancing diagnostic capabilities, and revolutionising how medical care is delivered. By leveraging the capabilities of smart textiles, healthcare professionals can provide more personalised and efficient care to patients, leading to better health outcomes and quality of life.

11.2.3.2 Sports and Fitness

Smart textiles have significantly impacted the sports and fitness industry by introducing innovative applications that enhance performance, comfort, and safety for athletes and fitness enthusiasts. Based on their performance characteristics (Canan Çelikel 2020), these textiles are classified into passive, active, and ultra-smart textiles. Smart textiles have found widespread application in sports and fitness monitoring devices, such as activity trackers and wearable sensors. These devices, integrated into clothing or accessories, enable athletes to track their performance metrics, monitor vital signs, and analyse activity levels in real-time (Tabia et al. 2018). The data collected from these smart textiles can provide valuable insights for athletes and coaches to optimise training routines, prevent injuries, and improve overall performance.

Nanotechnology-enabled sports products, such as sportswear, shoes, and equipment, have provided numerous benefits to athletes and the sports sector compared to traditional gear (Rahman et al. 2023). Using stimuli-responsive materials in smart textiles has enabled the development of sportswear that can adapt to environmental conditions and user preferences. For example, incorporating shape-memory polymers in textiles allows for garments that can change shape or properties in response to external stimuli, providing athletes with customised and comfortable clothing options (Van Langenhove 2014). Moreover, integrating photochromic dyes in smart textiles enables clothing to change colour based on UV exposure, offering functional and aesthetic benefits (Kumar Gupta 2021). Smart textiles have also been utilised in sports equipment to enhance safety and performance. For instance, the integration of pressure sensors in sports gear can provide valuable feedback on muscle activity and movement patterns, aiding in technique improvement and injury prevention (Sugathan and Hendry 2017; Kumar Singh 2021; Ayvaz et al. 2020). Additionally, the development of piezoelectric textiles has enabled the creation of sportswear that can generate electrical energy from mechanical stress, offering a sustainable power source for wearable devices (Matsouka and Vassiliadis 2018).

In conclusion, applying smart textiles in sports and fitness has transformed how athletes train, compete, and recover. Smart textiles offer many benefits for individuals involved in sports and fitness, from performance-enhancing sportswear to injury-preventing equipment. As technology advances, smart textiles are poised to play an increasingly significant role in optimising athletic performance, improving training methodologies, and enhancing the overall sports experience for athletes and enthusiasts.

11.2.3.3 Military and Safety

Smart textiles have significantly impacted the military and safety sectors by providing innovative solutions that enhance protection, communication, and performance in various applications. These textiles, integrated with advanced technologies, are extensively used in military operations, border control, surveillance, and safety monitoring (Yaacoub 2018). Incorporating smart textiles in military gear, such as protective GPS suits, has notably enhanced the safety and effectiveness of military personnel in challenging environments (Iftekhar Shuvo et al. 2021). A key area where smart textiles have proven beneficial is enhancing safety features for military personnel. These are the textiles specifically designed to protect from hazardous chemicals, extreme temperatures, and radiation, ensuring the safety and well-being of individuals in high-risk situations (Cabrera 2015). Additionally, smart textiles with specialised interconnectivity to online applications have been developed to improve communication and situational awareness in military operations (Cabrera 2015).

Smart textiles have also been instrumental in developing camouflage materials for improved concealment and stealth capabilities in military settings. Electrochromic textiles, capable of changing colour in response to external stimuli, have been utilised for military purposes to offer adaptive camouflage for soldiers and equipment, enhancing their tactical advantage (Camurlu and Toppare 2013). Furthermore, integrating smart textiles into military uniforms and equipment aims to enhance functionality and performance. Shape memory polymers integrated into textiles provide waterproofing, crease recoverability, and seam sewing, enhancing the durability and comfort of military garments (Thakur and Hu 2017). Additionally, exploring thermosensitive textiles in diving suits aims to provide better thermal insulation in cold waters, showcasing the versatility of smart textiles in addressing specific military needs (Jovancic et al. 2014).

Smart textiles are crucial in monitoring and protecting individuals in hazardous environments in safety applications. Equipped with sensors and actuators, these textiles can detect and respond to potential risks, offering real-time feedback and alerts to ensure user safety (Yaacoub 2018). Moreover, smart textiles with antifouling, flame-retardant, and water-repellent properties have been developed to enhance safety and well-being in various settings, including industrial environments and emergency response situations (Javaid et al. 2024). The future of smart textiles in military and safety applications holds significant potential for further innovation and advancement. Ongoing research in nanotechnology, wearable technology, and material science is expected to drive the development of even more sophisticated smart textiles for military and safety purposes. By leveraging the capabilities of smart textiles, the military and safety sectors can continue to enhance operational efficiency, safety standards, and overall effectiveness in challenging and dynamic environments.

In summary, smart textiles have emerged as a transformative technology in the military and safety sectors, offering advanced protection, communication, and performance enhancement solutions. Smart textiles are reshaping how military personnel operate, from adaptive camouflage materials to sensor-equipped uniforms. In safety applications, these textiles are crucial in monitoring and safeguarding individuals in hazardous conditions, contributing to improved safety standards and risk mitigation strategies.

11.2.3.4 Fashion and Wearables

Integrating smart textiles into the fashion and retail industry represents a groundbreaking shift that merges technology with traditional clothing. Smart textiles, embedded with electronic components and advanced materials, offer various functionalities, from interactive and adaptive clothing to enhanced retail experiences. This chapter explores smart textiles' diverse applications in fashion and retail, highlighting their potential to revolutionise consumer experiences, retail operations, and design innovation.

Interactive fashion includes the application of colour-changing fabric, LED, and display integration (Cherenack and Van Pieterson 2012). One of the most captivating applications of smart textiles in fashion is the development of colour-changing fabrics (Huang et al. 2016). These textiles, embedded with thermochromic or photochromic materials, can alter their colour in response to changes in temperature or light (Li et al. 2022). For instance, a jacket might change colour when exposed to sunlight (Ge et al. 2021), offering a unique and customisable aesthetic. This technology allows designers to create dynamic, versatile fashion pieces that adapt to different environments and moods. Fabrics embedded with LEDs (Takamatsu et al. 2015) and flexible displays (Mi et al. 2021) enable garments to display patterns, images, or messages. These textiles are controlled via smartphone apps and offer an interactive platform for personal expression. For example, a dress might display different designs or animations based on the wearer's mood or social settings. This fusion of technology and fashion enhances the aesthetic appeal and provides a medium for communication and personal branding.

Regarding health monitoring wearables, biosensor-embedded clothing (Sonawane et al. 2017) and posture analysis are vital in consumer fashion. Fashion is not just limited to the outlook but to material function. Integrating biosensors into textiles has opened new avenues in health and fitness apparel. Smart garments with sensors can monitor vital signs such as heart rate, respiration, and body temperature in real-time (Choudhry et al. 2023). For athletes and fitness enthusiasts, these smart textiles provide valuable insights into physical performance, enabling optimised training regimes and health monitoring (Ferraro 2015). Smart textiles embedded with motion sensors can analyse posture and movement, providing feedback and corrective measures (Tognetti et al. 2007). Such technology is beneficial for individuals seeking to improve their posture, as well as for athletes aiming to refine their techniques. These garments can alert wearers to improper movements or postures, helping to prevent injuries and improve overall physical well-being (Cho et al. 2011).

Enhanced retail experience is another dimension that is being explored using augmented reality (AR) and virtual reality (VR) (Fernandes and Morais 2021). AR and VR technologies are transforming the retail experience by allowing customers to try on clothes virtually (Fernandes and Morais 2021). Smart mirrors in stores equipped with AR enable shoppers to see how different outfits look without physically changing garments (Ogunjimi et al. 2021). Similarly, VR applications can create immersive shopping experiences where customers explore virtual stores and try on clothes digitally. These innovations enhance the shopping experience and reduce the need for extensive physical inventories (Fernández-Caramés and Fraga-Lamas 2018a, b). Smart fitting rooms with RFID tags and interactive displays streamline shopping (Yao et al. 2015). As customers try on garments, the smart fitting room can suggest complementary items or alternative sizes and colours available in the store. Integrating smart textiles and digital technology enhances customer satisfaction and encourages more informed purchasing decisions.

Smart textiles in sustainable fashion include resource efficiency and environmental impact monitoring. Smart textiles contribute to sustainable fashion by promoting more efficient use of resources. Textiles embedded with sensors can monitor wear and tear, alerting users when garments need repair rather than replacement (Fernández-Caramés and Fraga-Lamas 2018a, b). This approach extends the lifespan of clothing, reducing waste and promoting sustainable consumption. Additionally, smart textiles can be designed using recycled materials or be made for easy disassembly and recycling, supporting circular fashion models. Smart textiles with embedded environmental sensors can monitor and report on environmental conditions. For instance, garments can detect pollutants or allergens in the air, providing real-time data on environmental quality (Khalil et al. 2004). This application enhances the functionality of fashion items and raises awareness about environmental issues, aligning with the growing consumer demand for environmentally responsible products.

RFID, IoT, and blockchain for authenticity and transparency are next-generation supply chain and inventory management requirements through smart textiles (Nayak 2019; Tan and Sidhu 2022). Integrating RFID tags and Internet of Things (IoT) technology into smart textiles facilitates real-time tracking of garments throughout the supply chain (Luo et al. 2020; Fernández-Caramés and Fraga-Lamas 2018a, b). This capability enhances inventory management, reduces theft, and improves supply chain transparency. Retailers can efficiently manage stock levels, ensuring popular items are always available while minimising overproduction and waste. Blockchain technology can be integrated with smart textiles to ensure authenticity and transparency in the supply chain (Dutta et al. 2020). Each garment can be tracked from production to sale, providing consumers with verified information about the product's origins and production processes. This transparency builds trust and enhances brand reputation, particularly for ethically conscious consumers (Badhwar et al. 2023).

Personalised shopping experiences are another avenue where smart textiles are useful through data-driven customisation (Park and Jayaraman 2017; Schwarz et al. 2010). Smart textiles can collect consumer preferences and behaviour data, offering valuable insights for personalised marketing. For example, garments embedded with sensors can track how often and in what conditions they are worn. This data can be used to recommend similar products, suggest care instructions, or offer complementary accessories. Personalised shopping experiences increase customer satisfaction and loyalty, fostering a deeper connection between the brand and the consumer.

Smart textiles are poised to transform the fashion and retail industry by offering innovative and functional clothing solutions. From interactive fashion and health monitoring wearables to enhanced retail experiences and sustainable practices, the applications of smart textiles are vast and varied. As technology advances, integrating smart textiles into fashion and retail will likely accelerate, offering even more exciting possibilities for the future. Retailers can capitalise on this trend by offering a new category of health-focused apparel catering to a growing health-conscious consumer market. Overcoming usability, energy harvesting, and material durability challenges will be pivotal in unlocking the full potential of smart textiles and ensuring their widespread adoption.

11.2.3.5 Home and Environmental Applications

Integrating smart textiles into home and environmental settings marks a significant advancement in material science and technology. These textiles, imbued with electronic and intelligent capabilities, offer a range of functionalities that enhance comfort, efficiency, and sustainability in our living spaces. This chapter delves into the various applications of smart textiles in the home and environmental domains, highlighting their potential to transform everyday life through innovation and technology.

Smart textiles are revolutionising home furnishings by integrating advanced materials and technologies into everyday textile products, enhancing comfort, functionality, and aesthetics within residential spaces. Smart curtains and blinds utilise sensors and actuators to automate opening and closing, optimising natural light and privacy levels (Adiono et al. 2018; Venturini Degli Esposti et al. 2022). Intelligent upholstery and furniture incorporate sensors for ergonomic adjustments, promoting proper posture and comfort (Krauter et al. 2024; Venturini Degli Esposti et al. 2022). Interactive carpets and rugs feature sensors for detecting footsteps and triggering actions such as lighting control or security alerts (Yu et al. 2020). These textiles offer not only practical benefits but also aesthetic enhancements, with customisable colours, patterns, and textures (Tabor and Tushar 2019). Furthermore, smart textiles seamlessly integrate with home automation systems, enabling centralised control and management (Verma et al. 2016; Venturini Degli Esposti et al. 2022). As a result, smart textiles in home furnishings contribute to creating personalised, efficient, and technologically advanced living environments.

Moreover, smart textiles seamlessly integrate with home automation systems, enabling centralised control and management, thereby creating personalised, efficient, and technologically advanced living environments (Venturini Degli Esposti et al. 2022). In terms of comfort and convenience, smart textiles in home environments include temperature-regulating properties using phase-change materials, moisture-wicking fabrics for enhanced breathability, and self-cleaning capabilities through hydrophobic coatings (Wolniak and Grebski 2023). Smart bedding solutions utilise sensors to track sleep quality, adjust settings for personalised comfort, and voice-activated control of home furnishings (Hsu et al. 2020; Canan Çelikel 2020). Incorporating smart textiles in residential spaces enhances comfort and promotes energy efficiency and sustainability (Qian et al. 2016). These textiles seamlessly integrate with popular smart home platforms such as Amazon Alexa, Google Assistant, or Apple HomeKit, creating a cohesive, automated living environment that harmonises with other smart devices.

Furthermore, smart textiles are revolutionising safety and security applications in home environments by integrating advanced materials and technologies into everyday textile products (Abu-Thabit 2016; Stoppa and Chiolerio 2014). Fire-resistant textiles provide valuable protection against fire hazards in curtains, upholstery, and bedding (Soukup et al. 2014). Smart sensing fabrics incorporate sensors capable of detecting smoke, carbon monoxide, or other environmental hazards, triggering alarms or automated responses to mitigate risks (He et al. 2022; Zou et al. 2023; He et al. 2022). Anti-microbial textiles promote hygiene and reduce the risk of infections in home furnishings (Abu-Thabit and Basheer 2014). Impact-resistant fabrics offer protection against injuries by cushioning impacts and reducing the severity of accidents (Wang et al. 2013, 2022a, b; Venkatraman and Tyler 2015). Child safety textiles incorporate features designed to protect infants and young children from common household hazards, ensuring a safe living environment (Chico-Morales et al. 2022; Dominique and Crégo 2018; Gaissmaier et al. 2020). Intrusion detection fabrics utilise textile-based sensors to enhance home security and deter potential burglaries (Atwa et al. 2015).

In the realm of health monitoring and wellness, smart textiles integrate advanced materials and technologies into everyday textile products to empower individuals to proactively manage their health and well-being in the comfort of their homes (Malins et al. 2012; Mečņika et al. 2014). Wearable health-monitoring textiles incorporate biometric sensors for real-time tracking of vital signs such as heart rate and body temperature (Ahsan et al. 2022). Posture-correcting textiles support proper body alignment and reduce the risk of musculoskeletal pain (Visser 2018; Mendes et al. 2024). Stress-reducing textiles promote relaxation and reduce stress levels (van der Lugt and Feijs 2019). Pain-relief textiles alleviate discomfort and promote muscle relaxation (Liu et al. 2020; Goncu Berk 2018). Hydration-monitoring textiles track fluid intake and hydration levels, supporting optimal hydration habits and overall health (Jang et al. 2022; Balaban and Blecha 2022). By seamlessly integrating health-monitoring and wellness features into textiles, smart textiles contribute to enhancing comfort, well-being, and health in home environments (Ahsan et al. 2022; Malins et al. 2012).

To summarise, smart textiles are pivotal in transforming home and environmental applications by offering various functionalities that enhance comfort, efficiency, safety, security, and health monitoring. These textiles represent a fusion of advanced materials and technologies that reshape living spaces to be more personalised, efficient, and technologically advanced.

11.3 Manufacturing Techniques

Various techniques are used to manufacture smart textiles and wearable technology, including weaving and knitting with conductive fibres to create multifunctional fabrics, while embroidery and sewing enable precise electronic integration. Textile structures can be rapidly produced using printing technologies such as screen and 3D printing. Coating, lamination, and chemical vapour deposition can also enhance textile properties. Further advancements in smart textiles include plasma treatment, laser cutting, ultrasonic welding, nanotechnology, electrospinning, extrusion, microencapsulation, and embossing (Stoppa and Chiolerio 2014; Ahmed et al. 2020; Tseghai et al. 2020; Dulal et al. 2022; Root et al. 2020).

11.3.1 Weaving and Knitting of Conductive Fibers

Weaving techniques have been utilised to integrate components like hetero-core optical fibers, conductive fibers, and batteries into smart textiles (Koyama et al. 2018; Qu et al. 2015; Khandelwal et al. 2022). These weaving processes facilitate the creation of advanced textile sensors, multifunctional fabrics, and body-conforming stretch textiles for seamless woven fashion (Gong et al. 2019; Wang et al. 2009; Moon et al. 2018). Weaving not only allows for the integration of electronic components but also enhances the structural integrity and design flexibility of smart textiles (El-Dessouky and Saleh 2018; Labeeb et al. 2018a, b).

11.3.2 Embroidery and Sewing Techniques for Electronic Integration

The combination of weaving with techniques like embroidery further enhances the functionality and wearability of smart textiles (Labeeb et al. 2018a, b; Choudhry et al. 2022). Conductive embroidery, involving the stitching of conductive materials onto fabric, has emerged as a key method for creating smart apparel (Mecnika et al. 2014; Roh 2018; Chen et al. 2022; Goncu Berk 2018; Choudhry et al. 2023). This technique enables the integration of electronic components into textiles, allowing for the development of smart garments and wearable antennas (Gil et al. 2019; El Gharbi et al. 2022). Embroidery provides advantages such as dimensional stability, reproducibility, and rapid prototyping, making it a preferred method for creating smart textile structures (Goncu Berk 2018). Additionally, sewing techniques are utilised to integrate electronic components into textiles, facilitating the production of flexible circuits and electronic systems (Domskiene et al. 2023). These methods enable the seamless integration of technology into textiles, paving the way for innovative smart textile applications.

11.3.3 Printing Technologies for Smart Textiles

Printing technologies are essential in the manufacturing of smart textiles and the integration of electronics into textiles. Screen printing, digital printing, and 3D printing are commonly used techniques for these purposes. Screen printing is valued for its simplicity, speed, cost-effectiveness, and high-throughput capabilities in creating smart textiles (Tian et al. 2022). On the other hand, 3D printing, also called additive manufacturing, allows for rapid production of smart textile structures by layering objects using digital design data (Goncu-Berk et al. 2020). This technology has been pivotal in producing flexible circuits, sensors, antennas, and conductive tracks on textiles, facilitating the seamless integration of electronic components (Spahiu et al. 2020; Eutionnat-Diffo et al. 2019). Moreover, 3D printing has been employed to develop smart fibres, textiles, and garments with enhanced functionalities (Cao et al. 2019; Zhang et al. 2019; Eutionnat-Diffo et al. 2020). These printing methods provide innovative solutions for producing smart textiles with electronic integration, advancing wearable electronic systems.

11.3.4 Coating and Lamination Techniques

Coating and lamination technologies are another essential method in manufacturing smart textiles and integrating electronics into textiles. These processes involve applying functional layers onto textile substrates to enhance their properties. (Choudhry et al. 2023, 2022). Various coating methods, such as spray-coating, dip-coating, and microencapsulation, have been utilised to deposit conductive materials onto textiles, enabling the development of smart textile structures (Tian et al. 2022; Elsayed et al. 2020; Lin et al. 2023). Lamination techniques, including thermal lamination and laser engraving, have bonded functional layers like electrodes and electronic components onto fabrics, facilitating the creation of wearable electronic systems. (Loss et al. 2016; Saremi et al. 2020). Additionally, nitrocellulose coatings have been explored to functionalise textiles for various applications, including smart textiles (Khan et al.). These technologies enable the production of innovative smart textiles with enhanced functionalities and electronic integration.

11.3.5 Chemical Vapour Deposition

Chemical vapor deposition (CVD) processes involve depositing thin films on textile substrates through chemical reactions between precursors. These techniques are widely used in producing high-quality inorganic layers, functional polymer films, and crystalline materials on textiles, enabling the development of smart textile structures with enhanced functionalities (Shahidi et al. 2016; Hu et al. 2015; Alf et al.

2010; Wang et al. 2017). CVD methods provide excellent thickness control and versatile platforms for fabricating various polymer thin films, making them ideal for electronic integration into textiles (Singh et al. 2009; Xiong et al. 2006; Coclite et al. 2013). The technology has been successfully applied in synthesizing graphene, carbon nanotubes, and various functional coatings on textiles, highlighting its significance in advancing smart textile applications (Ullah et al. 2021; Zhu et al. 2020; Ozaydin-Ince et al. 2012). Overall, CVD technologies offer a powerful means to tailor the properties of textiles for electronic integration and smart textile development.

11.3.6 Plasma Treatment

Plasma treatment involves modifying textile surfaces to enhance properties like adhesion, wettability, and dyeing selectivity without altering the fundamental textile characteristics (Das et al. 2022; Azanova et al. 2019; Kim et al. 2023; Verschuren et al. 2007). This technology is widely used to improve the anchoring of coatings on fibres, resulting in smooth and homogeneous coatings (Kim et al. 2023). Extensive research has been conducted on plasma treatment for its ability to enhance textile finishing processes, such as mercerisation and dyeing, by improving surface properties (Azanova et al. 2019). It is recognised as a promising and environmentally friendly alternative to traditional wet-chemical processing techniques in the textile industry (Jelil 2015). Plasma treatment can enhance mechanical properties, provide antistatic finishing, improve surface wettability, and convert normal fabrics into flame-retardant materials (Reema et al. 2022). By combining plasma treatment with nanoparticles, significant enhancements in textile fibre properties have been achieved {Katouah 2021 #1145}. Overall, plasma treatment technologies offer versatile solutions for modifying textile surfaces and advancing smart textile applications.

11.3.7 Laser Cutting and Ultrasonic Welding

Laser cutting is widely used in the textile industry to achieve precise cuts, intricate designs, and reduced material waste, making it a preferred method for smart textile production {Angelova, 2020 #1146}. Laser welding, including hybrid laser welding techniques, offers high precision and efficiency in joining textile components, enhancing joint performance in smart textile applications (Sonia et al. 2024; Fromme et al. 2021). Ultrasonic welding provides a useful approach for connecting textile electronics to conductive wires, enabling the seamless integration of electronic components into textiles (Micus et al. 2021).These advanced techniques play a significant role in enhancing the functionality and performance of smart textiles, paving the way for innovative wearable electronic systems.

11.3.8 Nanotechnology Integration

Nanotechnology enables the enhancement of textile properties through the incorporation of nanoparticles and sensors into textile materials. Nanoparticles are utilized to improve physicochemical behaviours such as self-cleaning, UV protection, flame resistance, and antibacterial capabilities in textiles, contributing to the development of innovative and smarter textiles with multifunctional properties (Hassabo et al. 2022; Abou El-Kheir and El-Gabry 2022; Salman et al. 2019). Nanotechnology also facilitates the functionalization of synthetic fibers, allowing for the creation of textiles with a variety of functions (Abou El-Kheir and El-Gabry 2022). By utilizing nanotechnology, textiles can be produced with enhanced properties like antibacterial, UV protection, easy-clean, water-and stain repellent, and anti-odour characteristics (Patra 2013). Moreover, the application of nanotechnology in textile engineering enables the production of fabrics with special functions, including stain resistance, flame retardancy, wrinkle resistance, moisture management, and antimicrobial qualities (Shah et al. 2022; Hassan et al. 2019). Overall, nanotechnology integration in smart textiles enhances their functionality, performance, and versatility, paving the way for the development of advanced wearable electronic systems.

11.3.9 Electrospinning and Extrusion

The electrospinning technique allows for the creation of composite nanofibers and yarns with enhanced properties by incorporating various materials such as nanoparticles, conductive polymers, and thermoplastic polyurethane. Electrospinning enables the fabrication of nanofibers with unique characteristics like high surface area, porosity, and mechanical strength, highly conductive, and highly resistive, making them ideal for applications in smart textiles, wearable electronics, and energy storage devices (Moradi et al. 2023; Niu and Yuan 2021). By utilising electrospinning, researchers have developed functional textiles with features such as energy conversion, stretchable conductors, and stimuli-responsive functionalities, expanding the possibilities for smart textile applications (Viswanathan et al. 2006; Wang et al. 2022a, b; Ramirez et al. 2021). Electrospinning plays a vital role in advancing smart textiles by enabling the production of innovative materials with tailored properties for electronic integration and wearable technology.

Extrusion incorporates conductive or functional materials into fibres during the extrusion process, enabling the production of inherently smart fibres. Later technologies like fused deposition modelling (FDM; Melnikova et al. 2014) and direct ink writing (DIW) (Wan et al. 2019) are widely used in 3D printing textiles to create intricate 3D structures efficiently (Li 2023). These methods facilitate the production of smart textiles with customised designs and functionalities, allowing for the seamless integration of electronic components into textile structures (Li 2023).

11.3.10 Microencapsulation

Controlling release or activation of these components can be achieved by encapsulating active ingredients or sensors within microcapsules embedded into the textile matrix (Islam 2008). Melamine–formaldehyde (MF) microcapsules obtained through in situ polymerisation are commonly used in smart textiles to leverage microencapsulation technology due to their mechanical resistance and durability (Shaid et al. 2016; Sánchez-Navarro et al. 2015). This technique allows for incorporating various materials into textiles, enhancing their functionalities and properties (Mohaddes et al. 2014). Microencapsulation and functionalisation using biocompatible vehicles and polymers have shown promise in creating smart and bio-functional textiles, offering innovative solutions for improving textile performance and functionality (Lis Arias et al. 2018). Application of microencapsulation techniques in smart textiles enable the development of advanced materials with tailored properties for electronic integration and wearable technology applications.

11.3.11 Embossing

With the embossing technique, imprinting patterns or circuits onto textiles, the process creates areas with specific functionalities such as touch sensitivity, enhancing smart textiles' aesthetic appeal and functionality (Castano and Flatau 2016; Grancarić et al. 2018). This technique creates textured surfaces that can serve as touch-sensitive interfaces or provide visual and tactile feedback in wearable electronic systems. Embossing is a versatile method that can be used to add both decorative and functional elements to textiles, making it a valuable tool in the development of smart textiles with enhanced interactive capabilities (Castano and Flatau 2014; Khumpuang et al. 2011).

11.4 Opportunities in the Production of Smart Garments

The world of fashion and technology is merging, creating a new frontier known as smart garments. These are not just clothes but wearable devices that integrate technology into fabric to create clothing that can interact with the wearer's environment or monitor their physical condition.

One of the most exciting opportunities in this field is the potential for technological innovation (Castenetto 2022). As technology continues to advance rapidly, the possibilities for smart garments expand. For example, we see garments that can monitor heart rate, body temperature, and even the wearer's emotional state. These innovations are particularly beneficial in the health and fitness sector. For instance, a smart sports bra can monitor vital signs and track physical activity, providing real-time feedback to the wearer and promoting a healthier lifestyle.

Another opportunity lies in the realm of sustainability. Traditional clothing production is notoriously wasteful (Islam 2021), but smart garments have the potential to change this. For example, if a smart garment can adapt to changes in the wearer's size or style preferences, it could significantly extend its lifespan, reducing waste. Personalisation is another significant opportunity. Smart garments can be designed to adapt to the wearer's body and needs, providing a level of comfort and functionality that traditional clothing cannot match. For instance, a smart jacket could adjust its temperature based on the wearer's body temperature and the surrounding environment, ensuring optimal comfort at all times (Lee and Baek 2021; Abro et al. 2018).

However, the path to smart garment ubiquity is not without its challenges. One of the most significant is the high cost of production. The materials and processes required to produce smart garments are often more expensive than those used in traditional clothing production. This can make smart garments prohibitively expensive for many consumers. Durability is another challenge (Hossain and Bradford 2021). While traditional clothes can withstand washing and daily wear and tear, the same cannot always be said for smart garments (Won and Yun 2022). For example, how does one wash a shirt embedded with electronic sensors? And how long will the battery last before it needs to be replaced?

User acceptance is another hurdle. Despite the many benefits of smart garments, some consumers are uncomfortable with the idea of wearing technology. They may find the garments unattractive or be wary of the potential privacy and security risks associated with garments that collect personal data. To summarise, while the world of smart garments is full of exciting opportunities, it also presents significant challenges. Overcoming these will require innovation, consumer education, and, perhaps most importantly, a commitment to addressing the ethical implications of this new technology.

11.5 Challenges in the Production of Smart Garments

Smart materials are indeed innovative solutions designed to address specific needs or improvements in various industries, including fashion and textiles. These materials can respond to environmental changes, such as temperature, light, pressure, or electricity, and adjust their properties accordingly. However, as these are new and cutting-edge solutions, standardisation in terms of durability, ergonomic attributes, performance efficiency, and analysis can be challenging.

For instance, consider the use of phase change materials (PCMs) in clothing (Mohaddes et al. 2014). These materials can absorb, store, and release heat, making them ideal for use in clothing designed for extreme temperatures. However, the durability of these materials, particularly after repeated washing and wearing, is a concern that needs to be addressed. Standardised tests for durability are yet to be developed, making it difficult to compare the performance of different products.

Another example is using shape memory alloys (SMAs) in wearable technology. SMAs can return to their original shape after being deformed, making them useful in applications like smart watches or fitness trackers (Srivastava et al. 2022). However, the ergonomic attributes of these materials, such as comfort and fit, can vary widely depending on the application and user. Standardising these attributes can be challenging due to the wide range of potential uses and user preferences.

In terms of performance efficiency, consider using conductive textiles in smart clothing. These materials can transmit electricity, making them useful for integrating electronic components into clothing. However, the efficiency of these materials can vary depending on factors like the type of textile used, the method of integration, and the specific electronic components involved. Standardised tests for performance efficiency are needed to compare different products and solutions. While smart materials offer exciting possibilities for innovation in the fashion and textile industry, there are challenges in standardisation (Shuvo et al. 2021; Luo et al. 2023). Developing standardised tests and measures for durability, ergonomic attributes, performance efficiency, and analysis will be crucial in ensuring the reliability and effectiveness of these innovative solutions.

Smart materials, although innovative and promising, do come with their own set of challenges, including technological limitations and high production costs.

11.5.1 Technological Limitations

The integration of smart materials into wearable technology often requires complex manufacturing processes and advanced technology (Angelucci et al. 2021). For example, integrating electronic components into clothing using conductive textiles often requires specialised equipment and techniques to ensure the components are properly embedded and functional. Additionally, these components need to be able to withstand the rigours of daily wear and tear, including washing and drying, which can be a significant technological challenge (Mokhtari et al. 2020).

Another technological limitation is the current battery technology (Mokhtari et al. 2020). Many smart garments require a power source to function, and traditional batteries can be bulky, rigid, and require frequent recharging. While advancements are being made in flexible and wearable power sources, these technologies are still in their early stages and have limitations in capacity and durability.

11.5.2 High Production Costs

The production of smart materials and their integration into wearable technology can be expensive (Cherenack and Van Pieterson 2012). For example, the production of conductive textiles often involves the use of precious metals such as silver, gold and stainless steel, which can significantly increase the cost (Muhammad Sayem et al. 2020).

Furthermore, the specialised equipment and techniques required for the production and integration of smart materials can also contribute to high production costs (Angelucci et al. 2021). For instance, producing clothing with integrated phase change materials (PCMs) requires specialised manufacturing processes to ensure the PCMs are properly embedded in the fabric and will function correctly.

In addition, the research and development costs associated with creating and improving smart materials can be substantial (Stoppa and Chiolerio 2014). For example, developing new types of shape memory alloys (SMAs) or improving the performance of existing ones can involve significant investment in research and development.

11.5.3 Sustainability and Eco-friendly Production

The fashion industry, a significant contributor to the global economy, is urged to address its environmental and social impacts. Currently, the industry contributes to a significant portion of global CO_2 emissions, water consumption, microplastic pollution, and textile waste. To address these issues, the United Nations has outlined several Sustainable Development Goals (SDGs) that the industry should strive to meet. These include promoting sustainable industrialisation and innovation (Bigger et al. 2023), ensuring sustainable consumption and production patterns, and taking urgent action to combat climate change.

11.5.4 Issues with Durability and Maintenance

Durability, maintenance, and end-of-life solutions are also significant considerations when it comes to smart materials in the fashion and textile industry.

Smart materials need to be durable enough to withstand the rigours of daily use. For instance, clothing with integrated electronic components needs to be able to withstand not just wear and tear, but also regular washing and drying. However, maintaining the functionality of these components over time can be a challenge. For example, conductive textiles may lose their conductivity over time due to repeated washing.

The maintenance of smart garments can also be more complex than that of regular clothing. They may require special care when washing to prevent damage to the integrated components. In some cases, they may not be machine washable at all, which could be a significant inconvenience for the user.

Finally, end-of-life solutions for smart garments are a critical consideration as the industry is grappling with circular economy transition (van der Velden et al.

2015). Traditional clothing can be recycled or disposed of relatively easily, but smart garments with integrated electronic components present a more significant challenge. These components may need to be removed before the garment can be recycled or disposed of, which can be a complex and time-consuming process. Alternatively, if the garment is simply disposed of, it could contribute to electronic waste, which is a growing environmental concern.

Although smart materials offer exciting possibilities for innovation in the fashion and textile industry, they also present significant challenges in terms of durability, maintenance, and end-of-life solutions. Addressing these challenges will be crucial for the sustainability and success of these innovative materials.

11.6 Opportunities in the Distribution of Smart Garments

The distribution of smart garments, like their production, presents a unique set of opportunities and challenges. As the intersection of fashion and technology continues to evolve, the ways in which these innovative products reach consumers are also changing (Fernández-Caramés and Fraga-Lamas 2018a, b).

One of the most significant opportunities lies in the rise of e-commerce (Pal and Jayarathne 2022). Online shopping platforms have made it possible for smart garment manufacturers to reach a global audience (Jamal and Kapoor 2022). For instance, a small start-up producing smart fitness wear in Melbourne can easily sell its products to customers in London or Los Angeles. This global reach, facilitated by the internet, has the potential to significantly boost sales of smart garments.

Another opportunity is the potential for partnerships and collaborations. By partnering with tech companies, fashion brands, or even healthcare providers, smart garment manufacturers can tap into new markets and expand their customer base (Lee and Baek 2021; Abro et al. 2018). For example, a smart garment company could partner with a popular fitness app, offering customers a discount on their smart workout gear when they sign up for a subscription to the app.

11.7 Challenges in the Distribution of Smart Garments

However, the distribution of smart garments is not without its challenges. One of the most significant is consumer perception. Despite the many benefits of smart garments, some consumers may be hesitant to embrace this new technology (Castenetto 2022). They may be wary of the potential privacy and security risks, or they may simply find the idea of wearing technology to be unappealing. Overcoming this resistance will require education and marketing efforts to highlight the benefits of smart garments and address any concerns.

Regulatory and legal hurdles can also pose challenges. As a relatively new product category, smart garments may face regulatory scrutiny in different markets. For example, a smart garment that monitors health data may be classified as a medical device in some jurisdictions, subjecting it to a different set of regulations.

Finally, logistics and supply chain complexities can also pose challenges. The production of smart garments often involves a range of different components, some of which may need to be sourced from different suppliers. This can complicate the supply chain and make distribution more challenging (Pal and Jayarathne 2022).

Although the distribution channels of smart garments present exciting opportunities, it also comes with significant challenges. Overcoming these will require strategic planning, innovative thinking, and a deep understanding of both the fashion and technology sectors.

11.8 Future Prospect of Smart Textiles and Wearable Technology

11.8.1 Predicted Market Growth

The global smart textile market, valued at USD 2.82 billion in 2022, is projected to grow significantly, reaching USD 17.94 billion by 2031. This growth, at a CAGR of 22.80% from 2023 to 2031, is driven by advancements in smart textile materials, which have revolutionised the textile industry and expanded its reach into high-tech applications (straitsresearch 2024). Smart textiles and fabrics integrated with computing power offer additional functionalities like monitoring, communication, and stimulation. The growth of the wearable electronics market, trends of miniaturisation in modern electronics, and increasing demand for smart devices are key drivers of this market growth (Júnior et al. 2022). Furthermore, the advent of nanotechnology, quantum computing, RFID, and sensor technology in textiles also boosts the market. However, the high cost of these textiles could potentially hinder market growth.

11.8.2 Potential Innovations and Developments

The future of smart textiles and wearable technology is likely to be shaped by several exciting innovations and developments (Persson et al. 2018). For example, advancements in nanotechnology could lead to the creation of textiles with enhanced properties, such as increased strength, improved thermal insulation, or the ability to change colour in response to environmental changes. Additionally, the development of more efficient and flexible power sources could enable the creation of wearable technology with longer battery life and improved comfort.

Another potential area of innovation is the integration of AI and machine learning into wearable technology (Cioffi et al. 2020). This could enable the creation of smart garments that can monitor health metrics and provide personalised feedback or recommendations. For example, a smart shirt could monitor a user's heart rate and breathing during exercise and provide real-time feedback on their performance.

11.8.3 Role of Smart Textiles in the Post-COVID World

The COVID-19 pandemic has highlighted the potential role of smart textiles and wearable technology in monitoring health and preventing disease (Persson et al. 2018). For example, smart masks have been developed that can monitor the wearer's breathing and alert them if they are showing symptoms of respiratory illness. Similarly, wearable devices that can monitor vital signs such as temperature, heart rate, and oxygen saturation could play a crucial role in early detection and monitoring of diseases.

In the post-COVID world, we could also see an increased demand for smart textiles in the workplace. For example, smart uniforms could be used to monitor the health and safety of children and workers in industries such as healthcare, construction, and manufacturing. These uniforms could monitor vital signs, detect exposure to harmful substances, and even provide feedback on ergonomic posture (Angelucci et al. 2021).

The future of smart textiles and wearable technology looks promising, with significant market growth predicted, exciting innovations on the horizon, and a potentially crucial role to play in the post-COVID world (Lam Po Tang and Stylios 2006). However, these developments will need to be balanced with considerations of sustainability, affordability, and user comfort and convenience (Muhammad Sayem et al. 2020; Underwood and Islam 2024).

11.9 Conclusion

In conclusion, the transition towards a circular economy within the textile and fashion value chain is a complex but necessary endeavour. It involves increasing resource efficiency, preventing material waste, and revaluing post-consumer 'waste' as new resources. This transition requires a shift in mindset, one that can creatively navigate and integrate multiple overlapping systems, including economic, social, ecological, and political dimensions.

The development of smart materials is no exception to this. These innovative solutions, while promising, come with their own set of challenges, including technological limitations, high production costs, durability, maintenance, and end-of-life solutions. Addressing these challenges requires a similar shift in mindset, one that considers not just the economic potential of these materials, but also their social, ecological, and political impacts.

In the end, the success of both the circular economy and smart materials in the fashion and textile industry will depend on our ability to navigate these complex systems and make decisions that are sustainable and beneficial in the long term. This will require ongoing research, innovation, and most importantly, a commitment to sustainability at every level of the value chain.

References

Abou El-Kheir A, El-Gabry L (2022) Potential applications of nanotechnology in functionalization of synthetic fibres (a review). Egypt J Chem. https://doi.org/10.21608/ejchem.2022.106369.4891

Abro GEM, Shaikh SA, Soomro S, Abid G, Kumar K, Ahmed F (2018) Prototyping IOT based smart wearable jacket design for securing the life of coal miners. International Conference on Computing, Electronics & Communications Engineering (iCCECE), 134–137

Abu-Thabit NY (2016) Chemical oxidative polymerization of polyaniline: a practical approach for preparation of smart conductive textiles. J Chem Edu 93(9):1606–1611

Abu-Thabit NY, Basheer RA (2014) Synthesis of highly conductive cotton fiber/nanostructured silver/polyaniline composite membranes for water sterilization application. Mater Res Exp 1(3):035010

Adiono T, Feranti Anindya S, Fuada S, Yusuf Fathany M (2018) Curtain control systems development on mesh wireless network of the smart home. Bull Electr Eng Inf 7(4):615–625. https://doi.org/10.11591/eei.v7i4.1199

Ahmed A, Hossain MM, Adak B, Mukhopadhyay S (2020) Recent advances in 2D MXene integrated smart-textile interfaces for multifunctional applications. Chem Mater 32(24):10296–10320. https://doi.org/10.1021/acs.chemmater.0c03392

Ahmed A, Adak B, Mukhopadhyay S (2022) Smart textile-based interactive, stretchable and wearable sensors for healthcare. In: Nanosensors for futuristic smart and intelligent healthcare systems. 1st Ed. CRC Press

Ahsan M, Teay SH, Sayem ASM, Albarbar A (2022) Smart clothing framework for health monitoring applications. Signals 3(1):113–145

Akram SV, Malik PK, Singh R, Gehlot A, Juyal A, Ghafoor KZ, Shrestha S (2022) Implementation of digitalized technologies for fashion industry 4.0: opportunities and challenges. Sci Program 2022:1–17. https://doi.org/10.1155/2022/7523246

Al Mahmud A, Wickramarathne TI, Kuys B (2020) Effects of smart garments on the well-being of athletes: a scoping review protocol. BMJ Open 10(11):e042127. https://doi.org/10.1136/bmjopen-2020-042127

Alf ME, Asatekin A, Barr MC, Baxamusa SH, Chelawat H, Ozaydin-Ince G, Petruczok CD, Sreenivasan R, Tenhaeff WE, Trujillo NJ, Vaddiraju S, Xu J, Gleason KK (2010) Chemical vapor deposition of conformal, functional, and responsive polymer films. Adv Mater 22(18):1993–2027. https://doi.org/10.1002/adma.200902765

Andersen AB, Mihovska A (2019) Wireless smart monitoring of patient health data in a hospital setup. In: Lecture notes of the institute for computer sciences, social informatics and telecommunications engineering. Springer International Publishing. https://doi.org/10.1007/978-3-030-23976-3_4

Angelucci A, Cavicchioli M, Cintorrino I, Lauricella G, Rossi C, Strati S, Aliverti A (2021) Smart textiles and sensorized garments for physiological monitoring: a review of available solutions and techniques. Sensors 21(3):814. https://doi.org/10.3390/s21030814

Arik B (2024) Chapter 16—Smart bio-textiles for medicine and healthcare applications. In: Mondal MIH (ed) Smart textiles from natural resources. Woodhead Publishing. https://doi.org/10.1016/B978-0-443-15471-3.00020-0

Atwa Y, Maheshwari N, Goldthorpe IA (2015) Silver nanowire coated threads for electrically conductive textiles. J Mater Chem C 3(16):3908–3912. https://doi.org/10.1039/c5tc00380f. https://uwspace.uwaterloo.ca/bitstream/10012/9565/5/Atwa_Yahya.pdf

Ayvaz U, Elmoughni H, Atalay A, Atalay Ö, Ince G (2020) Real-time human activity recognition using textile-based sensors. In: Lecture notes of the institute for computer sciences, social informatics and telecommunications engineering. Springer International Publishing. https://doi.org/10.1007/978-3-030-64991-3_12

Azanova AA, Khisamieva LG, Minnebaeva RG, Semenova EY, Davletbaev IG (2019) The effect of low-temperature plasma on the wicking properties of the textile materials based on natural cellulose fibres. Textile Res J 71(1):49–56. https://doi.org/10.1177/004051750107100108

Badhwar A, Islam S, Tan CSL (2023) Exploring the potential of blockchain technology within the fashion and textile supply chain with a focus on traceability, transparency, and product authenticity: a systematic review. Front Blockchain 6. https://doi.org/10.3389/fbloc.2023.1044723

Bagarello A (2016) Technological innovation as solution for the fashion e-commerce gap: 3D body scanners and smart measuring tapes for size optimization. https://api.semanticscholar.org/CorpusID:114625235

Balaban J, Blecha T (2022) Textile sensor for skin hydration measurement. IEEE, 1665465891

Bigger EE, Ahrens-Wels H, Kelbel HC (2023) Fashion ex machina: human–machine collaboration to support sustainability through customized design and production. In: Accelerating sustainability in fashion, clothing and textiles. Routledge

Cabrera LY (2015) Rethinking human enhancement: social enhancement and emergent technologies. Palgrave Macmillan. https://doi.org/10.1057/9781137402240

Camurlu P, Toppare L (2013) Electrochromic polymers, In: Encyclopedia of polymeric nanomaterials. Springer Berlin Heidelberg. https://doi.org/10.1007/978-3-642-36199-9_32-1

Canan Çelikel D (2020) 'Smart e-textile materials. Adv Funct Mater. IntechOpen. https://doi.org/10.5772/intechopen.92439

Cao WT, Ma C, Mao DS, Zhang J, Ma MG, Chen F (2019) MXene-reinforced cellulose nanofibril inks for 3D-printed smart fibres and textiles. Adv Funct Mater 29(51):1905898. https://doi.org/10.1002/adfm.201905898

Castano LM, Flatau AB (2016) Smart textile transducers: design, techniques, and applications. In: Hosseini M, Makhlouf ASH (eds) Industrial applications for intelligent polymers and coatings. Springer International Publishing, Cham. https://doi.org/10.1007/978-3-319-26893-4_6

Castano LM, Flatau AB (2014) Smart fabric sensors and e-textile technologies: a review. Smart Mater Struct 23(5):053001. https://doi.org/10.1088/0964-1726/23/5/053001

Castenetto C (2022) Redefining fashion ecommerce: a comprehensive study on the transformative impact of technologies on user experience. https://hdl.handle.net/10589/218654

Chang C-W, Riehl P, Lin J (2021) Alignment-free wireless charging of smart garments with embroidered coils. Sensors 21(21):7372. https://doi.org/10.3390/s21217372

Chatterjee S, Chi-Leung Hui P (2019) Stimuli-responsive hydrogels: an interdisciplinary overview. Hydrogels Smart Mater Biomed Appl. IntechOpen. https://doi.org/10.5772/intechopen.80536

Chen G, Li Y, Bick M, Chen J (2020) Smart textiles for electricity generation. Chem Rev 120(8):3668–3720. https://doi.org/10.1021/acs.chemrev.9b00821

Chen L, Su Z, He X, Chen X, Dong L (2022) The application of robotics and artificial intelligence in embroidery: challenges and benefits. Assem Autom 42(6):851–868. https://doi.org/10.1108/aa-07-2022-0183

Cherenack K, Van Pieterson L (2012) Smart textiles: challenges and opportunities. J Appl Phys 112(9):091301. https://doi.org/10.1063/1.4742728

Chico-Morales I, Narváez-Pupiales S, Umaquinga-Criollo A, Rosero-Montalvo P (2022) Application of embedded accident prevention system for infant crawling stage in intelligent textiles. Wearable Technol 3(1):56–62

Cho G, Jeong K, Paik MJ, Kwun Y, Sung M (2011) Performance evaluation of textile-based electrodes and motion sensors for smart clothing. IEEE Sens J 11(12):3183–3193. https://doi.org/10.1109/JSEN.2011.2167508

Choudhry NA, Shekhar R, Rasheed A, Arnold L, Wang L (2022) Effect of conductive thread and stitching parameters on the sensing performance of stitch-based pressure sensors for smart textile applications. IEEE Sens J 22(7):6353–6363. https://doi.org/10.1109/JSEN.2022.3149988

Choudhry NA, Shekhar R, Khan IA, Rasheed A, Padhye R, Arnold L, Wang L (2023) Fabrication and characterization of single-layer textile-based flexible pressure sensors for smart wearable electronics applications. Adv Eng Mater 2201736. https://doi.org/10.1002/adem.202201736

Cioffi R, Travaglioni M, Piscitelli G, Petrillo A, De Felice F (2020) Artificial intelligence and machine learning applications in smart production: progress, trends, and directions. Sustainability 12(2):492. https://doi.org/10.3390/su12020492

Coclite AM, Howden RM, Borrelli DC, Petruczok CD, Yang R, Yagüe JL, Ugur A, Chen N, Lee S, Jo WJ, Liu A, Wang X, Gleason KK (2013) 25th anniversary article: CVD polymers: a new paradigm for surface modification and device fabrication. Adv Mater 25(38):5392–5423. https://doi.org/10.1002/adma.201301878. http://openlib.tugraz.at/download.php?id=5d38377d00ef3&location=browse

Daniel Shadrach F, Santhosh M, Vignesh S, Sneha S, Sivakumar T (2022) Smart Virtual Trial Room For Apparel Industry. 2022 IEEE International Conference on Distributed Computing and Electrical Circuits and Electronics (ICDCECE), 1–5

Das R, Dash C, Bisoyi DK (2022) A review of cold plasma treatment on textile fibre. Technology 202(14):3427–3449

Dominique P, Crégo P (2018) Wearables, smart textiles and smart apparel. Elsevier. ISBN: 9781785482939

Domskiene J, Mitkute M, Grigaliunas V (2023) Sewing and adhesive bonding technologies for smart clothing production. Int J Cloth Sci Technol 35(4):581–595. https://doi.org/10.1108/ijcst-02-2022-0028

Duarte JP, Fernandes RJ, Silva G, Sousa F, Machado L, Pereira JR, Vilas-Boas JP (2022) Lower limbs wearable sports garments for muscle recovery: an umbrella review. Healthcare 10(8):1552. https://www.mdpi.com/2227-9032/10/8/1552

Dulal M, Afroj S, Ahn J, Cho Y, Carr C, Kim I-D, Karim N (2022) Toward sustainable wearable electronic textiles. ACS Nano 16(12):19755–19788. https://doi.org/10.1021/acsnano.2c07723

Dutta P, Choi T-M, Somani S and Butala R (2020) Blockchain technology in supply chain operations: applications, challenges and research opportunities. Transp Res Part E Logist Transp Rev 142:102067. https://doi.org/10.1016/j.tre.2020.102067. https://www.sciencedirect.com/science/article/pii/S1366554520307183

El Gharbi M, Fernández-García R, Gil I (2022) Embroidered wearable antenna-based sensor for real-time breath monitoring. Measurement. 195. 111080: 1–9. https://doi.org/10.1016/j.measurement.2022.111080

El-Dessouky HM, Saleh MN (2018) 3D woven composites: from weaving to manufacturing. In: Recent developments in the field of carbon fibers. InTech. https://doi.org/10.5772/intechopen.74311

Elsayed EM, Attia NF, Alshehri LA (2020) Innovative flame retardant and antibacterial fabrics coating based on inorganic nanotubes. Chem Select 5(10):2961–2965. https://doi.org/10.1002/slct.201904182

Eutionnat-Diffo PA, Cayla A, Chen Y, Guan J, Nierstrasz V, Campagne C (2020) Development of flexible and conductive immiscible thermoplastic/elastomer monofilament for smart textiles applications using 3D printing. Polymers 12(10):2300. https://doi.org/10.3390/polym12102300

Eutionnat-Diffo PA, Chen Y, Guan J, Cayla A, Campagne C, Zeng X, Nierstrasz V (2019) Stress, strain and deformation of poly-lactic acid filament deposited onto polyethylene terephthalate woven fabric through 3D printing process. Sci Rep 9(1). https://doi.org/10.1038/s41598-019-50832-7

Fernandes CE, Morais R (2021) A review on potential technological advances for fashion retail. dObra[s]—revista da Associação Brasileira de Estudos de Pesquisas em Moda (32):168–186. https://doi.org/10.26563/dobras.i32.1372

Fernández-Caramés T, Fraga-Lamas P (2018a) Towards the internet of smart clothing: a review on IoT wearables and garments for creating intelligent connected e-textiles. Electronics 7(12):405. https://doi.org/10.3390/electronics7120405. http://ruc.udc.es/dspace/bitstream/2183/21668/3/Tiago_M._Fern%c3%a1ndez-Caram%c3%a9s_2018_Towards_The_Internet_of_Smart_Clothing.pdf

Fernández-Caramés TM and Fraga-Lamas P (2018b) Towards the internet of smart clothing: a review on IoT wearables and garments for creating intelligent connected e-textiles. Electronics 7(12):405. https://www.mdpi.com/2079-9292/7/12/405

Ferraro V (2015) Smart textiles and wearable technologies for sportswear: a design approach. European Conference on Software Architecture. https://api.semanticscholar.org/CorpusID:55438133

Ferri J, Llinares Llopis R, Moreno J, Ibañez Civera J, Garcia-Breijo E (2019) A wearable textile 3D gesture recognition sensor based on screen-printing technology. Sensors 19(23):5068. https://doi.org/10.3390/s19235068

Fromme NP, Li Y, Camenzind M, Toncelli C, Rossi RM (2021) Metal-textile laser welding for wearable sensors applications. Adv Electron Mater 7(4):2001238. https://doi.org/10.1002/aelm.202001238

Gaissmaier M, Karlsson A, Aschan Eriksson S, Kosmack Vaara E, Komazec K, Fernaeus Y (2020) Designing for workplace safety. TEI '20: Proceedings of the Fourteenth International Conference on Tangible, Embedded, and Embodied Interaction: 53–65. https://doi.org/10.1145/3374920.3374932

Ge F, Yu W, Zhang W, Yin Y, Wang C (2021) Sunlight-responsive photothermochromic fabric with reversible color changing based on photothermal conversion. Solar RRL 5(7):2100135. https://doi.org/10.1002/solr.202100135

Gil I, Fernández-García R, Tornero JA (2019) Embroidery manufacturing techniques for textile dipole antenna applied to wireless body area network. Text Res J 89(8):1573–1581. https://doi.org/10.1177/0040517518770682

Goncu Berk G (2018) Design of a wearable pain management system with embroidered TENS electrodes. Int J Cloth Sci Technol 30(1):38–48

Goncu-Berk G, Karacan B, Balkis I (2020) Embedding 3D printed filaments with knitted textiles: investigation of bonding parameters. Cloth Text Res J 40(3):171–186. https://doi.org/10.1177/0887302X20982927

Gong Z, Xiang Z, Ouyang X, Zhang J, Lau N, Zhou J, Chan CC (2019) Wearable fiber optic technology based on smart textile: a review. Materials 12(20):3311. https://doi.org/10.3390/ma12203311

Grancarić AM, Jerković I, Koncar V, Cochrane C, Kelly FM, Soulat D, Legrand X (2018) Conductive polymers for smart textile applications. J Ind Text 48(3):612–642. https://doi.org/10.1177/1528083717699368

Hassabo A, Elmorsy H, Gamal N, Sediek A, Saad F, Hegazy B, Othman H (2022) Applications of nanotechnology in the creation of smart sportswear for enhanced sports performance: efficiency and comfort. J Text Color Polym Sci. https://doi.org/10.21608/jtcps.2022.181608.1147

Hassan B, Islam G, Haque A (2019) Applications of nanotechnology in textiles: a review. Adv Res Text Eng 4(2):1038

He H, Liu J, Wang Y, Zhao Y, Qin Y, Zhu Z, Yu Z, Wang J (2022) An ultralight self-powered fire alarm e-textile based on conductive aerogel fiber with repeatable temperature monitoring performance used in firefighting clothing. ACS Nano 16(2):2953–2967

Heikenfeld J (2016) Non-invasive analyte access and sensing through eccrine sweat: challenges and outlook circa 2016. Electroanalysis 28(6):1242–1249. https://doi.org/10.1002/elan.201600018

Hossain MM, Bradford PD (2021) Chapter 3—Durability of smart electronic textiles. In: Ehrmann A, Nguyen TA, Nguyen Tri P (eds) Nanosensors and nanodevices for smart multifunctional textiles. Elsevier. https://doi.org/10.1016/B978-0-12-820777-2.00003-0

Hsu W-L, Chen W-T, Kuo H-H, Shiau Y-C, Chern T-Y, Lai S-C, Fan W-H (2020) Establishment of smart living environment control system. Sens Mater 32(1):183–195. https://doi.org/10.18494/SAM.2020.2581

Hu LC, Wang CJ, Lin YW, Wei TC, Lee CC, Chang JY, Chen IC, Kawai Y, Li TT (2015) Investigation of electron cyclotron resonance chemical vapor deposition process for a-Si:H deposition, film characterization and in situ plasma diagnostics. ECS J Solid State Sci Technol 4(7):P213–P219. https://doi.org/10.1149/2.0141507jss. http://jss.ecsdl.org/content/4/7/P213.full.pdf

Huang G, Liu L, Wang R, Zhang J, Sun X, Peng H (2016) Smart color-changing textile with high contrast based on a single-sided conductive fabric. J Mater Chem C 4(32):7589–7594. https://doi.org/10.1039/c6tc02051h

Ielo I, Giacobello F, Sfameni S, Rando G, Galletta M, Trovato V, Rosace G, Plutino MR (2021) Nanostructured surface finishing and coatings: functional properties and applications. Materials 14(11):2733. https://doi.org/10.3390/ma14112733

Iftekhar Shuvo I, Decaens J, Lachapelle D, Dolez IP (2021) Smart textiles testing: a roadmap to standardized test methods for safety and quality-control. Text Funct Appl Intechopen. https://doi.org/10.5772/intechopen.96500

Islam S (2008) Development of automotive textiles with antiodour/antimicrobial properties. Masters thesis. https://researchrepository.rmit.edu.au/esploro/outputs/graduate/Development-of-automotive-textiles-with-antiodourantimicrobial/9921861434501341

Islam S (2021) 15—Waste management strategies in fashion and textiles industry: challenges are in governance, materials culture and design-centric. In: Nayak R, Patnaik A (eds) Waste management in the fashion and textile industries. Woodhead Publishing. https://doi.org/10.1016/B978-0-12-818758-6.00015-6

Jamal F, Kapoor V (2022) Smart clothing and wearables: a review of fashion technology. IUP J Brand Manage 19(4):50–63

Jang M, Kim H-D, Koo H-J, So J-H (2022) Textile-based wearable sensor for skin hydration monitoring. Sensors 22(18):6985

Javaid S, Saleem N, Ur Rehman S (2024) Polymeric nano-emulsion in functional textile finishing. Nanoemul Des Appl. IntechOpen. https://doi.org/10.5772/intechopen.1004397

Jelil RA (2015) A review of low-temperature plasma treatment of textile materials. J Mater Sci 50(18):5913–5943. https://doi.org/10.1007/s10853-015-9152-4

Jovancic P, Petrusic S, Molina R (2014) Novel synthesis pathways for PNIPAAm-based hydrogels and their application in thermosensitive textiles. In: Handbook of smart textiles. Springer Singapore. https://doi.org/10.1007/978-981-4451-68-0_12-1

Jung-Sim R (2018) Conductive yarn embroidered circuits for system on textiles. In: Jesús Hamilton O (ed) Wearable technologies. IntechOpen, Rijeka. https://doi.org/10.5772/intechopen.76627

Júnior HLO, Neves RM, Monticeli FM, Dall Agnol L (2022) Smart fabric textiles: recent advances and challenges. Textiles 2(4):582–605. https://doi.org/10.3390/textiles2040034

Karuppusamy S, Vengatesh P, Kulandainathan MA (2015) Eco-friendly cellulose–polymer nanocomposites: synthesis, properties and applications. In: Advanced structured materials. Springer India. https://doi.org/10.1007/978-81-322-2473-0_15

Khalil SE, Yuan J, El-Sherif MA (2004) Development of smart textiles with embedded fiber optic chemical sensors. Proceedings of SPIE, 5270:38–49. https://doi.org/10.1117/12.515068

Khan IA, Thekkekara L, Waqar S, Choudhry N, John S (2021) Supercapacitors fabrication and performance evaluation techniques. In: Supercapacitors for the next generation. https://doi.org/10.5772/intechopen.101748

Khandelwal G, Dahiya AS, Dahiya R (2022) V2O5 nanowires coated yarn based temperature sensor for smart textiles. In: 2022 IEEE International Conference on Flexible and Printable Sensors and Systems (FLEPS), Vienna, Austria, 10th–13th July ISBN 9781665442732. https://doi.org/10.1109/FLEPS53764.2022.9781524

Khumpuang S, Miyake K, Itoh T (2011) Characterization of a SWNT-reinforced conductive polymer and patterning technique for applications of electronic textile. Sens Actuators A 169(2):378–382
Kim ML, Otal EH, Sinatra NR, Dobson K, Kimura M (2023) Washable PEDOT:PSS coated polyester with submicron sized fibers for wearable technologies. ACS Omega 8(4):3971–3980. https://doi.org/10.1021/acsomega.2c06671
Koncar V (2018) Smart textiles and their applications-visual perceptions. In: 9th International Symposium on Graphic Engineering and Design. https://doi.org/10.24867/GRID-2018-p1
Kongahage D, Foroughi J (2019) Actuator materials: review on recent advances and future outlook for smart textiles. Fibers 7(3):21. https://doi.org/10.3390/fib7030021. https://www.mdpi.com/2079-6439/7/3/21/pdf
Koyama Y, Nishiyama M, Watanabe K (2018) Smart textile using hetero-core optical fiber for heartbeat and respiration monitoring. IEEE Sens J 18(15):6175–6180. https://doi.org/10.1109/JSEN.2018.2847333
Krauter C, Angerbauer K, Sousa Calepso A, Achberger A, Mayer S, Sedlmair M (2024) Sitting posture recognition and feedback: a literature review. In: CHI '24: Proceedings of the 2024 CHI Conference on Human Factors in Computing Systems 943:1–20. https://doi.org/10.1145/3613904.3642657
Krifa M (2021) Electrically conductive textile materials—application in flexible sensors and antennas. Textiles 1(2):239–257. https://doi.org/10.3390/textiles1020012
Gupta KV (2021) Photochromic dyes for smart textiles. In: Dyes and pigments—novel applications and waste treatment. IntechOpen. https://doi.org/10.5772/intechopen.96055
Singh KM (2021) Textiles functionalization—a review of materials, processes, and assessment. In: Textiles for functional applications. IntechOpen. https://doi.org/10.5772/intechopen.96936
Labeeb A, Elgory Z, Sobhy S, Eltopshy S, Swielam E (2018) Embroidery on textiles as a smart solution for wearable applications. Int Des J 8(4):81–86. https://doi.org/10.21608/idj.2018.84143
Labeeb AM, Elgory ZM, Sobhy SK, Eltopshy SM, Swielam EM (2018) Embroidery on textiles as a smart solution for wearable applications. Int Des J 8(4):81–86. https://doi.org/10.21608/idj.2018.84143. https://idj.journals.ekb.eg/article_84143_f160751eb68a1529cd87d714833f3695.pdf
Lam Po Tang S, Stylios GK (2006) An overview of smart technologies for clothing design and engineering. Int J Cloth Sci Technol 18(2):108–128. https://doi.org/10.1108/09556220610645766
Lee H, Baek K (2021) Developing a smart multifunctional outdoor jacket with wearable sensing technology for user health and safety. Multim Tools Appl 80(21–23):32273–32310. https://doi.org/10.1007/s11042-021-11166-7
Li S (2023) Review on development and application of 4D-printing technology in smart textiles. J Eng Fibers Fabr 18:155892502311774. https://doi.org/10.1177/15589250231177448
Li P, Sun Z, Wang R, Gong Y, Zhou Y, Wang Y, Liu X, Zhou X, Ouyang J, Chen M, Hou C, Chen M, Tao G (2022) Flexible thermochromic fabrics enabling dynamic colored display. Front Optoelectron 15(1). https://doi.org/10.1007/s12200-022-00042-3
Liao C, Zhang M, Yao MY, Hua T, Li L, Yan F (2015) Flexible organic electronics in biology: materials and devices. Adv Mater 27(46):7493–7527. https://doi.org/10.1002/adma.201402625
Lin M-T (2022) The chameleonic garment integrated POF fabric with a tricolour LED and wearable device technology. Int J Cloth Sci Technol 34(1):41–51. https://doi.org/10.1108/ijcst-06-2020-0084
Lin Y, Chen X, Lu Q, Wang J, Ding C, Liu F, Kong D, Yuan W, Su W, Cui Z (2023) Thermally laminated lighting textile for wearable displays with high durability. ACS Appl Mater Interf 15(4):5931–5941. https://doi.org/10.1021/acsami.2c20681
Lis Arias MJ, Coderch L, Martí M, Alonso C, García Carmona O, García Carmona C, Maesta F (2018) Vehiculation of active principles as a way to create smart and biofunctional textiles. Materials 11(11):2152. https://doi.org/10.3390/ma11112152. http://hdl.handle.net/2117/123610

Liu M, Ward T, Young D, Matos H, Wei Y, Adams J, Yang K (2020) Electronic textiles based wearable electrotherapy for pain relief. Sens Actuat A 303:111701

Liu Z, Jin P, Yin Y, Yin F (2022) Mapping the knowledge domains of smart textile: visualization analysis-based studies. J Text Inst 113(12):2651–2659

Loss C, Gonçalves R, Lopes C, Pinho P, Salvado R (2016) Smart coat with a fully-embedded textile antenna for IoT applications. Sensors 16(6):938. https://www.mdpi.com/1424-8220/16/6/938

Luo C, Gil I, Fernández-García R (2020) Wearable textile UHF-RFID sensors: a systematic review. Materials 13(15):3292. https://doi.org/10.3390/ma13153292

Luo Y, Abidian MR, Ahn J-H, Akinwande D, Andrews AM, Antonietti M, Bao Z, Berggren M, Berkey CA, Bettinger CJ (2023) Technology roadmap for flexible sensors. ACS Nano 17(6):5211–5295

Majumder S, Mondal T, Deen M (2017) Wearable sensors for remote health monitoring. Sensors 17(1):130. https://doi.org/10.3390/s17010130

Malins J, Steed J, Fairburn SM, Robertson S, Cruickshank LM, Scott K (2012) Future textile visions: smart textiles for health and wellness. Robert Gordon University. http://hdl.handle.net/10059/772

Matsouka D, Vassiliadis S (2018) Piezoelectric melt-spun textile fibers: technological overview. In: Piezoelectricity—organic and inorganic materials and applications. InTech. https://doi.org/10.5772/intechopen.78389

Mečņika V, Hoerr M, Krieviņš I, Schwarz A (2014) Smart textiles for healthcare: applications and technologies. Rural Environ Educ Person 7:150–161

Mecnika V, Hoerr M, Krievins I, Jockenhoevel S, Gries T (2014) Technical embroidery for smart textiles. Mater Sci Text Cloth Technol 9:56–63

Melnikova R, Ehrmann A, Finsterbusch K (2014) 3D printing of textile-based structures by fused deposition modelling (FDM) with different polymer materials. IOP Publ 1:1757–1899

Mendes CR, Tugas CF, da Silva MR, Pinto AM, da Silva SB, Urbano EO, dos Santos MPF, do Vale Sampaio R, (2024) Development of a smart lumbar posture correction vest. Stud Health Sci 5(2):e3459–e3459

Mi H, Zhong L, Tang X, Xu P, Liu X, Luo T, Jiang X (2021) Electroluminescent fabric woven by ultrastretchable fibers for arbitrarily controllable pattern display. ACS Appl Mater Interf 13(9):11260–11267

Micus S, Rostami SG, Haupt M, Gresser GT, Meghrazi MA, Eskandarian L (2021) Integrating electronics to textiles by ultrasonic welding for cable-driven applications for smart textiles. Materials 14(19):5735. https://doi.org/10.3390/ma14195735

Mohaddes F, Islam S, Shanks R, Fergusson M, Wang L, Padhye R (2014) Modification and evaluation of thermal properties of melamine-formaldehyde/n-eicosane microcapsules for thermo-regulation applications. Appl Thermal Eng 71(1):11–15. https://doi.org/10.1016/j.applthermaleng.2014.06.016. https://www.sciencedirect.com/science/article/pii/S1359431114004955

Mokhtari F, Cheng Z, Raad R, Xi J, Foroughi J (2020) Piezofibers to smart textiles: a review on recent advances and future outlook for wearable technology. J Mater Chem A 8(19):9496–9522. https://doi.org/10.1039/d0ta00227e

Moon SH, Lee JS, Sul IH (2018) Ray-tracing-based modeling of clad-removed step-index plastic optical fiber in smart textiles: effect of curvature in plain weave fabric. Adv Mater Sci Eng 2018:1–16. https://doi.org/10.1155/2018/1672369

Moradi A, Szewczyk PK, Stachewicz U (2023) Bridging a gap in thermal conductivity and heat transfer in hybrid fibers and yarns via polyimide and silicon nitride composites. Small 19(52). https://doi.org/10.1002/smll.202305104

Muhammad Sayem AS, Hon Teay S, Shahariar H, Luise Fink P, Albarbar A (2020) Review on smart electro-clothing systems (SeCSs). Sensors 20(3):587. https://doi.org/10.3390/s20030587

Nasri M, Helali A, Maaref H (2021) Energy-efficient fuzzy logic-based cross-layer hierarchical routing protocol for wireless internet-of-things sensor networks. Int J Commun Syst 34(9). https://doi.org/10.1002/dac.4808

Nayak R (2019) Radio frequency identification (RFID) technology and application in fashion and textile supply chain. https://doi.org/10.1201/9781351238250

Nesenbergs K, Selavo L (2015) Smart textiles for wearable sensor networks: review and early lessons. 2015 IEEE International Symposium on Medical Measurements and Applications (MeMeA) Proceedings, Turin, Italy, 2015:402–406. https://doi.org/10.1109/MeMeA.2015.7145236

Niu Z, Yuan W (2021) Smart nanocomposite nonwoven wearable fabrics embedding phase change materials for highly efficient energy conversion-storage and use as a stretchable conductor. ACS Appl Mater Interf 13(3):4508–4518. https://doi.org/10.1021/acsami.0c19674

Oatley G, Choudhury T, Buckman P (2021) Smart textiles for improved quality of life and cognitive assessment. Sensors 21(23):8008. https://doi.org/10.3390/s21238008

Ogunjimi A, Rahman M, Islam N, Hasan R (2021) Smart mirror fashion technology for the retail chain transformation. Technol Forecast Soc Chang 173:121118. https://doi.org/10.1016/j.techfore.2021.121118

Ozaydin-Ince G, Coclite AM, Gleason KK (2012) CVD of polymeric thin films: applications in sensors, biotechnology, microelectronics/organic electronics, microfluidics, MEMS, composites and membranes. Rep Prog Phys 75(1):016501. https://doi.org/10.1088/0034-4885/75/1/016501

Pal R, Jayarathne A (2022) Chapter 15—Digitalization in the textiles and clothing sector. In: MacCarthy BL, Ivanov D (eds) The digital supply chain. Elsevier. https://doi.org/10.1016/B978-0-323-91614-1.00015-0

Park S, Jayaraman S (2017) The wearables revolution and big data: the textile lineage. J Text Inst 108(4):605–614. https://doi.org/10.1080/00405000.2016.1176632

Patel S, Park H, Bonato P, Chan L, Rodgers M (2012) A review of wearable sensors and systems with application in rehabilitation. J Neuroeng Rehabil 9(1):21. https://doi.org/10.1186/1743-0003-9-21

Patra K (2013) Application of nanotechnology in textile engineering: an overview. J Eng Technol Res 5(5):104–111. https://doi.org/10.5897/jetr2013.0309

Persson NK, Martinez JG, Zhong Y, Maziz A, Jager EWH (2018) Actuating textiles: next generation of smart textiles. Adv Mater Technol 3(10):1700397. https://doi.org/10.1002/admt.201700397

Proesmans R, Verleysen A, Vleugels R, Veske P, De Gusseme V-L, Wyffels F (2021) Modular piezoresistive smart textile for state estimation of cloths. Sensors 22(1):222. https://doi.org/10.3390/s22010222

Qian Z, Wu K, Bi Z (2016) The wireless sensor network of the family environment monitoring system research. In: 6th International Conference on Machinery, Materials, Environment, Biotechnology and Computer. https://doi.org/10.2991/mmebc-16.2016.115

Qu H, Semenikhin O, Skorobogatiy M (2015) Flexible fiber batteries for applications in smart textiles. Smart Mater Struct 24(2):025012. https://doi.org/10.1088/0964-1726/24/2/025012. http://arxiv.org/pdf/1301.1266

Rahman KT, Moin TS, Chowdhury MFM, Khan MN (2023) Emerging nano-enable materials in the sports industry. Emerg Appl Nanomater 141:75–100

Ramirez M, Vaught L, Law C, Meyer JL, Elhajjar R (2021) Electrospinning processing techniques for the manufacturing of composite dielectric elastomer fibers. Materials 14(21):6288. https://doi.org/10.3390/ma14216288

Reema KRR, Bailung H, Sankaranarayanan K (2022) Review of the cold atmospheric plasma technology application in food, disinfection, and textiles: a way forward for achieving circular economy. Frontiers in Physics, 10. https://doi.org/10.3389/fphy.2022.942952

Rijavec T (2010) Standardisation of smart textiles. Glasnik Hemičara Tehnologa i Ekologa Republike Srpske 4:35–38

Roh J-S (2018) Conductive yarn embroidered circuits for system on textiles in Wearable Technology, EDS Ortiz H.J (8):161–174

Root W, Bechtold T, Pham T (2020) Textile-Integrated thermocouples for temperature measurement. Materials 13(3):626. https://doi.org/10.3390/ma13030626

Sajovic I, Kert M, Boh Podgornik B (2023) Smart textiles: a review and bibliometric mapping. Appl Sci 13(18):10489. https://doi.org/10.3390/app131810489

Salman A, Metwally F, El-Bisi M, Emara G (2019) Applications of nanotechnology and advancements in smart wearable textiles: an overview. Egypt J Chem. https://doi.org/10.21608/ejchem.2019.18223.2112

Sánchez-Navarro MM, Pérez-Limiñana MÁ, Arán-Ais F, Orgilés-Barceló C (2015) Scent properties by natural fragrance microencapsulation for footwear applications. Polym Int 64(10):1458–1464. https://doi.org/10.1002/pi.4941

Saremi R, Borodinov N, Laradji AM, Sharma S, Luzinov I, Minko S (2020) Adhesion and stability of nanocellulose coatings on flat polymer films and textiles. Molecules 25(14):3238. https://www.mdpi.com/1420-3049/25/14/3238

Schwarz A, Van Langenhove L, Guermonprez P, Deguillemont D (2010) A roadmap on smart textiles. Text Prog 42(2):99–180. https://doi.org/10.1080/00405160903465220

Selvasudha N, Sweety JP, Dhanalekshmi UM, Devi NSD (2021) 15—Smart antimicrobial textiles for healthcare professionals and individuals. In: Mondal MIH (ed) Antimicrobial textiles from natural resources. Woodhead Publishing. https://doi.org/10.1016/B978-0-12-821485-5.00001-9

Sempionatto JR, Lasalde-Ramírez JA, Mahato K, Wang J, Gao W (2022) Wearable chemical sensors for biomarker discovery in the omics era. Nat Rev Chem 6(12):899–915. https://doi.org/10.1038/s41570-022-00439-w

Shah MA, Pirzada BM, Price G, Shibiru AL, Qurashi A (2022) Applications of nanotechnology in smart textile industry: a critical review. J Adv Res 38:55–75

Shahidi S, Wiener J, Ghoranneviss M (2016) Plasma-enhanced vapor deposition process for the modification of textile materials. Plasma Sci Technol Prog Phys States Chem React. InTech. https://doi.org/10.5772/62832

Shaid A, Wang L, Islam S, Cai JY, Padhye R (2016) Preparation of aerogel-eicosane microparticles for thermoregulatory coating on textile. Appl Therm Eng 107:602–611. https://doi.org/10.1016/j.applthermaleng.2016.06.187. https://www.sciencedirect.com/science/article/pii/S1359431116311012

Shekhar R, Choudhry NA, Islam S, Ahnood A, Pirogova E, Troynikov O (2023) A novel elastic conductive yarn for smart textile applications. Adv Eng Mater 25(22). https://doi.org/10.1002/adem.202300572

Shuvo II, Decaens J, Lachapelle D, Dolez P (2021) Smart textiles testing: a roadmap to standardized test methods for safety and quality-control. IntechOpen London, UK

Singh N, Gargate R, Banerjee D, Patil A (2009) Using dip pen techniques for synthesis of nanostructures. In: Proceedings Volume 7318, Micro- and Nanotechnology Sensors, Systems, and Applications; 731809. https://doi.org/10.1117/12.819071

Smith AA, Li R, Tse ZTH (2023) Reshaping healthcare with wearable biosensors. Sci Rep 13(1):4998. https://doi.org/10.1038/s41598-022-26951-z

Sonawane A, Manickam P, Bhansali S (2017) Stability of enzymatic biosensors for wearable applications. IEEE Rev Biomed Eng 10:174–186. https://doi.org/10.1109/RBME.2017.2706661

Sonderegger A (2013) Smart garments—the issue of usability and aesthetics. In: UbiComp '13 Adjunct: Proceedings of the 2013 ACM conference on Pervasive and ubiquitous computing adjunct publication, 385–392 https://doi.org/10.1145/2494091.249596

Sonia P, Mahesh PV, Nijhawan G, Hlail SH, VR, Rao AK (2024) Review on hybrid welding techniques for improved joint performance. E3S Web Conf 505:01022. https://doi.org/10.1051/e3sconf/202450501022

Soukup R, Blecha T, Hamacek A, Reboun J (2014) Smart textile-based protective system for firefighters. In: Proceedings of the 5th Electronics System-integration Technology Conference (ESTC), Helsinki, Finland, 2014, 1–5. https://doi.org/10.1109/ESTC.2014.6962821

Spahiu T, Canaj E, Shehi E (2020) 3D printing for clothing production. J Eng Fibers Fabr 15:155892502094821. https://doi.org/10.1177/1558925020948216

Srivastava R, Alsamhi SH, Murray N, Devine D (2022) Shape memory alloy-based wearables: a review, and conceptual frameworks on HCI and HRI in industry 4.0. Sensors 22(18):6802. https://doi.org/10.3390/s22186802
Stoppa M, Chiolerio A (2014) Wearable electronics and smart textiles: a critical review. Sensors 14(7):11957–11992. https://doi.org/10.3390/s140711957. https://www.ncbi.nlm.nih.gov/pmc/articles/PMC4168435
straitsresearch (straitsresearch) (2024) Smart textile market. straitsresearch.com website. https://straitsresearch.com/report/smart-textile-market. Accessed 2 Jul 2024
Sugathan M, Hendry MD (2017) Market forecasts and personal adoption of smart textiles in fitness sector. Int J Technol Diff 8(3):57–75
Tabia K, Wattez H, Ydée N, Sedki K (2018) Data analytics and visualization for connected objects: a case study for sleep and physical activity trackers. In: Lecture notes in computer science. Springer International Publishing. https://doi.org/10.1007/978-3-319-92058-0_66
Tabor J, Tushar G (2019) Building and construction textiles in High Performance Technical Textiles, Eds Paul R, Page 319–352
Takagi T (1990) A concept of intelligent materials. J Intell Mater Syst Struct 1(2):149–156. https://doi.org/10.1177/1045389x9000100201
Takamatsu S, Yamashita T, Itoh T (2015) Meter-scale large area LED-embedded light fabric for the application of fabric ceilings in rooms. Microsyst Technol 21(6):1209–1217. https://doi.org/10.1007/s00542-014-2174-z
Tan WC, Sidhu MS (2022) Review of RFID and IoT integration in supply chain management. Oper Res Perspect 9:100229. https://doi.org/10.1016/j.orp.2022.100229. https://www.sciencedirect.com/science/article/pii/S2214716022000070
Thakur S (2017) Shape memory polymers for smart textile applications. Text Adv Appl Intech. https://doi.org/10.5772/intechopen.69742
Thakur S, Hu J (2017) Polyurethane: a shape memory polymer (SMP). Aspects Polyureth Intech. https://doi.org/10.5772/intechopen.69992
Tian B, Fang Y, Liang J, Zheng K, Guo P, Zhang X, Wu Y, Liu Q, Huang Z, Cao C, Wu W (2022) Fully printed stretchable and multifunctional e-textiles for aesthetic wearable electronic systems. Small 18(13):2107298. https://doi.org/10.1002/smll.202107298
Tognetti A, Bartalesi R, Lorussi F, De Rossi D (2007) Body segment position reconstruction and posture classification by smart textiles. Trans Inst Meas Control 29(3–4):215–253. https://doi.org/10.1177/0142331207069487
Tseghai GB, Malengier B, Fante KA, Nigusse AB, Van Langenhove L (2020) Integration of conductive materials with textile structures, an overview. Sensors 20(23):6910. https://doi.org/10.3390/s20236910
Ullah S, Yang X, Ta HQ, Hasan M, Bachmatiuk A, Tokarska K, Trzebicka B, Fu L, Rummeli MH (2021) Graphene transfer methods: a review. Nano Res 14(11):3756–3772. https://doi.org/10.1007/s12274-021-3345-8
Underwood J, Islam S (2024) 15—Garment machinery for regenerative manufacturing. In: Paul R, Gries T (eds) Sustainable innovations in the textile industry. Woodhead Publishing. https://doi.org/10.1016/B978-0-323-90392-9.00017-3
United Nations (2015) Adoption of the Paris agreement. https://unfccc.int/resource/docs/2015/cop21/eng/l09r01.pdf
van der Lugt B, Feijs L (2019) Stress reduction in everyday wearables: balanced. In: UbiComp/ISWC '19 Adjunct: Adjunct Proceedings of the 2019 ACM International Joint Conference on Pervasive and Ubiquitous Computing and Proceedings of the 2019 ACM International Symposium on Wearable Computers, pp 1050–1053. https://doi.org/10.1145/3341162.3349575
Van Langenhove L (2014) Smart textiles: past, present, and future. In: Handbook of smart textiles. Springer Singapore. https://doi.org/10.1007/978-981-4451-68-0_15-1
van der Velden NM, Kuusk K, Köhler AR (2015) Life cycle assessment and eco-design of smart textiles: the importance of material selection demonstrated through e-textile product redesign.

Mater Des 84:313–324. https://doi.org/10.1016/j.matdes.2015.06.129. https://www.sciencedirect.com/science/article/pii/S0264127515300174

Venkatraman P, Tyler D (2015) Applications of compression sportswear. In: Materials and technology for sportswear and performance apparel. CRC Press. https://doi.org/10.1201/b19359-8

Venturini Degli Esposti E, Bedon C, Jonaitiene V, Kazak JK, Liotta LF, Priniotakis G, Stachewicz U (2022) Smart textiles in building and living applications: WG4 CONTEXT insight on elderly and healthcare environments. Buildings 12(12):2156. https://doi.org/10.3390/buildings12122156

Verma H, Jain M, Goel K, Vikram A, Verma G (2016) Smart home system based on Internet of Things. Proceedings of the 3rd International Conference on Computing for Sustainable Goal Development. https://ieeexplore.ieee.org/stamp/stamp.jsp?tp=&arnumber=7724631

Verschuren J, Kiekens P, Leys C (2007) Textile-specific properties that influence plasma treatment, effect creation and effect characterization. Text Res J 77(10):727–733. https://doi.org/10.1177/0040517507078820

Visser F (2018) Haptic feedback in a posture correcting wearable. Bachelors Thesis. University of Twente. https://essay.utwente.nl/75537/1/Visser_BA_EEMCS.pdf

Viswanathan G, Murugesan S, Pushparaj V, Nalamasu O, Ajayan PM, Linhardt RJ (2006) Preparation of biopolymer fibers by electrospinning from room temperature ionic liquids. Biomacromole 7(2):415–418. https://doi.org/10.1021/bm050837s

Wan X, Wei H, Zhang F, Liu Y, Leng J (2019) 3D printing of shape memory poly (d, l-lactide-co-trimethylene carbonate) by direct ink writing for shape-changing structures. J Appl Polym Sci 136(44):48177

Wang X, Ng FMC, Hu J, Seto Y-c (2009) Shapeable stretch textiles via simple weaves for seamless woven fashion. Text Res J 79(18):1715–1724. https://doi.org/10.1177/0040517509103552

Wang F, Zhu B, Shu L, Tao X (2013) Flexible pressure sensors for smart protective clothing against impact loading. Smart Mater Struct 23(1):015001

Wang M, Wang X, Moni P, Liu A, Kim DH, Jo WJ, Sojoudi H, Gleason KK (2017) CVD polymers for devices and device fabrication. Adv Mater 29(11):1604606. https://doi.org/10.1002/adma.201604606

Wang L, Zhang F, Liu Y, Leng J (2022a) Shape memory polymer fibers: materials, structures, and applications. Adv Fiber Mater 4(1):5–23. https://doi.org/10.1007/s42765-021-00073-z

Wang S, Ning H, Liu F, Hu N, Zhang H, Zou R, Wen J, Huang K, Wu X, Song Z, Xiang C, Wang Z (2022b) Wearable multifunctional graphene-based aerogel/spacer fabric composites for sensing and impact protection. Adv Mater Technol 7(9):2200010. https://doi.org/10.1002/admt.202200010

Wolniak R, Grebski W (2023) The usage of smart thermostats in smart home. In: Scientific papers of Silesian University of Technology. Organization and Management Series No. 189:759–769. https://doi.org/10.29119/1641-3466.2023.189.48

Won AY, Yun C (2022) Effects of maintenance and wear on the electrical resistance of silver-based conductive textiles. Fibers Polym 23(4):977–984. https://doi.org/10.1007/s12221-022-4101-8

Xiaopei Wu J, Li L (2019) An introduction to wearable technology and smart textiles and apparel: terminology, statistics, evolution, and challenges. In: Smart and functional soft materials. IntechOpen. https://doi.org/10.5772/intechopen.86560

Xiong R, Wissmann PJ, Gallivan MA (2006) An extended Kalman filter for in situ sensing of yttria-stabilized zirconia in chemical vapor deposition. Comput Chem Eng 30(10–12):1657–1669. https://doi.org/10.1016/j.compchemeng.2006.05.032

Yaacoub E (2018) An efficient channel-aware aloha-like OFDMA-based wireless communication protocol for IoT communications in wireless sensor networks. In: Advances in systems analysis, software engineering, and high performance computing. IGI Global. https://doi.org/10.4018/978-1-5225-2845-6.ch004

Yao Y, He N, Chen W, Yu J, Chen X (2015) Novel optically transparent antenna for RFID smart fitting room application. Asia-Pacific Microwave Conference (APMC). https://doi.org/10.1109/APMC.2015.7413048

Yu A, Wang W, Li Z, Liu X, Zhang Y, Zhai J (2020) Large-scale smart carpet for self-powered fall detection. Adv Mater Technol 5(2):1900978. https://doi.org/10.1002/admt.201900978

Zhang M, Zhao M, Jian M, Wang C, Yu A, Yin Z, Liang X, Wang H, Xia K, Liang X, Zhai J, Zhang Y (2019) Printable smart pattern for multifunctional energy-management e-textile. Matter 1(1):168–179. https://doi.org/10.1016/j.matt.2019.02.003

Zhang Y, Xia X, Ma K, Xia G, Wu M, Cheung YH, Yu H, Zou B, Zhang X, Farha OK, Xin JH (2023) Functional textiles with smart properties: their fabrications and sustainable applications. Adv Funct Mater 33(33):2301607. https://doi.org/10.1002/adfm.202301607

Zheng Y-L, Ding X-R, Poon CCY, Lo BPL, Zhang H, Zhou X-L, Yang G-Z, Zhao N, Zhang Y-T (2014) Unobtrusive sensing and wearable devices for health informatics. IEEE Trans Biomed Eng 61(5):1538–1554. https://doi.org/10.1109/tbme.2014.2309951

Zhu W, Si J, Zhang L, Li T, Song W, Zhou Y, Yu J, Chen R, Feng Y, Wang L (2020) Growth of GaN on monolayer hexagonal boron nitride by chemical vapor deposition for ultraviolet photodetectors. Semicond Sci Technol 35(12):125025. https://doi.org/10.1088/1361-6641/abb71d

Zou T, Zhang D, Xu T, Peng X, Zhang H, Du Y (2023) Smart fire-safety cotton fabric with fire-warning capability via dual working mechanisms. Cellulose 30(9):6015–6030. https://doi.org/10.1007/s10570-023-05227-3

Chapter 12
Role of Digital Technologies and Digital Marketing in the Fashion and Textile Supply Chain

Nghia Thi Minh Luu, Phuong Thanh Phung, Sang My Hua, Anh Thi Van Nguyen, Anushka Siriwardana, and Ai-Phuong Hoang

Abstract This chapter is a systematic literature review of research papers on the role of digital technologies and digital marketing in fashion and textile supply chain management. Over the last decade, the fashion and textile industries have faced criticism over poor working conditions, employee exploitation, and human rights violations. This has led to a growing interest in how technology can transform the fashion and textile supply chain. Despite the negative perception associated with 'fast fashion', which is criticized for harming the environment and fueling consumers' instant gratification, digital technologies in general and digital marketing in particular offer a pathway to improve supply chain operations. Research findings from a careful examination of 74 papers indicated four interwoven key research themes: digital transformation in fashion and textile supply chains, sustainable supply chain and circular economy, digital resilience in the fashion and textile industry post-COVID-19, and evolving business and supply chain models. In theme 1, prominent technologies, including blockchain, 3D-virtual technologies, and the Internet of Things, were major motors driving the supply chain transformations. Emerging

N. T. M. Luu (✉) · P. T. Phung · S. M. Hua · A. T. Van Nguyen · A. Siriwardana · A.-P. Hoang
RMIT University, Ho Chi Minh City, Vietnam
e-mail: Nghia.luuthiminh@rmit.edu.vn

P. T. Phung
e-mail: phuong.phung@rmit.edu.vn

S. M. Hua
e-mail: sang.huamy@rmit.edu.vn

A. T. Van Nguyen
e-mail: anh.nguyenthivan3@rmit.edu.vn

A. Siriwardana
e-mail: anushka.siriwardana@rmit.edu.vn

A.-P. Hoang
e-mail: phuong.hoangai@rmit.edu.vn

R. Nayak et al. (eds.), *Use of Digital and Advanced Technologies in the Fashion Supply Chain*, Springer Series in Fashion Business,
https://doi.org/10.1007/978-981-97-7528-6_12

advanced technologies, including AI, robotics, and cloud computing, are instrumental in enhancing supply chain operational transparency and efficiency. Digital marketing and e-commerce technologies further the advancement of supply chain transparency and efficiency in creating a demand-driven supply chain model, which results in not only shortened lead time but also complicated the issue of supply chain sustainability. Findings on Theme 2 on supply chain sustainability and Theme 3 on the impact of COVID-19 reinforce the interwoven characteristics of the topics. While sustainability is a sure concern of supply chain management, Covid-19 heightened the urgency of sustainability as a pressing issue, accelerated the development of digital technologies, and eventually led to the rise of new business models in supply chain management. Findings in theme 4 on business models further confirm that digital technologies enable new models within four categories of models, embracing both upstream and downstream supply chains, and addressing both pertinent supply chain concerns of lead-time and sustainability. The review identified research gaps and proposed future research directions, including but not limited to the adoption of digital technologies for disruptive situations and the integration of advanced technologies in a more specific, process-oriented approach, a broader context for the impact of digital marketing and e-commerce on the supply chain, a holistic approach to how digital technology application would impact sustainability and the evolution of multiple business models in the fashion supply chain. The chapter contributes to understanding how digital technologies and digital marketing are reshaping the fashion and textile supply chain, highlighting the potential for improvements in sustainability, efficiency, and resilience.

Keywords Digital transformation · Fashion and textile supply chain · Sustainability · Supply chain management · COVID-19 · Digital resilience · Digital marketing technologies

12.1 Introduction

The fashion and textile sector has endured significant changes in the past two decades, primarily due to the major disruptions caused by the COVID-19 pandemic and advancements in digital technologies (Wu et al. 2023). These technologies have revolutionized traditional supply chain procedures and influenced customer behavior, market dynamics, and corporate strategies in the industry (Lopez et al. 2023).

Over the past two decades, research in the field of fashion and textile supply chains has developed to address emerging trends and challenges driven by digitalization (Arribas and Alfaro 2018; Oguntegbe et al. 2023). However, there is a lack of research exploring the importance of digital technologies and digital marketing in the transformation of fashion and textile supply chain post COVID-19. This chapter provides an in-depth investigation of the evolving fashion and textile supply chains, explaining the role of digital technologies, the evolving trends and key research themes in the fashion supply chain throughout two decades (2006–2024), and the related research gaps in applying digital technologies for digital transformation in the fashion supply chain.

This chapter aims to provide insights into the transformative power of technology that shapes fashion and textile supply chains, with the research objectives: (1) to identify the main themes of digital transformation research in the fashion and textile supply chain domain; (2) to evaluate the role of digital technologies in the digital transformation of the fashion and textile supply chain, (3) to examine innovative business models in the fashion and textile supply chain, and (4) to identify emerging research trends, and (5) identifying research directions for future academics in the domain.

The study employed a multi-faceted approach to guarantee the quality, comprehensiveness, and depth of the literature review and analysis to offer valuable insights gathered from 74 articles over two decades (2006–2024). The investigation resulted in four main themes that encapsulate the transforming dynamics within the fashion and textile supply chains. Theme 1 investigates the process of digitizing supply chains, focusing on implementing advanced technologies. Theme 2 examines the growing discussion on sustainable supply chains and circular economy ideas in the fashion and textile industry (Heim and Hopper 2022; Hmamed et al. 2023). Theme 3 delivers an understanding of the digital resilience strategies embraced by the fashion and textile industries in response to the COVID-19 pandemic. Lastly, theme 4 examined the evolution of business and supply chain models in the fashion and textile industry. It encompasses a range of models, such as circular and sustainable value chains, omni-channel retailing, and fast fashion paradigms (Jocevski et al. 2019; Abbate et al. 2023; Harper and Pal 2022).

The findings reflected the evolving nature of the industry and the need to accept innovation to be competitive and sustainable in a rapidly changing environment. Themes such as digital transformation, sustainable supply chains, adoption of circular economy, and post-COVID-19 resilience have received significant attention from both scholars and practitioners (Garzoni et al. 2020; Howard et al. 2022; Heim and Hopper 2022; Hmamed et al. 2023; Acquila-Natale et al. 2022). These themes include other subtopics, including the integration of modern digital technology and the study of new business models and supply chain models, which have become the primary research fields.

12.2 Methodology

12.2.1 Review Type

The systematic review form is used in this paper to provide a comprehensive review of the supply chain in the fashion and textile industry. A systematic review is a process for studying existing literature by employing a comprehensive pre-planned strategy to locate existing literature, evaluate their contribution, analyze and synthesize the findings, and present the evidence to draw conclusions about what is known and not known (Denyer and Tranfield 2009). A systematic literature review can summarise and classify existing literature based on themes and provide future suggestions (Seuring et al. 2005). Thematic analysis, a method for identifying and interpreting patterns of meaning across qualitative data (Clarke and Braun 2017), is used to classify existing studies based on themes of this area. Therefore, this review chapter aims to consolidate and synthesize the findings of studies pertaining to the key themes of digital technologies and digital marketing in the fashion and textile supply chain and propose future research suggestions in this field.

12.2.2 Key Definitions

Digital transformation has been a crucial phenomenon in strategic information system research (Bharadwaj et al. 2013; Piccinini et al. 2015) and for practitioners (Fitzgerald et al. 2014; Westerman et al. 2011). The fashion industry underwent a digital transformation that impacted the entire value chain, bringing significant changes in customer relationships and supply chain operations (Arribas and Alfaro 2018).

According to a definition developed by Vial (2019, p. 121) after reviewing 282 works on digital transformation from Information System literature, digital transformation is "a process that aims to improve an entity by triggering significant changes to its properties through combinations of information, computing, communication, and connectivity technologies." Vial (2019) concluded that the eight building blocks of the digital transformation process are the use of digital technologies, disruptions, strategic responses, value creation paths, organizational barriers, structural changes, negative impacts, and positive impacts. In the scope of this study, we use the definition and the eight building blocks of the digital transformation process of Vial (2019).

A supply chain is a group of three or more entities (organizations or individuals) that actively participate in the upstream and downstream flows of products, services, finances, and information from a source to a client (Mentzer et al. 2001). In more recent research, LeMay et al. (2017) gathered supply chain management definitions from various sources, including journals, textbooks, universities, and industry associations, and online, to propose a more overarching definition of supply chain management. They concluded that "Supply chain management is the design and coordination of a network through which organizations and individuals get, use, deliver, and dispose of material goods; acquire and distribute services; and make their offerings available to markets, customers, and clients" (LeMay et al. 2017, p. 1446). In the scope of this study, we use the definition of Lemay et al. (2017).

12.2.3 Review Scope and Process

The present study adopted a multi-faceted approach to guarantee the quality, comprehensiveness, and profundity of our literature search (Ott and Michailova 2018). The data collection process is presented in Fig. 12.1.

In step 1, we performed a keyword search on the Scopus database to gather data from three bibliometric fields: titles, abstracts, and keywords. The search was delimited by three sets of keywords to confine the research scope. The first group comprised keywords of the fashion and textile business: fashion, textile, clothing, and garment. The second set of keywords was designed to filter articles related to supply chain management, including supply chain, logistics, value chain, supply network, and supply operation. The third and final set of keywords pertained to digitalization-related terminologies, including digital transformation, digitalization, digital technology, digital platform, and digital business model. The search results were limited to three discipline areas: Business and Management, Economics and

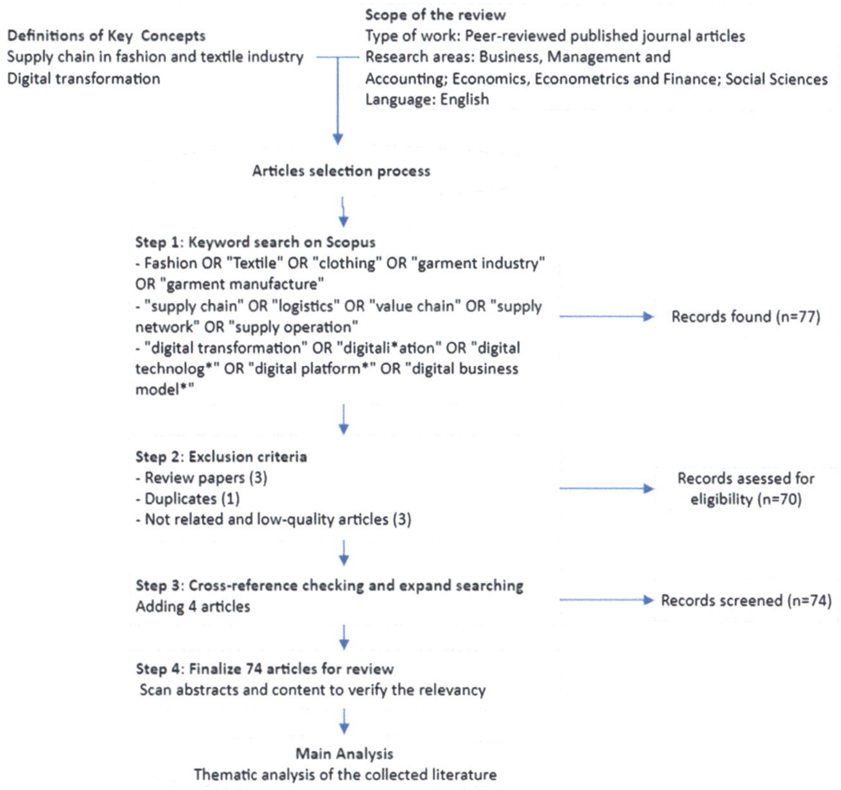

Fig. 12.1 Data collection process

Finance, and Social Science. After the initial search, 77 articles were obtained and briefly reviewed to ascertain their relevance to the research topic.

In step 2 of the research methodology, duplicate, irrelevant, and low-quality articles were identified and eliminated, resulting in seven documents being excluded from the data collection. To ensure the reliability of the exclusion process, the second author reviewed and verified the excluded documents and confirmed the remaining 70 articles.

In Step 3, a cross-referencing process was conducted to identify highly relevant papers that could potentially be included in the final dataset. In step 4, the identified documents were then meticulously scrutinized, and five additional articles that met the inclusion criteria were ultimately incorporated into the final dataset of 74 papers. Finally, the main content of individual articles was analyzed, and a classification process based on research themes was carried out. To ensure the reliability of the classification process, two teams of researchers conducted a cross-check of the process.

12.3 Main Research Themes in the Fashion and Textile Supply Chain

12.3.1 Theme 1: Digital Transformation in Fashion and Textile Supply Chains

12.3.1.1 Digital Technology Adoption and Transformation in the Fashion Supply Chain

Prior research has looked at the impact of digital transformation on supply chains across different firm sizes. The timely adoption of digital technologies can enhance supply chain performance and help firms gain competitive advantages (Russo et al. 2023; Shahadat et al. 2023). In the context of SMEs, a four-level approach to engagement in digital technologies adoption is observed, namely (1) digital awareness, (2) digital requirement, (3) digital collaboration, and (4) digital transformation, with the supply chain's involvement becoming crucial at levels 3 and 4 (Garzoni et al. 2020). Technologies play a critical role in collaboration between business functions and within the supply chain at level 3, where custom application software can be replicated within the respective supply chain at level 4 (Garzoni et al. 2020). Garzoni et al. (2020) proposed a digitization framework consisting of three key components: (1) supply chain traceability and precision farming, (2) product-process maintenance services, and (3) smart PPE.

Research showed that digital supply chains significantly enhance the capabilities of ready-made garment companies, creating a competitive advantage for firms' supply chain performance (Shahadat et al. 2023). Russo et al. (2023) further explored the digital transformation of the downstream supply chain, identifying a specific digital resource category and its four foundations—technology, competency, policies, and control—crucial for firms to manage resources across their supply chain to defend their competitive advantage. They also suggested that firms must first search internally and among their network of suppliers for the critical resources needed to digitalize their sales channels successfully (Russo et al. 2023).

However, the limitation of this research lies in its analysis of different industries, including agri-food, clothing, footwear, and mechanics-mechatronics, rather than focusing solely on the fashion and textile industries. Moreover, the supply chain was only one component of this broad strategic digital transformation study.

12.3.1.2 Advanced Digital Technologies in the Fashion and Textile Supply Chain

Blockchain

Blockchain technology, a peer-to-peer distributed database system powered by a computational algorithm, facilitates the transparent exchange of data and information while ensuring users' anonymity (Iansiti and Lakhani 2017). It enables secure, auditable, and verifiable smart contracts among supply chain partners through digital notes, thereby allowing all transactions to be recorded and synchronized across multiple partners for enhanced transparency and traceability in the supply chain (Wang et al. 2019; Manupati et al. 2020). This technology is critical in monitoring and optimizing supply chain performance, reducing operational costs, and minimizing carbon emissions (Manupati et al. 2020).

As supply chain transparency becomes increasingly important, the challenge of balancing the need for disclosure with protecting trade secrets in a competitive landscape arises. Blockchain technology addresses this concern by implementing discretionary disclosure management mechanisms through a public and private key system, thus maintaining trade secrecy while fostering transparency (Heim 2022). A private blockchain ensures trust among supply chain participants, enabling them to maintain their strategic advantage without fully disclosing methods and information to competitors. This approach provides controlled access to approved and identifiable participants at various stages of the fashion supply chain, promoting traceability while protecting sensitive information (Agrawal et al. 2021).

Nevertheless, the practical implementation of blockchain in the fashion supply chain faces several challenges. The technical requirements for blockchain integration pose significant barriers, including the lack of universally accessible applications, common data standards, and the complexities of data collection and transfer. The relative immaturity of the technology, the absence of a universally accepted platform, and limited resources further complicate its adoption (Oguntegbe et al. 2023; Heim 2022).

3-Dimensional Digital and Virtual Technologies

Within the literature on digitalization in the fashion supply chain, 3-dimensional digital and virtual technology (3D DVT) emerges as the most frequently cited technology, encompassing 3D design software, 3D modeling, 3D printing, 3D virtual garment fitting visualization, digital twinning, and 3D computer-aided design (CAD) alongside virtual reality (VR) and augmented reality (AR). This technology offers many benefits across the value chain, from design and development to manufacturing, retailing, and distribution, enhancing the creative process for designers and improving communication among designers, suppliers, and manufacturers (Casciani et al. 2022a, b; Arribas and Alfaro 2018). The principal focus of 3D technologies is product design and development, facilitating designers in experimenting with different ideas, testing fit and aesthetic features through 3D virtual prototypes before physical production, and incorporating professional knowledge with consumer demand to visualize digital garments (Casciani et al. 2022a, b).

In the downstream supply chain, 3D DVT technology enables an immersive retailing experience through digital try-on and large-scale customization. VR is employed for personalized fit and style visualization, and AR is used for creating personal wardrobes and visualizing assorted styles on smartphones (Casciani et al. 2022a, b). This leads to the possibility of a digital make-to-measure approach, offering highly personalized and precisely fitted garments based on customer body measurements (Sharma et al. 2021).

Despite the broad application of 3D DVT in the fashion industry, implementing 3D DVT within the fashion industry faces several challenges. The initial challenge is establishing of a new digital organizational culture for effective technology adoption (Arribas and Alfaro 2018). It is worth noting that 3D DVT, still in its early development stages, requires further technological advancements. At the individual level, technical challenges hinder the mutual understanding and collaboration between fashion designers and manufacturers, with engineers struggling to understand the designer's perspective and designers finding difficulties in using 3D modelling software developed from an engineering perspective (Sun and Zhao 2018). In addition, fashion industry professionals need to acquire new programming knowledge. However, limited accessibility to training programs, along with the industry's limited options for 3D software that facilitates effective collaboration, poses significant hurdles (Sun and Zhao 2018).

Internet of Things (IoT)

The integration of the Internet of Things (IoT) in the supply chain introduces technological devices attached to physical items, enabling them to transmit data over the Internet, thus facilitating IoT-supported traceability technologies like barcodes, QR codes, NFC, RFID, and Bluetooth low energy (BLE) (Gubbi et al. 2013). These technologies have become increasingly accessible, especially with their integration into smartphones, broadening their applications in the fashion and textile supply chain (FTSC) (Gubbi et al. 2013; Akram et al. 2022). In current literature, IoT's deployment notably focuses on two primary areas: smart warehouse management and smart clothing.

In smart warehouse management, products equipped with RFID tags communicate with code readers, providing vital information on storage, retrieval, tracking, and supporting the automation of these processes (Khan et al. 2022). This application of IoT enhances the efficiency and accuracy of inventory management, contributing significantly to the optimization of supply chain operations.

Meanwhile, in the domain of smart clothing, IoT technology leverages cloud computing to further enhance users' life experiences. It is utilized for a variety of functions, including product tracking and feedback, chronic disease management, emotional care, and training for auxiliary athletes, demonstrating the versatile potential of IoT to transcend traditional supply chain management and penetrate consumer-centric applications (Akram et al. 2022). This broad application spectrum of IoT in the fashion supply chain highlights its role in bridging the gap between operational efficiency and enhanced consumer engagement.

Emerging Tech: AI, Robotics, and Cloud Computing in FTSC

Recent academic research underscores the importance of investing in cloud computing, IT, robotics, and machine learning technologies as crucial drivers for achieving a higher level of digital transformation within textile and fashion companies (Špiler et al. 2023). This investment allows firms to leverage the potential of advanced technologies to streamline operations, enhance product quality, and foster innovation.

Given its diverse applications, the adoption of AI and machine learning in the fashion industry is particularly noteworthy. These technologies are employed not only for predicting health-related issues of users but also for forecasting fashion trends and recommending apparel based on environmental data (Akram et al. 2022). Such predictive capabilities allow fashion companies to stay ahead of market trends, personalize customer experiences, and contribute to sustainable fashion practices by aligning product offerings with actual consumer needs and preferences.

Furthermore, the integration of robotics and AI aims primarily at reducing costs, increasing revenue, and enhancing the user experience (Špiler et al. 2023). Robotics, for instance, automates repetitive and labour-intensive tasks, thus optimizing production processes, reducing human error, and enabling a more efficient allocation of human resources to creative and strategic tasks. The convergence of these technologies within the fashion industry augments operational efficiencies and fosters a culture of innovation.

12.3.1.3 Digital Strategies in FTSC: Marketing, E-Commerce, and Omnichannel Trends

Several studies have explored the role of digital marketing and communication within FTSC, focusing on aspects such as e-commerce, omnichannel strategies, social media, and brand strategy alongside cross-border promotion.

The exploration of e-commerce adoption within the FTSC highlights various governance frameworks—market, modular, relational, captive, hierarchy, and multiple. These frameworks are selected based on transaction complexity, the ability to codify transactions, supply base e-operation capabilities, and inter-firm knowledge transfer capacities, indicating the strategic considerations firms undertake in managing e-commerce ventures (Mola et al. 2017). Gornostaeva (2023) underscored the shift towards multichannel wholesaling models by emerging fashion designers in London, particularly noting an increase in e-commerce influenced by the COVID-19 pandemic, highlighting the adaptability of fashion firms to changing market conditions.

In the context of omnichannel strategies, studies reveal that using out-store technologies enhances omnichannel purchase intentions and customer experiences. However, the impact of in-store technologies on purchase intentions is minimal. Notably, there is a positive relationship between showrooming purchase intentions and social-physical customer experiences, and webrooming intentions with cognitive-affective experiences, underscoring the nuanced effects of technology on consumer behaviour in a multichannel retail environment (Szozda 2022).

Another study examined social media's influence on fashion companies' innovation orientation (Scuotto et al. 2020). It was found that social media platforms' structural, relational behaviour, cognitive dimensions, and knowledge transfer practices positively influence ambidextrous innovation orientation in fashion firms (Scuotto et al. 2020).

Recent discussions have also touched upon brand strategy and cross-border promotion, highlighting the need for a flexible digital supply chain to meet consumer demands for speed, personalized customization, and multiple SKUs in clothing (Zhang and Gong 2023). Munizu et al. (2024) further elaborated on how digital marketing, an integrated supply chain, and innovation capabilities enhance competitiveness and performance in the creative industry, demonstrating the significant impact of digital marketing and integrated supply chains on these outcomes.

12.3.2 Theme 2: Sustainable Supply Chain and Circular Economy in the Fashion and Textile Market

Recent years have witnessed significant growth in studies on sustainable supply chains in the fashion and textile market, emphasizing the circular economy. This includes exploring circular economy adoption processes (Howard et al. 2022) and the technology adoption for the digital transformation of the circular supply chain (Heim and Hopper 2022; Hmamed et al. 2023). In particular, applying business models designed to foster a circular economy has been a sub-theme of interest. Studies have examined various models, including product-service systems (Pal 2016), digital-based circular business models investigated (Huynh 2021), and the textile-to-textile recycling system (Sandvik and Stubbs 2019).

Another dominant theme is the role of digital technologies in enhancing a sustainable supply chain. Notable technological trends being examined included blockchain (Heim and Hopper 2022), the Internet of Things (Prajapati 2022), and digital twins technology (Wagner and Kabalska 2023). Additionally, the literature delves into the supply chain transformation process of fashion and textile companies within industry 4.0 and 5.0 frameworks. For instance, Hmamed et al. (2023) analyzed the impact of organizational factors on the implementation of industry 4.0 technologies towards sustainable goals, while Kazancoglu et al. (2023) tackled the challenges businesses face in the textile and apparel supply chain during the transition from 4.0 to 5.0.

12.3.3 Theme 3: Digital Resilience in the Fashion and Textile Industry Post-COVID-19

The COVID-19 pandemic has significantly impacted the global fashion and textile industry, leading to supply chain disruptions and changing consumer behaviors. These changes are for a move towards digital technologies for resilience and innovation. The outbreak revealed many vulnerabilities of traditional supply chain models, characterized by lockdown measures, factory closures, transportation delays, and fluctuating consumer demand, all of which contributed to inventory stockouts and revenue losses (Rao et al. 2021). In response, digital platforms emerged as crucial enablers of remote collaboration, providing real-time visibility into inventory levels and establishing e-commerce platforms as alternative sales channels, thus offering a lifeline to the industry (Ornati and Kalbaska 2022).

As such, much attention has been given to the impacts of digital technologies and potential solutions, resulting in a distinct representation of this subject before and after the outbreak (Acquila-Natale et al. 2022). Digital technologies enable firms to endure disruptions, adapt to new market conditions, and secure a favorable position for long-term success post-pandemic (Acquila-Natale et al. 2022). Notably, a study examining the effects of COVID-19 on the fashion retail industry in the Gulf Cooperation Council (GCC) countries explored the transformation in customer behavior, supply chain dynamics, and business operations due to lockdown measures, social distancing protocols, and economic uncertainty (Rao et al. 2021). Proposed strategies for industry reimagination include leveraging data analytics, optimizing inventory levels, personalizing marketing, investing in omnichannel retailing, and fostering customer loyalty. The importance of collaboration and partnerships within the industry ecosystem for innovation and resilience was also highlighted, offering practical strategies for the post-pandemic era (Rao et al. 2021).

Another study offered insights into the challenges faced by Indian startups during the pandemic, including supply chain disruptions and financial instability (Ajgaonkar 2022). Various strategies are proposed, including digital technologies, supply chain diversification, agile business practices, solid networks, partnerships, and customer-centric approaches for recovery and growth (Ajgaonkar 2022). The Swedish fashion sector also witnessed disruptions, such as a decline in consumer spending and an evaluation of market strategies, remote work, and alternative sales channels. Techniques for resilience proposed include focusing on digital marketing, product diversification, and sector collaborations, providing critical insights into the industry's capacity to adjust and recover in a post-pandemic world (Wulff 2022).

On a global scale, the pandemic created many challenges for the apparel business, including factory closures, transportation delays, and worker shortages (Castañeda-Navarrete et al. 2021). Kanat and Atilgan (2022) suggested leveraging technology, flexible production methods, sourcing strategy diversification, and supply chain partner collaboration to address these issues, emphasizing risk management strategies and sustainability initiatives for resilient supply chains.

A more recent work on Italian fashion businesses focuses on the disruptions in manufacturing processes, supply chains, and customer demand caused by the pandemic (Di Maria et al. 2023). The findings further emphasized the role of the digitalization process in overcoming pandemic-related challenges. In particular, brands need to enhance their manufacturing capabilities to produce essential goods, adopt sustainability practices, and invest in digital platforms such as e-commerce, virtual showrooms, and augmented reality experiences. Such an initiative would increase brand recognition, customer base expansion, and revenue growth (Di Maria et al. 2023) (Table 12.1).

12.3.4 Theme 4: Evolving Business and Supply Chain Models in the Fashion and Textile Industry

Associated with the word 'model', as in 'business model' or 'supply chain model', the following terms were identified from the systematic review: circular, sustainable value chain, resilient supply chain, cross-border reverse logistics, small-series production, omnichannel, real-time fashion, ultra-fast fashion, fast fashion, and slow fashion. In total, there are 10 unique word associations with 'model' as illustrated in Fig. 12.2.

Table 12.1 Journal articles where the different business models were researched

No.	Tittle	Publication year	Journal	Authors	Models
1.	Reshaping sustainable value chain model under post pandemic disruptions: A fast fashion supply chain analysis (Wu et al. 2023)	2023	International Journal of Production Economics	Wu, K.-J., Tseng, M.-L., Yang, W.-H., Ali, M.H. and Chen, X.	Fast-fashion model, Sustainable value chain model
2.	From Fast to Slow: An Exploratory Analysis of Circular Business Models in the Italian Apparel Industry (Abbate et al. 2023)	2023	International Journal of Production Economics	Abbate, S., Centobelli, P. and Cerchione, R.	Circular business model, Slow fashion model, Fast fashion model
3.	Small-series supply network configuration priorities and challenges in the EU textile and apparel industry (Harper and Pal 2022)	2022	Journal of Fashion Marketing and Management	Harper, S. and Pal, R.	Small-series production model
4.	Digital value chain restructuring and labour process transformations in the fast-fashion sector: Evidence from the value chains of Zara and H&M (López et al. 2021)	2021	Global Networks	López, T., Riedler, T., Köhnen, H., and Fütterer	Fast-fashion model, ultra-fast model
5.	Shein: The (not so?) Shining Growth of Ultra-Fast Fashion (Plé and Yacoub 2022)	2022	Journal of International Business Education	Plé, L. and Yacoub, G.	Ultra-fast model real-time fashion model
6.	Transitions towards omni-channel retailing strategies: a business model perspective (Jocevski et al. 2019)	2019	International Journal of Retail and Distribution Management	Jocevski, M., Arvidsson, N., Miragliotta, G., Ghezzi, A. and Mangiaracina, R.	Omni-channel model

(continued)

Table 12.1 (continued)

No.	Tittle	Publication year	Journal	Authors	Models
7.	Comparison of Cross-Border Reverse Logistics of a Fast Fashion Brand in China (Wahab et al. 2013)	2023	Operations and Supply Chain Management	Wahab, S.N., Tan, A. and Roche, O.	Cross-border reverse logistic model
8.	Toward a resilient supply chain model: critical role of knowledge management and dynamic capabilities (Irfan et al. 2022)	2022	Industrial Management and Data Systems	Irfan, I., Sumbal, MSUK, Khurshid, F. and Chan, F.T.S.	Resilient supply chain model
9.	Changing the game to compete: Innovations in the fashion retail industry from the disruptive business model (Jin and Shin 2020)	2020	Business Horizons	Jin, BE and Shin, D.C.	Disruptive business model

Source Authors compiled from 9 journal articles on business models in fashion supply chain management

Fig. 12.2 Ten unique word associations with "model" in Theme 4. *Source* Authors compiled from 9 research articles on Theme 4

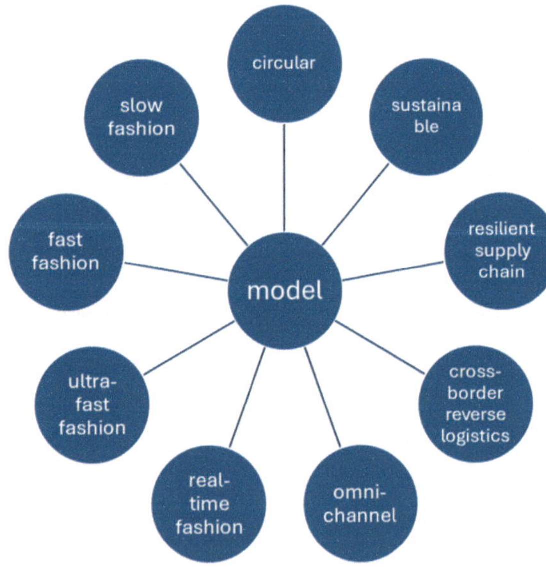

12.3.4.1 Categorization of These Distinct Types of Models/Word Associations with Models

Within this theme, the models in these nine papers can be categorized into two main types: the overall business models in fashion that were enabled by digital technologies, and the supply chain model that results from new business models enabled by digital technologies. The two articles focus on the supply chain innovation model created by new business models enabled by digital technologies: the reverse logistics model and small-series production model. The reverse logistics model is a new supply chain model resulting from the ultra-fast fashion business model (Wahab et al. 2023), and the same is true for the small-series production model (Harper and Pal 2022). Table 12.2 provides a detailed categorization of the models.

The first level of categorization includes a subgroup of terms related to '**sustainability**', where the three terms 'circular model', 'sustainable value chain model (SVM)', and 'resilient model' all refer to the overarching theme of sustainability in business and, more specifically, in supply chain management (Abbate et al. 2023). While the sustainable business model (SBV), synonymous with SVM, and the circular business model (CBV) focus primarily on the environmental impact of the supply chain, the resilient supply chain model emphasizes the dynamic capabilities of the supply chain in adapting to environmental changes, representing another dimension of sustainability (Irfan et al. 2022). Irfan et al. (2022) also advocate integrating supply chain resilience and sustainability in their research article. Additionally, it is noteworthy that Abbate et al. (2023) compare SBM and CBM, highlighting that CBM is more concerned with the effective and efficient use of resources. In contrast, SBM or SVM addresses all three pillars of sustainability: economic, social, and environmental.

The following subgroup within the models is the retail model, which represents the downstream part of the supply chain. There are two types of retail models: one is based on the level of innovation, encompassing the three disruptor models, and the other, the omnichannel model, revolves around the use of both digital and physical channels. This includes web-based stores, mobile applications, and social media, alongside brick-and-mortar stores, to provide a seamless customer experience across all distribution channels. Key features of this omni-channel approach include integrated data analytics and an effective supply chain management system (Jocevski et al. 2019).

The third subgroup of models pertains to those based on the speed of lead time. Over time, with advancements in digital technologies, the model has evolved from the traditional slow fashion model, which had a lead time of a few months, to the fast fashion model, and further to the ultra-fast or real-time fashion model, which boasts a lead time of only about 8–9 days from order to delivery. The ultra-fast fashion model can also be called the 'real-time' fashion model, as products are produced immediately upon customer order placement (Plé and Yacoub 2024). The nearly one-week lead time of Fast Fashion 2.0 represents a significant acceleration compared to Fast Fashion 1.0, which could take a few weeks for the product cycle (Lopez et al. 2023). However, there is growing pressure on fast fashion models to slow

Table 12.2 Categorizations of digital-technology-enabled models in fashion and textile supply chain management

First level categories	2nd levels categories	3rd level Categories	Company cases
"Sustainable" Model	1. Circular model (CBM)	None	21 Italian fashion companies
	2. Sustainable value chain model (SVM)	None	H&M Taiwan
	3. Resilient model	None	Pakistani company
Retail model (downstream models)	1. Disruptive model	Born-digital startup	Bonobos Warby Parker
		AI-enabled demand forecasting and product design	Stitch Fix Amazon
		Collaborative consumption	Rental Service Platform: B2C: Rent the Runway, Le Tote Peer-2-peer platform: C2C: Tradesy and Poshmark, Style Lend in the US and Rentez-Vous in the UK
	2. Omni-channel model	None	ePrice Luxottica OVS Three more detailed cases within the set of 13 examined companies
Model based on the delivery lead time	1. Slow fashion	None	Not specified
	2. Fast fashion	None	H&M Taiwan Zara, H&M in Spain and Germany
	3. Ultra-fast fashion	None	Shein
	4. Real-time fashion	None	Shein
Supply chain innovation model (upstream)	1. Cross-border reverse logistics (CBRL)	None	Zara Alibaba
	2. Small-series (SS) production model	SS-A: small series through postponement SS-B: small series through postponement and on-demand SS-C: small series through on-demand or customization	Sample of 10 companies in Europe: Sweden (4), Italy (3), Germany (1), Denmark (1) and Belgium (1)

Source Authors compiled from 9 research articles on Theme 4

down if they are to address sustainability issues effectively. Notably, slow fashion is advocated as a model encouraging the adoption of circular business models (CBM), aiming to reduce the environmental impact of this second-most polluting industry (Abbate et al. 2023).

The fourth subgroup encompasses two models of the supply chain that emerge from the fast fashion model, leveraging a global value chain network. The first is the cross-border logistics model (CBLM), which tackles specific challenges in cross-border or international e-commerce. This model addresses situations where products may be returned because they do not meet customer expectations and need to be promptly resold upon return. The second model focuses on small-series production, catering to the requirement of configuring the supply chain to produce a small quantity of products. This need arises because ultra-fast fashion aims to cater to niche product designs—fulfilling real-time demand. Within the small series production model (SSPL), three approaches involve postponement, customization, on-demand production, or a combination of these strategies to meet customer needs (Harper and Pal 2022). CBLM and SSPL are primarily concerned with production, sourcing, and the transportation network, especially in the upstream of the supply chain.

12.4 Summary of Digital Technologies Enabling These Different Models and Their Technological Challenges

Table 12.3 shows the application of enabling digital technologies across these models alongside the technological challenges identified in the research. It is observed that the integration of different technologies poses a common challenge in nearly all cases.

Taking a detailed look at the small series production model as a specific example, it is evident that digital technologies facilitating on-demand production and customization are crucial for this model. However, this model confronts significant challenges in reconciling various demands from producers and brands, which often include concerns about sustainability, cost, speed, and quality (Harper and Pal 2022). According to the authors, the most significant challenge faced by this model, as well as by others, is technological integration.

The below summary table does not include the slow fashion model, as it is regarded as the traditional approach rather than a new model that has emerged from the application of digital technology, especially when considering the aspect of lead time.

Table 12.3 Enabling digital technologies and empowered processes of business models in fashion supply chain management and technological challenges

Model	Enabling digital technologies and empowered processes	Technological challenges
Small-series production	On-demand, customization technologies, digitalized production system, IT system supporting customer communication and co-design	Digitalization processes in balancing the conflicting requirements (sustainability, costs, speed, quality, materials, flexibility, competence availability, etc.) Data securities, integration of data, digital customer relationship
Cross-border reverse logistics	AI for sorting and processing Automated customer support system Real-time logistics tracking	Lead time and inventory management Integration with custom policies and procedures, 3rd party system
Fast fashion model Ultra-fast model	Digital value chain restructuring: digitized retail processes, digital supply chain management, specifically: RFDI, cloud-computing, robotic automation 3D design software for sample making or digital sewing machine networks, innovative technologies for real-time performance monitoring, digital store management system	Digital integration, labor process transformation: non-compatibility of digital production technologies by different companies, a lack of compatibility with existing systems Various levels of digitization and integration at various parts of the supply chain network
Disruptive retail models	All three disruptors based on a combination of existing technologies: digital devices, social media, and key technologies of Industry 4.0 (e.g., big-data analytics, AI, robotics) Some specifics: Virtual try-on, One-on-one styling service, AI in demand forecasting and design, big data analysis, camera monitoring, robotic processes, machine learning, big data algorithms, peer-to-peer platforms	Identification of what technologies could address what current challenges of the fashion retailers
Omni-channel model	Retail digitization: webrooming, magic fitting room, in-store interactive digital kiosk, click-n-collect, digital content creator, reverse routing, opening delivery points, customers data tracking tool	Integration, additional data

(continued)

Table 12.3 (continued)

Model	Enabling digital technologies and empowered processes	Technological challenges
Sustainable Value Chain Model	Virtual reality services, digital information in sustainability, integrated social media, digital techniques for enhancing production efficiency, Google Assistant and Holome, fuzzy synthetic method—decision-making trial and evaluation laboratory (FSM-DEMATEL), Facebook	Integration of social media and qualitative information into the model for sustainability enhancement
Circular business model	Product take-back system in fashion retail Digital technology management (Internet of Things, blockchain) Social media, chatbot on website, customer relationship management system E-commerce for direct communication and sales to customers Digital tracking system for the whole process, RFID, QR code	Not discussed
Resilient supply chain model	Enterprise Resource Planning software, mobile knowledge management system	Integration, upgrading

Source Author compiled from 9 research articles on Theme 4 (digital technologies empowered business models in fashion supply chain management)

12.5 Discussion and Future Research Direction

12.5.1 Direction 1: Digital Transformation in the Fashion and Textile Supply Chain (FTSC)

12.5.1.1 Adoption of Digital Technologies

The study by Garzoni et al. (2020) on the digital transformation of SMEs within the Fashion and Textile Supply Chain (FTSC) outlines a four-level approach. It emphasizes the importance of future research to validate this proposition. This involves exploring various case studies of organizations in the phase of digital transformation, adopting different analytical approaches, and developing key performance indicators to monitor the progress of their digital efforts. Complementing this perspective, Russo et al. (2023) highlight the critical need for future studies to delve into the impact of digital resources on enhancing responsiveness and resilience, especially during severe operational and supply chain disruptions.

12.5.1.2 Integration of Advanced Digital Technologies

Prior works on this theme reveal a significant gap in understanding the practical integration of these technologies. Researchers call for more empirical research, particularly in the form of case studies, to develop a theoretical framework for identifying various applications, impactful factors, and outcomes associated with the integration of advanced digital technologies in the supply chain (Arribas and Alfaro 2018; Oguntegbe et al. 2023). Such theoretical frameworks would then need to be empirically validated in real-world scenarios to test their applicability and effectiveness (Manupati et al. 2020). This research gap underscores the need for a detailed investigation into the practical challenges hindering the widespread adoption of technologies like blockchain in sustainable fashion supply chains. Identifying and addressing these obstacles, including the technical requirements specific to different contexts and sharing successful strategies, is crucial for enhancing the technology's adoption and impact.

Sharma et al. (2021) suggest that future studies should broaden the scope to include other emerging technologies, such as the Internet of Things (IoT), machine learning, robotics, and artificial intelligence (AI). For instance, while IoT has seen application in warehouse management and smart clothing, its potential across other supply chain segments remains largely untapped. This calls for focused research on how IoT and other advanced technologies can be effectively integrated across different stages of the fashion supply chain to foster a more comprehensive digital transformation.

Furthermore, the integration of AI, robotics, and machine learning into the FTSC digitalization has been primarily evaluated for their general effectiveness, with less attention paid to their specific operational mechanisms and application processes. Future studies should further explore these technologies, particularly their contributions to the sustainable development of the FTSC, to broaden our understanding and application of digital transformation strategies in the sector.

12.5.2 Direction 2: Digital Marketing and Communication in the Fashion and Textile Supply Chain

Mola et al. (2017) advocate for future research to explore governance frameworks and supply chain reconfigurations across different sectors or countries to enhance the generalizability of findings. They suggest conducting quantitative research to understand the dynamics between governance choices, e-commerce capabilities, and knowledge transfer capacities. Gornostaeva (2023) also recommends investigating the digital commerce practices of emerging fashion designers in various global fashion capitals for comparative analysis and assessing the long-term effects of the COVID-19 pandemic on the adoption of digital commerce and the internal capabilities of fashion designers.

Szozda (2022) recommends further exploring the impacts of in-store technologies and their integration with omnichannel strategies in supply chains across different retail sectors beyond just the fashion industry and the case study of Poland. This approach would offer insights into how in-store technologies contribute to omnichannel adoption in varied contexts.

Additionally, Scuotto et al. (2020) highlight the need for future studies to broaden the sample of firms to include SMEs operating in different countries, emphasizing comparative analyses on the role of social media platforms in fostering ambidextrous innovation orientation within fashion companies. Such insights would reveal how social media influences innovation in the fashion industry across different national contexts, providing valuable perspectives on global digital commerce practices and innovation strategies.

12.5.3 Direction 3: Addressing Challenges and Leveraging Opportunities Post COVID-19, Towards a Sustainable Future

The pandemic accelerated the transition to online purchasing and usage of digital platforms, leading to an increase in digitalization and e-commerce (Acquila-Natale et al. 2022). This transition highlights the importance of additional funding in e-commerce infrastructure, including user-friendly interfaces, enhanced virtual try-on experiences, and seamless omnichannel integration to offer customers a unified buying experience (Acquila-Natale et al. 2022).

In addition, the pandemic emphasized the role of collaboration and partnerships in driving innovation and resilience within the industry ecosystem (Rao et al. 2021). In the future, it may be possible to enhance collaboration among brands, suppliers, and technology providers to co-create sustainable solutions, share resources, and collaboratively manage risks (Rao et al. 2021).

Advanced manufacturing technologies present another promising area for development, potentially enhancing productivity, adaptability, and personalization in the manufacturing process (Di Maria et al. 2023). As such, allocating resources toward research and development is also crucial for fostering future innovation and maintaining a competitive advantage in the market (Wulff 2022).

Most authors agree that sustainability is a promising future research direction despite being in its early stage because it contributes to value creation (Pal 2016; Howard et al. 2022). Future research could further explore the application of digital technologies towards sustainable supply chains (Pal 2016; Kazancoglu et al. 2023; Hmamed 2023) or assess the effectiveness of technology applications on the circular economy (Wagner and Kabalska 2023). Additionally, a systematic review of the business models and implementation of the circular economy is necessary for a holistic understanding of the theme (Howard et al. 2022).

12.5.4 Direction 4: Evolving Business and Supply Chain Models

The evolution of business and supply chain models covers a broad spectrum, including the upstream and downstream of the supply chain. It also addresses some of the most critical concerns of supply chain management: lead time (i.e., implications on inventory management, supply network configuration, etc.) and sustainability.

The adoption and integration of digital technology have created multiple models within the fashion and textile industry, such as drop-shipping, on-demand production, direct-to-consumer, and subscription service models (Wen et al. 2019). Notable, on-demand and direct-to-consumer models have been examined multiple times in the context of disruptor models. On the one hand, disruptive technologies have given rise to startups (Jin and Shin 2020). On the other hand, there is a distinction between digitally new-born companies and established firms, suggesting the need for further research on how established firms can adapt to new business models through digital technologies (Casciani et al. 2022a, b).

The research on other models, namely the cross-border reverse logistics model and the resilient supply chain model, remains limited. The resilience of the supply chain is a prominent issue, especially in developing countries where additional capabilities, if needed, should be built quickly at lower costs (Irfan et al. 2022).

12.6 Conclusion

This chapter explored the transformative impact of digital technologies, including digital marketing, on the fashion and textile supply chains. Through a review of relevant literature, we identified four main themes that underscore the evolution within the industry: digital transformation, sustainable supply chain practices, resilience in the post Covid-19 pandemic, and innovative business and supply chain models.

Our findings highlight how digital technologies revolutionize supply chain operations by enhancing transparency, efficiency, and responsiveness. In addition, digital marketing helps to align customer demand with supply chain innovations and strengthen customer engagement. As such, digital transformation drives long-term sustainability and resilience in the fashion and textile sector. Potential future research directions are identified in light of these findings.

References

Abbate S, Centobelli P, Cerchione R (2023) From fast to slow: an exploratory analysis of circular business models in the Italian apparel industry. Int J Prod Econ 260:108824

Acquila-Natale E, Chaparro-Peláez J, Del-Río-Carazo L, Cuenca-Enrique C (2022) Do or die? The effects of COVID-19 on channel integration and digital transformation of large clothing and apparel retailers in Spain. J Theor Appl Electron Commer Res 17(2):439–457

Agrawal TK, Kumar V, Pal R, Wang L, Chen Y (2021) Blockchain-based framework for supply chain traceability: A case example of textile and clothing industry. Comput Indus Eng 154:107130

Ajgaonkar M (2022) The "d'you" story: gearing the startup during the pandemic. Emerald Emerg Markets Case Stud 12(2):1–25

Akram SV, Malik PK, Singh R, Gehlot A, Juyal A, Ghafoor KZ, Shrestha S (2022) Implementation of digitalized technologies for fashion industry 4.0: opportunities and challenges. Scientific Programming

Arribas V, Alfaro JA (2018) 3D technology in fashion: from concept to consumer. J Fashion Market Manage 22(2):240–251

Bharadwaj A, El Sawy OA, Pavlou PA, Venkatraman NV (2013) Digital business strategy: toward a next generation of insights. MIS Quart 471–482

Casciani D, Chkanikova O, Pal R (2022) Exploring the nature of digital transformation in the fashion industry: opportunities for supply chains, business models, and sustainability-oriented innovations. Sustain Sci Pract Policy 18(1):773–795

Casciani D, Chkanikova O, Pal R (2022) Exploring the nature of digital transformation in the fashion industry: opportunities for supply chains, business models, and sustainability-oriented innovations. Sustain Sci Pract Policy 18(1):773–795

Castañeda-Navarrete J, Hauge J, López-Gómez C (2021) COVID-19's impacts on global value chains, as seen in the apparel industry. Dev Policy Rev 39(6):953–970

Clarke V, Braun V (2017) Thematic analysis. J Positive Psychol 12(3):297–298

Denyer D, Tranfield D (2009) Producing a systematic review

Di Maria E, Bettiol M, Capestro M (2023) How Italian fashion brands beat COVID-19: manufacturing, sustainability, and digitalization. Sustainability 15(2):1038

Fitzgerald M, Kruschwitz N, Bonnet D, Welch M (2014) Embracing digital technology: a new strategic imperative. MIT Sloan Manage Rev 55(2):1

Garzoni A, De Turi I, Secundo G, Del Vecchio P (2020) Fostering digital transformation of SMEs: a four levels approach. Manage Decis 58(8):1543–1562

Gornostaeva G (2023) The development of digital commerce in the fashion industry: The typology of emerging designers in London. Technol Forecast Social Change 186:122122

Gubbi J, Buyya R, Marusic S, Palaniswami M (2013) Internet of Things (IoT): a vision, architectural elements, and future directions. Future Gen Comput Syst 29(7):1645–1660

Harper S, Pal R (2022) Small-series supply network configuration priorities and challenges in the EU textile and apparel industry. J Fashion Market Manage

Heim H (2022) Digital fashion revolutions: supply chain transparency, digitalization and the non-disclosure paradox. Fashion Pract 14(3):329–351

Heim H, Hopper C (2022) Dress code: the digital transformation of the circular fashion supply chain. Int J Fashion Des Technol Educ 15(2):233–244

Hmamed H, Cherrafi A, Benghabrit A, Tiwari S, Sharma P (2023) The adoption of I4.0 technologies for a sustainable and circular supply chain: an industry-based SEM analysis from the textile sector. Bus Strat Environ 1–20

Howard M, Böhm S, Eatherley D (2022) Systems resilience and SME multilevel challenges: a place-based conceptualization of the circular economy. J Bus Res 145:757–768

Huynh PH (2021) Enabling circular business models in the fashion industry: the role of digital innovation. Int J Prod Perform Manage 71(3):870–895

Iansiti M, Lakhani KR (2017) The truth about blockchain. Harvard Bus Rev 95(1):118–127

Irfan I, Muhammad Saleem Ullah KS, Khurshid F, Chan FTS (2022) Toward a resilient supply chain model: critical role of knowledge management and dynamic capabilities. Indus Manage Data Syst 122(5):1153–1182

Jin BE, Shin DC (2020) Changing the game to compete: innovations in the fashion retail industry from the disruptive business model. Bus Horiz 63(3):301–311

Jocevski M, Arvidsson N, Miragliotta G, Ghezzi A, Mangiaracina R (2019) Transitions towards omni-channel retailing strategies: a business model perspective. Int J Retail Distrib Manage 47(2):78–93

Kanat S, Atilgan T (2022) Effects of Covid-19 pandemic on supply chain management in the clothing sector and possible solutions. Fibres Text Eastern Europe 30(2):8–16

Kazancoglu Y, Mangla SK, Berberoglu Y, Lafci C, Madaan J (2023) Towards industry 5.0 challenges for the textile and apparel supply chain for the smart, sustainable, and collaborative industry in emerging economies. Inf Syst Front 1–16

Khan MG, Huda NU, Zaman UKU (2022) Smart warehouse management system: architecture, real-time implementation and prototype design. Machines 10(2):150

LeMay S, Helms MM, Kimball B, McMahon D (2017) Supply chain manage: the elusive concept and definition. Int J Logist Manage 28(4):1425–1453

Lopez G, Galimova T, Fasihi M, Bogdanov D, Breyer C (2023) Towards defossilised steel: supply chain options for a green European steel industry. Energy 273:127236

Manupati VK, Schoenherr T, Ramkumar M, Wagner SM, Pabba SK, Inder Raj Singh R (2020) A blockchain-based approach for a multi-echelon sustainable supply chain. Int J Prod Res 58(7):2222–2241

Mentzer JT, DeWitt W, Keebler JS, Min S, Nix NW, Smith CD, Zacharia ZG (2001) Defining supply chain management. J Bus Logist 22(2):1–25

Mola L, Russo I, Giangreco A, Rossignoli C (2017) Who knows what? Reconfiguring the governance and the capabilities of the supply chain between physical and digital processes in the fashion industry. Prod Plan Control 28(16):1284–1297

Munizu M, Alam S, Pono M, Riyadi S (2024) Do digital marketing, integrated supply chain, and innovation capability affect competitiveness, and creative industry performance? Int J Data Netw Sci 8(2):1025–1034

Oguntegbe KF, Di Paola N, Vona R (2023) Communicating responsible management and the role of blockchain technology: social media analytics for the luxury fashion supply chain. TQM J 35(2):446–469

Ornati M, Kalbaska N (2022) Looking for haptics. Touch digitalization business strategies in luxury and fashion during COVID-19 and beyond. Digital Bus 2(2):100035

Ott DL, Michailova S (2018) Cultural intelligence: a review and new research avenues. Int J Manage Rev 20(1):99–119

Pal R (2016) Extended responsibility through servitization in PSS: an exploratory study of used-clothing sector. J Fashion Market Manage 20(4):453–470

Piccinini E, Gregory RW, Kolbe LM (2015) Changes in the producer-consumer relationship-towards digital transformation. Changes 3(4):1634–1648

Plé L, Yacoub G (2024) Shein: the (not so?) shining growth of ultra-fast fashion. Neilson Journals Publishing

Prajapati D, Chan FT, Chelladurai H, Lakshay L, Pratap S (2022) An internet of things embedded sustainable supply chain management of B2B E-commerce. Sustainability 14(9):5066

Rao PHN, Vihari NS, Jabeen SS (2021) Reimagining the fashion retail industry through the implications of COVID-19 in the Gulf cooperation council (GCC) countries. FIIB Bus Rev 10(4):327–338

Russo I, Mola L, Giangreco A (2023) Digitalisation for survival: managing resources in digitalizing operations and processes in the fashion industry. Prod Plan Control 1–19

Sandvik IM, Stubbs W (2019) Circular fashion supply chain through textile-to-textile recycling. J Fashion Market Manage 23(3):366–381

Scuotto V, Arrigo E, Candelo E, Nicotra M (2020) Ambidextrous innovation orientation effected by the digital transformation: a quantitative research on fashion SMEs. Bus Process Manage J 26(5):1121–1140

Seuring S, Müller M, Westhaus M, Morana R (2005) Conducting a literature review—the example of sustainability in supply chains. In: Research methodologies in supply chain management: in Collaboration with Magnus Westhaus, pp 91–106

Shahadat MH, Chowdhury AHMY, Nathan RJ, Fekete-Farkas M (2023) Digital technologies for firms' competitive advantage and improved supply chain performance. J Risk Finan Manage 16(2):94
Sharma S, Koehl L, Bruniaux P, Zeng X, Wang Z (2021) Development of an intelligent data-driven system to recommend personalized fashion design solutions. Sensors 21(12):4239
Špiler M, Gostimirović L, Milosević D, Beslać M, Miškić M, Jevtić B (2023) Investments in digital technology advances in textiles. Indus Text 74(1):90–97
Sun L, Zhao L (2018) Technology disruptions: exploring the changing roles of designers, makers, and users in the fashion industry. Int J Fashion Des Technol Educ 11(3):362–374
Szozda N (2022) Omnichannel as a driver of digitalization: evidence from the emerging market in the fashion industry. J Fashion Market Manage (ahead-of-print)
Vial G (2019) Understanding digital transformation: a review and a research agenda. J Strat Inform Syst 28(2):118–144
Wagner R, Kabalska A (2023) Sustainable value in the fashion industry: a case study of value construction/destruction using digital twins. Sustain Dev 31(3):1652–1667
Wahab SN, Tan A, Roche O (2023) Comparison of cross-border reverse logistics of a fast fashion brand in China. Oper Supply Chain Manage 16(1):25–35
Wang Y, Han JH, Beynon-Davies P (2019) Understanding blockchain technology for future supply chains: a systematic literature review and research agenda. Supply Chain Manage 24(1):62–84
Wen X, Choi TM, Chung SH (2019) Fashion retail supply chain management: a review of operational models. Int J Prod Econ 207:34–55
Westerman G, Calméjane C, Bonnet D, Ferraris P, McAfee A (2011) Digital transformation: a roadmap for billion-dollar organizations. MIT Center Dig Bus Capgemini Consult 1:1–68
Wu K-J, Tseng M-L, Yang W-H, Ali MH, Chen X (2023) Reshaping sustainable value chain model under post pandemic disruptions: a fast fashion supply chain analysis. Int J Prod Econ 255:108704
Wulff G (2022) Changes in market organisation due to exogenous shocks—the case of the transformation of the Swedish fashion industry caused by the COVID-19 pandemic. Int Rev Retail Distrib Consum Res 33(3):276–299
Zhang C, Gong T (2023) The brand strategy and cross-border promotion of Han Chinese clothing under the digital economy. Electron Commerce Res 23(1):257–277

Chapter 13
Conclusions, Challenges, and Future Directions of Advanced Technologies in Fashion Supply Chain

Huy Truong Quang, Rajkishore Nayak, and Rudrajeet Pal

Abstract Application of Industry 4.0 (I4.0) in fashion and textile industries helps to produce high quality products at a cheaper price. Further, the use of digital technologies covered under I4.0 in fashion and textiles has several benefits for the planet and people while making profit. Digital technologies can be helpful to achieve the triple bottom line of sustainability, which relates to the planet, people, and profit. The implementation of digital technologies can help to improve the efficiency and productivity, improve the quality of the products, and reduce process and material waste. However, there are several downsides of using digital technologies, which needs to be addressed to make the technology adoption popular among the businesses. This chapter will discuss the major challenges of using digital technologies, which include high initial investment cost, high running and maintenance cost. The lack of skilled staff and infrastructure to accommodate the digital technologies during operation is another major challenge. There are other issues relating to the cybersecurity, failure of the IT system, compatibility issues, and lack of digital culture in many organisations. Various ethical issues, such as data privacy, lack of legal policies, and legal issues, are also some of the challenges that need to be overcome for making the digital technology successful in fashion and textile industries. This chapter also involves some of the findings of a survey conducted with Vietnamese fashion manufacturing industries. The survey revealed that digital technologies can

H. T. Quang (✉)
The Business School, RMIT University, Ho Chi Minh City, Vietnam
e-mail: huytruong.quang@rmit.edu.vn

R. Nayak
School of Communication and Design, RMIT University, Ho Chi Minh City, Vietnam
e-mail: rajkishore.nayak@rmit.edu.vn

R. Pal
Swedish School of Textiles, University of Borås, Borås, Sweden

Department of Industrial Engineering and Management, University of Gävle, Gävle, Sweden

R. Pal
e-mail: rudrajeet.pal@hb.se

R. Nayak et al. (eds.), *Use of Digital and Advanced Technologies in the Fashion Supply Chain*, Springer Series in Fashion Business,
https://doi.org/10.1007/978-981-97-7528-6_13

produce quality products at cheaper price; however, they can also lead to elimination of local craftsmanship in addition to job losses.

Keywords Ethical issues · High cost · Cybersecurity · Compatibility · System failure · Skilled workforce

13.1 Introduction

Technology integration in garment industry has the prospects of bringing about positive outcomes, such as increased efficiency, greater transparency, and more data-driven decisions. However, this transformation is filled with obstacles that can impede the implementation. Firstly, the initial cost of acquisition might be prohibitive, particularly for small and medium-sized enterprises (SMEs). The increased expenses associated with operation and upkeep place further pressure on available resources, necessitating a healthy financial condition (Dal Forno et al. 2023). The fast rate of technological progress also necessitates a skilled workforce capable of operating advanced systems and resolving problems (Pal and Jayarathne 2022). Nevertheless, there is frequently a notable disparity in the accessibility of proficient personnel, worsened by a deficiency of comprehensive training initiatives centred on digital proficiencies (Fromhold-Eisebith et al. 2021). Moreover, the growing interconnectedness and flow of data increase the likelihood of cyberattacks, which can result in unauthorised access to data and disruptions to operations (Manglani et al. 2019).

The absence of a strong and reliable IT infrastructure, together with compatibility problems between new and current systems, can lead to failures that undermine reliability (Küsters et al. 2017). Finally, ethical issues arise as one of the key concerns. The digital transformation of supply chains is complicated by contractual uncertainty, ethical considerations over data usage, ambiguous policies, and legal challenges (Akhtar et al. 2022). There have been several research publications focusing on the use of digital technologies in fashion and textiles. However, the number of publications summarising the challenges and ethical issues while using digital technologies is limited. Therefore, this chapter thoroughly examines the challenges, analysing each issue and providing valuable insights into ethical concerns around such challenges before setting out the future directions of applying advanced technologies in fashion supply chain. The data for this chapter are collected both from primary and secondary resources. The primary data collection involves Vietnamese industries using advanced technologies. Similarly, the secondary data were collected from database such as Google Scholar, EBSCOhost, and Science Direct. This chapter will provide additional knowledge to the industries involved in the use of advances technologies.

13.2 Challenges of Using Digital Technologies

There are several challenges of using digital technologies, which can be related to installation cost, technical knowledge, maintenance cost, cybersecurity, and lack of digital culture. The following section summarises the challenges of using digital technologies in fashion and textiles.

13.2.1 High Investment Cost

The fashion and textile industry has significant obstacles in implementing cutting-edge digital technologies owing to cost constraints. Incorporating advanced technologies like augmented reality (AR) and virtual reality (VR) necessitates a substantial initial financial investment (Davila Delgado et al. 2020). Nevertheless, these technologies have enormous promise. AR/VR can create immersive design experiences, allowing customers to virtually "try on" clothes, while integration with the Metaverse offers exciting possibilities for enhanced brand engagement (Madhu 2024). These expenses include the expenditures related to acquiring and upkeeping computer equipment, software programs, and the establishment of essential infrastructure (Kumari and Polke 2019). Using artificial intelligence (AI) for tasks like improving material science, predicting demand, or creating customer service chatbots requires a significant amount of computer resources and skill in the data science (Górriz et al. 2020). Moreover, the integration of additional digital technologies presents an additional degree of financial constraints.

The use of radio frequency identification (RFID) technology improves the supervision of the supply chain (Kgobe and Ozor 2021), while the application of big data analytics provides an important understanding of customer behaviour (Holmlund et al. 2020). Nevertheless, both need advanced technology and software systems, which necessitate a significant initial cost commitment. Deploying robotic systems for automated production, employing machine learning techniques for design optimisation, and embracing computer-aided design (CAD) and computer-aided manufacturing (CAM) technologies all need a substantial upfront investment (Nagy et al. 2023). Despite its cost-effectiveness and environmental friendliness, 3D printing necessitates a significant initial investment in terms of equipment and resources (Thakar et al. 2022). Integrating blockchain technology into supply chain transparency requires the integration of this technology with current information systems, which involves allocating additional resources (Habib et al. 2022). The significant upfront expenses pose an especially difficult barrier for smaller businesses and conventional producers. These companies could be reluctant to justify the expenditure unless there are clearly measurable and advantageous returns on investment.

13.2.2 High Running and Maintenance Cost

The overwhelming allure of cutting-edge digital technology in the fashion and textile industries is impeded by the continuing expenses associated with their operation. AR/VR and Metaverse systems need regular upgrades and significant bandwidth, leading to ongoing costs for software maintenance and data use (Lee et al. 2021). Moreover, the optimisation and retraining of Chatbots and AI systems are crucial for guaranteeing their ongoing triumph, necessitating a consistent investment in data scientists and engineers (Sharma et al. 2022). RFID technology, although advantageous for inventory management, requires the maintenance of scanning equipment and software, as well as periodic tag replacement (Want 2022). In addition, big data analytics systems need ongoing data cleansing and infrastructure maintenance, which in turn requires specialised IT people and strong data centres (Pothukuchi et al. 2021).

Robotics and automation systems also require routine servicing and parts replacement, escalating operational costs (Mia and Shuford 2024). The sustained efficacy of ML (machine learning) models hinges on their continual recalibration with new data streams. This technique necessitates substantial computing resources and the specialist knowledge of data scientists to guarantee the precision and dependability of the model (Tariq et al. 2021). Furthermore, CAD and CAM systems need frequent software updates and the availability of proficient personnel who can promptly address any potential problems (Cheng et al. 2023). Deploying IoT (Internet of Things) devices requires ongoing surveillance and regular implementation of security updates to address any potential weaknesses (Tawalbeh et al. 2020). Furthermore, the use of 3D printing machinery requires meticulous adherence to established calibration protocols and the continuous replenishment of resources, both of which incur substantial costs and need a considerable workforce (Pramanik et al. 2020). Implementing blockchain technology requires ongoing maintenance of decentralised networks to maintain security and system performance, leading to substantial operational costs (Habib et al. 2022). The aggregation of these expenses might particularly hinder SMEs, obstructing the overall assimilation of these advanced technologies in the fashion and textile industry.

13.2.3 Lack of Skilled Staff

A major challenge to training competent workers is the widespread use of high-tech digital tools in the textile and clothing industries. Professional knowledge in areas like 3D modelling, immersive environment design, and user experience optimisation is now necessary for users to successfully engage with these new technologies like the Metaverse and AR/VR (Lee et al. 2021). These abilities are generally not covered in conventional fashion courses. The successful implementation and long-term maintenance of chatbots and intelligent systems necessitates a profound understanding and proficiency in natural language processing, machine learning, and data analytics, thereby demanding a significant level of technical expertise (Izadi and Forouzanfar 2024). Efficient inventory control with RFID devices requires comprehension of hardware and software integration (Nayak et al. 2015).

The field of big data analytics and machine learning requires individuals to possess a specialised skill set that includes statistical analysis, data mining, and algorithm creation. These abilities are essential for obtaining practical and useful insights from large datasets (Halwani et al. 2022). Expertise in mechatronics, programming, and systems engineering is necessary for the successful incorporation of automated and robotic systems into manufacturing processes. Furthermore, using CAD and CAM systems effectively requires expert knowledge of specialist software as well as a thorough understanding of digital design and production processes (Mikhalev and Yanyushkin 2020). The successful establishment of IoT device connectivity and the implementation of robust data protection measures require a high level of proficiency in sensor technology, network configuration, and cybersecurity (Altulaihan et al. 2022).

Finally, 3D printing requires specialised skills in additive manufacturing processes and material science (Haleem and Javaid 2020). Proficiency in cryptographic concepts and decentralised systems is necessary to comprehend blockchain technology (Alam 2022). The industry has traditionally depended on skilled artisans and designers. However, there is currently a scarcity of individuals who possess the requisite technical proficiency to proficiently oversee and leverage the complex digital technology employed in the domain (Alam 2022). Obtaining the necessary advanced skills to utilise these technologies in the fashion and textile industry may present difficulties in terms of both complexity and expense. This is a substantial obstacle for several organisations, particularly SMEs, to fully exploit the potential benefits provided by these technologies.

13.2.4 Cybersecurity Issues

The interconnected digital systems generate vast amounts of customer information, design knowledge, and operational details. This wealth of data, while instrumental for innovation and efficiency, presents a growing challenge—its vulnerability to cyberattacks (Neumeyer et al. 2020). Malicious actors, often referred to as hackers, are increasingly drawn to these interconnected systems. Their motivations can range from intellectual property theft, aimed at stealing valuable design knowledge, to operational disruption, which could cripple entire production chains. Perhaps the most concerning threat lies in the potential for breaches of confidential consumer data (Roberts 2023). The Metaverse and AR/VR encounters give rise to apprehensions over data privacy and user safety inside these simulated realms (Dwivedi et al. 2023).

Technological advancements in the fashion and textile sector, like CAD, software and cloud-based storage, have revolutionised design processes and production. However, these advancements are only as secure as their implementation. Lax access controls and inadequate encryption can leave even the most sophisticated technology exposed, creating vulnerabilities for data breaches (Dal Forno et al. 2023). The ever-expanding IoT, which seamlessly connects devices throughout the supply chain, offers immense operational efficiency. However, this interconnectedness also creates new attack vectors (Bhushan et al. 2021). Robust security frameworks are crucial to prevent unauthorised access and data interception. While blockchain technology promises a more open and secure supply network, its effectiveness hinges on strong cryptographic measures. These measures deter fraudulent activities like counterfeit goods entering the market (Kurpjuweit et al. 2021). A critical knowledge gap and the lack of robust security practices within the industry leave companies susceptible to costly data breaches and reputational damage. These cybersecurity challenges underline the need for the fashion and textile sector to implement sophisticated protective measures alongside continuous monitoring.

13.2.5 Lack of Infrastructure (IT Facilities)

A resilient and reliable IT infrastructure is crucial for maximising the potential of technologies like AI, big data analytics, and the IoT. These technologies generate vast amounts of data, requiring robust computing capability and secure storage alternatives (Lanza et al. 2022). Furthermore, the implementation of RFID tags for supply chain monitoring or the deployment of chatbots with natural language processing requires a network infrastructure that is both dependable and capable of handling increased demands (Hassija et al. 2020). Obsolete computer systems may hinder the functionality of even widely used technologies like CAD and CAM (Larshin et al. 2021).

The emerging Metaverse and fascinating AR/VR experiences offer a future characterised by engaging and interactive encounters. Nevertheless, these technological progressions rely heavily on a strong digital framework, namely fast internet connection and potent graphics processing units (GPUs) (Huynh-The et al. 2023). Furthermore, the IoT and blockchain technologies both largely depend on strong IT infrastructure to enable networked devices and provide safe and transparent transactions (Da Xu et al. 2021). In addition, advancements such as 3D printing need significant digital and physical resources (Iftekar et al. 2023). For some organisations, particularly smaller entities, the substantial expense of modernising or completely overhauling their IT infrastructure is a considerable obstacle. The financial obstacle to entering the market may worsen the current disparity in access to digital resources, further extending the gap between well-funded firms and others who are striving to stay up (Arewa 2022).

13.2.6 Compatibility Issues

The fashion and textile industries have major compatibility challenges when integrating new digital technology, which impedes smooth operations. Emerging technologies with the capacity to enhance design and captivate consumers encompass the Metaverse as well as AR/VR. Nevertheless, the successful execution of these solutions frequently requires the utilisation of specialised hardware and software, which might not integrate seamlessly with the existing systems (Huynh-The et al. 2023). AI-driven chatbots are transforming customer service and customisation. Nevertheless, it is essential to thoroughly evaluate their compatibility with the current infrastructure (Ghosh et al. 2024). The utilisation of RFID technology presents a compelling resolution for the management of inventory, particularly when it can be seamlessly integrated with enterprise resource planning (ERP) systems. However, difficulties occur because of compatibility concerns (Nayak 2019). The disparities between RFID and current databases or customer relationship management (CRM) systems might result in data inaccuracies and impede operational effectiveness (Marín Díaz et al. 2021).

Big data analytics, which are crucial for making strategic decisions, need the alignment of many data sources, which is frequently impeded by differences in data formats and standards (Jha et al. 2020). Robotics and automation, which are essential for CAD and CAM processes, need coordinated communication between mechanical and software components. Nevertheless, this task may provide challenges owing to the absence of established methods (Campi et al. 2022). The IoT requires a unified network structure to connect various devices. However, the presence of diverse communication protocols might hinder the capacity of devices to operate together (Bansal and Kumar 2020). 3D printing technology requires compatible design and production software (Friedrich et al. 2022), while blockchain technology for secure supply chains has to be integrated with pre-existing financial and logistical systems (Wecken 2021). These compatibility issues underscore the complexity of adopting advanced technologies in the fashion and textile industry, necessitating standardised frameworks and greater emphasis on interoperability to ensure cohesive and efficient technological integration (Wan et al. 2024).

13.2.7 Failure of the System

The fashion and textile industry has a unique challenge when using cutting-edge digital technology. While technologies like robotics, AI, big data analytics, and the IoT offer interesting possibilities, they may be complex systems that are prone to faults. These errors may result in substantial costs and interruptions across all aspects of the production process. For example, coding errors in AI-powered design tools could lead to nonsensical or unusable designs (Liao et al. 2023). Similarly, the malfunctioning of a robotic arm within a production line has the capacity to cause disruptions and halt the manufacturing process. Likewise, unfinished projects like the Metaverse and AR/VR might encounter technological glitches that break user immersion and perhaps make them queasy or lightheaded (Creed et al. 2024). Furthermore, if a single point of failure happens, IoT networks—which include a large number of linked devices—may be susceptible to cascade failures (Horak et al. 2021).

The consequences of system failure can range from production delays and financial losses to reputational damage if customer data is compromised in a malfunctioning chatbot or RFID-based tracking system (Hassija et al. 2020). Robotics and automation in CAD and CAM processes depend on the seamless operation of both software and hardware; any malfunction can halt production, leading to costly downtime (Sahoo and Lo 2022). 3D printing technology, reliant on precise coordination, can produce defective prototypes if any component fails (Arefin et al. 2021). Blockchain systems, used for secure supply chains, are not immune to cyberattacks or software bugs, jeopardising transaction integrity (Agarwal et al. 2022).

13.2.8 Lack of Digital Culture

The fashion and textile industry, with its rich history rooted in physical craftsmanship, is facing a fascinating hurdle as it attempts to integrate modern digital tools. This challenge stems from a gap in "digital fluency," a combination of awareness, skill, and enthusiasm for these technologies throughout the industry (Le and Pole 2023). Take, for example, the exciting potential of AR/VR to create immersive design experiences. Without a strong foundation in digital literacy, their effectiveness may be hampered (Alalwan et al. 2020). Similarly, the success of the Metaverse for virtual try-on sessions and digital fashion ownership hinges on two key factors: consumer openness to this new digital space and the industry's own ability to navigate it with expertise (Lee et al. 2021).

Implementing AI-powered chatbots for customer service or utilising RFID for supply chain management requires staff who can not only manage these technologies but also analyse the data they generate (Gande 2020). Moreover, using big data to predict trends or implement machine learning algorithms for efficient manufacturing processes requires a mindset change towards making decisions based on the data (Lăzăroiu et al. 2022). Insufficient utilisation of well-established technology such as CAD and CAM might occur when the workforce lacks proficiency in digital design processes (Cheng et al. 2023). The IoT, which is transforming connections on manufacturing floors, and 3D Printing, which allows for customised manufacture on demand, are other instances where a lack of digital culture might hinder the advancement (Jimeno-Morenilla et al. 2021). Implementing blockchain technology to achieve supply chain transparency requires both technical proficiency and a cultural transformation towards placing faith in decentralised systems (Varriale et al. 2021).

13.3 Ethical Issues

In addition to several challenges mentioned above, the use of digital technologies also associated with some ethical issues (Thomas 2017). Although digital technologies can assist to achieve the TBL (triple bottom line) of sustainability, they are associated with some ethical issues, which are discussed in the following section.

13.3.1 Privacy in Data Protection

The use of digital technologies can help in managing personal data relating to size and choices to improve customer experience. Analysis of a large-scale data can help the brands to develop new products and services as per the customer demand, which can increase brand's profitability. These data can also be used for accurate forecasting of fashion trends and consumer demand. However, there are a lot of challenges during storage, communication and usage of personal data of customers (Akram et al. 2022). In the past, there were incidents of leakage of personal data which had led to serious consequences. It is essential to protect the confidential information of customers, maintain private rights and security while using personal data. Breach of privacy in data protection creates tensions among consumers, manufacturers, retailers and regulators.

13.3.2 Ethical Issues Relating to Job Losses

Digital technologies and automation can do the jobs faster and more accurately. Replacing labour-intensive jobs with automation and advanced technologies may lead to job-losses as technologies can perform multiple jobs (Parschau and Hauge, 2020). For example, one semi-automatic machine to attach the collar of a shirt can replace the work done by 3–4 people. To avoid this, the technology providers and the companies installing digital technologies should ensure to take care of the people who lose their jobs. Government should also ensure that the regulations instruct the companies to take care of the employees. On the other hand, there are some job creations to program and operate these machines, which claim more skillset.

13.3.3 Inequality and Digital Division

Digital technology applications in fashion and textiles can lead to inequalities in the workplace. The technology applications can also create digital division. For example, the people who are digitally savvy will be using the technologies and feel advantageous; on the other hand, employees with limited access to technology will feel isolated and disadvantageous (Casciani et al. 2022). Furthermore, digitally savvy employees will be getting higher salary and career growth opportunities. Hence, for a sustainable company, these points can raise ethical concerns as the digital technology creates division among the employees. It is the responsibility of the brands and manufactures of fashion to provide equal digital opportunities to all the employees irrespective of their culture and socioeconomic status.

13.3.4 Decision Uncertainties

The integration of digital technologies leads to the decision-making process (based on algorithms) to be dependent on the technologies (Nouinou et al. 2023). The digital technologies depend on all the input parameters to make right decisions. Missing a data during decision making process can lead to inaccurate decision making. The technology-based decision-making processes may not be empathetic and unable to see the nuances that can be looked by human-based decision making. It may not be possible to take a decision based on transparency and accountability.

13.3.5 Lack of Policies and Legal Issues

The manufacturing of fashion and textiles are mainly located in developing countries. Some manufacturers and retail businesses take the advantages of lack of policies in these countries to reduce the manufacturing cost. In some instances, although the policies exist, they are not practiced well. Brands not following the existing regulations lead to legal issues. Until now, there are no established policies focusing on the use of digital technologies in fashion and textile manufacturing. However, it should be the strategy of fashion businesses to be ethical while implementing digital technologies. Many popular global fashion brands are following ethical practises into their production, supply chain, and retail management. Other should follow them to make digital technologies successful in fashion and textile manufacturing.

13.3.6 Other Challenges

There can be other challenges associated with the use of advance technologies such as blockchain-based cryptocurrencies can lead to illegal financial transactions. Some of the immediate impacts include money laundering, illegal pornography, black markets for drugs, and firearms (Akram et al. 2022). The application of digital technologies is associated with potential misuse of the technology by individuals or the organisations. The misuse of AI has been reported in different areas in recent times. Regulations should be developed to take care of the society being not harmed by digital technologies. Newly installed digital technologies are superseded by advanced technologies after few years. This leads to the creation of large quantities of e-wastes, which creates environmental impacts.

13.4 Survey Findings

Vietnam is one of the major exporters of fashion and textiles in the global marketplace. This sector houses more than 6000 fashion and textile industries that employees about 3 million people (Nayak et al. 2019a, b). The export revenue from this sector contributes 15% of the total export from Vietnam, which largely contribute towards the GDP of Vietnam. The government is targeting to achieve the export value of $60-$80 billion USD by the year 2030 and create about 1 million new jobs. In addition to the major destination of the US, Vietnam is also gaining popularity in Asia and Africa. Due to increased importance of Vietnam in the global fashion and textile sector, we attempted to include the findings of a survey involving Vietnamese fashion and textile industries.

A qualitative survey was conducted involving three SMEs and three large enterprises (LE) in Vietnam. The industries were selected based on their ownership status and the use of at least one digital technology in the supply chain process. Further, these industries were operating for at least five years in Vietnam. As per RMIT's ethical guidelines name of the industries is not disclosed, but the findings are discussed in this section. Open-ended questions were asked to the owners or managers of these companies to collect their views on the use of digital technologies in fashion and textiles. The industries were coded as: SME1, SME2 and SME3; and LE1, LE2 and LE3; to anonymise their identity. The survey findings were included in this chapter to provide broader perspective and status on the use of digital technologies.

13.4.1 Benefits of Digital Technology

The survey findings revealed that the SMEs and LEs are aware of the benefits of the digital technology. They understood the use of various technologies support to improve the quality of the products (Nayak et al. 2024). The recent trend in manufacturing fashion and textiles is to implement digital technologies to meet the customer's demand. Various other manufacturing sectors have already implemented new technologies such as RFID, AR/VR, artificial intelligence, blockchain and IoT. However, these technologies are still at their infancy in fashion and textile sector (Nayak 2019). Availability of cheap labour, low price of fashion items, and lack of strict regulations are some of the factors that prevent the implementation of digital technologies (Nayak 2020). It was found that several LEs are at forerun of implementing digital technologies as per their strategic plans. Several large manufactures in developing countries have implemented digital technologies as per the requirements from global fashion brands. However, the SMEs are not that much advanced in applying digital technologies. They face several challenges while adopting digital technologies, which can be related to high cost, technical knowledge, and low price of the products in the local marketplace (Nayak et al. 2019b). These findings are explained in the quotes below.

Quote 1 (LE 2): "*All our buyers want new digital manufacturing technologies to be used in entire operational stages of manufacturing. Hence, we have to build our infrastructure with the advanced technologies. Some of the major technologies that we use recently is RFID and ERP. RFID technology supports for easy manufacturing of products and components as the information flow is more accurate. ERP integrates the information from several departments and presents as a package whenever needed. Although these new technologies are expensive, they pay-off due to the benefits that we receive in terms of quality and productivity*".

Quote 2 (SME 3): "*We understand that advanced technology is better for good quality of garments. We can create more intricate designs using the technology like CAD. However, the investment cost of these technologies is very high. Also, the infrastructure development cost (such as laptops, systems etc.) cost us a lot more money. We are small companies with very low turnover and our people can manage it without technologies. We have no skilled people to take care and operate these technologies. May be in the future we can think to invest in these technologies when our revenue increases*".

13.4.2 Drawbacks of Digital Technology

The survey findings also brought forward some drawbacks of using digital technology. One of the major drawbacks that was agreed by both the LEs and SMEs is the loss of traditional skills due to digitisation. As the digital technologies can work much faster and produce better products at cheaper price compared to the traditional technologies, it creates challenges for the artisans who have the traditional skill of making crafted products. The rising labour cost and pressure from digitalisation is leading to the elimination of some crafts that was practiced in the family for long periods of time. The new generation are not willing to continue the family tradition as they struggle to get enough income. In addition to this, the LEs explained job loss as another challenge they need to deal with as digital technologies make redundancy of some employees. Hence, taking care of these employees is essential for ethical fashion manufacturing. On the other hand, LEs expressed that the local manufacturing facilities does not need to be that much advanced in applying technology as many consumers don't know the role of digital technology in the process of manufacturing. For the local market the stylish design of the product and cheap price is essential, and the technology application is immaterial. They focus more on designing stylish products with experienced designers and tailors. The findings are explained in Quote 3 and Quote 4.

Quote 3 (LE1): "*The application of digital technology has several advantages and some downsides as well. Digital technologies can perform the work much faster, which can help to keep the cost of products low. However, they are a major threat to the locals, who use traditional art and craft for making textiles. Due to rising labour cost, the product prices produced by manual operations is increasing. This makes difficult for the local communities to continue with their traditional work. In addition to these digital technologies also lead to job cuts ad the organisations should consider alternatives for the employees who lose their job*".

Quote 4 (SME 2): "*Our business is not worried about digital technology as customers are not aware of the use of digital technology. They want the products to be stylish and available to them at a cheaper price. We focus more on the design aspects of products by experienced designers and trained tailors rather than applying digital technology. Digital technology is a problem for the local craftmanship from where we source some of our products due to rising labour cost. It leads to termination of some crafts and job losses as well*".

13.5 Conclusions

The incorporation of digital technologies in garment manufacturing offers a multitude of prospects, but also entails substantial obstacles. Significant obstacles include considerable high costs associated with investment of digital technologies, and the cost associated with continuous running and maintenance of these technologies. Furthermore, the fashion sector is confronted with a shortage of skilled labour, demanding an improvement in technological expertise and digital proficiencies of employees, which are sometimes lacking in conventional fashion education. The use of digital technology becomes more challenging by cybersecurity issues, which result in a heightened susceptibility to cyberattacks and data leakages. There have been several instances of cyberattacks leading to leakage of personal information of consumers. The recent problem of Facebook users' data leakage due to cyberattack is one such example.

The absence of a strong and reliable IT infrastructure, as well as compatibility problems between new and current systems, hinder the smooth integration, resulting in operational delays. Specifically, complexity of digital systems results in system failures, which cause substantial costs and disruptions in production and supply chain processes. The industry's dependence on manual craftsmanship has led to a deficiency in digital literacy, impeding the efficient integration and use of cutting-edge technologies. The digital revolution of the sector is made more complex by ethical challenges such as contractual uncertainty, data privacy concerns, and the lack of defined laws. Consequently, to fully harness the benefits of digital technologies in improving efficiency, transparency, and innovation in the fashion and textile industries, it is essential to address these complex difficulties.

The findings of the survey conducted in Vietnamese fashion industries provide primary knowledge. It was found that the digital technologies play a major role for large fashion enterprises than the SMEs. Large fashion enterprises need to have higher speed of production and better quality of products, which is only possible using digital technologies. For SMEs it is important to have stylish products available to consumers at cheaper price. Hence, the use of digital technology is not a major issue for the SMEs. Both the SMEs and LEs agreed that the use of digital technologies is creating challenges for the local artisans to compete with the products from large industries, which is much cheaper. The recent generations are not willing to carry their tradition forward due to difficulties in selling these products at competitive price. Further, the use of digital technologies leads to job losses mainly in large enterprises, which is against the ethical practices of the LEs.

13.6 Future Directions

Garment manufacturing in many developing countries is still done manually using the traditional technologies. Although significant developments have transformed the other manufacturing sectors, the fashion and textile manufacturing are still done with manual operations in many developing countries. The integration of Industry 4.0 with digital technologies can transform the garment industries from labour-intensive processes to technology-integrated operations. For example, the use of RFID tags in manufacturing can store information about the size, component details, and steps to complete specific operations. By following these instructions, garments can be manufactured more accurately, which can facilitate higher productivity and improve the passing rate during quality assurance. A range of data analytics and techniques can be applied to investigate the possibility of device failure, which can be saved by the predictive maintenance approach. Predictive maintenance can save the breakdown of the machines, improve the productivity of the departments, and reduce idle time.

There has been tremendous growth in e-commerce in fashion and textiles, like the other sectors. More and more consumers are moving to online purchasing after the Covid-19 pandemic. Consumers' expectations from fashion brands are increasing, and they want hassle-free service in addition to getting advice on personal styling or choices. The fashion brands are using innovative technologies to provide a more personalised experience to the consumers. Advanced technologies are helping brands produce customised products for consumers, which are produced in a sustainable manner following ethical guidelines.

Virtual sampling is one of the major areas of improvement in fashion manufacturing using Industry 4.0. The traditional process of physical sample development by skilled patternmakers and tailors can be done using virtual reality technologies. Virtual garment prototypes can be created using 3D garment-making software, and then they can be rendered in different manikin forms. This can help to evaluate the fit and aesthetics of different garments without developing the real prototypes. The product techpacks can be shared by cloud computing with the buyer, and feedback can then be received instantly. This process can reduce the sampling time from several weeks to only a few days.

Consumers can use 'Virtual try-on' software that can generate their own 3D avatars and help them select the right design and style of the product before making the real purchase. Big data analysis can help to analyse the data set of consumers' choices for different fabric trends or styles while designing their products. Similarly, automated chatbots or virtual style assistants can help customers find their desired products much more easily without spending too much time. AI integration can give feedback to customers regarding their styling choices based on their purchase history. All these technologies facilitate customers to have a better shopping experience with their favourite brands, which improves customer relationship management (CRM).

Hence, it is clear from the above discussions that there are several advantages of using digital technologies in fashion and textile industries. This chapter have discussed some of the challenges of implementing digital technologies. The benefits achieved from digital technologies outweighs the drawbacks and challenges. Several fashion brands have already started using digital technologies in the entire supply chain process. It is now high time for others to make strategic plans to implement digital technologies for a better future in the global competitive marketplace.

References

Agarwal U, Rishiwal V, Tanwar S, Chaudhary R, Sharma G, Bokoro PN, Sharma R (2022) Blockchain technology for secure supply chain management: a comprehensive review. IEEE Access 10:85493–85517

Akhtar WH, Watanabe C, Tou Y, Neittaanmäki P (2022) A new perspective on the textile and apparel industry in the digital transformation era. Textiles 2:633–656

Akram SV, Malik PK, Singh R, Gehlot A, Juyal A, Ghafoor KZ, Shrestha S (2022) Implementation of digitalized technologies for fashion industry 4.0: opportunities and challenges. Sci Program 2022(1):7523246

Alalwan N, Cheng L, Al-Samarraie H, Yousef R, Alzahrani AI, Sarsam SM (2020) Challenges and prospects of virtual reality and augmented reality utilization among primary school teachers: a developing country perspective. Stud Educ Eval 66:100876

Alam A (2022) Platform utilising blockchain technology for eLearning and online education for open sharing of academic proficiency and progress records. In: Smart data intelligence: proceedings of ICSMDI 2022. Springer, pp 307–320

Altulaihan E, Almaiah MA, Aljughaiman A (2022) Cybersecurity threats, countermeasures and mitigation techniques on the IoT: future research directions. Electronics 11:3330

Arefin AM, Khatri NR, Kulkarni N, Egan PF (2021) Polymer 3D printing review: materials, process, and design strategies for medical applications. Polymers 13:1499

Arewa OB (2022) Scarcity amidst plenty: regulating digital transformation. Front Res Metrics Anal 7:1004369

Bansal S, Kumar D (2020) IoT ecosystem: a survey on devices, gateways, operating systems, middleware and communication. Int J Wirel Inf Netw 27:340–364

Bhushan B, Sahoo C, Sinha P, Khamparia A (2021) Unification of blockchain and internet of things (BIoT): requirements, working model, challenges and future directions. Wirel Netw 27:55–90

Campi F, Favi C, Germani M, Mandolini M (2022) CAD-integrated design for manufacturing and assembly in mechanical design. Int J Comput Integr Manuf 35:282–325

Casciani D, Chkanikova O, Pal R (2022) Exploring the nature of digital transformation in the fashion industry: opportunities for supply chains, business models, and sustainability-oriented innovations. Sustain Sci Pract Policy 18(1):773–795

Cheng K, Davis MK, Zhang X, Zhou S, Olechowski A (2023) In the age of collaboration, the computer-aided design ecosystem is behind: an interview study of distributed cad practice. Proc ACM Human Comput Interact 7:1–29

Creed C, Al-Kalbani M, Theil A, Sarcar S, Williams I (2024) Inclusive AR/VR: accessibility barriers for immersive technologies. Univ Access Inf Soc 23:59–73

Da Xu L, Lu Y, Li L (2021) Embedding blockchain technology into IoT for security: a survey. IEEE Internet Things J 8:10452–10473

Dal Forno AJ, Bataglini WV, Steffens F, Ulson de Souza AA (2023) Industry 4.0 in textile and apparel sector: a systematic literature review. Res J Text Appar 27:95–117

Davila Delgado JM, Oyedele L, Beach T, Demian P (2020) Augmented and virtual reality in construction: drivers and limitations for industry adoption. J Constr Eng Manage 146:04020079

Dwivedi YK, Kshetri N, Hughes L, Rana NP, Baabdullah AM, Kar AK, Koohang A, Ribeiro-Navarrete S, Belei N, Balakrishnan J (2023) Exploring the darkverse: a multi-perspective analysis of the negative societal impacts of the metaverse. Inf Syst Front 25:2071–2114

Friedrich A, Lange A, Elbert R (2022) Supply chain design for industrial additive manufacturing. Int J Oper Prod Manage 42:1678–1710

Fromhold-Eisebith M, Marschall P, Peters R, Thomes P (2021) Torn between digitized future and context dependent past—how implementing 'Industry 4.0'production technologies could transform the German textile industry. Technol Forec Social Change 166:120620

Gande A (2020) Emerging AI & ml-based technologies & applications in supply chain management (scm): future prospects. Int J Market Technol 10:1–6

Ghosh S, Ness S, Salunkhe S (2024) The role of AI enabled chatbots in omnichannel customer service. J Eng Res Rep 26:327–345

Górriz JM, Ramírez J, Ortíz A, Martinez-Murcia FJ, Segovia F, Suckling J, Leming M, Zhang Y-D, Álvarez-Sánchez JR, Bologna G (2020) Artificial intelligence within the interplay between natural and artificial computation: advances in data science, trends and applications. Neurocomputing 410:237–270

Habib G, Sharma S, Ibrahim S, Ahmad I, Qureshi S, Ishfaq M (2022) Blockchain technology: benefits, challenges, applications, and integration of blockchain technology with cloud computing. Future Internet 14:341

Haleem A, Javaid M (2020) 3D printed medical parts with different materials using additive manufacturing. Clin Epidemiol Global Health 8:215–223

Halwani MA, Amirkiaee SY, Evangelopoulos N, Prybutok V (2022) Job qualifications study for data science and big data professions. Inf Technol People 35:510–525

Hassija V, Chamola V, Gupta V, Jain S, Guizani N (2020) A survey on supply chain security: application areas, security threats, and solution architectures. IEEE Internet Things J 8:6222–6246

Holmlund M, Van Vaerenbergh Y, Ciuchita R, Ravald A, Sarantopoulos P, Ordenes FV, Zaki M (2020) Customer experience management in the age of big data analytics: a strategic framework. J Bus Res 116:356–365

Horak T, Strelec P, Huraj L, Tanuska P, Vaclavova A, Kebisek M (2021) The vulnerability of the production line using industrial IoT systems under DDoS attack. Electronics 10:381

Huynh-The T, Pham Q-V, Pham X-Q, Nguyen TT, Han Z, Kim D-S (2023) Artificial intelligence for the metaverse: a survey. Eng Appl Artif Intell 117:105581

Iftekar SF, Aabid A, Amir A, Baig M (2023) Advancements and limitations in 3D printing materials and technologies: a critical review. Polymers 15:2519

Izadi S, Forouzanfar M (2024) Error correction and adaptation in conversational AI: a review of techniques and applications in chatbots. AI 5:803–841

Jha AK, Agi MA, Ngai EW (2020) A note on big data analytics capability development in supply chain. Decis Support Syst 138:113382

Jimeno-Morenilla A, Azariadis P, Molina-Carmona R, Kyratzi S, Moulianitis V (2021) Technology enablers for the implementation of industry 4.0 to traditional manufacturing sectors: a review. Comput Indus 125:103390

Kgobe P, Ozor P (2021) Integration of radio frequency identification technology in supply chain management: a critical review. Oper Supply Chain Manage 14:289–300

Kumari S, Polke N (2019) Implementation issues of augmented reality and virtual reality: a survey. In: International conference on intelligent data communication technologies and internet of things (ICICI) 2018. Springer, pp 853–861

Kurpjuweit S, Schmidt CG, Klöckner M, Wagner SM (2021) Blockchain in additive manufacturing and its impact on supply chains. J Bus Logist 42:46–70

Küsters D, Praß N, Gloy Y-S (2017) Textile learning factory 4.0–preparing Germany's textile industry for the digital future. Proc Manuf 9:214–221

Lanza M, Sebastian A, Lu WD, Le Gallo M, Chang M-F, Akinwande D, Puglisi FM, Alshareef HN, Liu M, Roldan JB (2022) Memristive technologies for data storage, computation, encryption, and radio-frequency communication. Science 376:eabj9979

Larshin V, Lishchenko N, Babiychuk O, Piteľ J (2021) Computer-aided design and production information support. Herald Adv Inf Technol 2:111–122

Lăzăroiu G, Andronie M, Iatagan M, Geamănu M, Ştefănescu R, Dijmărescu I (2022) Deep learning-assisted smart process planning, robotic wireless sensor networks, and geospatial big data management algorithms in the internet of manufacturing things. ISPRS Int J Geo Inf 11:277

Le D, Pole A (2023) Beyond learning management systems: teaching digital fluency. J Polit Sci Educ 19:134–153

Lee L-H, Braud T, Zhou P, Wang L, Xu D, Lin Z, Kumar A, Bermejo C, Hui P (2021) All one needs to know about metaverse: a complete survey on technological singularity, virtual ecosystem, and research agenda. arXiv preprint arXiv:2110.05352

Liao QV, Subramonyam H, Wang J, Wortman Vaughan J (2023) Designerly understanding: Information needs for model transparency to support design ideation for AI-powered user experience. In: Proceedings of the 2023 CHI conference on human factors in computing systems, pp 1–21

Madhu A (2024) Immersive innovation: augmented and virtual reality in fashion marketing. In: Emerging paradigms and challenges in multidisciplinary education and research.

Manglani H, Hodge GL, Oxenham W (2019) Application of the internet of things in the textile industry. Text Prog 51:225–297

Marín Díaz G, Carrasco RA, Gómez D (2021) RFID: a fuzzy linguistic model to manage customers from the perspective of their interactions with the contact center. Mathematics 9:2362

Mia MR, Shuford J (2024) Exploring the synergy of artificial intelligence and robotics in industry 4.0 applications. J Artif Intell General Sci. ISSN: 3006-4023 1

Mikhalev ON, Yanyushkin AS (2020) CAD/CAM-system module for the design of automatic production. Industry 4.0 5:59–62

Nagy M, Lăzăroiu G, Valaskova K (2023) Machine intelligence and autonomous robotic technologies in the corporate context of SMEs: deep learning and virtual simulation algorithms, cyber-physical production networks, and industry 4.0-based manufacturing systems. Appl Sci 13:1681

Nayak R, Singh A, Padhye R, Wang L (2015) RFID in textile and clothing manufacturing: technology and challenges. Fash Text 2:1–16

Nayak R (2019) Radio frequency identification (RFID) technology and application in fashion and textile supply chain. CRC press

Nayak R, Nguyen L, Nguyen T, Gaimster J, Panwar T, Morris R (2019) The challenges for sustainability marketing approach: an empirical study in Vietnamese fashion SMEs. Int J Trade Econ Financ 10(4):104–107

Nayak R, Akbari M, Far SM (2019) Recent sustainable trends in Vietnam's fashion supply chain. J Clean Prod 225:291–303

Nayak R (ed) (2019) Sustainable technologies for fashion and textiles. Woodhead Publishing

Nayak R, Panwar T, Nguyen LVT (2020) Sustainability in fashion and textiles: a survey from developing country. In: Sustainable technologies for fashion and textiles, pp 3–30

Nayak R, Panwar T, Grover T, Singh A (2024) Recent trends in sustainable clothing and textile manufacturing. In: Sustainable manufacturing practices in the textiles and fashion sector. Springer Nature Switzerland, Cham, pp 75–93

Neumeyer X, Santos SC, Morris MH (2020) Overcoming barriers to technology adoption when fostering entrepreneurship among the poor: the role of technology and digital literacy. IEEE Trans Eng Manage 68:1605–1618

Nouinou H, Asadollahi-Yazdi E, Baret I, Nguyen NQ, Terzi M, Ouazene Y, Yalaoui F, Kelly R (2023). Decision-making in the context of industry 4.0: evidence from the textile and clothing industry. J Clean Prod 391:136184

Pal R, Jayarathne A (2022) Digitalization in the textiles and clothing sector. In: The digital supply chain. Elsevier, pp 255–271

Parschau C, Hauge J (2020) Is automation stealing manufacturing jobs? Evidence from South Africa's apparel industry. Geoforum 115:120–131

Pothukuchi AS, Kota LV, Mallikarjunaradhya V (2021) A critical analysis of the challenges and opportunities to optimize storage costs for big data in the cloud

Pramanik PKD, Mukherjee B, Pal S, Upadhyaya BK, Dutta S (2020) Ubiquitous manufacturing in the age of industry 4.0: a state-of-the-art primer. In: A roadmap to Industry 4.0: smart production, sharp business and sustainable development, pp 73–112

Roberts L (2023) Countermeasures for preventing malicious infiltration on the information technology supply chain. Purdue University

Sahoo S, Lo C-Y (2022) Smart manufacturing powered by recent technological advancements: a review. J Manuf Syst 64:236–250

Sharma S, Singh G, Islam N, Dhir A (2022) Why do SMEs adopt artificial intelligence-based chatbots? IEEE Trans Eng Manage

Tariq Z, Aljawad MS, Hasan A, Murtaza M, Mohammed E, El-Husseiny A, Alarifi SA, Mahmoud M, Abdulraheem A (2021) A systematic review of data science and machine learning applications to the oil and gas industry. J Petrol Explor Prod Technol 1–36

Tawalbeh L, Muheidat F, Tawalbeh M, Quwaider M (2020) IoT privacy and security: challenges and solutions. Appl Sci 10:4102

Thakar CM, Parkhe SS, Jain A, Phasinam K, Murugesan G, Ventayen RJM (2022) 3d printing: basic principles and applications. Mater Today Proc 51:842–849

Thomas S (2017) Fashion ethics. Routledge

Varriale V, Cammarano A, Michelino F, Caputo M (2021) New organizational changes with blockchain: a focus on the supply chain. J Organ Chang Manage 34:420–438

Wan Y, Liu Y, Chen Z, Chen C, Li X, Hu F, Packianather M (2024) Making knowledge graphs work for smart manufacturing: Research topics, applications and prospects. J Manufac Syst 76:103–132

Want R (2022) RFID explained: a primer on radio frequency identification technologies. Springer Nature

Wecken RA (2021) The value of blockchain: potential and applications within design engineering

Index

R. Nayak et al. (eds.), *Use of Digital and Advanced Technologies in the Fashion Supply Chain*, Springer Series in Fashion Business, https://doi.org/10.1007/978-981-97-7528-6

V

W

Z

The manufacturer's authorised representative in the EU is Springer Nature Customer Service Centre GmbH, Europaplatz 3, 69115 Heidelberg, Germany. If you have any concerns regarding our products, please contact ProductSafety@springernature.com

Printed and bound by CPI Group (UK) Ltd, Croydon, CR0 4YY
01/10/2026
02225932-0009